A Naturalist in Costa Rica

A Palmito (*Euterpe* sp.) and tree ferns at the forest's edge.

A Naturalist in Costa Rica

Alexander F. Skutch

UNIVERSITY PRESS OF FLORIDA
GAINESVILLE/TALLAHASSEE/TAMPA/BOCA RATON/
PENSACOLA/ORLANDO/MIAMI/JACKSONVILLE

Copyright 1992 by the Board of Regents of the State of Florida
First edition copyright 1971 by the State of Florida Board of
Trustees of the Internal Improvement Trust Fund
Printed in the United States of America
All rights reserved

The University Press of Florida is the scholarly publishing agency for the State University System of Florida, comprised of Florida A & M University, Florida Atlantic University, Florida International University, Florida State University, University of Central Florida, University of Florida, University of North Florida, University of South Florida, and University of West Florida.

University Press of Florida
15 Northwest 15th Street
Gainesville, FL 32611

Library of Congress Cataloging-in-Publication Data

Skutch, Alexander Frank, 1904-
   A naturalist in Costa Rica / Alexander F. Skutch.
     p.   cm.
   Includes bibliographical references and index.
   ISBN 0-8130-1148-5 (acid-free paper)
   1. Skutch, Alexander Frank, 1904-. 2. Natural history—Costa Rica. 3. Birds—Costa Rica. 4. Naturalists—United States—Biography. 5. Ornithologists—United States—Biography.
I. Title.
QH31.S59S3   1992   92-8140
508.7286′092—dc20   CIP
[B]

To
WINSLOW R. HATCH

in remembrance of
journeys together

Acknowledgments

For help with the identification of organisms mentioned in this book, I am indebted to the following, some of whom are no longer with us: Paul H. Allen (flowering plants), Oakes Ames (orchids), S. F. Blake (Compositae), William C. Burger (flowering plants), C. H. Lankester (orchids and butterflies), E. C. Leonard (Acanthaceae), William R. Maxon (ferns), Douglas Robinson (lizards and frogs), Louis O. Williams (flowering plants), and Alvaro Wille T. (wasps). I am especially indebted to C. V. Morton of the Smithsonian Institution, who identified the bulk of my Costa Rican botanical collections and through the years has kept me informed of nomenclatural changes.

For permission to reproduce the drawing of the Laughing Falcon in chapter 7, which first appeared in *Animal Kingdom*, I thank the New York Zoological Society and the artist, Don R. Eckelberry. My son, Edwin, kindly provided the drawing of the moth at the head of chapter 21. Chapter 10 first appeared, in slightly different form, in *The Scientific Monthly*. For permission to include this, as well as certain photographs that were published in this extinct journal, I thank the American Association for the Advancement of Science.

Finally, I acknowledge my debt of gratitude to Eugene Eisenmann for helpfully criticising the manuscript.

A.F.S.

Contents

Introduction   1

PART I   A NATURALIST'S WANDERINGS

1. Into the Wilderness   7
2. Homemaking Amid the Forests   16
3. A Fragrant Summit   27
4. Two Drops of Blood   37
5. Backwoods Neighbors   44
6. The Mountain of Death   55
7. The Snake Eater   71
8. In Quest of the Quetzal   82
9. Winding Creek   100
10. The Hummingbirds' Brook   112

PART II   A NATURALIST'S HOMESTEAD

11. A Farm in the Wilderness   133
12. The House   141

13.	The Garden and Its Birds	149
14.	The Lives of Some Tropical Flowers	172
15.	The River	191
16.	Forest Trails	206
17.	A Last Home of Mystery	225
18.	The Coffee Grove	240
19.	Social Insects, Their Homes and Enemies	255
20.	Farming Without a Plow	279
21.	Butterflies and Moths	296
22.	In the Caribbean Lowlands	313
23.	Conclusion: Vicissitudes of a Valley	335
Appendix 1: Birds of Los Cusingos and the Valley of El General		343
Appendix 2: The Author's Published Writings		358
Appendix 3: The Author's Honors and Awards		367
Index		369

Illustrations follow pages 130 and 342.

Introduction

This book is a record of some of the more noteworthy observations, as well as some of the more memorable personal experiences, of a naturalist who has spent forty years in wilder parts of tropical America, about thirty-five of them in Costa Rica.

What is a naturalist? If he makes systematic observations, keeps careful records, and tries to interpret them, he is certainly a scientist, yet he differs profoundly from other scientists, even from other biologists. Many a scientist is never happier than when he can bring into his laboratory whatever phenomenon he is investigating, isolate it, and study it under controlled conditions. His triumph is to summarize his observations in a neat graph or a mathematical formula. He lives in middle-class comfort like any other professional man. To the true naturalist, the concrete experience of living things in their natural setting is at least as precious as any generalization or "law" that he can derive from his observations. To

Headpiece: The author in search of a farm, March 1941. Fording a stream on Bayon.

gain this experience, he is willing to endure discomforts and privations in far places.

The pioneer naturalists of the tropics risked their lives, and whatever fortunes they had, to explore the marvels of tropical nature, then little known in the North. They traveled by the most primitive means, shared the squalor of native huts, suffered hardships of every sort, fell ill of tropical diseases without medical care, and risked death at the hands of hostile natives. For months or years, they were cut off from civilized society and even the possibility of communicating with home. Their collections, made at such great sacrifice, were sometimes lost in ill-conditioned vessels.

The contemporary successors of these courageous pioneers work under conditions totally different. If equipped with a doctorate degree, they are, as a rule, generously supported by their university or a research foundation; they do not risk their own fortunes. Their lives are probably safer than they would be on the perilous highways of their homeland, for the tropical diseases that so often struck down the pioneers have been largely brought under control. In any case, they are rarely more than a few hours distant from a modern hospital. They travel in ease by airplane or car; they provide for themselves most of the comforts and even many of the luxuries they had at home. If they do not take their wives and children into the field, they are seldom long without communication with their families.

Just as the conditions of work in tropical biology have changed over the years, so have the procedures. The great pioneers were, necessarily, to a large extent, collectors, for until the organisms of which they wrote had been properly described and classified with the aid of collected specimens, nobody could be sure what they were talking about. But they were also indefatigable observers, interested in everything from the structure of the earth, the atmospheric phenomena, the appearance of the vegetation, and the habits of insects to the customs and even the languages of the exotic races among which they traveled. Many of the more striking aspects of tropical nature, such as the ants that live in the hollow stems or thorns of plants and defend them with their stings, the fishes of the Orinoco region that give electric shocks, and the decorated gardens of certain Papuan birds, came under their observation. Naturally, with so many new and marvelous things claiming their attention, they could describe them only in broad outlines. The finer details were left for their successors to study.

The contemporary naturalist in the tropics who wishes to contribute something new, rather than retell the tales of his forerunners, must take a different course. If he collects such taxonomically well-known groups as birds or butterflies anywhere except in the most remote nooks in the interior of the great continents and islands, he is wasting his time and perpetrating a useless slaughter, for he is unlikely to find an undescribed species. To add to the sum of knowledge, he must specialize. Much remains to be learned about the habits and ways of life of tropical organisms of all kinds, from flowers and insects to birds and mammals. Their ecology, or interactions with their physical environment and each other, is a fruitful field of study. The long migrations or more limited movements of many birds, mammals, and insects remain to be traced and explained. We need to know much more about the physiology of tropical organisms and the factors controlling their distribution.

In almost every respect, my own work, as reported in this book, has fallen between that of the great pioneers and that of recent students of tropical nature. While a graduate student of botany at Johns Hopkins University, I spent the summer of 1926 in Jamaica, visiting the island with a party from the botanical department and remaining to carry on research on a banana plantation for two months after the rest of the group returned to the United States. Two years later, having received a doctor's degree in botany, I went to Panama on a fellowship for botanical research. During six delightful and rewarding months at the United Fruit Company's research station beside the Changuinola Lagoon in the Almirante Bay region, I became deeply interested in the marvelously rich bird life around me. Looking into the subject after my return to well-stocked libraries, I learned that the birds of Central America had been so thoroughly collected and described that the probability of finding a new species was remote but that very little was known about the lives of these beautiful creatures. In Robert Ridgway's great descriptive catalogue, *The Birds of North and Middle America*, I found, for genus after genus, the terse remark "Nidification unknown." On a long visit to the Lancetilla Research Station in northern Honduras in the following year, my interest in tropical birds deepened. Gradually there grew upon me the determination to devote my life to filling in some of the great gaps in our knowledge of their habits. In no other way, it seemed to me, could I make such creative use of whatever abilities I had.

In the midst of the Great Depression of the early 1930s, it was not easy to find support for my project of studying the habits of tropical American birds, especially since my formal training had been in another field. During that period, most ornithological work in the tropics was financed by museums, whose chief interest was the acquisition of specimens. But I had no desire to shoot birds and make them into "skins"; I wished to study them alive. Not to be deterred by lack of support, I used my small savings to finance two long visits to Guatemala, the first to the Motagua Valley, the second to the western highlands, where I lived for a whole year amid forests of pine and oak above eight thousand feet. For my own interest, I made a collection of the fascinating mountain flora. Later I discovered that there was a market for my botanical specimens and that by selling them I could support my ornithological studies. For the next seven years, I combined botanical collecting with bird study. Then for six months, I traveled in South America with one of the rubber survey parties sent out by the United States Department of Agriculture. At the conclusion of this trip, I bought the farm in southern Costa Rica where I have since resided, farming on a small scale, studying the life around me, and writing.

I have not ventured so far beyond the frontiers of what we call civilization nor taken such risks as the great pioneer naturalists of the tropics did. Although for long periods I lived primitively among struggling settlers in the backwoods, I was at least among people who knew, and mostly obeyed, the basic laws of a modern state. I managed to preserve excellent health, save for a few mild bouts with tropical diseases that were promptly cured by modern treatments. Except for an interval of seven weeks during the Costa Rican revolution of 1948 when I was absolutely isolated and exposed to violence from lawless mercenaries, I have never been long out of communication with distant friends. And although most of the time I paid my own way, just as the pioneers did, I have been helped by two fellowships from the John Simon Guggenheim Memorial Foundation and, in recent years, have had generous support from the Frank M. Chapman Memorial Fund of the American Museum of Natural History of New York City, which I here gratefully acknowledge.

Although there is much about birds in this book, I have included only a small fraction of my observations on them so that I might have space to tell of other things: mountains and rivers, trees and flowers, insects of many kinds, reptiles and mammals, primitive agriculture on rough tropical lands, and something about the people among whom I have dwelt. Those who might wish more information about some of the birds mentioned may find it in the three volumes of *Life Histories of Central American Birds*, published from 1954 to 1969 by the Cooper Ornithological Society at Berkeley, California; in *Life Histories of Central American Highland Birds*, published in 1967 by the Nuttall Ornithological Club at Cambridge, Massachusetts; and in numerous papers published in journals and listed in systematic order in an appendix to the third volume of the first-mentioned work.

PART I

A Naturalist's Wanderings

Headpiece: Young Jacaranda trees (*Jacaranda copaia*). The huge, twice-compound, deciduous leaves play the role of branches.

1

Into the Wilderness

AS THE SUN ROSE brilliantly over the mountains on a morning in late November, 1935, I stepped down from the little trolley car that ran the length of San José's principal avenue and, knapsack on shoulder, walked across the street to La Sabana, the airport on the outskirts of the capital. In my pocket was a ticket for San Isidro del General. The day before, I had delivered my botanical collecting outfit, extra clothes, and other equipment to the office of the Empresa Nacional de Transportes Aéreos in the center of the city.

Of the many parts of the earth to which the term "a naturalist's paradise" has been applied by enthusiastic naturalists, none deserved this praise more than Costa Rica as it then was. This little republic in southern Central America owes its floral and faunal wealth to its strategic situation near the junction of two great continents, biologically quite different, from each of which it has received large contributions. It has been

Headpiece: Valley of the Río Buena Vista in 1936. At the valley's head, the continental divide.

able to support such a great number of natural groups of both northern and southern origin and to provide a field for their further diversification into distinct races and species because of its varied terrain, which includes very wet and moderately arid regions and mountain chains reaching heights of eleven and twelve thousand feet. These serve as the isolating barriers essential for the origination of new forms of life.

Moreover, in the mid-1930s, Costa Rica was still largely unspoiled. Its population of less than half a million people, mostly of European descent, was concentrated in the narrow Meseta Central, or central plateau, and along the railroads leading down from the capital, San José, to Puerto Limón on the Caribbean Sea and Puntarenas on the Pacific Ocean. Paved roads, passable at all seasons, extended hardly twenty miles on either side of the railroads and only in the highlands. Beyond this narrow belt of intensive cultivation were small settlements, connected by rough trails threading the vast forests, which at that time covered possibly three-quarters of the twenty-three thousand square miles of the nation's territory. In these tiny villages and on outlying farms, the naturalist not too squeamish or careful of his comforts could often find accommodations of sorts, while he observed or collected.

Other advantages that Costa Rica offered to the naturalist were its political stability and the friendliness of its people. Although not without an occasional bloody revolution, Costa Rica has a record of continuous, orderly constitutional government that scarcely any other country of Latin America can match. Thus, the naturalist working in some remote spot was not likely to have his studies suddenly interrupted or his thin lines of communication cut by a violent civil upheaval, as has happened to many in Latin America and elsewhere. Without an army to devour the lion's share of a slender national budget, Costa Rica has been able to devote a large portion of its revenues to education, with the result that the majority of its citizens can at least read and write, and a minority are highly cultured.

Before the problems created by wars and a too-rapidly expanding population had heightened the tension of life everywhere, the friendliness of the people was accompanied by a delightful informality. Having entered the country with only a tourist's visa, I desired to prolong my sojourn, and I was advised to apply to the governor of the province of San José. I found Señor Volio in a large, sparsely furnished office in an unpretentious building. After I had explained why I wished to stay longer, he took my passport and wrote in it: "Extend the bearer's permission to remain in Costa Rica until he has finished the studies for which he came." What a pleasant and courteous contrast to the vexatious regulations that I have since encountered in this and other countries!

Despite the hard times in the midst of the Great Depression, my friend Dr. William R. Maxon, director of the National Herbarium in Washington, persuaded half a dozen of the most important museums and botanical gardens of the United States and Europe to purchase duplicate sets of Costa Rican plants, which would be identified by him and his colleagues at the Smithsonian Institution. When the arrangements for my botanical collecting had been completed by a lengthy correspondence, as I was already in Costa Rica, the long rainy season was drawing to an end and I was eager to take to the wilderness. I chose for exploration the southwestern quarter of the Republic, which was then largely covered with heavy, well-watered forests, interrupted here and there by a small settlement with its surrounding clearings. Recently, the more important of these villages had been connected with the capital by an air service, which took one in an hour or less to points that a few years before could be reached only by days of toilsome travel over rough trails.

The largest and best known of the inland settlements in this wild, southern Pacific quarter of Costa Rica was Buenos Aires de Osa. Entering the office of the Empresa Nacional de Transportes Aéreos to buy my ticket for this point, I fell into conversation with Eric Murray, manager of the company. He suggested that San Isidro del General, nearer the head of the Térraba Valley, would be better for my work. I knew nothing of San Isidro, but since it was the first stop south of San José, I said that I would go there and look around. Thus, on the spur of the moment, I decided to visit the locality where I was destined to remain for the greater part of my life.

While waiting to board the airplane, I drank in the splendid panorama that spread on every side of the broad, level field. On the north and east, three lofty volcanoes, Poás, Barba, and Irazú, rose into the clear, early morning air. Irregular masses rather than regular cones, their form failed to suggest their character. To the south, and much closer, towered the first of the high mountains over which we would fly. A huge cross stood out prominently on its eastern spur.

The three motors of the big, silver-sided Ford plane were already whirling the propellers as they warmed up for the take-off. A great variety of baggage was being stowed away in the fuselage and wings. There were locked canvas bags containing the mail, bales of clothes, sacks of bread, boxes of canned foods, tins of kerosene, drums of barbed wire for fences, and even a little calf, tied up in a coffee sack with only his head outside, terrified by the roar of the motors and his strange treatment, struggling desperately to escape. Although the tariff for air freight was much higher than it afterward became, the overland trail was so long and difficult that the airplanes promptly took the traffic away from the pack trains, to the great relief of the poor, saddle-galled horses and mules that were driven over it with blows and curses.

The thirteen passengers, including an infant in arms, had been weighed and were now called to take their seats; the motors redoubled their roar, and soon we were soaring over the city, looking down upon the checkerboard pattern of avenues and streets intersecting at right angles. Almost before we were well up in the air, we had reached the edge of the narrow central plateau and were flying over the nearest of the mountain ridges. At first we rushed over a broken terrain completely shorn of forest from narrow valley to sharp ridge. Coffee plantations, shaded by low trees that made them resemble squares and rectangles of woodland, occupied the sheltered valley lands; open pastures covered the steep slopes. As we receded from the centers of population, forests began to appear on the ridges. Soon they became more extensive, and the clearings, with their tiny houses and cattle dwarfed by distance to the size of toys, were restricted to the wider and more open valleys. Far away to the right, the blue waters of the Pacific stretched away to a vastly distant horizon. After a few minutes more, the last clearing and farmhouse fell behind, and unbroken forest covered all the land.

The terrain over which we flew was now all sharp ridges and deep, abysmal valleys, with scarcely any level ground in sight. It was thrilling to a naturalist to gaze down upon the rounded, green crowns of millions and millions of trees, which glided swiftly astern to be replaced by as many more. We flew low, and as we shot over the crests of the ridges, the treetops went skimming by so close below that we could distinguish the forms of the foliage. On these summits, slender palms (*Euterpe*) with spreading crowns of great feathery leaves were the dominant vegetation. From between the trees, on the slopes that rose steeply to our left, graceful waterfalls shot out abruptly and fell in tall, slender columns. From the foot of each waterfall stretched a narrow ribbon of white, marking the course of a tumultuous mountain torrent that lashed itself into foam as it rushed down the valley over a rocky bed between long slopes clad in sylvan green. On the left, too, the steep slopes of the Cordillera de Talamanca rose so abruptly that the lofty summits were cut off from view by the wing beneath which I sat.

I had flown too little to have the marvel of mechanical flight dulled to the commonplace, and I traveled as though in a dream. It seemed so unreal to be gliding swiftly and smoothly over the roof of the forest, which now fell away abruptly to the white thread of a stream, now rose steeply to the next palm-crowned ridge, then fell, and rose, and fell once more. It was the most difficult sort of mountainous country, and, in Guatemala, I had traveled by horse and foot over such terrain enough to know that it would take hours of hard toil, struggling up and slipping down forbidding slopes, hacking constantly at the undergrowth to open a passage, to cross any one of those great ridges over which we rushed magically in the airplane in a minute or two.

I looked out sharply for birds, but on the whole journey over the forest I saw only one, which flew into the crown of a great tree standing above its neighbors. Most of the birds seemed to remain beneath the canopy.

After we had flown for many minutes over forest interrupted only by the white ribbons of slender mountain torrents, we again began to see clearings beneath us in the valleys. Then of a sudden, the mountains, which had formed a single, continuous mass, parted into two chains. That on the left was very high, rising into craggy pinnacles bare of trees; but the range on the right was much lower, permitting us to view the ocean over its rounded, forest-clad summits. Between the Cordillera de Talamanca and the lower coastal range stretched a broad, comparatively level valley, the Valley of El General, as the expanded basin at the head of the drainage of the Río Grande de Térraba is called.

We arrived before the rising sun had dissolved the mist that had settled over the valley during the night. It covered most of the lower ground with a fleecy blanket that stretched far away to the southeast, white and billowy like a frozen polar sea. The landing strip was completely hidden, and, for a quarter of an hour, we circled around, waiting for the air to clear. Sometimes we dived through the gray fringes of the blanket of cloud, but more often we flew over parts of the valley that were clear of fog. This delay was not unwelcome to me, for it provided an opportunity to see what this new region was like. The impression it made was decidedly favorable. Beneath us were long strips of forest, separated by clearings that were devoted to grazing, or earlier in the year had been planted with maize. Scattered throughout these clearings were thatched cabins in front of which stood knots of people gazing up at the circling airplane. After a while, the fog dissolved enough to reveal the landing strip, and the pilot brought his wide-winged machine gently to earth, only an hour after leaving San José.

We had come down in the midst of a sterile, scrubby area several miles from the village of San Isidro. The baggage from the airplane was loaded into an oxcart to be hauled there, but I found no taxis waiting for the passengers—indeed, there was no motor vehicle in the whole valley. I set off on foot for the village. The morning was still so young and fresh that I enjoyed that walk along the deep-rutted cart road, through open fields and stretches of woodland, where the birds had not yet fallen silent in the midday heat. Most were kinds that I already knew; but there were others, restricted to this region, that I had never seen.

From the mouth of the Gulf of Nicoya southward into the Panamanian province of Chiriquí, the rainfall is more copious and evenly distributed throughout the year than it is on most of the Pacific side of the North American continent, until one reaches high latitudes in Oregon and Washington. Accordingly, the forests are taller and denser, more like the Caribbean rain forests, than elsewhere on the Pacific slope for long distances to the northwest and the south or, more properly, to the east, when one recalls the curvature of the Isthmus. The isolation of this heavily forested region from similar forests, by the Cordillera de Talamanca to the north, by the savannas of central Panama to the east, and by drier woodland to the northwest, has favored the evolution of a number of endemic birds, including such colorful species as the Fiery-billed Araçari, the Golden-naped Woodpecker, the Orange-collared Manakin, the Turquoise Cotinga, and the Riverside Wren.* The relative isolation of the Térraba Valley seems also responsible for the absence of other birds that one expects in Central America: I have never seen a resident oriole or a jay in the valley.

As I followed the grassy cart road toward the village, I heard the clear little trills of Blue-crowned Manakins coming from adjoining patches of woodland. From time to time, velvety black tanagers with intensely scarlet rumps flew across the road or flitted among the surrounding trees. These mature males were accompanied by more numerous females clad in nondescript shades of olive and brown; but I noticed that on some the breast and rump were orange, a color far brighter than I had ever seen on a female Scarlet-rumped Black Tanager in the Caribbean lowlands, where the species is so prominent. It was interesting to find that, although the males of the Caribbean and the Pacific races of this tanager are indistinguishable, the females of the latter are more richly colored—a phenomenon which systematists have called heterogynism. The males of the Pacific race are, in my experience, more songful than their counterparts across the Cordillera.

I was delighted to find myself in a region where so much forest remained so close to a settlement, for in most parts of Central America that I had visited the forest had been cut and burned in every direction around the villages, and it was necessary to go far in order to reach it. The recent date of colonization in the valley explained the large amount of uncut woodland. Twenty-five years earlier, the site of San Isidro had been a wilderness. Before I even reached the village, I had decided that this was the place for me, and I asked Mr. Murray, who had accompanied me on the airplane, to please send down my baggage on the next

*Capitalized names of animals and plants refer to definite species, of which the scientific designations are given in the index.

flight. I had left it in his care in San José, until I decided where I would work.

The village itself was not attractive. The main street was unpaved and muddy, for the rainy season was just ending. With one exception, the houses were all of a single story, and most were crudely built. Some were constructed of sawed boards, others of planks roughly split from trunks; a few of the better ones had walls of white plaster. Scarcely any of the buildings were painted. The roofs were of corrugated sheet iron or were thatched with the leaves of the sugarcane or more rarely of tiles. There were a church, a school, and half a dozen little stores, called *pulperías*, some owned by native Costa Ricans, others by Chinese; in each the wares displayed were of sufficient variety to satisfy most of the simple needs of the barefoot customers. I was amused by the sign in front of the smithy, announcing that he would undertake to repair watches as well as to shoe horses!

In a tiny hut with a thatched roof, a black Jamaican, the only Negro in San Isidro, served rice and beans and coffee in enamelware plates and cups on a bare wooden board to guests who sat on backless, four-legged stools. The rough board walls of this rustic cafeteria were papered with pages from old magazines and newspapers with which the patrons could entertain themselves while waiting to be served. But there was no hotel or inn, and I might have passed an uncomfortable night under the open sky if the agent of the aviation company had not kindly shared his room with me.

In the center of the village was a large, square, open space called the plaza. In most Central American towns, the central park is an attractive spot, laid out with paved walks and flower beds, planted with palms and other trees and shrubs with colorful foliage, and provided with benches where one can rest and chat with friends in the shade. Perhaps there will be a fountain and a statue or two, and almost always in the center there is a pavilion, where the band plays in the evenings. But San Isidro was still so small and new, and everybody had been so busy building his own house and making a living that nobody had found time to beautify the plaza, which was merely an open, grassy field, where the boys played soccer, here known as "football." Around the edges of the field, small casuarina trees had been planted. Each was enclosed in a little pen of barbed wire to protect it from wandering horses and cattle. The people called these trees "pines" and supposed them to be the same as the pine trees of the North. But they had never seen true pines, which do not grow wild south of Nicaragua, and their error in identification was excusable.

At the southeastern corner of the plaza was the *jefatura*, a low wooden building which might be called the city hall of San Isidro, and beside it stood the shack that sheltered the post office and radio station. El General depended on two of the most modern inventions, the airplane and the radio, to keep in touch with the outside world. Here was the interesting phenomenon of a community that had jumped directly from the most primitive means of communication to the most advanced, without ever having passed through those intermediate stages represented by the railroad and the telegraph, the automobile and the telephone. There were many people, especially among women and children who had never been outside the valley, who had never seen these inventions that the rest of the world considered so important. Not until a decade later, when construction began on that part of the great Inter-American Highway which traverses southern Costa Rica, did the first motor vehicles reach the valley.

When I set out for southern Costa Rica, it had been my intention to build a rancho in the forest, a temporary structure with a roof thatched with palm fronds, walls of split palm trunks, and no floor except the hard-packed ground. Such a shelter, adequate during dry weather, would be neither comfortable nor healthful during the long rainy season, which here lasts eight or nine months. If I had not, on the day following my arrival, visited the *Jefe Político,* or civil administrator of the district, I might have carried out my original plan of spending only the dry season in the valley and never have come to dwell here as long as I have.

On entering the *jefatura,* I found a tall, gaunt man with a week's stubble on a face that reminded me of Abraham Lincoln's. When I learned that this was the person I sought, my anticipations fell. But it did not take me long to discover that behind that rough exterior lurked a deep and sympathetic understanding and somewhat more than the average man's share of human kindness. His name was Juan Schroeder, and we were, after a fashion, compatriots; his father had been a North American who came to Costa Rica from Wisconsin many years before, one of a group of immigrants who attempted to form an agricultural colony in San Carlos in the northern part of the country. But the colony had failed for lack of a road to transport its produce. Don Juan's father had remained in the country and married one of its daughters. Don Juan had not inherited his father's language, and our conversation was, accordingly, carried on in Spanish.

When I had introduced myself and explained the purpose of my visit and my intention of building a temporary shelter in the forest, the *Jefe Político* suggested an alternative arrangement which he thought would prove more practicable. His home was in Rivas, a district on the upper side of the basin of El General, at the foot of the main Cordillera, higher and cooler than San Isidro. Recently, he had bought a piece of land adjoining his own, and on this was a rustic dwelling which he did not need. He had removed the boards from the walls and floor; but the sturdy framework was still intact, and the roof, although it contained gaps, might be easily repaired. He thought that for a small expenditure I could make the place habitable, and he offered me the use of it free of rent. He happened to be going up to Rivas that same afternoon and invited me to accompany him. I eagerly seized the opportunity.

Don Juan found a horse that for a colón I could hire for the journey, and toward evening we set forth for Rivas. The little black mare, no taller than a pony, was even smaller than most of the horses in the valley. After I mounted, my feet nearly touched the ground, making me feel ridiculous as we rode through the village. But the little horse was not lacking in energy; she trotted with a will beneath her disproportionate load.

We traveled along a rough, unpaved road, over gently rolling country, pleasantly diversified with woodland and open pastures and cornfields. In the pastures, the sticky, strong-scented Calinguero grass was in full bloom, tinting whole hillsides with the delicate pinkish lavender of its inflorescence, which covered them softly like an unsubstantial, clinging mist. Always ahead loomed the great rampart of the Cordillera de Talamanca, its high summits veiled by the afternoon clouds. As night fell, we approached a large river, whose presence was proclaimed, even before it came into view, by the loud rumbling and roaring of water rushing along a rocky channel. This, my companion informed me, was the Río Buena Vista, which flowed through Rivas. The road led for a while along the bank of the stream, beneath great gnarled Sotacaballo or Riverwood trees, whose far-spreading branches were heavily burdened with a great variety of ferns, orchids, aroids, and other air plants, some of which were trees growing on the bigger trees. All this heavy mass of vegetation cast a deep gloom over the stream and the road. Soon we crossed the river by a wooden bridge and followed it up the eastern side of the valley, now narrowed between steep ridges, with the roaring of the river always in our ears. Night was almost upon us when my companion reined his horse before a low wooden farmhouse with a tiled roof and announced, in the courteous manner of countries where Spanish is spoken: "Here is your home, señor."

Although neither of us suspected it at the time, these words proved to be more than a courteous formula; they were prophetic.

2

Homemaking Amid the Forests

I WAS WELL PLEASED with the site of Rivas. It was situated at the lower end of the long, narrow valley of the Buena Vista River, a large, rushing mountain stream whose ceaseless roar filled all the vale with a sound that told of wild, untameable power. After I had lived close beside the river for many weeks, I grew so accustomed to its voice that most of the time I was not conscious of hearing it; but ever and again, especially when the breeze blew the sound toward me with increased volume, I would awaken with a start to a renewed realization of its presence and be glad that I had that mighty murmur always with me.

The level floor of the valley was narrow and so rocky that it could not have been plowed, even if any of the settlers had possessed a plow. Here all the forest had been destroyed, and the land was occupied by bushy pastures, little patches of sugarcane, little groves of coffee or of bananas and plantains. Almost half of the valley floor was covered by low thickets,

Headpiece: The author's residence in Rivas, December 1935–June 1937. Miguel Esquivel and Bayon.

which had promptly taken possession of neglected fields. The bushes in these thickets were now so dense, so bound together with vines, that it was impossible to move through them without cutting the way with a machete, a long knife so indispensable here that every man and boy of Rivas carried one almost everywhere he went.

The valley floor was about three thousand feet above sea level. On either side, the enclosing slopes rose abruptly and steeply to summits that were increasingly high as one advanced up the river, until they merged with the lofty main ridge of the Cordillera. These slopes were for the most part covered with forest, except near their feet, where the trees had been felled to make way for cornfields and pastures and here and there, at greater heights, where some more daring settler had made his clearing and his homestead, revealed from afar by a patch of more vivid green set amid the dark verdure of the ancient trees. Far up at its head, the beautiful vista of the valley was closed by a long stretch of the mighty ridge of the Cordillera, whose broad flank was darkly covered with unbroken forest, and whose high, nearly even summit separated the waters which flowed into the Pacific from those that found their way to the Caribbean Sea.

One could hardly call Rivas a village or even a hamlet, the dwellings were so widely separated. The diminutive ranchos, of the rudest and most primitive construction, often with no floor other than the hard-packed earth, were scattered along both sides of the river for several miles, and a few even perched upon the slopes of the enclosing mountains. The broad, grassy road that paralleled the river was so rough with projecting rocks and large boulders that even the lumbering oxcarts toiled along it rarely and with difficulty. At the lower end of the valley, near Juan Schroeder's house, stood the one-roomed schoolhouse and the church, to which a priest came from San Isidro once in every month or two to hear confessions and perform the Mass. The church was a low wooden structure without a steeple and almost devoid of ornamentation. But to bring the corrugated iron roofing to this remote spot had been costly; considering the fewness of the people and their poverty, the construction of this humble church was for Rivas almost as pretentious an undertaking as the erection of St. Paul's for London or of St. Peter's for Rome.

Rivas was one of those happy places without a history, save such as was connected with its name. It was evidently named for that Rivas in the neighboring republic of Nicaragua where Juan Santa-María, Costa Rica's national hero, had advanced under rifle fire to ignite the building in which the army of the filibuster, William Walker, had fortified itself. That campaign to hurl a North American adventurer from Central American soil, few as were the men engaged in it, furnished the epic theme of Costa Rican history. Happy the nation which can recount no more sanguinary wars!

On the morning after my arrival in Rivas, I employed a young man to show me the trails through the surrounding forest. For a while, I considered establishing myself temporarily in the next valley, that of the Río Chirripó, which was wilder, although here too was a small settlement called Canaán. But the trail into this valley was so wretched that I finally decided to accept Don Juan's dismantled dwelling.

As it turned out, I was glad that I chose Rivas rather than Canaán. For work with both birds and plants, a district half-forested can be more favorable than unbroken woodland; and this is particularly true where there are alternating bands of forest and clearing, such as I found in the Valley of El General. Unless hunting has been excessive—which happily was not so here—the remaining forest will have an almost complete representation of the region's fauna, except some of the largest mammals, which in any case are rarely seen. The flora of the surviving half of the woodland will be an excellent sample of the whole. But in addition to the natural wealth of the forest, there will be in the cleared lands a largely different, and by no means uninteresting, aggregation of plants and birds, kinds which prefer the sunlight and, arriving mysteriously, begin to establish themselves in the new clearings surprisingly soon. Moreover, the forest's edge is the best place to collect the taller trees and vines, whose flowers are usually difficult to see from the woodland depths but which here are frequently displayed in greater profusion and nearer the ground. The edge of the forest and isolated trees standing near it are likewise the best stage for watching the treetop birds, so difficult for earthbound man to glimpse from the midst of the woods; here their nests are most readily discovered and may be most advantageously studied.

The framework of the cabin placed at my disposal was of heavy timbers, from trees that had been cut in the neighboring forest, hewn square with the adze in the spots where they had fallen, then drawn by yoked oxen to the site of the building. As I had been told, the boards had been removed from the walls and floor. About two miles farther up the valley was a tiny sawmill with a jig saw operated by a homemade, wooden waterwheel—the whole set up and afterward sold by the *Jefe Político*, a most versatile man. Here I bought lumber to rehabilitate the dwelling. When the boards arrived in the oxcart they were still unseasoned and very rough, for there was no planing machine at the mill. No matter! My cabin would be wholly in the rustic style. I had decided to enclose only one of the two rooms, each eleven feet square, of which the dwelling had originally consisted, leaving the other half to serve as a porch, where I could eat and work at the arrangement of my plants in the open, at least in the dry weather. After the rains began, I found it advisable to enclose this side, too. At the rear, separated from the main structure by a narrow passage, was a kitchen with walls and roof still intact.

At another time, I should have enjoyed rebuilding my cabin with my own hands, but now I was eager to finish the job as quickly as possible so that I might start promptly to collect the plants which were everywhere coming into flower with the beginning of the dry, sunny weather. Moreover, I had no tools, except my machete, which, despite its many uses, is not well fitted for driving nails. Accordingly, I sought the services of the local carpenter, but he was hardly better equipped than myself. Like me, he was a newcomer here, and, to raise money to bring his family and establish a home, he had sold his tools. So he was obliged to work with such instruments as helpful neighbors could lend: a dull saw, two planes, and a chisel. Sometimes he had a hammer, but when the owner needed this article, he was reduced to driving nails with the back of an adze. There was neither spirit level nor square, and for a plumb line the carpenter tied the hammer (when he had it) to the end of a string! When, after three days' work, the cabin was ready for occupancy, I could not find a tight joint in the whole construction, but there was many a gaping one. This did not trouble me greatly; I was happy to have a little shelter all to myself, where I could work alone and undisturbed.

In any case, to have given more care to finishing the cabin would have been a waste of effort. My new boards had been trees such a short while before that they had not time to dry. In the days that followed, they shrank rapidly, and, where nails prevented their uniform shrinkage, they were forced to split. Often during the early afternoon, when the air was driest, I would be startled by a sudden, loud report, almost as sharp as a rifle shot, which advised me tersely that another of my boards had cracked. Before the dry season was over, many of the floor boards had separated from their neighbors by nearly half an inch, and there was a wide gap down the center of my table. Fortunately, the wall boards had been nailed up with an overlap, which prevented the appearance of gaps between them. Some of the neighbors had neglected this precaution, with the result that their walls and floors both gaped. The one-roomed schoolhouse was especially well ventilated. You could stand in front and see through both walls the trees along the river behind!

Then there was the roof to be mended. The great fronds of certain palms make the best thatch, but those in the neighboring forest were not well suited for this purpose. The long, narrow leaves of the sugarcane were almost universally used for roofing, save by those few who could afford locally made tiles and had dwellings substantial enough to bear their great weight. Rods of the Wild Cane that grew tall and slender in the river bottoms served admirably to support the sugarcane leaves, which, in small bundles, were doubled over them.

José, the young man who had at first guided me through the neighboring woods, agreed to remain with me as cook, field assistant, and general factotum, all for the monthly wage of forty colones (then about seven dollars) and meals, a remuneration quite liberal by local standards. He was about twenty-two, somewhat less than half Indian, able to outwalk me despite the shortness of his legs, excessively vain of his small, dark, regular features and his ridiculously meager mustache, and as great a gossip as any beldam. As one of his first tasks, I requested, at about nine o'clock one bright morning, that he go into a neighboring cane field and gather dry leaves to mend the gaps in our roof. But he objected, telling me that the old cane leaves were already so dry and brittle that they would break as he pulled them from the canes. In dry weather, they should be gathered in the early morning while still wet and soft with dew. He promised to go at the following dawn to do my bidding. I had much to learn from him.

I had things to learn, too, about loading a packsaddle. It became necessary to go down to San Isidro for more nails to finish the cabin. Wishing to bring up some of my baggage at the same time, I hired a mare from a neighbor. I rode down to the village on the packsaddle, a hard seat. On reaching the office of the aviation company, where my things were stored, I asked the agent to help me load the horse. Each of us had watched packsaddles being loaded, but neither had done it himself—and there is a tremendous difference between these two kinds of experience. Yet, ashamed to request assistance, thereby admitting incompetence in an art so necessary in this part of the world, we tied on the bulky parcels as best we could. Thanking the agent for his assistance, I started homeward with the mare, pleased with the nicely balanced load that we had achieved.

Everything went well until we came to a stream on the outskirts of the village. Sending the mare ahead over the ford, I crossed by the log that served as a footbridge, to keep my shoes dry. Before I could overtake the horse on the farther side, the end of a rope worked loose and began to drag. This frightened the nervous little creature and she broke into a run, soon shaking off her burden and dragging it in the mud. Only when she had become so thoroughly entangled in the ropes that she could no longer move did she halt. Shamefacedly, I trudged back toward the village with a parcel under each arm, continuing until I met a man who compassionately volunteered to reload my mare. Incidentally, he found a most attentive pupil as he tied the ill-assorted bundles on the wooden frame.

The difference between his method and mine was slight, merely a matter of the positions of two knots; but it made a vast difference in the results. This time the cargo stayed in place, and, by the light of the rising moon, I led the mare up the peaceful valley to my new home.

The furnishings of this home were simple, both for economy, very necessary to me at that time, and because I found it interesting to adapt local products to my uses. For a bed, the carpenter made me a folding cot of the kind known as a *tijereta*, from the Spanish word for scissors. To finish it properly we needed heavy canvas, but none was available in the local emporium, so we tacked three new coffee sacks over the wooden frame. At first they stretched a good deal, letting me rest nearer and nearer the floor as the frame spread, until I was obliged to shorten them.

Nights were cool, especially toward dawn in the dry season, when air chilled by radiation on the frosty heights at the head of the valley flowed strongly down it. To keep out the cold from below, it was necessary to cover my burlap cot with some sort of mat or mattress. An *estera de vena* was the local answer to my need, and a boy who lived nearby volunteered to supply it. He collected a number of the biggest of the giant leaves of the banana, cut the heavy midribs from their broad blades, dried these midribs in the sun, then tied them closely side by side in a single layer with twine that he made from the fibers in the fleshy, swordlike leaves of the Cabuya, an agavelike plant. My mat of banana midribs full of air spaces gave excellent insulation, but at first I found it rather hard. However, as the nights passed, I grew harder by lying on it, at the same time that the mat became softer and more flexible from my tossing about on it. Thus, by a process of mutual adaptation, I came at length to sleep on my rustic cot as sweetly as though I lay upon the softest mattress that man has devised.

Local pillows were made of flour sacks stuffed with rags or shredded, dry corn husks. Since I had not yet dwelt in Rivas long enough to accumulate rags, I used the husks. These made a headrest sufficiently soft for one who had spent an active day afield, but they were not wholly silent. Whenever I turned my head, they complained with a soft and drowsy rustling, as of a gust of wind stealing through an October cornfield in the North, where I grew up. So I slumbered the more soundly. Later, when I found a ceiba tree shedding the copious buff-colored down in which its seeds are embedded, I stuffed my flour sack with kapok, thereby disproving the local superstition that such a pillow induces baldness.

For the rest, there were a couple of four-legged stools, standard equipment in all the neighboring ranchos, which I would not lightly have exchanged for chairs, because they provided an excellent excuse for reading in bed when I came home from tramping over the hills. Long shelves for herbarium specimens along one wall, rows of nails for hanging things along the opposite one, substituted for chests and cupboards.

The kitchen was equipped in a manner equally simple. In place of a stove, there was a wooden platform, supported on four stout legs, with a high rim that surrounded a thick layer of clay. The fire, kindled upon the hard, dry clay in the center of the platform, was kept in place between two rows of stones. The cooking pots were hung on wires or supported on bars of iron laid across the stones, as in most of the neighboring cabins. A few feet above the hearth was a screen of boards with narrow spaces between them to shield the thatched roof from sparks, which might have started a fire that would have consumed my whole establishment in a twinkling. Chimneys were unknown in Rivas; the smoke from the wood fires found its way out beneath the eaves and through the thatch as best it could. When cooking was in progress, a newcomer might have supposed that the cabin was burning.

In this fashion, for eighteen months, I lived very much like my neighbors, perhaps even a little more comfortably than some whose poor huts were without floors and had wide chinks in the walls. It was gratifying to discover with how little a man could live contentedly and accomplish the work on which he had set his heart. My chief lack was a library, for I soon ran through the Tauchnitz paperbacks that I had bought in San José; but I did not discover this need until the wet season came with its long, rainy afternoons and evenings. What was important to me now was that I had wild nature all around me, with woods and thickets teeming with multitudes of the most brilliant and interesting birds. And if I worked hard at my plant collecting, my time would soon be my own for studying them.

I had not dwelt many days in my cabin before I discovered that José and I were not its only occupants. A Southern House Wren slept nightly in the cane-leaf thatch above us, while her mate slipped every evening into the heart of a bunch of green bananas growing in the yard. Later, becoming uneasy when I watched too closely as he retired, he moved to the roof and slept near the female. Their presence did not surprise me, for at almost every dwelling where, in my wanderings through tropical America, I had resided for a period or received only a lodging for the night, a pair of these cheerful little brown birds had been present. It made no difference whether the house was the great and luxurious mansion of some wealthy planter or the wretched hovel of a poor peasant, whether it stood in the midst of rich farmlands or was hidden in some remote clearing in the forest: the wrens had made their home there and were content, paying generously for their lodgings with ebullient liquid song. These house wrens differ little in appearance from the familiar bird of temperate North America and by some are classified in the same species, but to my mind they are superior songsters.

Throughout my sojourn in Rivas, with brief interruptions, this same pair of wrens continued to sleep in my roof and to be my nearest neighbors. As our intimacy grew, it seemed but fitting to give them names. By his tireless repetitions of a variety of sweet liquid songs, the male earned the name Singing-Wren. His mate, who acknowledged the conjugal bond by replying with a simple little twitter, sometimes followed by a brief, clear trill, was called Twittering-Wren. In March of the first year, I tied a gourd for my wrens in an orange tree close beside the cabin, where I could watch it through the window. In this they raised three broods during the first year and four in the second. I watched carefully over all these nestings except the last. From each I learned something new, and soon my notes on the house wrens became more voluminous than those on any other kind of bird. To do justice to the energy, versatility, and adaptability of Twittering-Wren and her mate would require a small volume.

Singing-Wren always helped his mate to build her successive nests in the gourd, but usually while work was in progress he was so busy singing that he accomplished less than she did. After the foundation of coarse sticks was completed to Twittering-Wren's satisfaction, and she proceeded to line the hollow at the back of the gourd with soft materials, he often continued to bring superfluous twigs, sometimes earning a peck for his stupidity. At times Twittering-Wren removed his twigs from the overstuffed gourd. She alone incubated her speckled eggs, four or, more rarely, three in a set; but while she sat warming them, he came from time to time to look in and see how she fared. Then, after the eggs hatched, he took an equal share in bringing insects, caterpillars, and spiders to the nestlings, although he never brooded them. After the young took wing, the parents led them in the evening to some snug shelter: back again into the gourd, to the thatch of the cabin, or to a cavity in a stump, where, as a rule, their mother slept with them. Sometimes it was difficult for the fledgling wrens, who still flew weakly, to enter the dormitory their parents had chosen for them. When this happened, the adults would instruct and encourage the fledglings by flying in and out, in and out, many times over, to the accompaniment of much song from Singing-Wren, until at last the little ones succeeded in following their example.

During the first year, the parent wrens drove away their offspring of one brood about the time the succeeding brood hatched. But in the second year, they were more tolerant, Twittering-Wren permitting her older children to sleep beside her in the gourd while she incubated the following set of eggs and brooded the younger brothers and sisters. As a result of this close association, the older juveniles regularly helped to feed the nestlings of the following brood. On one occasion, this help was so efficient that Twittering-Wren and her mate proceeded to build a new nest in a neighboring gourd before their current brood had fledged. Although rather rare among birds, such overlapping of broods has been recorded in a number of species, in most of which the parents do not receive assistance.

Above Rivas, high on the slope that flanked the valley on the east, was an old, abandoned cornfield, overgrown with bushes and weeds, among which stood a number of scattered, fire-killed trees. Such a clearing beside the forest is the best possible place to learn the habits of birds which sleep and nest in cavities in trees. There I often went to pass the last hour of the day, to watch the sun set behind the opposite ridge and the birds retire into the woodpeckers' holes and other cavities so numerous in these decaying trunks. Or else I would arrive at dawn to see the birds come forth and begin their day.

For a year and a half, I followed the fortunes of a pair of beautiful Golden-naped Woodpeckers, who every night slept together in a deep chamber that they had carved in a tall, branchless trunk. They continued to sleep together in this chamber even while it contained eggs and nestlings. By day they took turns incubating and brooding, and, of course, both fed the young, with food brought visibly in their bills rather than by regurgitation. The latter method of feeding is followed chiefly by woodpeckers that consume many ants.

In the first year, these Golden-napes raised three fledglings. After flying from the nest, these young woodpeckers were led back by the parents to roost in it with them, and even to take shelter there from a heavy shower. The whole family of five continued to lodge in the old nest hole, until one vanished prematurely and the others left a short while before the following breeding season, as is customary in this species.

I have only twice, in many years, known Golden-napes to try to raise two broods in a season; but when this occurred, the young of the first brood slept in the hole where the parents were attending the second brood. On one of these occasions, two or three young females of the first brood brought a little food to their younger brother and sister in the nest, but they delivered it clumsily. After the second brood fledged, the whole family used the latest nest as a lodging, which each night sheltered the two parents, three females of the first brood hatched late in March, and a male and female of the second brood hatched late in June—seven sleepers in all. When this chamber fell, the young woodpeckers helped their parents to carve a new one. The young male engaged in this work only three weeks after he left the nest, when he was slightly under two months of age.

A pair of Red-crowned Woodpeckers, close relatives of the North American Red-bellied Woodpecker, whom I watched on the hillside above Rivas for an equal period, had customs quite different from those of their near neighbors, the Golden-napes. The male and female Red-crowned Woodpeckers invariably slept apart, the female often in an abandoned dormitory of her more industrious mate, who was always chiseling out new cavities in the soft wood of dead burío trees. Yet, these woodpeckers also remained paired throughout the year, as indeed do most of the Central American members of the family. Since the male's newer and sounder dormitory became the receptacle of his mate's eggs, it was but natural that during the night he should take charge of them and the nestlings that hatched from them. By day, the two sexes shared all the duties of the nest, as is usual among woodpeckers. The fledglings, far from being led back to sleep in the hole they had just left, were repulsed with pecks when they tried to join their father in the evening or rudely evicted if they entered before him. After passing a number of nights clinging to a trunk in the open, the juveniles finally succeeded in finding old cavities for their accommodation, always sleeping one by one.

The pair of Fiery-billed Araçaris who occupied this clearing always slept together in an old hole of one of the larger woodpeckers, except while the female was incubating the two white eggs. Then her mate sought a dormitory apart but came in the morning and took his turn in the nest. Elsewhere I found as many as five of these middle-sized toucans entering the same old woodpecker's hole at nightfall, folding their tails over their backs to save space.

The shy, brown Streaked-headed Woodcreepers always slept singly in crannies in trees. They were among the last of the diurnal birds to retire, seeking their inconspicuous nooks in the gathering dusk when it was difficult to follow their movements, and they were among the first to leave their dormitories at dawn. A pair of Masked Tityras, plump, whitish members of the cotinga family with bright red bare cheeks, nested in holes carved by the Golden-naped Woodpeckers, but, when not incubating or brooding, they roosted in the neighboring forest, where I could not follow them. Thus, while I learned how to keep house for myself amid the forests, I discovered how wild creatures of a number of kinds kept theirs. In the course of these studies, I never molested nor destroyed their homes, always treating them with the same respect as I desired them to preserve for mine.

During all my long sojourn in Rivas, I was scarcely ever out of hearing of the Buena Vista River, for its tireless murmur followed me far up on the slopes of the enclosing ridges when I went to watch birds or collect plants. Only while I was in the midst of the forest, where the murmur was muffled by the trunks and foliage of the crowded trees, did it fail to reach my ears. This sound came in time to be part of the undercurrent of my consciousness, conveying a constant reassurance of home and peace and well-being, as the roar of the surf to men who dwell beside the sea or the dull rumble compounded of a thousand different noises to those who love the life of a great city. During the long nights of the wettest months, I would sometimes lie sleepless, listening to the now far louder voice of the torrent, and fancy that I could distinguish in its overtones a deep and stirring harmony, a sweet and elemental music, like the strains of some great church organ heard faintly from afar. And, in truth, it was the voice of Nature that sang to me then, a voice whose harmonies had sounded so for aeons before I drew breath and would continue in the same lofty strain long after I had passed away. How can one who has dwelt long in an atmosphere saturated with such cosmic sounds, calm and soothing in their unhurried sameness and secular duration, ever sleep soundly again amid the sharp and fretful noises of a city?

3

A Fragrant Summit

WITH THE ADVANCE of that first December that I passed in El General, the days became brighter and drier, the afternoon rains fewer and lighter. As almost everywhere in Central America, the beginning of the dry season was the most delightful time of the year; not only was the weather then most agreeable, but the face of the earth was most beautiful. Then bright blossoms adorned the landscape more profusely than at any other period. During the long wet season, there had been too much rain and too little sunshine to bring forth a great variety of flowers. After the dry season had continued for several months, the soil in the clearings became so desiccated that vegetation languished and few plants bloomed. But now, at the outset of the dry weather, the sky was full of sunshine, while much water remained in the soil, which for months had received an almost daily soaking—a combination of circumstances that favored the blossoming of a great variety of

Headpiece: Rain forest in the mountains of southern Costa Rica. In the Upper Tropical Zone, altitude nearly 4,000 feet.

plants. Yet few birds sang at this season, and those beautiful, bright days were all too silent. The silence of the birds during the early months of the dry season, when earth and air and sky seem most to invite song, is doubtless one of the causes of the preposterously false belief that tropical birds, bedight in the brightest colors, are poor songsters. In Central America, bird song is at its peak in April, whether this month is very dry, as in western Guatemala, or rainy, as in southern Costa Rica.

Here it was easy to understand why colonists from Spain, a land with a Mediterranean climate of rainy winters and dry summers, gave the name *verano* (summer) to the dry season, while the wet season, when the air is frequently damp and disagreeable and the skies often dark and frowning, is called *invierno* (winter). These designations are used throughout much of tropical America without reference to temperature or the position of the sun in the sky; they refer to rainfall alone. So strong has the association between rainfall and the two cardinal seasons grown that, in periods of changeable weather, my neighbors might call a dry day *verano* and the following wet day *invierno*. In spite of its position in the Northern Hemisphere, Costa Rica has its lushly green "winter" while North America and Europe are enjoying summer and its "summer" while the northern lands are in winter's harsh grip.

By Christmas, the valley of the Río Buena Vista was bright with a multitude of blossoms. The roadsides and weedy pastures were gay with the flowers of shrubs, vines, and tall herbs, prominent among which were golden marigolds, purple mints, white begonias, pink or purple morning glories, white or pink melastomes, and acacias with fluffy balls of little white florets. In the thickets that covered the lower slopes of the mountains where crops had once been grown and the land was afterward permitted to rest, tall shrubs of the composite family displayed great masses of white or the purest gold, visible as one looked over the tops of the thickets from a distant height. Among the many woody cousins of the daisy and the aster that flowered at this season was *Oliganthes discolor*, a tree of the more open parts of the forest that attained a height of ninety feet with a trunk two feet thick. Its small heads, each consisting of only two white disk florets, were displayed in generous, flat panicles.

In the forests there were fewer blossoms, and scarcely any of the giant trees had yet come into flower. The heavy forest guards its moisture well, and deep-rooted trees can bloom later in the season, when herbs and shrubs in the clearings are languishing in the drought.

As soon as we were settled in the cabin in Rivas, we began the work of collecting specimens of the multitude of plants now coming into bloom. Before a week had passed, we had fallen into the routine that was continued, with slight variations, throughout the next three months. Like everybody in Rivas, we always rose at dawn. José, after the custom of his class, slept in his work clothes and was the sooner ready to begin the day's tasks. On arising, he folded his blanket and rolled up the banana-leaf mat upon which he had lain on the floor, washed his face at the river, then started the fire and had breakfast on the way, while I washed, shaved, and dressed. I rarely neglected the daily use of the razor, even in the most solitary places, for this is often the first step toward slovenly living. Breakfast usually consisted of oranges, of which Rivas provided an abundance of the best throughout the year, oatmeal, eggs, and tortillas of maize. This over, José washed the dishes, while I tidied the cabin and swept the floor.

While the sun still hung low above the forest that crowned the eastern ridge, the housework was done, and we set off for the woods. José bore the wooden frame in which the plants were carried and was sometimes requested to scramble up a tree, machete in his belt, to cut down a flowering branch. But he had long intervals of rest, while I bent over the open press arranging specimens. Sometimes we returned to the cabin for lunch, but more often we carried this meal and did not come home until the afternoon. Usually my first thought was to bathe in the cold, refreshing water that the river brought down from cool heights. José, remembering the local proverb, *mejor tierra en cuerpo que cuerpo en tierra* (better earth on the body than the body in the earth), mistrusted this chilling stream and did not often immerse himself. He kept busy cooking supper and also the beans and rice to carry for lunch the next day, while I removed dry specimens from the corrugated cardboards and placed between them those that we had just collected.

Returning from the forest one day, we opened the cabin to find that a neighbor's hen had flown over the wall, settled on the bundle of corrugated cardboard driers hanging above the little kerosene stove and, finding the tops soft with the moisture that the heat had driven up from the plants, scratched a hollow in them to make a comfortable nest. As proof of what had happened, a fresh egg lay among the fragments of cardboard in this depression. When one is working far from a source of supplies, little mishaps of this sort are so upsetting that they are long remembered. I sent to Washington for more driers, and, to prevent a repetition of the disaster, we gave the room an open ceiling of wild canes.

Twice we climbed the steep slope on the western side of the valley to a brook that flowed through a narrow, wooded vale at an altitude of four thousand feet. Even in the Blue Mountains of Jamaica, that stronghold of ferns, I never saw them growing in greater profusion than along this rivulet; but here were fewer of the filmy ferns that abound in similar situations on that cloud-bathed insular range and a greater variety of stouter ferns with wide-spreading fronds, chiefly species of *Dryopteris*, *Diplazium*, and *Asplenium*. They were so abundant that I opened the plant press on the little-used trail and worked half a day in this one spot, arranging the ferns between the papers while José brought me more. When I closed the press in the middle of the afternoon, it contained as many specimens as I could dry. I always arranged the herbarium specimens in the field, and, as I put them into the driers in the evening, I gave them some final touches, smoothing out doubled leaves and spreading them more evenly over the paper.

While I was putting away ferns beside this rivulet, some Chestnut-mandibled Toucans, which José called *quioros*, flew back and forth among the boughs of the tall trees overhead. Presently, they descended lower, as though to see what I was doing. Two of the big, black, yellow-breasted birds alighted on branches not fifteen feet from me and looked on with such unmistakable curiosity that I was almost persuaded that they were eager to learn how botanical specimens are prepared. One cocked his head and enormous bill to one side and peered down intently with a large, brown eye set in a patch of pale green skin in a yellow face. The other toucan soon became more interested in the fruit of some forest tree that it carried and began to pull it apart with the hooked extremity of its bill, while holding it against a branch with a foot. Here, where they had not been persecuted, the *quioros* were not at all shy; even when I stood up to look at them, they were in no hurry to go.

Returning with his hands full of ferns, José announced that he had found a hummingbird's nest. He led me to a point where the rivulet flowed between rocky walls lushly overgrown with ferns and other plants. Here the great, elongated leaves of a heliconia or wild plantain arched over the narrow channel. As often happens with these huge leaves and those of the related banana, the blades had somehow been torn, from margin to massive midrib, into strips of varying width. Beneath one of these strips hung a roomy cup, which with admirable skill a hummingbird had fastened to the slippery surface. In this pensile cradle, under the green roof formed by the downward-curving strip of leaf, slept two ugly, naked nestlings, which I could see by raising a mirror above the cup. Partly hidden amid the luxuriant vegetation, I watched until a long-billed Green Hermit Hummingbird approached; but she was too shy to feed her homely babies in my presence. Her behavior and my observations at similar nests left no doubt that she was their mother.

On a later visit, I found the nest empty and pulled it apart to learn its composition. As was appropriate in this ferny dell, the chief ingredient was the long, narrow, brown scales of a tree fern. Mixed with these were some fine, fibrous rootlets. Strands of cobweb, thickly applied, held these materials together and, wrapped around the back of the leaf, bound the nest firmly to the strip.

In another part of the forest, we found a Green Hermit perching in the undergrowth and repeating monotonously, with clocklike regularity, a single, unmelodious note. While calling, he wagged his long, white-tipped tail rhythmically up and down. Doubtless, he was a male advertising his presence to the other sex all day long, as is the way of male hermit hummingbirds.

A favorite walk, whether for collecting plants or watching birds, was down the valley of the Río Buena Vista to its junction with that of the Chirripó. Pedestrians crossed this broad, impetuous torrent on two great trunks, flattened on the upper face, each of which stretched from one of the banks to a tiny islet in the center of the channel. A vine and a steel cable stretched beside these narrow bridges made shaky handrails. Horsemen and oxcarts forded the river, which, when swollen, had taken several lives. Not far beyond the crossing, a roadway led up a long slope, through alternating patches of forest and clearings with rude huts, to a new settlement called Santa Cruz. The broadness of the road through the woodland made it especially favorable for scanning the treetops for flowers, the earliest migrant birds in autumn, and the latest to depart in the spring.

At an altitude of about three thousand feet, great oak trees became abundant in the forest. Although this was the lowest point where I found a concentration of oaks in El General, scattered trees grew at least six hundred feet lower. In Guanacaste, *Quercus oleoides*, a small oak with a gnarled trunk covered with rough, gray bark, grew in almost pure stand on volcanic soil only a few hundred feet above sea level. It has diminutive acorns which contrast strikingly with those up to two and a quarter inches in diameter produced by some of the oaks of El General. The oaks at Santa Cruz dropped their acorns, which are slightly larger than those of the White Oak, in late July and August. Early in the latter month, the trail was thickly strewn with them, and at intervals we heard the *plop* made by the fall of yet another. In mid-October, these oaks were shedding their leaves, and by early December most of them were nearly bare. They contrasted so strongly with the full verdure of the surrounding trees that it was difficult to resist the impression that they had been blighted and were dying, but, if one looked sharply, he could see that some were already putting forth new foliage. Soon they were in full leafage again.

Here was a colony of Acorn Woodpeckers, hardly distinguishable from their relatives in California. With their harlequin attire of black, white, and red, their rollicking calls, their constant activity and unusual habits, they are among the most entertaining of birds. They are so constantly associated with oaks that later I lived for many years about two miles from a colony of them without ever once seeing one on my farm, where there are no oaks. Their habit of storing countless acorns in little holes, each just big enough to hold a single one of these fruits snugly, which they carve into wood or thick bark, is well known and has been observed in Honduras and western Panama. Yet it is not invariable, for in both Guatemala and Costa Rica I have spent much time watching these woodpeckers without seeing one insert an acorn into a specially made, close-fitting niche; but they often tucked whole acorns or fragments into natural crannies in trees or amid the epiphytes with which the trees were covered.

Late in May, I found, amid the oaks at Santa Cruz, feathered nestlings looking from the doorway of a hole sixty feet up in a barkless trunk. At least four grown birds, two males and two females, were feeding them, chiefly with insects skillfully captured on aerial sallies and carefully prepared in a crevice in a tree before being carried to the nest. In a very tall charred trunk, a mile or so above my cabin in the Buena Vista valley, was a nest hole in which a single female and three or four males were taking turns at incubation. I never saw other incubating birds change about so frequently. The average length of one hundred eight sessions on the eggs that I timed was only five minutes; the longest was seventeen minutes. Do these woodpeckers nest communally, in the manner of anis, or is a mated pair assisted in the care of the nest by unmated helpers, probably their own offspring of an earlier brood, as occurs occasionally in Southern House Wrens and Golden-naped Woodpeckers and regularly in White-tipped Brown Jays and wrens of the genus *Campylorhynchus*? Without being able to count the eggs or young in these inaccessible nests, I could not decide between these alternatives, although available evidence points to the latter as correct. Even in California, where likewise Acorn Woodpeckers' nests have numerous attendants, the problem has not, to my knowledge, been settled.

By February, orchids of many kinds were in flower. Especially delightful were the species of *Oncidium* which the Costa Ricans aptly call *lluvia de oro* (golden shower). They often grew on boughs of trees overhanging the rivers; above the rushing current drooped the long, profusely branched inflorescence, aglow with myriad yellow blossoms of medium size. The little schoolchildren, who had learned that I would buy *parásitas* and *toritos* (as they called the orchids), made pretty pictures as they came shyly up to the cabin of the awesome stranger with golden sprays longer than themselves draped around their necks. Most would let me decide the price, but a few came demanding an exorbitant sum and went away with less than the others. Since most orchids are exceedingly troublesome to dry into herbarium specimens, I could not afford to pay high prices for them. In the same group as the *lluvia de oro*, but of very different aspect, was the charming, little, yellow-flowered *Oncidium titania*, only an inch or two high when in bloom. This dwarf orchid grew abundantly on low, thin twigs in gardens and thickets, often on Guava trees.

Another noteworthy orchid of this district was a wild vanilla, *Vanilla pfaviana*, a slender vine that formed great festoons among the branches of trees along the rivers, as well as on the moister ridges, up to at least thirty-five hundred feet. Its large flowers are greenish, its leaves broader and thinner than those of the vanilla of commerce. The drying pods quite fail to develop the delicious aroma of vanilla.

One of our more strenuous collecting trips was to the first high summit on the eastern side of the Buena Vista valley. On its riverward side, this rounded eminence fell away in a verdant precipice. In order to reach it, we followed the long ridge that began between the confluence of the Buena Vista and Chirripó rivers and, alternately rising and sinking, led gradually upward to the continental divide. We set out along the forest trail that crossed this ridge from Rivas to Canaán. Now in December, at the end of the wet season, this path had been churned by the feet of men and quadrupeds into an interminable series of mud puddles, and to travel along it was an ordeal. Picking our way, we had little time to look upward into the crowns of the trees that towered above us, which, in any case, had few flowers at this season. We noticed only the white, clustered stamens of some blossoming Ingas. At intervals, the mellifluous triple whistles of Thrush-like Manakins reached our ears, but we never glimpsed the brown birds lurking behind the dense wall of verdure that bordered the trail on either side.

We were relieved when, at the crest of the ridge, the muddy trail dipped down the farther side toward Canaán, and we parted company with it. We found an old passageway, probably a surveyor's line, leading upward along the crest of the ridge, but it was so cluttered with fallen logs and branches, with vines and young shoots through which we had to cut our way, that we soon decided to leave it and open our own path through the unbroken forest. The going was now easier, and soon we came to a narrow bridge of land, just wide enough to walk across safely, between the precipices on both sides. Beyond this, the ridge became broader and inclined more sharply upward. Stately feather palms (*Euterpe*) now dominated the crest of the ridge, in places almost to the exclusion of other vegetation. The chief impediments to our march were now fallen, dead palm fronds, which we frequently cut with our machetes so that we could pass. The soft, moss-covered ground also made walking difficult.

Two hours after leaving the Canaán trail, we reached our objective, a summit where my aneroid read five thousand feet, two thousand feet above our cabin in Rivas. No exhilarating view rewarded our toilsome climb, for we were surrounded by vegetation that permitted only narrow glimpses over the valleys below us. But this vegetation was most unexpected. The summit was covered with the same palm trees that grew so thickly on the ridge leading up to it, but here they were shorter. After the palms, the most abundant tree was a Clusia, about twenty-five feet high with large, broadly elliptical leaves that were dark green and very thick. These trees were just coming into bloom, and their large, white flowers shed a delicious fragrance over the mountaintop. The male and female flowers were on different trees. The former, which were slightly the larger, measured nearly two inches in diameter and consisted of five or six fleshy petals with many stamens clustered in the center. I carefully selected twigs with the greatest number of open flowers, which was rarely more than two or three. But I labored in vain; as usually happens with Clusias, most of the petals fell before I could put the specimens into the driers. The scent was more enduring than the flowers; a tin box in which I placed some remained fragrant for weeks. My specimens were later identified as *Clusia flava*, a South American species not hitherto known in North America.

Beneath the palm and the Clusia trees, the ground on this mountaintop was thickly carpeted with a luxuriant growth of green bog moss. Yet here was no rockbound basin to hold water, such as I once found on a sphagnum-covered summit in the state of Maine; instead, the moss was kept sufficiently wet by the rain and cloud mist, which much of the time bathed this summit. Now, at the end of a sunny morning, the sphagnum moss dripped when I squeezed it like a sponge which had been freshly immersed.

The most conspicuous and abundant plant among the sphagnum was *Carludovica leucocarpa*, a relative of the palms, whose large, cleft leaves, springing in generous clusters from each short stem, held their twin apices seven feet above the moss. It bore fleshy, fruiting spikes in all stages of development, some already turning red, but with difficulty we found two freshly opened inflorescences, still surrounded by their white spathes. Among the Carludovica plants grew the curious fern, *Oleandra costaricensis*, terrestrial here amid the moss, although it usually perches high on trees. Its slender, scaly, rootless, rodlike stems, sometimes eight feet long, leaned against the surrounding vegetation and bore long, narrow, simple leaves, much like those of a hart's-tongue fern. A large polypody, *Polypodium fraxinifolium,* was also abundant amidst the bog moss.

It was so easy to keep to the crest of the ridge up which we had climbed that we did not take the trouble to mark a trail to lead us down. As one ascends a mountain, its spurs converge so that it is difficult to go astray. On the downward course, they diverge, sometimes so imperceptibly that, in forested country where one has no outlook, it is all too easy to take the wrong one. Starting homeward in the middle of the afternoon, we hurried down through the open palm forest until the aneroid indicated forty-three hundred feet. Here, according to a notation that I had made on the way up, we should have reached the narrow bridge of land, but we failed to find it. Apprehensive now, we nevertheless continued downward, until we found our way blocked by a dense stand of Bracken fern higher than our heads, which we had not seen as we ascended. Even by vigorously swinging the machete, we could hardly make any progress through this; we turned down the side slope to our right, hoping to cross the intervening depression to the ridge we should have followed.

The forest was so entangled with underbrush and fallen trunks, the slope so steep and treacherous, that we wandered about confusedly. The wise course would have been to have turned upward again as soon as we discovered that we were on the wrong ridge, for thereby we would assuredly have come to the right one. But now the clouds blew in, dimming the light beneath the trees. With disconcerting visions of a night in the wet forest without a bite to eat, a match, or any cover thicker than a cotton shirt, we pressed doggedly downward, slashing our way through the undergrowth, until at last we reached a long-abandoned clearing, where the tangled second growth brought the machete into still more continuous action. Finally, we crossed a rivulet into a neglected banana plantation, through which led a newly cut trail. Following this, we passed the ruins of a cabin and a cane press, beyond which we came to the Canaán trail.

We had come out in the valley of the Chirripó instead of that of the Buena Vista, and now we had twice as far to trudge over that miserable passageway as we would have had if we had not gone astray. Nevertheless, we were immensely relieved to see this familiar ribbon of mire and sloshed along it as fast as we could. Just at nightfall, we reached our cabin with our fragrant Clusia blossoms and memories of that perfumed summit that would endure for many years as rewards for our toil.

Walking homeward, I recalled that, two years earlier, my guide had lost us on Volcán Zunil in Guatemala by just this same mistake of taking the wrong one of two diverging spurs while descending a wooded mountain. Then he and I had passed a cold, blanketless night in the forest, in view of the lights of the village of Santa María and within hearing of the house dogs and the cars passing along the highway but unable to proceed farther in the dark, because we were hemmed in on three sides by deep ravines. And I solemnly vowed never again to ascend a wooded ridge in unfamiliar terrain without marking a trail to lead me down again. For many years I have kept that vow and have never again been lost.

4

Two Drops of Blood

THROUGH MUCH of the four-month dry season, the men of Rivas were busy cutting down the forest on the mountain slopes above their valley to make fields for their crops, the chief of which was maize. Not that there was any lack of land that had already been cleared. Well over half of the deforested areas in the valley and on the lower reaches of the enclosing slopes, which had borne crops in past years, was now lying idle, while the exuberant native vegetation shot up taller and taller. The longer this process continued and the heavier the second growth became, the more thoroughly would the land recover from the effects of the last burning and sowing and yield a richer harvest when it was again brought into cultivation by the same crude method. Each new settler in El General was eager to take possession of as much land as he could for this rough sort of agriculture, and, before he could acquire legal title to a farm, he was obliged by law to clear and plant at least half its

Headpiece: Thatching my kitchen roof. Humberto Gamboa is doubling sugarcane leaves over the rods of wild cane, while Efraim Flores assists.

area. Hence, each dry season, he zealously renewed his attack upon the dwindling forest.

January and February were the chief months when the woods were leveled. At intervals throughout the mornings, I would hear the dying groan of some great tree as it began to strain the shrinking band of wood between the axe cuts on opposite sides. Then came the billowy swish of myriad leaves rushing madly downward through the air and a thunderous, earth-quivering thud that reverberated far across the valley as the huge tree crashed down upon its final resting place, shattering many branches by its impact. Next came the scattered, sharp reports made by larger branches, which more tardily snapped under the mighty strain that had so suddenly been thrust upon them. Finally, there was silence, punctuated by the blows of axes as the laborers attacked another tree.

José and I sometimes visited the places where the men were chopping down the trees, in the hope of procuring flowers which some towering forest giant had displayed high above the ground, where neither he nor I could have climbed to them. Or, perhaps, we might find the flowers of an orchid, aroid, or other epiphyte, or a rare fern that grew only on high branches; or maybe the blossoms of some great liana, thick as a man's thigh and hundreds of feet long, which for years had plotted and schemed its way from branch to branch and from tree to tree, striving ever upward, strangling old supporters that it no longer needed, like some master of diplomacy, so that at long last it might spread its inflorescence at the very top of the forest.

Before they felled the tall trees, the laborers cleared away all the underbrush with their machetes. This made the forest parklike and most inviting, with longer vistas beneath the trees than one ordinarily enjoys in tropical woodland and attractive glades through which we could wander without fighting our way through bushes and vines. But this idyllic state was usually of short duration. Soon the big trees were attacked and overthrown, the noble forest reduced to a scene of chaos and ruin. The tangle and confusion of prostrate trunks, splintered branches, and intertwined vines concealed the ground; to struggle across it demanded the greatest exertion. Only by walking along the horizontal trunks, clean and branchless, jumping from one to another, was it possible to make much headway. When we left these slender bridges, we sank from waist-deep to head-deep in such a litter of boughs, twigs, creepers, and leaves that it was hardly possible to move as much as two steps either forward or backward. José, barefoot like almost everyone in Rivas, walked along the trunks more securely than I did, for with shoes I was more likely to slip.

In return for the effort of struggling through this terrible wreckage, we found few good specimens. The trees were nearly always thrown down the steep slopes, and the heavier ones fell with such terrific impact, one on top of another, that their crowns were thoroughly shattered. Often it was difficult to gather half a dozen flowering twigs in good condition from the branches of what had once been a huge tree. The confusion was so great that, even when a good specimen was found, it was often hard to tell whether it belonged to a big tree, a small one, or a liana.

The sun beat down into these new clearings unopposed by any leaf, sending the full intensity of his rays upon ground that for centuries had never felt more than stray, foliage-filtered beams. Many of the fallen trees had contained hives of wild bees of several kinds. Their homes destroyed, the little bees wandered lost and aimless over the wreckage of the forest, alighting on the sweaty skin of our faces, necks, and hands, annoying us greatly as we struggled through the tangles, exposed to the full force of the morning sunshine. Fortunately for the laborers who fell the trees, the meliponine bees of the tropical American forests are stingless, but the same is not true of the wasps of many kinds. Myriads of ants, likewise homeless, crawled over the branches and foliage, thence upon our clothes and skin. Although they did not often sting or bite, their journeys over the tender skin of neck and shoulders were extremely irritating.

Some of the men told me that they greatly enjoyed the work of cutting down the trees, strenuous though it was and with the ever-present danger of being struck by a falling dead limb or crushed beneath a heavy trunk. They took childish delight in watching the huge trees topple over and hearing the loud crash. Then, too, there was always the possibility of finding the hives of wild bees and taking their honey. These people were fond of wild honey and used it in household remedies: a mixture of honey and banana vinegar, taken internally, was supposed to be beneficial in cases of severe contusions. The beeswax served to light the huts of those too poor to buy tallow candles or kerosene for lamps.

When José was in the woods with me, he never ceased to look for the funnel-shaped or tubular entrance, made of yellowish or blackish wax, which projects from the side of a bee tree and leads to the hive in the hollow center of the trunk. His eyes were keen to detect these spouts where the bees continually swarm in and out; he was constantly calling out that he had found another beehive, until I grew weary of hearing about them. Although he always promised to return later with axe and kettle to bring home some honey, I never sent him, and he never went.

One day we visited a new clearing early in the afternoon, when the axe men had finished their day's work, and watched them remove honey from a hive of small, black meliponine bees, situated in a thick, hollow branch of a huge tree that had been felled in the morning. The man who chopped away the outer shell of wood to uncover the hive was so skillful that he rarely cut into one of the cells that contained the honey, although with each stroke the edge of his axe came scarcely an inch from them. As more and more of the hive was revealed, everyone was surprised by its great size; the watching children were so delighted that they could hardly stand still. The honey, instead of being stored in small, hexagonal cells regularly spaced, as in the hives of domestic bees, filled several scores of globular cells, arranged irregularly one above another, each somewhat smaller than a hen's egg and made of blackish wax. These filled the big cavity in the branch.

One of the little boys had been sent down the mountain to fetch a kettle from the house, but he misunderstood directions, or perhaps was lazy, and returned with a very dirty one that held only a gallon and proved too small to contain that huge hive, which must have held at least a gallon of pure honey. When the hive was sufficiently exposed, it was lifted bodily out of the great, irregular cavity in the branch, with very little loss of liquid. Now the three children, vibrant with joy, stuck their little hands, all dirty as they were, into the dripping sweetness and licked them again and again. Managing to get hold of some of the broken, egg-like cells, they squeezed and sucked them as long as they would yield a taste of the delicious fluid. Since the hive was too big to fit into the kettle, the honey was pressed out and allowed to flow into the vessel. This was done with unwashed hands, soiled from a morning's work at felling trees; but neither the dirty hands nor the unappetizing kettle seemed to trouble anybody—except me! Nevertheless, I plucked a large leaf and, folding it into a cup, caught some of the clear, freely flowing liquid that was offered to me and found it deliciously sweet. I also sampled some of the yellowish beebread, composed chiefly of pollen and stored in globular cells like those that held the honey, and I enjoyed its piquant sweetness.

In January, there was little rain; in February and most of March, almost none. When the fallen trees had dried under the rays of the bright summer sun, burning began. Later in the season, some of the older, taller, second-growth thickets, covering land that had lain idle for several years after removing a crop, were also cut for burning. They dried more quickly than the great trees of the forest and were sooner ready for the fire. Then, too, extensive stands of the tall, coarse Bracken fern, a cosmopolitan weed that took possession of land so sterile that scarcely anything else would grow on it, were at this season wantonly ignited.

Through February and March, the burning continued. On a single day, a dozen great columns of smoke might be seen ascending on all sides, rising higher and higher into the heavens until they resembled fat, white, cumulus clouds. The air lost the fine clarity that had made it so delightful during the earlier part of the dry season. The sunlight, filtering through dense clouds of smoke, often took on a wan, amber color; the atmosphere seemed to sicken. Charred bits of vegetation, especially small fragments of the great fronds of the Bracken, carried high into the air by the updraft above the blaze, drifted down everywhere, often at long distances from their source. These blackened remains soon became conspicuous on roadways, paths, and other bare ground. The afternoons at this season were often darkly overclouded, apparently with the great quantity of smoke sent into the upper atmosphere by the fires rather than with moisture-bearing clouds, for it almost never rained. By night, the glow of distant fires, hidden behind ridges or forest, illumined the sky here and there, while other blazes raged more vividly in full view.

March 6 was a day of fires. The whole long slope, just across the river from my cabin, was burnt off in the afternoon. A few weeks earlier, it had supported a tall, dense, second-growth thicket, which had been cut and allowed to dry. The fire made so much smoke that it masked the flames. A cabin had been built in the midst of the drying brush, which the occupants had not taken the trouble to remove to a safe distance from their walls. From across the river, the shack appeared to be enveloped in flame; I expected to see it become a lively bonfire. The occupants draped huge, green banana leaves over the ridgepole of their roof, where a man stood with a vessel of water, ready to dash it immediately upon any spark that might settle on the thatch of inflammable cane leaves. Others moved around the outside of the cabin, bearing buckets and kettles of water. It seemed that a miracle had occurred when the flames finally passed the shack, which would have burned like so much dry straw, leaving it standing unharmed in the midst of a blackened slope.

Another large field was burned off in the valley on our side of the river, not far above my cabin. All around, at greater distances, other columns of smoke rose into the air. The setting sun was hidden by the dense cloud of smoke that hung over the valley. The acrid fumes of burning wood irritated my nostrils. The air was murky, oppressive, menacing. The full moon, gliding up above the crests of the trees on the eastern ridge, shed down a weird, baneful light. I felt that on a night that began this way anything foul or evil might fitly happen. I almost expected some hideous tragedy.

As I sat at supper on the porch, while the last dim afterglow of the dead day faded in the west, of a sudden a drop of fresh, red blood fell upon a finger of my right hand, which was extended on the table, and another dropped into the dish of rice from which I had just served myself. How dark and ominous was the spot it made on the snowy white grains! I peered up into the high-peaked roof, rising above me dim and cavernous in the feeble light of a little kerosene lamp, but I could see nothing. I rushed into the sleeping room for my flashlight, but even its brighter rays revealed only the poles of the framework and the straw-colored leaves of the thatch—nothing that could shed red blood. After such an unexpected, inexplicable occurrence in such a setting, I felt perplexed, shaken, insecure. Might not those mysterious drops of blood portend some dreadful calamity?

My first thought was of the house wrens. They and the Lucias, the little, shiny, bronzy-backed lizards that earned my gratitude by eating the cockroaches and spiders that lurked in crannies of the cabin, were the only creatures with red blood that lived in the thatch; the drops of blood might have been shed by either of them. Perhaps a snake or a weasel had climbed into the roof and caught one of the wrens, then escaped before I could detect it in the flashlight's beam. But it would be impossible to learn, before the return of the morning light, whether anything had befallen the birds.

I was not allowed much time to worry about the fate of my wrens. I went into the passageway between the house and the kitchen to wash the blood from my hand. Before I could return to the table to finish my meal, for which I now had little appetite, bloodcurdling shrieks pierced the stillness of the night. They seemed to issue from Don Juan's house, fifty yards distant. Then I heard Juan call José. My first surmise was that a snake, or possibly even a jaguar from the forest, had attacked Juan's wife or one of his four small children. Acting on this belief, I snatched up my readiest weapon, my machete, and rushed off in the direction of the shrieks. But before I had covered half the distance between the two dwellings, I noticed a thick column of smoke rising from a corner of my neighbor's house, which fortunately was roofed with tiles rather than with cane leaves. Immediately dropping the machete, I ran back to the kitchen for the bucket, which luckily I found half-full of water.

When I reached the interior of the burning house, Don Juan had quenched the blaze. A cupboard in a corner of the bedroom, filled with books and papers, was the site of the fire. My neighbor's wife had probably ignited it when she went to remove something by candlelight; then she had closed the door and was unaware of the blaze she had kindled until smoke began to pour out. The shrieks that had aroused me were her wails of distress, and they did not stop until she had been assured that the fire was extinguished. Her nerves had been overstrained by the double duty of teaching two grades in the one-roomed schoolhouse and raising four children of her own. As a result of the shock she had received that night, a fifth child was prematurely born, and for days she hovered between life and death.

After the last spark had been quenched, the children discovered a litter of kittens in the bottom of the cupboard, drenched by the water that had been poured upon the flames, but still squirming. The kittens' misfortune distressed the children more than the loss of the books and important papers that had been ruined, the danger that had threatened their home, or even the injury to their mother's health, which they could not yet understand.

As the night ended, I stood in front of the cabin to learn whether the wrens were still alive. I was delighted to see both fly out from among the cane leaves at their usual time. Singing-Wren sang long and cheerily, as though there were neither pain nor sorrow in all the world.

As to the two drops of blood, the explanations were various. Don Juan suggested that one of the little lizards had cut itself on the sharp edge of a cane leaf. José's sister was of the opinion that a vampire bat, which sometimes sucked blood from the horses and cows, had flown over my supper table fresh from its gory feast and still dripping warm blood. I never heard that these vampires bit any person in this valley; they seemed to confine their attacks to the grazing animals, who in the morning would sometimes be found with a little round hole in the ear or neck or back and a trickle of dried blood on the hair below it. I preferred not to pass judgment on these various suggestions and was content to let the drops of blood, which fell so mysteriously from my roof at the end of that day of fires, remain always a mystery.

5

Backwoods Neighbors

LONG AGO, the Valley of El General was inhabited by Indians of the Brunka tribe. To judge by the number and extent of their burial grounds, they were formerly fairly numerous, but now they have all but vanished as a pure race. When I first arrived, a pitiful remnant, consisting of only a few families, dwelt beside the Río Chirripó, at a point called Chimirol. Their white neighbors, themselves none too clean, said that these aborigines were filthy and asserted that they were dying out because of their dirty habits. I sometimes passed them on the trails, and once they came to sell me vegetables. The men had their front teeth filed to sharp points—certainly a painful operation. They refused to tell me the meaning of words in their native language that I heard them using. In the lower Térraba Valley, beyond Buenos Aires, were two large Indian villages, Térraba and Boruca. I was informed that these people led such a hand-to-mouth existence that they rarely had provisions to sell to travelers, and so I did not visit them. In all Costa Rica, only a few

Headpiece: The burial ground in the forest, Rivas, 1936.

thousand Indians remain, in contrast to the millions that persist, preserving their ancestral customs and languages, in the extensive highlands of such countries as Mexico, Guatemala, Ecuador, and Peru.

Here in El General, the burial grounds of the aborigines are commonly situated on the backs of the ridges rather than in the valleys. The reason for this seems obvious: in the rocky bottom lands, deep graves are difficult to dig. Moreover, these valley bottoms, limited in area, are the richest agricultural lands. The sides of the ridges are commonly very steep, leaving the flat tops as the most favorable sites for cemeteries. As in other regions, the deceased Indian was interred with his possessions. Possibly, there were cotton garments, woven *matates* for carrying burdens, headdresses, weapons, and the like; but these corruptible articles have long since rotted away, and, in the graves today, clay pottery and golden ornaments are the artifacts chiefly encountered.

The presence of the precious metal has led the recent inhabitants of El General to dig open the Indian graves in great numbers. The forest on the lower end of the ridge east of Rivas, once an extensive aboriginal burial ground, was broken by many deep, yawning pits, in the vertical sides of which the beautiful Blue-diademed Motmots sometimes dug their nest burrows. But as in other populations, wealthy individuals appear to have been in the minority among the Indians, and often the back-straining toil of uncovering one of the profound graves was rewarded by nothing more valuable than crude pottery for which there was no market. The most attractive and highly colored pottery found in Costa Rican Indian graves comes from the Chorotega culture of the province of Guanacaste. Still, with perseverance and a measure of luck, the gold ornaments, frequently in the form of a stylized bird with spread wings, could be found in numbers. One of the wealthiest men of the valley was reputed to have laid the foundations of his fortune by grave digging, and it was also darkly rumored that he suffered from some mysterious malady contracted in the course of these excavations. So widespread is the practice of grave digging that it has a special name. The Indian burials are called *huacas*—whence the verb *huaquear*, to open Indian graves. I never cared to indulge in this occupation. I felt that, having despoiled the unhappy aborigines of their lands, their culture, and all their sublunary possessions, we intruders of Old World origin might at least suffer their dust to rest undisturbed deep in the ground where their bereaved kindred laid them. "Irrational sentiment!" the reader may exclaim. A life devoid of sentiment is narrow and mean.

The actual inhabitants of El General have come chiefly from the densely populated central part of Costa Rica during the present century. The earliest immigrants, I was told, were mostly people who found it convenient, for one reason or another, to flee from the more civilized districts and conceal themselves amid the forests. Later colonists were of a different stamp. Many came from the *cantón* of Dota, southernmost outpost of the long-settled central region of Costa Rica. While I dwelt in Rivas, I would sometimes watch a family, newly arrived by way of the forbidding trail over El Cerro de la Muerte, file down the grassy roadway before my cabin. The men and older boys would travel afoot, usually with bulky packs on their backs. The mother would be riding a wiry little horse, often carrying an infant in arms wrapped in a flaming scarlet blanket. Perhaps there would be two small children mounted tandem upon a second horse. Sometimes there was a third horse bulkily laden with miscellaneous household articles, cooking pots much in evidence. These people had sold their small farms in more crowded regions and come with all their movable possessions to establish homesteads in this valley rich in promise.

Frequently these new immigrants would camp beneath the thatched roof of somebody's cane press until they could buy or build a rude dwelling of their own. The earliest settlers, who arrived before there were cane fields and these little factories for making crude sugar, must have endured many hardships until they became firmly established on their new farms. An ancient widow told me of days when matches and all other manufactured necessities were difficult to procure, and the embers of the cooking fire had to be carefully covered every night to keep them alive until morning, when Jaguars, already disappearing when I arrived, prowled around the flimsy huts. The first shopkeeper in the valley charged exorbitantly for essential commodities and laid the foundation of a modest fortune before competition reduced his prices. But in the mid-1930s, many settlers arrived by airplane and found essential articles sold at competitive prices in the many *pulperías* of San Isidro.

When I first knew El General, recently cleared valley lands yielded good crops with a minimum of cultivation and no fertilization. A competent farmer had little difficulty raising enough to feed his family. But to find money for clothing, utensils, and the few indispensable tools was a serious problem. Since nearly everybody else in the valley was also a farmer, the prices of agricultural products were low and the demand limited. The difficulties of overland transportation and the high rates for air freight made it profitable to export only the most valuable produce. Tobacco was perhaps the most reliable cash crop; beans and rice could profitably be sent to the cities of the interior only when a shortage raised prices above normal; maize was grown for local consumption only. Precisely because it was, of all the settled regions of Costa Rica, one of the most unfavorably situated for overland or water transport, El

General attracted several airlines, and resulting competition made the tariffs unusually low. In 1939, when I dwelt beside La Quebrada de las Vueltas below San Isidro, an airplane would pass overhead every morning, and on some days two or three. All this was changed when the United States hastily built a section of the Inter-American Highway from Cartago to San Isidro del General during the Second World War, when early Japanese victories in the Pacific made some Americans fear that the sea route between the Panama Canal and the West Coast might be controlled by the enemy.

For a while, an independent aviator, skillful but inadequately financed, operated an airplane between San Isidro and San José. He offered transportation at rates considerably below those of the well-established companies and had plenty of business, for my neighbors, when obliged to visit the capital, would ride in his little machine to save a dollar or so on the round trip. "Poor brave devils," I would say to myself, "to risk their necks for so little!" But after talking to them, I changed my opinion. Knowing nothing about motors or aerodynamics, they regarded flying as a sort of miracle; and after all, is it less miraculous to ride in an airplane in poor repair than in one adequately serviced? But I, who had once driven an ancient automobile and knew a little about the ailments to which a gasoline motor is susceptible, would never travel in the independent aviator's plane, which, before long, had an accident. Yet my neighbors considered me most valiant because I slept alone in the forest on the mountaintops, where they, if benighted, would sit up tending a fire through the hours of darkness for fear of the *tigre*. Since I had never heard of a Jaguar's attacking a man in Costa Rica, I had no fear, slept as soundly as the cold would allow, and did not imagine that I had done anything heroic. Courage, as the Greek philosophers contended, is largely a matter of knowing what is to be feared.

At first, my neighbors and I had considerable difficulty understanding each other. I had learned my Spanish chiefly in Guatemala, where many Indian words were used for common things. In Costa Rica, I had to learn new names for these things. My neighbors in El General spoke very rapidly with indistinct enunciation, many ellipses and provincialisms.

They were simple people, so simple—or was it goodness of heart?—that even at the beginning they did not take advantage of my newness among them to charge special prices. Until my cabin in Rivas was ready for occupancy, I boarded with a neighboring woman, who fed me amply for a week, at the end of which she charged me the equivalent of thirty cents and refused to take more, as this was the customary rate. This predisposed me in their favor. As I have found elsewhere south of the Río

Grande, my neighbors did not cultivate veracity as one of the noblest of their virtues; they did not hesitate to lie when it would shield them or their friends from admission of a fault. But the adage on which I had been raised, "Show me a liar and I'll show you a thief," hardly applied here. In matters of money or property, my neighbors were generally to be trusted. When I sent a boy to buy something, I could depend upon receiving the correct change, and thievery was rare.

Despite the poverty of these people, they were extraordinarily independent, proud, and sensitive. Their intolerance of a rebuke made the relation between employer and employee exceedingly delicate and difficult. The mildest reprimand would grow—chiefly, I surmise, during those long, rainy afternoons filled with endless gossip—to the proportions of an unpardonable insult. José, my first assistant, after serving me well for four months, finally departed in a huff because I reproved him for leaving a task undone and trying to cover the palpable omission with a lie. Although I had used no hard words, he became so incensed that it required some persuasion to make him receive the balance of his wage and take home a blanket that I had given him. His parting shot was that he had worked all his life without ever being reprimanded, and I, a stranger, had no right to come here and scold a native. What a poor pride, that of never being reproved! The tree that is never pruned fails to attain maximum fruitfulness.

Most of my neighbors' mendacity sprang, I believe, from their dread of being discovered in a fault. One day when I returned to the cabin, one of José's successors, a boy of about fifteen, told me that my apparatus for illuminating the interior of woodpeckers' nests was out of order and explained that in my absence another boy had entered to play with it. It was obvious that he would never have discovered the inconspicuous defect if he himself had not been playing with my simple electrical equipment. When I remarked that it was easier for me to pardon breakage than lying, he wept like a little child.

During my first two years in El General, I employed successively seven assistants. Although it was not easy to cook after spending a long day afield, and they had no real interest in the culinary art, I had, on the whole, no trouble with my boys as long as I kept them constantly with me and busy all day long. It was when I did not require their help in the field, and they had only to cook, gather firewood, and go in search of provisions, that difficulties arose; then they enjoyed too much leisure for gossip with their neighbors and would talk over little unguarded things that I said until they became monstrous and unpardonable crimes. Or the neighbor would magnify my acts of supposed injustice to make my helper leave in dudgeon and open a position for his own son, who would come applying for the job almost before the other boy was out of sight. After a week, I and my late helper would be friends again, and presently would come application for reappointment.

While I lived in Rivas, the community undertook the construction of a new church and a new schoolhouse. Both were built largely with funds raised locally at little fairs called *turnos,* for which the neighbors were asked to contribute articles to be sold. The more valuable contributions, such as calves, pigs, and household goods, were disposed of by raffles, for which crudely printed tickets were sold many days in advance. I regretted that I failed to win the pig for which I bought a ticket, for it would have provided great amusement for everyone, all my neighbors knowing my aversion to those shrill-voiced scavengers, which they themselves admitted into their homes. The schoolhouse was in use more than two hundred days in the year, the church possibly a dozen times in as many months. The old school was more badly decayed than the old church; yet the fairs for the benefit of the church were more generously supported, because a donation to this cause was regarded as a gift to the Virgin, who would protect the donor in life and facilitate his entry into heaven. It was obvious that these people, like the mystics of every religion, valued the soul far more than the mind. Yet the simple one-roomed school was completed within a year, while the more pretentious wooden church promised to be almost as long in building as a great medieval cathedral.

Despite the prevailing lack of interest in schools, I felt that my neighbors' children received an education admirably adapted to their future needs. In two or three years in the little schoolhouse, they learned to write, clearly if slowly, and enough arithmetic for the simple financial transactions of the valley. They were even given a little music. I would sometimes pass the aged music teacher, on horseback, making his rounds of the scattered schools, his fiddle beneath an arm. For the rest, the boys completed their education on their father's farm; the girls, in their mother's kitchen. The boys learned how to plant sugarcane and when to cut it, how to operate the cane press and boil the juice and pour it into molds to form *dulce.* They learned how to prepare a clearing, plant maize, beans, cassava, and plantains. Before they were twelve, some could manage a yoke of oxen. The earliest plaything of many was the machete, which would later be their chief tool. Barefoot lads of nine or ten would put me to shame by carrying a bunch of bananas, almost as heavy as themselves, down a precipitous hillside path on which I, in shoes, could hardly remain erect. They knew the price of labor, the value of everything the farm sold, and the cost of all that the family bought; there were no financial secrets, as in the homes of the wealthy. In short, when they reached the age of fifteen or sixteen, most of these children had an adequate conception of what life would involve for them, in cash expenditure as well as muscular exertion, and they were well prepared to meet its demands.

I fear that I and most of my classmates, when at the age of twenty-one or twenty-two we had completed the education that had occupied fifteen years or so of our lives and cost our parents and the state a respectable sum of money, were far less adequately prepared to meet the struggle ahead of us. We had been taught something about life in ancient Egypt and Rome; we had learned to extract square roots and had heard —and often forgotten—about the periodic table of elements and the Mendelian laws of inheritance. But I wonder how many of us knew what it cost our families to live in the style to which we had all our lives been accustomed; and I know for a fact that many of us were unprepared to earn all the unnecessary things that habit had made essential for our happiness. The children of Rivas received too few of the amenities of learning; we had received too few of the fundamentals. I am not sure that they were not given the more adequate education.

One of the most alert and enterprising of my neighbors was Humberto Gamboa. Small and wiry, I used to call him "the Yankee," although, with dark skin and bare feet, he was anything but a Yankee in appearance. In addition to attending his hillside farm, he manufactured excellent brooms with broomcorn that he raised himself. Since my rough floor wore out so many brooms, I was one of his best customers. I also employed him to mend my cane-leaf thatch, which was constantly developing leaks. He was proficient in the tonsorial art and, periodically, cut my hair while I sat on a stool in the dooryard. He seemed pleased when I told him, without flattery, that they did not give me a more satisfactory haircut in the capital. A pillar of the local church, he was the special friend of the visiting *padres*. His eldest daughter, Dora, a child of about ten when I first knew her, with a satiny, dark olive complexion and large, dark eyes, was one of the prettiest girls in Rivas. She and her sister used to bring me tortillas which their mother made. They thought nothing of walking a mile each way to deliver two or three cents' worth of food.

In December, Humberto and I climbed far up into the mountains, he to gather the more luxuriant mosses and lycopods of that altitude for his *portal* or Christmas garden, I to collect botanical specimens. In addition to many ferns and mosses, I found, growing in the forest between five and six thousand feet above sea level, a lovely shrub that was later identified as *Symbolanthus pulcherrimus*, of the gentian family. It grew to be twelve feet high and had large, glossy leaves and deep pink, trumpet-shaped flowers nearly three inches long. As evening approached, Humberto kept urging me to hurry, lest night catch us in the forest; but when at last I closed the plant press and started downward, he found some prettier mosses and had to stop to gather them. Between us, we delayed so long that we barely reached the valley before dark.

Humberto invited me to come on Christmas Eve to join in the festivities and see the garden. It occupied a corner of the *sala*, or central large room of his humble, floorless, thatched hut—his roof always leaking, he was so busy repairing others. Here he had arranged a mountainous landscape with moss for verdure and little palm trees—no paper imitations—standing everywhere. In the center was a long bridge, spanning a pond in which swans floated, between two palm-crowned peaks. These heights might have been copied directly from those which rose up behind Humberto's cabin and, at this season, were deliciously fragrant with the white blossoms of the Clusia trees that grew beneath the palms; but the celluloid swans were a fanciful addition to the local scene. In the background was a plain on which stood two magi looking down upon an empty manger, but the third king and the infant Jesus were conspicuous by their absence. The place of the latter was taken by a full-grown Christ who looked over the garden from the rear! Humberto and his wife, Blanca, were obliged to use such figures and decorations as their own cabin and the largess of tropical nature happened to supply. Here were no shops displaying a special Christmas stock that could fill deficiencies.

But where did Humberto find those beautiful ivory posts and rich ribbons of white satin that fenced the Christmas garden? How could he afford such extravagances? It took me a while to solve this puzzle. Slender leaf bases from the interior of the false stem of the banana plant made pillars straight and white and smooth and well-turned as though they had been skillfully cut from marble or the finest ivory. Long strips of tissue torn from the thin edges of these same inner leaf sheaths of the banana trunk were stretched like ribbons between the upright posts. Ivory and satin could not have made a more elegant guardrail. Yet the whole had cost Humberto and his good wife only their labor. I recalled how in Córdoba, far away to the north in Mexico, the Indian girls fashioned white cylindrical boxes from the interior portions of banana stems, which, being built up of concentric layers, lent themselves admirably to such purposes. These ivorylike boxes were filled with gardenia blossoms; when the little lid in the side was raised, a heavy fragrance escaped and persuaded tourists to buy them.

Humberto had invited many guests, who, dressed in their poor best, sat stiffly on wooden benches against the rough walls, listening to the strains of the accordion and the guitar played by neighbors. Later, Doña Blanca served tamales and soggy unleavened bread made of maize. I did not stay to the end of the festivities, which promised to continue through much of the night. These Christmas celebrations were held, one after another, through much of January. Sometimes, when alcoholic refreshments were served, they would be terminated by fights among the men, which my garrulous servant José would report to me with wearisome prolixity.

José was indeed a great gossip. He seemed to be related, in one degree or another, to half the people in the vicinity, and he would tell me endlessly about his third and fourth cousins, his brother-in-law's aunt and his sister-in-law's niece, until I could wish the whole tribe of them in ultima Thule. Although only twenty-two years of age, he suffered, in addition to the anile weakness of gossip, from several other of the infirmities of old age. He was constantly complaining of rheumatism, colic, his liver, his stomach, his teeth, and his feet, which pained him during the night when chigoes burrowed into them. He had evidently passed through a difficult childhood in the damp, floorless hut in the little forest clearing, but many of his troubles were shared by others as young as himself. It was not surprising that so many suffered from disordered stomachs, for they commonly bolted their rice and beans almost unchewed, alleging, as an excuse for this unwholesome habit, that many employers did not allow them sufficient time for eating—yet the fact was that most worked on their own lands. I was not a *patrón* of that stamp, and with some of my younger helpers I would play a game at mealtime to see whether they or I would finish last, the one who ate most slowly winning. Moreover, I would never permit our food to be soaked and rendered indigestible with an excess of heavy lard, which, until cheap vegetable fats and oils became available, was the bane of Central American cooking.

My neighbors' teeth were very bad, for few of them ever used a brush. When a few teeth became so decayed that extraction was necessary, they would, if they had the money, have them all pulled out and acquire a complete set of false teeth. This was done for economy, to save their hard-earned colones. False teeth do not need brushes and toothpaste; they do not require fillings nor costly bridgework; and the first cost is, for a long while, the only expense. It was strange to see whole dentures in the mouths of adolescents. One lad of seventeen, who worked for me a long while, suffered much from toothache, until I sent him to the dentist who had recently opened an office in San Isidro. The young dentist pulled out five teeth which had decayed beyond repair; he offered to replace them by bridges and fill the others for only ninety colones. I promised to pay half the modest price of this dental work if the boy or his father would pay the other half. After talking it over, the lad announced that his natural teeth were "too ugly"; he much preferred a pretty set of false teeth with a little gold stuck here and there on the front ones, where it would glitter when he smiled. They would cost only forty colones. I refused to aid or abet a procedure so unnatural—but perhaps I was too rigid in my point of view.

Despite all the organic troubles from which they suffered, the consequence of improper living due in part to poverty and even more to ignorance, my barefoot neighbors were amazingly resistant to wounds. These rarely festered severely, although they were often improperly disinfected and covered. Perhaps, too, septic germs were not so abundant in this sun-drenched, rain-washed, sparsely inhabited valley as in more crowded communities.

Infant mortality was still very high. This is certainly not an unmitigated evil in communities where, otherwise, families would become excessively large and the population soon exceed the productive capacity of the land—as it threatens to do before long in Costa Rica where, with better health services, the population is presently increasing at the alarming rate of four per cent per year. One afternoon while I dwelt in Rivas, a neighbor's little girl came to ask whether I would sell a small amount of refined sugar; her infant brother was sick, and they needed this as a remedy. I was the only person in the vicinity who happened to possess this luxury; I had not yet learned to depend on local products as completely as I later did. On learning why it was needed, I would accept no money for the sugar.

A few days later, another little white box was carried up the hillside, to be buried in the *panteón*, a weed-choked clearing in the forest, with its crude wooden crosses all awry, occupying part of the site of the ancient Indian burial ground. Whether a graveyard was called a *panteón* or a *huaca* depended upon whether people of one's own or of an alien race were laid to rest there. One morning, prowling about the vicinity of the cemetery in search of birds, I found Humberto with his machete making a mighty attack on the tall weeds that had overgrown it. After much strenuous work, he was able to point out to me the graves of some of his closest relations, scattered here and there in the narrow forest clearing.

About this time, I had my first visitor, an Englishman, the father of a family and an excellent naturalist. When I told him about the incident of the sugar, he accused me of murdering the infant. I protested: "How is a bachelor like me to know that white sugar is not good for sick babies? Besides, if it has indeed become an *ángel*, as our neighbors claim, I am sure it is now singing my praise in heaven."

It is pleasant to recall that during my years of travel among the people of Central America, I received almost unfailing courtesy from rich and poor alike—but, chiefly, I traveled and dwelt among the most humble.

I have sought hospitality in rude huts in the forest where the inmates had scarcely anything—yet received the best they had. Frequently, I have eaten the food of strangers and afterward found it difficult or impossible to pay them. Although few have understood the nature of my activities, many have been eager to help my work along.

In these years of travel, I can recall only one glaring instance of discourtesy. While I passed through the Indian village of Paraíso on the Isthmus of Tehuantepec, some small boys threw stones at me. But when, on my return through the same village, I took a wrong turn and lost my way, the schoolmaster was so affable and with so fine a courtesy sent his little son to put me on the trail, that even against Paraíso I harbor no resentment. But on the whole, my experiences with places called "Paradise," of which I can recall four, have been disappointing; they have failed dismally to live up to the name. The one that came nearest was practically all forest.

6

The Mountain of Death

THE VALLEY OF EL GENERAL was so shut in by high mountains and vast forests that its inhabitants referred to all the rest of the world as *Afuera* (Outside). When anyone went to Cartago or San José, or only as far as San Marcos de Tarrazú or Santa María de Dota, his neighbors would say that he had gone "Outside." By mid-March, I had thousands of botanical specimens ready to send to the United States and Europe, and, having also other matters to attend to, I decided to make a trip "Outside." The packages of plants were hauled in an oxcart to San Isidro for shipment by air to the capital. This would also have been the simplest way for me to make the journey, but I had heard so much about the trail over the mountains that I wished to go that way and see it for myself.

I looked for a horse that I could hire for the journey, but when my friend the *Jefe Político* offered to sell me a handsome bay gelding, saddled

Headpiece: A green Violet-ear feeds her nestlings. In a young cypress in the Guatemalan highlands. The mossy nest has been burst asunder by their growing bodies.

and bridled, for only one hundred colones (about sixteen dollars), I seized the opportunity. With an admixture of foreign blood, my new horse was so much bigger than most of his equine neighbors, many of which were no larger than ponies, that he was generally known as *El Caballón* (the Big Horse). He had no other name; so dropping the first syllable of this appellation, I came gradually to call him *'Ballón*, which I finally Anglicized to "Bayon."

Since the trip promised to be long and difficult, I reduced baggage and provisions to a minimum. My heavy Guatemalan blanket would be excellent for sleeping on those cold mountaintops; a thick sweater, worn at night, would give almost as much protection as a second blanket and weigh less. I rolled these up in a rubberized ground cloth and strapped them behind the saddle. The indispensable machete was tied at the pommel. For food, I took forty tortillas, heated nearly to dryness and wrapped in pieces of banana leaf that had been scorched over flames—the usual method of preparing them for a long journey. A couple of tins of oatmeal were also placed in my saddlebags. When I was too tired, hurried, or lazy to kindle a fire, I could mix the meal with sugar and water and eat it cold. These provisions, I thought, would suffice for three days, until I could reach the first village on the other side of the mountains.

Thus equipped and provisioned, I mounted my new horse on a brilliant morning in the middle of March and set forth on the trail that led to Cartago over El Cerro de la Muerte. Our way led up the valley of the Buena Vista through the whole length of Rivas to a stretch where the river was pressed closely by steep slopes, leaving scarcely any level ground along its shores. We forded the rushing stream beside the footbridge that, in the following wet season, fell beneath an unfortunate pedestrian, who was carried away by the swollen current and never seen again. At the farther bank, we began to climb the mountain, choosing what appeared to be the more frequented of the two paths that diverged from the ford. But I had guessed wrong; the path ended at a solitary cabin on the mountainside. We had to return to the river and take the less used trail to the right.

We passed through a bushy pasture, then the maimed, fire-scarred outskirts of the forest, into unspoiled forest more remote from the dwellings of men. The trail was a mere footpath, scarcely wide enough for two horses to pass, rough with rocks and the exposed roots of the great trees beneath which it lay. Soon the ascent became so steep that I decided to walk and lead Bayon in order to conserve his strength. The trail held closely to a narrow ridge, with the slopes falling away sharply on both sides. Here on the dry ridge, Euterpe palms were the most abundant trees; soon we were climbing upward through a forest of them. Their slender, gray trunks were tall, straight, and clean, holding high their spreading crowns of huge, feathery fronds. I paused long enough to measure a fallen trunk, which was sixty-six feet long but only six inches in diameter. Others, still standing, appeared even higher.

As we continued to climb, the palms gave way to a forest of great, broad-leafed trees, chiefly oaks whose leaves were entire rather than deeply indented like those of many northern species. We toiled upward through woodland filled with the sweet melody of Black-faced Solitaires, relatives of the robins and thrushes. For long intervals, their unhurried, pensive whistles were so constantly in our ears that a single songster seemed to be accompanying us, unseen among the treetops like a guardian spirit, to cheer our laborious ascent with song; but, doubtless, we were actually hearing a succession of birds as we continued upward. Hours passed before I glimpsed one of the sylvan minstrels, for they remained well hidden amid the foliage, and I could not afford to stop long to peer about for them. But in the late afternoon, I saw two of them perching side by side on a branch above the trail, where they obligingly delayed until I had examined them well through my field glasses. They were slate-gray with black faces, orange-red bills, and orange legs and toes.

The path led relentlessly upward, always through unbroken forest. All day long we met no other traveler. Bayon did not enjoy the climb and began to behave badly. Little, black, bloodsucking flies persecuted him mercilessly, settling on his eyelids in such multitudes that they formed black circles around his eyes. There were also deer flies that pierced him with long, sharp lances. When I tried to lead him, he would hang back and need to be hauled along, which soon exhausted his master. When I drove from behind, he would turn off the trail at the first opportunity, trying to find his way down the mountain; but the dense undergrowth soon halted these attempts to double back. When I rode, he would race ahead for a short distance, then stop from sheer exhaustion, his heart beating with hammerlike pulsations. He was scarcely four years old, accustomed to the nearly level roads of the valley, but untrained for work on trails like this. I regretted that I had not arranged to join some other traveler with a more experienced horse, who could show Bayon how to behave on a mountain trail.

Hour after hour, I urged the horse up that never-ending mountain. Having set forth on this journey, I did not wish to turn back. I knew that my horse was strong and far from exhausted; if ever he reached the summit of El Cerro de la Muerte, the rest of the way would be easier. But finally, as evening approached, he stopped dead in his tracks and adamantly refused to budge. To urge him onward was as useless as it is to coax forward, by words or blows, an automobile with an empty gasoline tank. The point where he stalled was in a deep trench, where the trail had been eroded until there were vertical banks, shoulder-high, on both sides, with hardly enough space between them for me to pass the horse. I hauled at the reins until my arms ached, then went behind and switched the recalcitrant animal until pity made me desist. Bayon's failure to kick, while I was belaboring him from the rear, showed that he was well-bred, even if he was a poor mountaineer. But all urgings were in vain.

Soon, to relieve my overwrought feelings, I began to expostulate with the steed; but, as was to be expected, words were no more effective than blows and tugs on the reins. By this time, I was quite ready to allow Bayon to go whichever way he chose; the important point was to reach some locality that provided forage and water, neither of which was available here in the forest. The closest spots where I was sure of finding these necessities were the open summit of El Cerro de la Muerte, about two thousand feet higher, and the valley that we had left five thousand vertical feet below us. But now Bayon as stubbornly refused to turn back as to continue upward; neither coaxing nor the switch could persuade him to take a single step.

The scattered sunbeams that found their way between the great trunks were becoming horizontal, warning me that little daylight remained. In any event, it was necessary to get my horse out of that deep trench, where he had stood immobile for the past half-hour. Once more, I pulled and pushed, coaxed and threatened, applied the switch, with no more encouraging result than before. Despair was settling deeper, when I heard travelers, the first I had seen all day, approaching down the trail. Soon a pedestrian, followed by a man riding a mare and a boy leading another, emerged from between the trees. They had come from Santa María and intended to sleep at the resthouse of La División. With the arrival of others of his kind, my forlorn horse revived. After all, it must be possible for horses to pass through this forest alive! With a little urging, Bayon followed the two mares, and all of us hurried down the steep trail.

Well over a thousand feet below, we came to the resthouse. It stood on a slope below the trail, from which it was hidden by trees. Although I had been told of its existence, I had seen nothing to indicate its presence as we toiled upward. Constructed by the government, it had two small rooms with walls thickly plastered to keep out the nocturnal chill, a roof of corrugated iron laboriously hauled from "Outside," and even a floor. But it was falling into disrepair and was uninvitingly dirty. Leaving it to the three travelers from Santa María, I went to camp beneath the trees. A short distance below the house flowed a rivulet of pure water, where horse and rider drank deeply after the long climb. Beyond was a level area with little undergrowth, which made an attractive camp site. Here I kindled a fire, on which I heated a few tortillas and cooked some oatmeal.

Poor Bayon fared badly that night, but it was his own fault. The only gramineous plant in sight was the bamboo. I cut for him all of this hard fodder that I could find, but there was much less here than higher on the mountain. He eagerly devoured a few of my tortillas, then concluded his meager supper by nibbling at the leaves of some shrubs. By morning, he was hungry enough to pluck moss from the rocks.

After supper, I sat before the campfire thinking what I should do on the morrow. I did not enjoy the prospect of returning to my empty cabin in the valley; but I knew that if Bayon had traveled badly on the first day, he would go even worse on the second after a night with little food. Finally, I decided that I would try to arrange with the downward-bound travelers to take my horse to San Isidro, while I continued upward afoot. This decision made, I spread my ground cloth on the dry leaves and lay down beneath my blanket.

In the night, the wind blew up and roared through the great trees on the ridge above me with the sound of surf on a rocky seashore, but it scarcely penetrated into the sheltered vale where I rested. Around midnight, the waning moon rose, and its pale light filtered down through the foliage. A goatsucker, of a kind unknown to me, called sadly a few times in a voice not unlike that of the Whippoorwill. I slept soundly, but Bayon was restless and twice chewed through the rope, by which he was tethered close beside me, to go and join the mares in whose company I found him at dawn.

At daybreak, I arose and went to the resthouse to broach to the pedestrian traveler the proposal I had formed beside the campfire. As I had surmised, he was glad enough to finish on horseback the journey begun on foot. He promised to deliver Bayon to the *Jefe Político* in San Isidro. Although the man's square chin suggested honesty, I should not have entrusted to a stranger a horse that I valued, but Bayon was still new to me and had made a most unpromising start. I gave Morales two colones for taking care of my horse and a note to my friend hastily scribbled on a leaf torn from my pocket notebook.

When the three wayfarers, now all mounted, had started down the trail, I hung my blanket roll, saddlebags, machete, and other impedimenta around me and continued upward alone. It took an hour's hard climbing to recover the precious altitude that I had so swiftly lost when forced to turn back on the preceding evening. The solitaires whistled pensively beneath the towering oak trees, as on the previous day. Presently I reached a place where the forest on the crest of the spur was lower and more open, permitting here and there an outlook over the long, wooded slopes of the main ridge to my right. Although on the long climb through the forest I had seen scarcely any flowers, here, where the more open canopy permitted sunlight to enter, there was no lack of bright blossoms. Shrubs with blue and red and yellow flowers bordered the trail, and birds also were more in evidence. Violet-ear Hummingbirds, perching on exposed twigs, tirelessly repeated their little dry songs. A pair of Hairy Woodpeckers, much like those of northern woodlands, hammered on a dead trunk while I paused to watch.

At a point where my pocket altimeter indicated ten thousand feet, the trail ceased to climb so steeply but continued along the nearly level summit of a mighty spur, which led into the central mass of El Cerro de la Muerte. For miles I walked along a stony path which rose and fell only with the gentle undulations of the crest, yet tended gradually upward. The forest was still largely of oaks, which here were lower and grew in a more open stand. Their foliage was dark and compact, with that sombre aspect typical of trees on a high, exposed, cloud-bathed ridge. Their boughs were heavily cloaked with mosses, which here and there formed thick cushions and huge swellings. Beneath the trees was a thicket of bamboos, so dense that I could push through it only with great difficulty. The ground was covered with mosses, ferns, and lycopods. Nightingale-Thrushes, of a kind different from the orange-billed species that I heard in Rivas throughout the year, sang from concealment among the bamboos. Little Wilson's Warblers, with black caps and bright yellow breasts, passing here the months when snow and ice covered their summer homes far in the north, darted briskly through the bushes beside the trail.

In many places along this lofty ridge, the trees had been scarred or killed by fires, which consumed the dry undergrowth and left the ground black and charred. For hundreds of feet, I hurried with narrowed eyes through the acrid smoke of smoldering fires, slowly but surely destroying the forest.

In the early afternoon, the trail inclined more definitely upward again, and soon I climbed out of the forest into the páramo that covered the open summit of the Mountain of Death. Here dwarf bamboos (*Chusquea subtessellata*) and low bushes with dark, compact foliage gradually replaced the trees of the lower slopes. The ground was softly carpeted with a thick, peaty layer of dead vegetation, which at this season was so dry that in many spots it smoldered with fires that had evidently been set on purpose by travelers. Yet every leaf and twig and blade of grass above ground was dripping with water that condensed from the heavy gray clouds that a strong east wind was driving over the mountaintop from the Caribbean Sea. Over large areas that had already been burned, the ground was covered with gray, powdery ash, into which I sank to my shoe tops.

The resthouse stood amid the páramo in a great semicircular depression, shaped like a vast amphitheater, on the eastern side of the rounded summit, several hundred feet below the highest point. Like that at La División, this had been well constructed at considerable expense because of the difficulty of bringing materials to this remote mountaintop. But it was becoming ruinous, because travelers sometimes tore off boards to make their fires, and it was filthy both inside and outside. A rill of pure, cold water, arising in a saddle between two crests of the mountain, flowed down a narrow channel between high, vertical banks, to end in front of the resthouse in a muddy hole, befouled by swine. The pigs were sometimes driven over the trail from El General and even Buenos Aires de Osa, to be sold, if they survived the grueling journey, in the markets of Cartago and San José. This was the first body of water that I had seen since the morning, and I drank eagerly, well above the part polluted by the pigs.

I did not relish the prospect of passing a night in the dirty resthouse and hoped that the sky would clear so that I might sleep on the clean sod beneath the stars. But the clouds continued until dusk to stream over the summit from the east, releasing a fine drizzle that drenched everything exposed to it, and I reluctantly surrendered to the necessity of sleeping under cover.

But what is this shrub whose boughs I am cutting for my bed? With its small, narrow, pointed leaves closely set along slender, wiry stems, it closely resembled a juniper; yet no conifer of northern type was known to grow spontaneously in Costa Rica. I thought I had made a discovery of first importance to botanists—until some small, yellow flowers told me plainly that the shrub I was cutting was a Saint-John's-wort and not a gymnosperm. But the changed identification failed to alter my plans for a bed, and a few generous armfuls of the leafy twigs, spread over the floor in a corner of the resthouse, made a couch somewhat softer and much cleaner than the unwashed boards.

Before I had been long at the resthouse, I began to understand the reason for this mountain's name of El Cerro de la Muerte. On arrival, I found two girls, about ten and thirteen years of age, barefoot and wearing only thin cotton dresses with short sleeves. They had brought no heavier garments to keep them warm on the bleak summit of the Mountain of Death, but sat around all afternoon with bare arms exposed to the chill, damp wind that drove the clouds across the mountain. Before nightfall, both had begun to sniffle. Their fathers were also barefoot, but they were taking better care of themselves than of their daughters: one wore a light jacket, while the other covered his shoulders with an empty sack. The whole party crowded around a small fire that they had kindled beneath the porch, but it was too feeble to keep anybody warm.

Just at dusk, three belated travelers, two men and a boy, hurried up to the resthouse from the direction of Santa María, no better prepared for the cold of the summit than the first party. The boy complained of feeling sick; he sat, drawn and pinched, as close to the fire as he could; but the upper half of his body was covered only by a thin cotton shirt. Like the other travelers, these men promptly removed from their sack a hard, round brick of solidified crude cane sap called *dulce*. With a machete, they shaved off a liberal heap of the brown sugar and dissolved it in hot water, preparing the popular beverage known as *agua dulce*. The custom of drinking this sweet, brown liquid when they arrived at the summit, exhausted by the long climb, must have been responsible for keeping many of these people alive, for it quickly supplied heat-producing sugar to the blood. It was characteristic that they offered me a cup of the steaming beverage, which I politely declined, knowing that nobody carried an excess of provisions on such a journey.

Soon after darkness fell, the eight of us disposed ourselves over the floor for the night. Some had nothing heavier than an old coffee sack to cover themselves, and the rest had only thin cotton blankets. With my thick sweater and heavy Indian blanket, I had several times as much protection as any of the others, but still I felt chilly. The sky cleared soon after nightfall, and the stars shone forth brilliantly. As the night advanced, it became intensely cold, or at least it felt so to us who had long been living in balmier regions. From time to time I awoke, shivering and uncomfortable, and listened with sympathizing amusement to the moans and groans of the others, who even called upon their saints out of their great misery. It was not surprising that travelers accustomed to milder climates, who came so poorly prepared to pass the night on this cold summit, should sometimes contract a fatal chill. Those who arrived feeble or sick would be the chief victims. It sometimes happened, too, that someone, passing this way for the first time, wandered from the poorly marked trail over the open summit while it was mantled in cloud mist, to die from sheer exhaustion before he could find it again. But the airplane was already robbing this stern summit of its victims.

At daybreak I arose, wrapped my blanket around me, and went out to watch the sunrise. The first gray light of the new day revealed all the open ground between the bushes covered with a heavy white frost—the first I had seen since I camped on the Sierra Cuchumatanes in Guatemala nearly two years earlier. I had expected to watch the sun rise out of the Caribbean Sea, but the long, serrated crest of a great eastern offshoot of the main ridge stood darkly outlined against the roseate orient sky. All around me, the Sooty Thrushes were caroling in the frosty dawn. Their songs were long-continued and much like that of the American Robin in form, but their voices seemed sad and strained, as though they, too, had suffered from the chill of the night. For a long while, I watched one of the thrushes who perched at the top of a low shrub to sing. When the light became stronger, I was struck by this bird's resemblance to the Blackbird of England and that incomparable mimic, the Black Thrush of the Guatemalan highlands. His plumage was everywhere almost black; his bill, eyelids, and legs were bright yellow. Standing against the open sky, in the clear, empty air of the mountaintop, he appeared much bigger than he actually was—nearer the size of a crow than that of a thrush.

After the sun rose, I filled my canteen at the rivulet, then climbed to one of the summits of the mountain to enjoy the scenery while I breakfasted. Among the rocks on the slope up which I scrambled grew the shrubby heath *Pernettia coriacea,* with urn-shaped white or pinkish flowers resembling those of the blueberry; two species of Saint-John's-wort with yellow blossoms; the lycopod *Lycopodium saururus*; and the slender, stiff fronds of *Jamesonia glutinosa,* a fern of Andean affinities.

The open top of the Mountain of Death was vast and irregular, with great, rounded bosses separated by wide, shallow vales. Here and there, projecting from the páramo, were rocky outcrops and craggy pinnacles, mostly too small to destroy the low, rounded outlines of the great domes on which they rested. As seen from the Valley of El General, this mountain over eleven thousand feet high is grim, sombre, and forbidding, with the vegetation on its upper half less verdant and luxuriant than that on neighboring elevations. The mountains of southern Costa Rica are not volcanoes and so contrast sharply with the chains of volcanic peaks, frequently active, in the central and northwestern parts of the country.

The scenery spread before me on every side was on the most magnificent scale. To one who delights in wild Nature, no spectacle that human hands have ever created can compare in interest, or produce such a feeling of exultation mingled with reverence, as the vast landscape which spreads before him from the pinnacle of some lofty mountain rising above a remote wilderness. To the southeast stretched the main range of the Cordillera de Talamanca to which El Cerro de la Muerte belongs. Long, almost even-topped, forested ridges linked together the higher mountain masses, which were treeless and open like the summit on which I stood, but with surfaces more broken and craggy. The third of these outstanding elevations was the highest peak of Chirripó Grande, 12,570 feet, the culminating point in all the thousand miles of rugged mountains between Guatemala's shapely volcanoes and Colombia's snowy peaks. Many square miles in extent, the bare, treeless summit of the Chirripó massif is surmounted by ragged outcrops of rock and high, craggy pinnacles, between which nestle lakes of pure, cold water.

To the east of the continental divide was a terrain the wildest and most broken that I had ever seen. Great mountain spurs, offshoots of the main ridge, were piled one behind the other as far as eye could see, the huge, jumbled masses stretching dim and vast far into Panama. It was inspiring to gaze over so many titanic ridges all clad in unbroken primeval forest, which, like a regal robe without a rent, covered each from its foot up to its lofty crown, revealing not a trace of man's destroying hand. Such a verdant mantle of forest is no less becoming to a mountain than the white drapery of snow and ice. A great carpet of white, billowy clouds, far beneath me, covered all the lower country to the northeast. To the west, the land dropped away sharply, and I looked across many a lesser height, seeming only a hill beside the lofty one on which I stood, to a dim and changing white line of surf on the Pacific shore, more than two vertical miles below. All the recent burning on this side of the country had made the atmosphere very hazy.

It was difficult to tear myself away from this fascinating scene, but I carried only a limited supply of food, and, if I did not wish to starve here on the mountaintop, it was imperative to push onward before this supply was exhausted. All through the morning I trudged northward along the narrow, stony trail over the rocky, treeless crest of the mountain, through the low thickets of bamboos and small-leafed shrubs of the páramo, or across open, grassy spaces. The path wound around some of the highest rounded domes and, at intervals, skirted a craggy outcrop; but on the more level stretches of the ridge, it ran so near the crest that I enjoyed a fine outlook on either side. I journeyed along the roof ridge of Costa Rica, which separates the waters that flow into the two oceans.

Here and there a half-burned trunk, lying where only shrubs and grasses were now to be found, was proof that small trees had once grown higher on this mountain. All the fires burning along the trail, and signs of earlier fires, helped to explain their disappearance. In Guatemala, six degrees farther north, pines, alders, and other trees grow on the mountains and volcanoes, a thousand feet higher than the summit of El Cerro de la Muerte.

Juncos, named for the Volcán Irazú, now and again flew across the trail or perched in the bushes beside it to watch the wayfarer with their large, bright yellow eyes, eyes that made them appear wise and very serious. Rufous-collared Sparrows sang *We're here too too too,* as though they wished to make sure that I noticed how they braved the frosts and biting winds of this mountaintop, as they do from the volcanoes of Chiapas and Guatemala to the Andes of Chile. Adaptable birds, through all this vast extent of country, they dwell in farmyards and city parks as well as on remote peaks. Little Slaty Flower-piercers punctured, with their hooked, uptilted bills, the bases of the bright corollas of the mountain shrubs and sucked out the sustaining nectar. Once a straggling flock of Long-tailed Silky-Flycatchers, thin and pale in suits of gray, wandered over the open ridge, giving the impression that they might be the restless ghosts of those who had perished in bleak nights on the Mountain of Death.

The path that ran northward over the narrowing mass of the mountain had been descending gradually, and in the afternoon I left the open summit to walk beneath trees again. Then for hours I marched through the forest that covered a mountaintop. The trees cut off all outlook over the surrounding country, and along much of the way, the top of the ridge was so broad and level that it was easy to imagine that I was crossing some forested lowland plain. But the slender black hand of my aneroid—which stuck persistently a trifle below ten thousand feet—the appearance of the trees above my head, and the kinds of birds that flitted among them, all united in testifying that I was still high in the air. Among the dense undergrowth of bamboos grew flowering shrubs with orange-red and purplish-red blossoms, before which glittering green hummingbirds hovered on wings beating so rapidly that they seemed to dissolve into a mist, as they pushed their long, slender bills into the long tubes of the flowers to draw out the abundant nectar.

My passage frightened up, from its perch beside the trail, a young Violet-ear Hummingbird, so recently out of the nest that it still flew weakly. Its mother fluttered around me, chittering excitedly, much agitated over her fledgling's safety. In a bamboo close by, I found a tiny cup composed almost wholly of green moss, doubtless the nest in which this young hummer was hatched and raised. Its father, as usual, did not appear; he was too busy singing to care for his offspring.

In the middle of the afternoon, I reached the third and last resthouse, called Ojo de Agua, situated in a narrow clearing in the midst of the forest. Here I found neighbors returning to Rivas from a visit "Outside" and already encamped for the night. The boy showed me the "Eye of Water" for which this point was named, so well hidden at the foot of a bank below the trail that without his guidance I might not have found it. At the little spring of cold water, I quenched my growing thirst, gave hands and face a much-needed washing, and filled my canteen. Then I bade farewell to my neighbors and continued onward for several hours along the level path through the forest on the back of the same lofty ridge.

As evening fell, I ended my day's march in a grassy opening amid the trees. The sedges, bog mosses, and irislike *Orthrosanthus chimboracensis* growing here attested that in the wet season this was a little marsh, but now it was quite dry, with not a drop of water to be found. I stacked a pile of firewood, cut into convenient lengths, beside the spot I had chosen for my bed, made a meager supper of oatmeal and tortillas, then lay down close beside my campfire. By adding a few sticks from time to time when I happened to awake, I kept a slow fire burning through the night and slept more warmly than I had done in the house on El Cerro de la Muerte. During the early hours of darkness, clouds now and again blew across the mountaintop. Each relinquished part of its moisture in the form of fine droplets which wet my blanket, then drifted onward to reveal a sky bright with many stars.

After a peaceful night alone in the midst of the vast solitude, I awoke at dawn when the Sooty Thrushes and the Black-billed Nightingale-Thrushes in the woods around my little opening joined their voices in a liquid chorus. I made a most frugal breakfast, for my provisions were nearly exhausted, and drank the last of my water. It was not easy to extinguish the campfire, which during the night had burned deep into the peaty soil—dust-dry after the long, rainless months—on which I had unsuspectingly kindled it. Attempts to trample or beat out the embers only stirred up the black humus at the bottom of the hole, making the fire burn more hotly. Next, I tried to remove all the live coals to the hard-packed trail, where they would soon die away and do no harm; but as the air became drier with the rising sun, the fire spread more quickly than I could carry it away. Finally, it occurred to me to cut a large bundle of the sedges and grasses that grew in the open space and were still green and wet with the nocturnal dew. Trampling these down hard upon the smoldering cinders, after a quarter of an hour I had the satisfaction of seeing the smoke die away, nor did it rise again when I lifted the green herbage and loosened the ashes. This stubborn blaze delayed my departure for more than an hour, but it helped to explain the many fires and marks of burning that I had seen along the trail. I could not extinguish all the fires that other travelers had carelessly or deliberately set, but I could at least preserve the forest from destruction through fault of mine. I traveled the more blithely without that blaze behind me.

A short walk through the forest on the level ridge, then a brief climb, brought me to the flat, open summit of El Cerro de las Vueltas. I surmised that it was called "The Mountain of the Turns" because it would be so easy for a traveler to get turned about and lose his sense of direction while crossing the broad, open spaces when the summit was shrouded by clouds. This was the northernmost outpost of the páramo, a vegetable formation characteristic of the high Andes of Colombia and Ecuador. In moister spots stood *Puya dasylirioides,* a terrestrial bromeliad that resembled a short, sword-leafed yucca surmounted by a tall, polelike inflorescence that reminded the botanist Paul Standley of a gigantic mullein stalk. Mixed with this exotic growth were tree ferns (*Lomaria wercklei*) with short, exceptionally stout trunks and stiff, once-pinnate leaves, more like the leaves of a cycad than the fronds of a fern. Both of these plants were the northernmost representatives of Andean genera. Great flocks of Band-tailed Pigeons, very similar to those of the western United States, rested in the trees around the edges of the open spaces or settled in the pokeberry bushes that flourished there to feast upon the little, juicy, purple berries.

Soon the trail began to incline downward, entering a noble forest of oaks with the usual undergrowth of bamboo. Perhaps the forest here was actually no more beautiful than that through which I had laboriously climbed while ascending El Cerro de la Muerte three days before, but, on the downward way, the pedestrian has more energy for the enjoyment of the scenes through which he passes, and this seemed the most magnificent stand of oaks I had ever beheld. One mighty trunk measured seven feet in diameter at the level of my shoulders; the tree's height I estimated at no less than one hundred and fifty feet. Three-wattled Bellbirds sounded their peculiar wooden notes in the lofty treetops; but, as usual, I peered upward in vain through the clouds of foliage to see one. At an altitude of eighty-five hundred feet, I noticed the first small palms.

After I had descended several thousand feet more, the forest, which at its lower edge was scarred by fire, came abruptly to an end. Before me yawned the great, empty valley of El Copey, with a small river flowing along its bottom between long slopes astonishing in their utter nakedness. The contrast between what I had just passed through and what lay before me was unbelievable; I seemed to have been somehow suddenly set down in another world. The long, desolate slopes swept downward for thousands of feet with hardly a bush, hardly a fence, to relieve their gaunt barrenness. In places they were black from the fires set to prepare them for still another crop of maize or beans, but over much of their expanse they supported only a stunted growth of Bracken ferns, which told unmistakably that continued mistreatment had quite exhausted their fertility. It saddened me to see how soil, which not many years before had been capable of nourishing the most noble trees, had been so impoverished by ignorance and carelessness that it was no longer able to support a corn plant. I had left the magnificent wilderness and returned to the long-established haunts of man, wondering whether the new lands of El General would in a few years be reduced to this same pitiful state.

Passing quickly along the trail that wound down those desolate slopes, where there was little to beckon me to pause, I reached the village in the valley. Here I bought the hot lunch of which I was so greatly in need and sent a radiogram to the *Jefe Político* in San Isidro, asking him to look out for the horse that he had sold to me. After a night in a flea-ridden house, I crossed the ridge of La Estrella, walking again for miles through the splendid oak woods that capped its lofty summit. Beyond this was still another ridge, which rose only fifteen hundred feet above the valley and seemed a small obstruction after the mighty ones that I had already surmounted. At sunset, from the brow of this final mountain, I looked down upon the earthquake-shaken town of Cartago, spread out at the farther side of a broad, intensively cultivated plain at the foot of the immense, sprawling Volcán Irazú. An hour after nightfall, I reached the town, ending my five-day journey. Others who traveled with experienced horses and paused less frequently to observe birds, plants, and scenery, made it in three. The following morning, a half-hour's ride by autobus over a fine concrete highway took me to San José. How strange to be back again among automobiles, streetcars, railroads, electric lights, telephones, and moving pictures, all the noise and bustle of a small but very lively city, after a long sojourn amid the peace and solitude of the wilderness!

Now that I was familiar with the trail, I was glad that I had sent back my horse. Much of the way was too steep or too rough for comfortable riding, and in places the path was so choked by bushes and projecting branches that it would have been necessary to dismount. Over such a trail I preferred to travel afoot, without leading a horse, for it is easier to find spots to set down two feet than six. Without Bayon, too, I could return swiftly and comfortably by airplane, without toiling up long slopes and passing cold nights on the summits. My journey had been packed with interest; I would not for anything have missed it; but there was no point in repeating it so soon. I felt that I had bought an exceptionally sagacious horse, who knew better than I did what was best for me!

I delayed in the capital only the few days necessary to post my botanical specimens and buy a few necessities, for I was impatient to return to my wrens, woodpeckers, trogons, toucans, and all the other birds now beginning to prepare their nests. I intended to suspend collecting for a few months and give my full time to them. On the return journey by air, I traveled at little more than half the average height of my northward passage by foot! Flying over that excessively broken terrain of the Pacific slope of the Cordillera, it was easy to understand why the trail, one of the most difficult in Central America, kept so closely to the continental divide. It required a tremendous climb to reach the roof ridge of the country, but, once there, you traveled along a fairly level course. A trail anywhere below the highest crests would have been one of endless ups and downs, and the sum of the many shorter climbs would greatly exceed the single long ascent to the summit of the Mountain of Death. I had scarcely time to turn these thoughts over in my mind when the airplane set me down in the new landing strip close beside San Isidro. In less than an hour, I had undone my five days' journey.

During my absence, a heavy rain had fallen, leaving puddles in the road and ending a severe dry season. In two hours more, I walked up to Rivas. As I came in sight of my cabin, I was happy to see Bayon grazing comfortably in the yard. But why that ugly saddle gall on his withers, when I had been so careful of the padding beneath the saddle? Things must have gone badly with the horse after he left me! Don Juan explained that, after arriving at San Isidro, Morales had not delivered Bayon as he had promised to do, but had continued to ride him about the countryside as though the horse were his own. He had even sold the saddle pad, and rode with only an old sack beneath the saddle; hence the sore on Bayon's withers. On receiving my radiogram from El Copey, the *Jefe Político* had sent a policeman to warn Morales that he would be arrested if he did not promptly deliver the horse. Bayon was, accordingly, turned over to Don Juan, who noticed that some of the equipment was missing and sent the policeman the second time to tell the rogue that the threat of arrest would hold until every last article had been surrendered. On my return, I found all my property in the cabin.

Soon after this, Don Juan, weary of judging in patriarchal fashion the endless petty disputes among his neighbors, resigned from the office of *Jefe Político*, to be succeeded by a man of very different character. The new incumbent appointed Morales policeman for Rivas, and he came to dwell in a cabin close to my own. He wore no uniform, but a big nickel badge pinned on his shirt front brilliantly proclaimed his authority, which the heavy revolver conspicuous at his hip was ready to enforce. Actually, Rivas was so law-abiding that the policeman had little to do except to see that the neighbors did their share in keeping the trails open and the grass cut down in the roadway and confined their pigs to their own land. Morales was careless about the pigs. Leading a life of ease, he remained in Rivas until discharged for drunkenness. In spite of that big revolver, as I passed him on the road, especially when riding Bayon, I found it difficult to preserve due gravity of countenance, recalling how the Agent of Police had arrived in El General.

A decade after my memorable journey over El Cerro de la Muerte, the Cartago–San Isidro del General link of the great Inter-American Highway, begun during World War II, was opened to traffic. Like the old mule trail that dated from colonial times or earlier, it passes over El Cerro de la Muerte, close to the sites of the old resthouses of La División, El Cerro, and Ojo de Agua, but it avoids El Cerro de las Vueltas and the steep descent into the valley of El Copey, being located on the ridge farther to the east. Before long, several bus lines were carrying passengers between San José and San Isidro, and the air service fell into disuse. In the years that followed, I crossed El Cerro dozens of times by motor, but none of these swift and easy trips could equal, for interest and enjoyment, that first strenuous crossing by balky horse and foot, while I was at life's prime.

7

The Snake Eater

IN DIVERSE PARTS of the world, birds of various kinds are famous as snake hunters: in Africa, the long-legged Secretary-bird; on the *campos* of Brazil, the Seriema; in the vast Amazonian forests, the trumpeters. In the Central American forests, the birds that I have seen eat large snakes are all hawks. One of the most stirring sights of the tropical forest is that of the beautiful White Hawk soaring above the treetops with a long snake dangling from its talons. Although I have known this bird to carry off a fledgling araçari toucan, it appears to subsist largely on serpents.

The most renowned killer of snakes in Central America is a hawk of medium size that in books is called the Laughing Falcon. But as often happens, the people who for generations have been neighbors of this bird, familiar with it all their lives, have hit upon a better name than has occurred to hurried scientific travelers with many interests. They call this strange bird "Guaco," an excellent paraphrase of its most common call.

Headpiece: The Guaco or Laughing Falcon.

For many years, the Guaco was for me only a voice and the figure of a bird, for I had not yet learned much about its habits. It was as a voice that the hawk was most familiar: from one end of Central America to the other, in humid regions covered with heavy rain forest and among the cacti and thorny scrub of arid valleys, I had heard that loud, hollow, tirelessly reiterated *wah-co wah-co wah-co* floating over all the countryside from a bird unseen in the distance. Some have compared this call to the agonized wail of a human in pain, but to me it never suggested suffering. On the contrary, the sentiment that it stirred in my spirit was of deep and inscrutable mystery. This impression of the mysterious was heightened by the time when I most often heard the call—in the evening twilight, when the landscape was fading from view and all familiar objects took on vague and shadowy forms. I had known the Guaco's far-carrying cry for years before I heard the lower *ha ha ha*, like forced guttural laughter, which sometimes preludes it and has earned for this bird its other, less appropriate, name of Laughing Falcon. The presumed mirthfulness of this most staid and serious fowl is also responsible for the scientific designation *Herpetotheres cachinnans*, the Laughing Reptile-hunter.

From time to time, at points widely scattered, I had met the author of those mysterious cries and almost always in the same manner. The hawk would be perching on an exposed branch of a tree standing at the forest's edge, or of one growing isolated in a clearing, and it would remain looking stolidly down at me while I moved around beneath it, giving me an excellent opportunity to examine its form and coloration, but revealing nothing of its mode of life. It was a stocky bird, about nineteen inches long; the big, whitish head slightly crested, with a broad, black mask covering the eyes and much of the cheeks; the upper plumage brown and the under parts white; the short tail broadly barred with brown and buffy white. It was always the inactive figure of a bird that I saw perching high in the trees; it never called nor ate and rarely even flew its slow and labored flight in my presence.

During my second year in Rivas, I had most of the boys in the neighborhood hunting birds' nests for me. When a child found a nest, he led me to it and received his remuneration, adjusted to the rarity of the bird and the number of nests of that particular kind that had been previously reported. Thenceforth, the nest was mine, and the finder agreed not to molest it—a promise that was scarcely ever violated. While the price of the nests of the common small birds of the valley soon fell to ten or even five céntimos each, the prize that I offered for the report of a Guaco's nest was five colones. (At that time, it took nearly six colones to make a dollar; but one was all that a farmhand earned for his morning's work.) Yet even with this offer, no one came to show me a Guaco's nest.

THE SNAKE EATER

One afternoon early in the year, Lalo, a barefoot lad of twelve, led me up to the back of the ridge on the eastern side of the valley to show me a Marbled Wood-Quail's nest on which he had stumbled in the forest near the rough, weed-choked clearing where the inhabitants of the little community were laid to rest. At the foot of the narrow path that wound up the steep, wooded hillside to the cemetery, stood an enormous tree buttressed by great, projecting ridges of wood that extended up the massive trunk to twice my height. As we passed beneath this mighty tree, my young companion, calling my attention to certain white splashes, the droppings of some large bird that were prominent on the foliage beneath it, conjectured that a Guaco had its nest above. But we peered up into the lofty crown without detecting an eyrie.

More than a month later, on the afternoon of March 1, Lalo again came to my cabin to take me to a wren's nest that he had found lower in the valley. As we walked together down the grassy roadway, a Guaco, flying from the river on our right, crossed ahead of us. From its talons dangled a slender snake about two feet long. This was the first time that either of us had seen a Guaco carry a snake, and we resolved to follow. The pursuit led us through a brake of tall wild cane, a small patch of sugarcane, a weedy banana grove, then an abandoned field densely overgrown with bushes and entangled vines, through which we struggled slowly. The bird had interrupted its labored flight toward the forest to rest in a Cecropia tree growing in the midst of the cane brake, and this delay permitted us to gain on it. Soon it resumed its journey, flying slowly, with the snake held parallel to its body and the reptilian tail trailing through the air behind its own. Pushing onward as fast as the tangled vegetation would permit, we were fortunate enough to see the Guaco reach its destination. Although still a good way off, through the field glasses we could follow the events that attended its homecoming.

The hawk alighted upon a thick, horizontal branch of a burío tree near the foot of the steep eastern ridge, close by the great tree with white splashes about its base, where Lalo had surmised the presence of an eyrie that we could not find. Here the bird, evidently the male, called softly, and his mate came flying down from the blasted top of the forest giant. Eagerly, with a low cry, she pounced upon the serpent, which the other willingly relinquished to her. But instead of straightway beginning to devour it, she laid it against the branch and held it there with a foot. For many minutes, she lingered in this attitude, while her mate delayed close beside her and from time to time voiced low, throaty notes. Soon he became restless and winged away over the forest. After more than half an hour of inaction, the female Guaco balanced the snake over the bough, head hanging down on one side and tail on the other. Leaving it so, she flew up into the top of the giant tree and vanished into a hollow in the trunk.

The cavity was about a hundred feet above the ground, and the great length of thick, branchless bole would have defied the efforts of the best climber in the valley to reach it. The opening faced the steep, wooded slope at the base of which the tree stood. Accordingly, it was invisible from the cleared land in the level valley, and when we climbed the hillside, foliage screened it from view. But now that we were certain that there was a nest in the tree, we continued to move around until we found a gap in the verdure through which we could plainly see the Guaco sitting in her eyrie. This was a big cavity, occupying most of the thickness of the trunk, which was still massive so high above its base. The opening in the side was nearly as wide as the hollow to which it gave access; the arched top rose well above the head of the hawk, which was resting motionless like a black-masked statue in a niche. A single stick, evidently carried in by one of the Guacos, projected through the doorway; no other nest material was visible. Although we had scrambled well up the slope, we were still far below the level of the eyrie.

We decided to enlarge the opening in the foliage above us to obtain a wider view of the nest and its surroundings. While we attacked the undergrowth with our machetes, the Guaco continued to look calmly down on us from her high eyrie, appearing undisturbed by all the noise of chopping and shaking of foliage caused by two earth-bound humans. When we had finished our work and were starting to leave, we saw her fly down from the nest, pick up the snake from the branch where she had left it balanced, and carry it up into the forest.

It was not a little humiliating to me to have passed many times beneath a nest that I sought, without becoming aware of its presence. During the weeks while the Guaco was incubating, I had walked almost daily along the path that led up into the forest on the ridge. But neither the books I consulted nor the people I questioned had informed me that the Guaco breeds in a hollow tree. I had been searching for a bulky nest of sticks, such as most hawks build.

On the day following our great discovery, I was busy with other things, but at dawn on the second day, I stationed myself on a little shelf cut into the steep hillside, whence I could watch the eyrie through the gap that we had made in the foliage of the underwood. Before me towered the great buttressed trunk of the Guacos' tree; beyond, nearly concealed by the foliage on the slope below, spread the level, rocky lands of the narrow valley, covered with thickets and bushy pastures and small patches of cultivation, with a brown thatched roof half-glimpsed amid the verdure here and there; in the background rose steep, forested ridges, with the spreading, feathery crowns of tall and slender palms prominent among the foliage on their crests. From the dawning to the fading of the day, I kept vigil on my shelf on the hillside, careful to lose no detail in the daily routine of the Guacos. They had so long been birds of mystery that I was doubly eager to throw back the veil of ignorance that shrouded their life's secrets from me.

Through the early morning hours, a Guaco, apparently the female, stayed almost continuously in her nest. Rarely she broke her silence with a low, soft call. Soon after eight o'clock, I heard the *how how how* of her unseen mate. A moment later, he dropped down to the same branch of the burío tree to which he had brought the snake on the afternoon when we found the nest. In his talons was another serpent. The white feathers on his belly and thighs were wet and soiled, as though he had struggled with his victim among dewy vegetation. This time, his prey was a venomous coral snake, which I estimated to be twenty inches long; its coral-red body was crossed by broad black bands, each divided in the center by a narrow yellow ring. The snake's head had already been removed; it hung limp and motionless in its captor's grasp.

Promptly on her mate's arrival, the female Guaco flew down beside him and took the serpent. Her first act was to bite its forward end, as though to make sure that the work of tearing off the head with its poison fangs had been thoroughly done by the male. Then she held the limp body against the perch and began the hymn of victory that celebrated her mate's return with the proof of his successful hunting. First she uttered a peculiar *how how how,* which she varied with a slightly different note sounding like *haw haw*; but before long this changed to a loud *wac wac wac,* which she continued without interruption for at least five minutes. Meanwhile, the male was tuning up with a slightly different sequence of notes. Soon he worked into his full-voiced *wah-co,* and the two shouted together at their loudest a triumphant paean that filled all the valley and echoed from the enclosing slopes, proclaiming to all hearers that still another serpent had fallen victim to the prowess of the hawks. Then, suddenly, the pair became silent.

Some minutes after the conclusion of this chant of victory, the female Guaco picked up the snake with its fore end in her bill. Holding it against the branch with her left foot, she slid the toes of her right foot along the slender, slippery body. Its muscles stimulated by this massage, the brilliant snake began to writhe and twist for the first time since its arrival. The male Guaco soon flew up to a lofty perch in the nest tree, and, a little later, the female rose to her eyrie, bearing the serpent in her bill. Standing in the cavity back outward, she voiced a low *wac wac,* to which her mate replied in subdued tones, then flew away.

Instead of at once beginning to devour the snake, the female Guaco, who had eaten nothing since daybreak, stood for a long while motionless in the hollow, holding the prey inertly in her bill. While she rested thus immobile, like a sculptured memorial of the supremacy of hawk over serpent, a downy nestling, tumbling about on the floor of its high nursery, came so near the outer edge that now, for the first time, I glimpsed it. This was my first definite intimation of the nest's contents. The Guaco chick was light buff in color, except for a black band around its downy head, a miniature of the mask worn by the adults. From time to time, it preened its fluffy plumage and called in a hoarse little voice for food. But still its mother rested motionless above it, holding the serpent in her bill, while carrion flies buzzed around the dead flesh.

After holding the snake's vivid body for fully two and a half hours, the mother Guaco suddenly dropped it to the bottom of the nest. For another hour, she stood above it, scarcely moving. Soon after midday, she flew from the nest to the burío tree, where she rested upon her left foot, scratching herself with the right. It was always so: her right foot was invariably used as a hand to manipulate a snake or to scratch herself; the left was for standing. She was right-handed and left-footed. She stretched her wings and spread her tail fanwise. Then she returned to the hollow in the tree.

It was now well past noon, and I, who had breakfasted early, had grown hungry, for the boy who cooked for me was late bringing my lunch. But I finished my meal, and still the Guaco, who had eaten nothing all day, rested motionless above her nestling and the food her mate had brought for both of them. Finally, at a quarter to two in the afternoon, she stretched up and, turning her tail toward me, held down the serpent with her feet while she tore pieces from its forward end with her bill. She always tackled her prey in this manner, eating tailward from the head. Doubtless, although I could not see, she placed bits of snake flesh in her nestling's mouth, but she devoured the greater part herself. To me, like most humans afflicted with a whole array of irrational prejudices and aversions and vulnerable sensibilities, this meal was decidedly not pleasant to watch, even through field glasses at a distance of more than two hundred feet; but, doubtless, the Guaco, more of a realist than myself, thoroughly enjoyed her food. Certainly she had waited long enough to develop a hearty appetite! For nearly half an hour, she ate steadily, then she settled down to brood the nestling.

As the sun dipped toward the palm-crested summit across the valley, the mother Guaco continued faithfully to guard her nestling. Except for another brief recess of a quarter of an hour in the burío tree in front of the nest, she stayed continuously in the cavity until her mate's return;

through the whole day, she was never out of sight of her eyrie. In the late afternoon, she consumed more of the coral snake.

From her lofty watchtower, the female sensed her mate's return before he was visible to me, immersed in the depths of the forest. *How how how* she called, then a more deliberate, emphasized how how, *how how* HOW, HOW, as though she demanded to know what he had been doing during their long separation and *how* he had caught the snake. For another snake he had, as I could see when she indicated his position by flying up to where he perched in a tall, dead tree on the slope to my right. Then followed another long-continued hymn of triumph, such as I had heard in the morning. At its conclusion, the mother Guaco seized in her bill the forward end of the thick, dark-colored serpent, which, like all the others that were brought to her, had its head already bitten away. She carried it down into the eyrie and promptly began to devour it. Her morning of fasting had raised an appetite that it took a good part of the afternoon to satisfy.

At the conclusion of her supper, the female Guaco resumed her patient brooding of the single nestling. As the sky grew dim above, her white breast and collar gradually fused with the gathering blackness of the hollow in the trunk. When I could distinguish her no longer, I ended my daylong vigil and walked homeward through the tranquil valley. Meanwhile, the male Guaco had flown off over the forest to pass the night I knew not where.

My long day with the Guacos had proved so interesting that I resolved to pass the following afternoon watching their eyrie. I wished especially to learn something of the variety of snakes that they capture; and whether my friend Humberto was right when he told me that they prey upon the insatiable Mica, archenemy of nesting birds; and whether they would bring venomous snakes with fangs more formidable than those of the coral, although none has a more virulent poison. Widespread through tropical America is a twining vine with heavy clusters of greenish flower heads and large, ovate leaves which, when they grow in the shade, are beautiful with deep velvety-green upper faces and rich purple markings below. This plant, a member of the composite family known to botanists as *Mikania guaco,* is called by the country people *hoja de guaco* (Guaco's leaf) and is reputed to be an efficacious remedy for snake bites. It is said that the Guaco, wounded in an encounter with a venomous serpent, eats these leaves and is cured. It is interesting that a similar myth has sprung up about another snake killer of a very different sort living on the other side of the world, the Mongoose of India. But there is little evidence that either the avian or the mammalian conqueror of venomous serpents can preserve its life otherwise than by avoiding the fangs of its adversary.

On the second afternoon, as on the first, the mother Guaco divided her time between sitting in the hollow with her nestling and perching in the burío tree in front, where she could keep a watchful eye on it. About the middle of the afternoon, while she rested quietly in this slender tree, I suddenly became aware that an animal was climbing the great tree toward the eyrie. By its uniform blackness, otterlike form, and long, bushy tail, I recognized it as a Tayra, a forest-dwelling member of the weasel family, the size of a raccoon. It ascended in a direct, unhesitating manner, as though it had already espied the nest from the ground, and it climbed the thick, vertical trunk with the ease of a squirrel. Nearer and nearer the nest drew the Tayra, and still the mother Guaco, standing guard in the burío tree, gave no sign that she had seen it.

Now the black animal was almost within reach of the wide entrance of the eyrie. Waiting breathlessly to learn how efficient was the unremitting guard that the hawk had been keeping over her nestling, I did nothing to alarm the invader. Only when the Tayra was on the verge of entering the hollow did the Guaco bestir herself. Uttering a low cry, she darted straight toward the animal. It snarled, baring sharp, white teeth. She dropped away, without having touched it, to return to her former perch and watch it advance toward her nestling.

The situation had been so fraught with possibilities of intense and dramatic action that I, torn as always in such moments between desire to prevent a tragedy and eagerness to observe the natural course of events, had delayed action until the last moment. I had expected that the mother Guaco would at least retard the Tayra's advance toward her nest, but her action had been so weak and ineffectual that it did not give me time to plan my next move, when convinced that she alone could not save the nestling. When she returned tamely to her lookout, leaving the invader at the very doorway of her eyrie, I was seized with a horrifying awareness of my helplessness and lack of preparation in this emergency. I had no weapon; a quick glance around revealed nothing that I could throw; indeed, the nest was too distant to be reached with effect except by a bullet. Since I could do nothing else, I shouted. By this time, the Tayra had its head and forelegs in the hollow. Alarmed by my loud outcry, the animal, who had been unaware of my presence, withdrew its head from the hole and looked around. With repeated shouts and much waving of arms, I drove it to the ground.

Although the Tayra had been frightened by my frantic cries, the more phlegmatic Guaco, much closer to me on her perch in the top of the burío tree, was heedless of all my noise and gesticulation. Perching motionless, she uttered excited *wa*'s, higher in pitch than any of the calls I had hitherto heard from her. Even after the assailant had retreated to the ground, she did not return to the nest. From her lofty perch, she could see into it, as from my lower station I could not. Nor could I decide whether my shouts had saved the nestling's life or had been raised a moment too late. For a long while, I watched in an agony of doubt. Had I, after long searching, found a Guaco's nest only to lose it so soon? Had the tardiness of my action cost the life of one of the most useful birds of tropical America, a protector not only of man but of every feathered creature whose nests are pillaged by snakes?

Again and again, during the next hour, the Tayra and its companion or mate, who had now appeared, started on the long climb to the eyrie, only to be driven back by my shouts and gesticulations and much waving of my shirt. Standing naked to the waist, I yelled until I was hoarse. Although the uproar that I made served to keep the Tayras from the treetop, it did not drive them away; they lurked in the neighboring undergrowth, waiting for a moment when my guard was relaxed to finish off the young Guaco. Tayras are canny predators, choosing a moment when nobody is watching to dash into a dooryard, seize a chicken, and drag it into the neighboring woodland before the householders, aroused by the poor fowl's pathetic squawks, can rush out and rescue it. They vary their diet with fruit.

The afternoon wore slowly on, and still the Guaco delayed on the same high perch, not returning to her nest after a short absence, as she had always done in the past. At intervals, she called in a subdued voice. With waning confidence, I kept my eyes fastened on the doorway of the eyrie, hoping to glimpse the nestling as it tumbled about on its high nursery's floor. But I watched in vain. It did not again reveal itself, as it had so often done on the preceding day. Examining the nest through my field glasses, I thought that I could detect the nestling's light buffy head, with a black band around it, showing just above the doorway's lower edge. For over an hour it remained immobile, and I was driven to the melancholy conclusion that the chick had been killed by the Tayra.

At last, as the sun sank low, the female Guaco bestirred herself, stretched her wings and spread her barred tail, then flew over to the eyrie and picked up the nestling in her bill. It hung limp and lifeless in her grasp.

She dropped the nestling and looked down at it for a minute or two. Then, holding the lifeless body beneath her feet, she began to tear it with her bill and to devour it piece by piece. The creature that she had brought into the world by weeks of patient sitting, kept warm with the heat of her own body, and guarded continuously by day and by night, had become for her—now that its vital spark was extinguished—what it really was, a piece of lifeless carrion, a bit of organic matter, whose only use was to supply a little nourishment to some animal still living. Why not to her who had given it life, rather than to the destroying Tayra, who only awaited my departure to return and claim its victim? Why should not Guaco remain Guaco, rather than become Tayra? Human sentiment protests at this, but the Guaco, although faithful in her attendance of her young, was evidently devoid of maternal feeling.

Let us not judge the bereaved parent too harshly. As I had already come to suspect, the snake eater was a thorough realist, and, if you can divorce your judgment from sentiment, I believe that you will concede that her action was beyond reproach. There is no logical reason why we should not eat, after it has expired, that which we faithfully attended as long as it lived. Indeed, such has been the practice of certain races of mankind, who believed that they honored their dead by devouring them. And to birds, it appears, there is no such thing as a dead bird; with the extinction of life, the feathered body, lying prostrate and distorted, is no longer recognized as a bird.

After I had reflected maturely on the matter, I could not censure the mother Guaco for not having made a furious attack on the Tayra as it climbed to her nest. Compared to fiercer birds of prey, such as the Peregrine and the Harpy Eagle, the Guaco's talons are weak, its bill small, its wings slow. She had no weapon to match the formidable jaws of the mammal. Had the latter allowed me a minute's unhurried reflection before pushing home its attack, I might have recognized the parent's inability to drive the assailant away and shielded her from the necessity of exposing herself to danger. Natural selection operates against parent animals that take desperate risks in the defense of their young, when they should preserve themselves in order to make repeated attempts to perpetuate their kind. For the mother Guaco to have sacrificed herself defending an offspring she was powerless to save would have been a heroic gesture, but a threat to the existence of the entire species of Guacos; without her, the nestling would doubtless have perished from exposure. Such a sacrifice would not have been realistic. Heroic self-sacrifice is, as a rule, consistent with the survival of the species only among social animals, whose orphaned young may be attended by other individuals. Yet, even though it is biologically unsound, we do from time to time witness such sacrifice among solitary creatures.

Meanwhile, the male Guaco was abroad hunting a snake for his family's supper, unaware of what had happened at the nest. Apparently, he had difficulty finding what he sought, for he returned late, when the light was fading. At last he arrived, bringing a small, black snake with an abruptly slender tail. Alighting on a neighboring branch, he called in a very low voice. His mate, continuing to devour the remains of their offspring, answered from the eyrie. After she had completed her meal, she stood in the entrance, facing outward, and called more loudly. The male replied, then picked up his burden and flew southward along the forest's edge. The female soon followed. Both were now screened from my view by foliage, so I hurried down the slope through the dusky underwood to the open ground of the valley. When I arrived in the clearing, I could see the two perching not far apart on an exposed limb of a tall tree, high above me on the hillside. In the twilight, the female was eating the serpent while her mate looked on.

The female Guaco consumed but little, then, leaving the snake balanced across the bough, she flew back to the burío tree in front of the desolate eyrie. The male soon followed and alighted on a branch near her. Then, in the last dim light of the dead day, when all purely diurnal birds had hushed their songs and the white-throated Pauraques were calling softly in the clearing, the pair of hawks raised their voices in full duet and continued to shout *wah-co* at their loudest for several minutes. The mysterious chant carried afar over the drowsing valley, widely proclaiming that, although a Tayra might kill a Guaco nestling, the race of Guacos was still vigorous and strong and would need more and more snakes for their daily nourishment. And I fancied that all the small birds within hearing, snuggling their heads down into their outfluffed plumage as they composed themselves for rest, would slumber with a greater feeling of security for this reassurance that the hawks who preyed upon their direst enemies had hunted successfully that day.

8

In Quest of the Quetzal

By MID-JUNE of 1937, I had tarried in Rivas somewhat over eighteen months, more than thrice as long as I had originally intended to stay. I had prepared and mailed to my subscribers six thousand specimens of plants, representing nearly a thousand "numbers," as a collector designates all the specimens of the same species gathered at the same time and place. A gratifying number of these plants turned out to be new species; but it is difficult to say how many, because as specialists have worked over various families through the years, they have established new species for plants that were at first classified in older species and placed in older species some that were originally described as new. Such changes in taxonomic judgment are constantly occurring in all groups of animals and plants. A small tree, with inconspicuous greenish flowers, that grew on the slopes above the Río Buena Vista, was described by two specialists as the type of a new genus, *Skutchia*; but almost before the ink was dry, Paul Standley, the leading authority on the

Headpiece: A male Quetzal looks into his nest. Photo by James A. Kern.

Central American flora, pointed out that, far from representing a new genus, this tree (*Trophis chorizantha*) was not even a new species!

During my year and a half in El General, I had identified in the field 218 species of resident and migratory birds, not including those that I saw in the mountains above thirty-five hundred feet. I and my young helpers had found the nests of 90 species, or well over half of those that appeared to breed around Rivas. I had succeeded in learning some of the principal facts about the lives of many of these birds: what they ate; how they slept; how they built their nests, incubated their eggs, and attended their young; and the lengths of the incubation and nestling periods. While working hard and living simply on a vegetarian diet, I had enjoyed excellent health in this salubrious climate.

Certainly, many species of plants remained uncollected, even in the forests over which I looked from my cabin, and much remained to be learned even about the birds that I had studied most carefully. But I faced diminishing returns, especially in the botanical collecting on which I depended for a livelihood, and so, reluctantly, I resolved to tear myself away from a place where I had lived long and happily and felt quite at home.

While I had many ties to hold me in Rivas, I had at least one strong incentive to go. For nine years, I had been increasing my familiarity with the birds of Central America, north and south, highland and lowland; but I had not yet studied the life of the most famous and magnificent of all, the justly renowned Quetzal, sacred to the Indians of old. This lovely creature was one of the very first birds of tropical America to come to my attention. While still a schoolboy, I possessed a Guatemalan postage stamp that depicted a brilliant green bird with a crimson belly, a ridged crest over the head, and a remarkably long, gracefully curving train. Later, I learned that this bird is called the Quetzal and, later still, that the Guatemalans had chosen it as their national emblem and pronounced its name with the accent on the last syllable. Symbol of liberty, the Quetzal, it was averred, would invariably die if confined in a cage.

During the years when I lived in Guatemala, I saw much of the Quetzal: on the national coat of arms which appeared over the portals of many public buildings and as a medallion in the center of the blue and white banner; on bank notes and postage stamps and the seal on official paper, without which one could not present a petition to the government; and gaudily portrayed on school and office walls. I spent no end of quetzales at hotels and in shops and paying my Indian porters, for Guatemala has named her monetary unit for this bird, as her sister republics have bestowed this doubtful honor upon the memory of famous men: Columbus (Colón), Balboa, Bolívar, Córdoba, Sucre, Lempira. I turned my head away at the sight of many a crudely mounted, moth-eaten Quetzal skin in private homes and shop windows—this was not the way I cared to remember the bird. It has long seemed to me that bird skins, which have their scientific uses, should be stored away on their backs, out of sight in museum drawers, and not set up in rigid attitudes to mock living nature with sightless glass eyes. Movement, vibrant life, is the essence of a bird; it has been wisely said that there is no such thing as a dead bird. When we cannot enjoy the living presence, we had best look at a well-done portrait, which is an accurate representation and has merit as a work of art. It is pleasant to have a portrait of a deceased friend before us, but who would care to have his mummy?

Although I saw so many stuffed Quetzal skins, it was long before I glimpsed a living Quetzal in the forest. Doubtless, the abundance of the stuffed skins explained the rareness of the living birds, for as too often happens, it was only after they had become rare in Guatemala that laws for their protection were made and enforced. Then, too, the Quetzal inhabits heavy mountain forests at middle altitudes, just the zone in the tropics where the human population is densest and the woods have been most completely shorn away—and with the forest goes the Quetzal. When I lived in the Caribbean lowlands where there were still vast forests, I was below the range of this bird; during the year I passed on the Sierra de Tecpam, above eight thousand feet in western Guatemala, I wandered through woodlands too high for it.

Then, at last, while traveling over rough trails in northern Guatemala, far beyond the reach of railroad and highway, I enjoyed my first glimpse of a living Quetzal. As we rode down a narrow, winding track through heavy forest on a steep mountainside in northern El Quiché, my companion, a young Guatemalan on vacation from the agricultural school in the capital, was telling me how in the preceding year he had seen a Quetzal here. Scarcely had he finished his story when two magnificent male Quetzals, flying out of the trees above us on the slope, undulated across the deep ravine beside which we rode, each an unforgettable vision in scintillating green, richest crimson, and snowy white, with a long train that rippled behind, carrying out the rhythm of the bird's undulations. It took the twain less than a minute to cross the open space and vanish among the foliage of the farther side of the gorge, but for years this was the only vision of the Quetzal that I cared to remember.

There was a glamor and mystery surrounding this bird, which, added to its beauty, made me the more eager to study it. Before the Conquest, the Indians of Mexico and Guatemala used its plumage in their featherwork and to decorate their headdresses; the long, flexible, green plumes of the male's train are prominent in pictorial representations of Aztec kings and chiefs. Royalty and the nobility alone had the right to wear them. It is reported that the Indians snared the living birds, plucked out their proudest ornaments, then released them to renew their plumage and reproduce their kind. They took more thought of conservation than the white men who wrested their lands from them. By the eighteenth century, the Quetzal had become so rare in all the more accessible districts of Central America that ornithologists of Europe listed it with such fabulous birds as the phoenix and the roc. Then, after its rediscovery early in the following century, a large and nefarious trade was carried on to supply museums and the cabinets of virtuosi in Europe with stuffed Quetzals, most of which came from Alta Verapaz in Guatemala.

In Guatemala, I was everywhere told that the national bird nests in a hole carved in a decaying trunk and provided with doorways on opposite sides, so that the male, when he takes his turn at warming the eggs, can pass in through one opening and out through the other, without turning around in the cavity and damaging his long train. This, incidentally, is formed, not by the tail feathers themselves, which are black and white, but by the great elongation of their upper coverts, which in most kinds of birds are much shorter than the tail. Most of my informants did not claim to have seen a Quetzal's nest, and the only scientific record known to me, published many years earlier by the English ornithologist Osbert Salvin, stated that the Quetzal nests in an old woodpecker's hole with a single doorway and inferred that the duller female, who lacks the long train, incubates alone.

The Quetzal is the most resplendent member of a family of lovely birds called the trogons, most abundant in the American tropics, but occurring also in the tropics of the Old World and represented by a single species as far north as Arizona. The males are glittering green or violet or blue on the upper parts, with red or vermilion or yellow on the abdomen. With their bright plumage, proud upright posture, gentle dignified manners, and the mellow notes of most species, they are exceptionally attractive birds, the perfect gentlemen of the avian community. For each of seven years, in localities ranging from Chiapas, Mexico, to the Isthmus of Panama, I had discovered the nest of another kind of trogon and learned something of the attendants' habits. I had found them breeding in cavities in decaying stumps, in chambers carved into the heart of hard, black termitaries, and in high, papery wasps' nests. In every case where I was fortunate enough to watch the process, the nest cavity was carved by the two sexes working alternately, and the male took a large share in the incubation of the two or three white or bluish eggs, as likewise in attending the young. None of these males, it is true, had a long train like the Quetzal's. Still, I felt confident that the male Quetzal incubates like his less ornate cousins, although I doubted the Guatemalan story of the nest with two doorways, which was denied by a Costa Rican mountaineer who told me about a nest that he had found on Volcán Irazú. Observations of my own on the Quetzal would not only settle these controversial points, but crown my series of studies of the noble family of birds to which it belongs.

Here, then, was incentive to move from Rivas, where the temperate and agreeable climate was still too warm for the Quetzal, to some higher region. Because of the greater area of forest at the higher altitudes, Quetzals are more abundant in Costa Rica than in the country which claims them as its emblem. I might have found these birds far up on the slopes at the head of the valley of the Río Buena Vista, but here were no dwellings, and the transportation of provisions would have been difficult. Since I planned to remain long in the haunts of the Quetzal, I wished to be fairly well-housed. In the rain-drenched forests where this bird lives, a moderately tight shelter is a necessity for man.

At the suggestion of my neighbor Juan Schroeder, I left El General by air and visited Vara Blanca in the north. Two miles below the hamlet, I saw from the road an attractive cottage with a porch around three sides, a corrugated iron roof, and red shutters. It stood on the back of a narrow, cleared ridge between two deep, wooded gorges. The farm was called "Montaña Azul," and it was just the place for watching birds. The cottage happened to be unoccupied, and the caretaker, who lived in a smaller house nearby, opened doors and shutters and allowed me to inspect the interior. He told me that Quetzals were numerous in the surrounding forest.

The dwelling belonged to a wealthy German coffee planter who resided near San José and was developing a dairy farm here in anticipation of the arrival of the new highway, slowly creeping up over the continental divide from the central plateau. So to San José I returned and visited the owner in his grand mansion a few miles from the city. His family used the cottage for short visits in the fine weather, and at first he was reluctant to rent it. But when I explained my objectives and presented letters of recommendation from friends in the city, he finally gave me a lease with restrictions. I did not like the restrictions, which permitted me to use only one side of the little house, but I was very eager to study the Quetzal—and houses and Quetzals are not often found close together. The caretaker's wife agreed to provide my meals.

From Tacaná on the Mexican border of Guatemala to Arenal in northwestern Costa Rica, a long file of volcanic cones, becoming lower toward the south, stands guard over the Pacific coast of Central America. In central Costa Rica, the line of volcanoes changes its direction, bending eastward and crossing the narrowing continent in a transverse range known as the Cordillera Central, in which stand the more or less active volcanoes Poás, Irazú, and Turrialba, and extinct Barba. With the shift in the direction of the range also comes a change in the character of the volcanic peaks, for while those in the long coastwise chain have in general a regular conical form, those in central Costa Rica are so irregular and sprawling that, without examining their summits, one would hardly suspect their volcanic nature—unless, indeed, they happened to be emitting smoke. The most regular of these volcanoes is Turrialba, the easternmost, which rises abruptly from the Caribbean coastal plain.

The broad southern flanks of these volcanoes, facing the populous central plateau, had been stripped of their forests and were devoted to agriculture, with coffee plantations at their feet, dairy and vegetable farms nearer their wooded summits, and here and there villages nestling on their gentle slopes. Their northern faces, turned to receive the full force of the moisture-laden winds from the Caribbean, were still wild and sparsely populated. It was on the forested northern slope of the Cordillera Central, between the volcanoes Poás and Barba, that I hoped to study the life of the Quetzal.

My new dwelling commanded a vast and varied panorama. Although the north-south profile, the mean descent of the range from its summits to the plains, was gentle, the terrain was everywhere excessively broken, intersected by profound and narrow gorges, through which rushed impetuous streams that took frequent and sometimes very high plunges. My front yard sloped rapidly off into the gorge of the Río Sarapiquí, five hundred feet deep, with a wonderful hanging forest displayed to my view on the farther wall. To the north and east, the forest on the ridges was without visible break. The narrow backs of these ridges sloped easily down to the lowlands of northern Costa Rica and eastern Nicaragua: hundreds of miles of the wildest country, its nearly level surface embossed with low, scattered ridges and covered with a dark mantle of almost unbroken forest. I liked to think that my view over these forests reached as far as Santo Domingo, where for four years Thomas Belt superintended gold mines and gathered material for his book of perennial interest, *The Naturalist in Nicaragua*. In the far northeast lay a segment of the Caribbean shore, dimly glimpsed. At least, I could see all this when clouds did not interfere, but all too much of the time we were enveloped in them.

Through this immense lowland area to my north, but hidden from view by the forest, flowed the Río San Juan, forming the boundary between Costa Rica and Nicaragua and, with the Lake of Nicaragua at its head, the route of the long-projected interoceanic canal. This broad belt of lowlands stretching from coast to coast separates the highlands of Costa Rica and Chiriquí in the south from the more extensive northern highland area that centers in Guatemala and extends into Chiapas on one side and into Honduras, El Salvador, and Nicaragua on the other. To me, this wide gap in the Central American highlands was of profound significance: when I recalled that warm lowlands form a barrier to the dispersal of organisms adapted to cool heights, it helped to explain the great differences between the life about me on my lofty perch and that with which I had earlier become familiar in the mountains of Guatemala. Here were none of the pines, junipers, firs, sweet gums, maples, sycamores, ashes, or hornbeams that I had found in Guatemala, and few other trees of northern types. Here also were far fewer birds of northern origin: no towhees, flickers, bluebirds, kinglets, brown creepers, nor Steller's Jays, all of which live in the mountains of northern Central America. Although many of the birds here were similar to those I knew in Guatemala, few were exactly the same. The Quetzal here, for example, had a train of plumes somewhat shorter and narrower than those of his counterpart in the northern republic.

In compensation for the absence of so many of the birds of North Temperate origin, I was pleased to find about me here a number of kinds with Andean affinities that I had not previously seen. These were chiefly shy, inconspicuous, brown denizens of the moss-draped forests, members of the ovenbird and the woodcreeper families.

What an inhospitable reception Montaña Azul gave me! I moved into the cottage in early July; in the middle of the month began a storm of wind and rain such as I had never anywhere experienced, not even during the exceptionally wet year that I had passed in the Guatemalan highlands. It lasted a full fortnight with brief intermissions. Over the Caribbean Sea and the lowlands to the north, with nothing to mitigate the full intensity of their sweep, the north winds drove the clouds and mist and rain, for hours together completely enshrouding us in chill, sombre grayness. One who has not actually felt it can hardly conceive the penetrating chill of moisture-laden winds on an exposed tropical mountainside, fifty-five hundred feet above sea level, even while the thermometer stands at fifteen degrees Fahrenheit above the freezing point. How hardy are the birds of these mountain forests! No wonder that few of the lowland species, and those the most adaptable, range so high!

To add to my discomfort during this storm, there were great chinks in the wooden walls of the cottage, through which the wind and mist rushed in. These walls were double; but as in my cabin at Rivas, the boards had been nailed up before they seasoned, and shrinkage had left wide gaps. Since there was scarcely any agriculture in this wet region, and the bottomless mud of the roadway up to the continental divide at Los Cartagos made everyone reluctant to transport aught but bare essentials, my diet for a considerable period was reduced to little more than black or red beans, rice, and tortillas. These had long been my mainstay, but without fruits and vegetables to act as a leaven and supply vitamins, they are grim fare. We persuaded a man who had a farm at lower altitudes to the north to bring oranges and bananas when he passed us on his trips "outside," but he soon abandoned the effort because of the difficulty of the trail. Never have I seen one deeper in mud!

Sometimes I hungered so for something green that I wished I could eat the foliage of trees, like the Two-toed Sloths that I sometimes saw in the surrounding forests. This sloth, which has two long, powerful nails on its forefeet and three on its hindfeet, was the only kind that I found at Montaña Azul. It lives even higher in the mountains, for, in a later year, I found it not uncommon on dairy farms on the Barba massif, up to at least seventy-five hundred feet above sea level. There I saw it not only in the woodland but in isolated trees that it could reach only by walking for some distance over the open pastures. In El General, around twenty-five hundred feet, I have, over a period of many years, met this sloth only twice and the Three-toed Sloth but once. In the lowlands, the latter is, in my experience, by far the more abundant of the two species.

The Two-toed Sloth is evidently fitted to withstand the cold of the high mountains by its heavier pelage. Long, coarse, and gray, it hangs loosely below the body when the sloth hangs beneath a branch, in its usual inverted position, munching foliage. The gray is tinged with green by the microscopic algae that grow on the thick hairs. The sloth's face is whitish, except for its short, abruptly projecting, black muzzle. At Montaña Azul, the animal's favorite food seemed to be the large, pinnately compound leaves of the Capulín, a tall, weedy tree abundant in second growth at middle altitudes. In El General, I watched a Two-toed Sloth eat the compound leaves of the Olivo. Although these sloths eat a variety of leaves, they reveal definite preferences. Higher in the mountains, I watched one clinging by its hindfeet to a slender, drooping branch of *Cornus disciflora*, whose foliage it disdained, while it stretched full length to reach with its forefeet a neighboring shrub of *Fuchsia arborescens*, the leaves and inflorescences of which it steadily consumed. Whenever it came to a spray of a rubiaceous shrub that grew beside the fuchsia, it sniffed the foliage and passed it by. The preference of the Three-toed Sloth for the large, palmate leaves of the guarumo or Cecropia is well known.

I have seen baby Two-toed Sloths, still carried by their mothers, in the Costa Rican mountains from early June until mid-September. The infant's fur is everywhere dense and soft, with no trace of the coarseness and harshness of the adult's pelage. Its head is a light cinnamon-buff with a black muzzle. The tips of the hairs over the body and limbs are likewise cinnamon-buff, but basally these hairs become gray, and the superposition of these two colors produces a shade difficult to describe. The little eyes are deep brown. While the mother forages, the single baby rides upright on her upturned ventral surface, clasping her pelage with its already long claws. In August, I watched a half-grown youngster push forward between the forelegs of its dam, who was foraging in a high treetop, pull a twig toward itself and devour the foliage just as she was doing. After a while, it left its mother's breast to cling to a branch beside her while it continued to browse. It always maintained contact with her, and, after a few minutes, it climbed back upon her. Here it rode, back upward in the usual fashion, while its inverted bearer moved slowly away.

In June of the following year, a boy brought me a Two-toed Sloth who had evidently lost its mother; it was only ten inches long and seemed too young to shift for itself. Placed in a small tree, it climbed restlessly over the branches without attempting to eat the leaves, but it seemed unable to climb up or down even a thin trunk. From time to time, it gave a low, bleating cry, perhaps a call for its mother. This call, clearly audible at a distance of a hundred feet, was the only cry I ever knowingly heard from a sloth; the soprano notes commonly attributed to these mammals by country people in Costa Rica, as well as in other parts of tropical America, are the song of a nocturnal bird, the Common Potoo, as I and other naturalists have proved.

The baby Two-toed Sloth showed more spirit than an adult male Three-toed Sloth that I kept for some days in Panama. When touched, the little one tried to defend itself by striking with a forefoot, but the blows were too slow to be effective. At the same time, it emitted a low hiss. Taken in hand, it tried to bite, and its tiny teeth commanded respect. Once it managed to seize the palm of my hand; although the dull teeth failed to pierce the tough skin, the grip was painful and left deep impressions of two incisors. When I tried to pull the baby from a branch, it clung tenaciously and protested with loud, bleating notes. We returned it to the woods whence it came, not very hopeful that it would survive.

Three kinds of monkeys, the Black Howler, the White-faced, and the Red Spider Monkey, braved the chilling downpours a mile above sea level. I sometimes heard the deep bass roar of the first-mentioned coming from the ridge across the gorge of the Río Sarapiquí, but I failed to glimpse them, and I saw little of the White-faces. On an excursion far down a heavily forested ridge, we met larger bands of spider monkeys than ever appeared near the cottage. Although called *mono colorado*, the local race was a shade between cinnamon and tawny, with darker hair on the face, crown, and limbs. Some had conspicuous, buff-colored circles around their eyes. The body was fairly stout, with a well-developed chest, a pot belly, and, contrasting with this, grotesquely long, thin limbs and tail. Of all the monkeys that I have watched, these were the most active and noisy. Racing through the tops of soaring trees, they took prodigious leaps from bough to bough, apparently unimpeded by the babies that rode on the backs of some. As long as we had them in sight, and for a considerable while after they passed from view, we heard an incessant clamor. The call of an individual monkey reminded me of the bark of a small, rather hoarse, and not very sweet-tempered dog. The whole band of them shouting together produced a volume and dissonance that might be compared to the yelping of numerous packs of hounds hot on a trail. Even a large flock of Mealy Parrots, those most raucous of the Central American Psittacidae, hardly makes, in its vesper chorus, as much earsplitting racket as a band of spider monkeys.

When not rushing wildly through the high treetops, these monkeys spent most of their time scratching themselves. One that we watched for many minutes scratched its body, arms, and legs in a frantic manner which suggested that a more than momentary cessation of this activity might have fatal consequences. It perched upon a slender branch and supported itself by entwining its tail about another close behind itself, while with long, sweeping strokes it scratched one arm with the other. Another method of scratching a forelimb was to suspend itself by one arm from a branch, let the other arm hang loosely in front of itself, and scratch this limp limb with both feet simultaneously.

The monkey interrupted this activity only long enough to snatch leaves from the nearest twigs and drop them to the ground. Once it broke off a slender stick about as long as its arm, waved it up and down in its hands as though it were the baton of a band leader who was beating time for a particularly lively tune, then let the stick fall. This dropping of leaves and branches was evidently done in defiance of the man and boy watching far below, but the simian never tried to throw in our direction. Whether scratching or dropping things to earth, it never ceased to bark. The Red Spider Monkey seems the very spirit of unrest, constitutionally incapable of either repose or silence.

I have watched spider monkeys eat the fruit of a forest tree and spit out the seeds, and they include much foliage in their diet. Once, at the edge of a clearing in the Pacific lowlands, I watched one hang by its tail above a young Cecropia tree while it ate the leaves, which are also an important food of howling monkeys. At another time, at the edge of the same clearing, I saw a spider monkey hang inverted from a vine while it plucked the three-lobed leaves of a climbing aroid from the trunk of a tree. It ate only the bases of the petioles, dropping the remainder of the leaves. Recalling that the tissues of aroids usually sting the human mouth, I sampled one of these petioles. Some minutes after I had chewed it, I felt a slight smarting in my mouth, less than I had expected from a plant of this family.

August favored us with a few pleasant days at Montaña Azul. I took advantage of them to climb Volcán Poás, whose long, green ridge, looking not in the least like a volcano, terminated my view in the west. But from time to time, a great, fat puff of white smoke, floating up above the verdant summit, betrayed its plutonic nature. I went on foot with Faustino Gómez, the tall, pleasant caretaker of Montaña Azul. Since the intervening country was extremely broken and heavily forested, we made a long detour to the south, passing chiefly through the pastures of the dairy farms that occupied the more accessible parts of this region. Although the volcanoes of central Costa Rica lack picturesque, shapely cones, they have long histories of activity, and the series of craters, extinct and active, that occupy their expanded summits make them unusually interesting.

Climbing upward through forests that gradually became lower, then through dense thickets of bayberry and flowering shrubs among which hummingbirds darted, we stood early in the afternoon on the rim of a vast, oval hollow, walled in by forbidding vertical cliffs hundreds of feet high. At first, we had only fleeting, indistinct glimpses of the bottom of this titanic pit, for it was filled with gray, wind-driven cloud mist mingled with volcanic vapors rising out of its depths. A strong odor of sulphur dioxide assailed our nostrils. When at length the atmosphere cleared, we saw that a broad, nearly round lake of greenish gray water occupied most of the bottom of the immense depression at our feet. A thin curtain of steam rose continuously from the seething liquid. While we watched, of a sudden we heard a loud roaring, such as might be made by a great quantity of steam escaping under high pressure from some cyclopean boiler. The liquid heaved up at a point near the center, then fell back causing sluggish waves, as a fat, dense column of white vapor rose slowly above the focus of disturbance.

On the northern shore of the turbid lake was a narrow line of fissures from which dense, white vapors escaped in steady streams. Around each of these fumaroles was a heavy deposit of sulphur, the pale yellow hue of which, deepening to orange in the center, was by far the brightest color in all that vast crater.

We found lodgings of a sort in a flea-ridden farmhouse high on the volcano, about a mile from the crater. During the night, we heard a loud explosion. In the clear, early morning, we visited an older crater situated about a quarter of an hour's walk from the active one. This broader depression was filled by a beautiful lake, circular in outline and about a mile in diameter. The deep blue of the center paled to perfect colorless transparency along the shores, where the pure, cold water lapped the white volcanic sand. Steep, verdant slopes swept completely around the basin and rose to a nearly level rim a hundred feet or more above the water. The surface of this lake was about eighty-five hundred feet above sea level, several hundred feet below the highest point of the volcano. How utterly different were these two lakes so close together: one discolored by volcanic impurities and seething still with earth's internal fires, hemmed in by sheer walls quite destitute of any verdant plant; the other pure and cold and serene as a pond in some far northern wilderness, rimmed with wooded slopes that revealed no trace of plutonic violence! This contrast made Poás, despite its unimposing aspect from a distance, one of the most impressive volcanoes that I have climbed.

Often at dawn, when the clouds permitted an outlook, I would behold from my bedroom window at Montaña Azul the whole, wide northern lowland covered with a nearly continuous blanket of white mist, billowy on its upper surface, which seemed to lie just above the treetops and was interrupted only by the long, low ridges that jutted above it free of cloud. On certain cool, dark mornings, it was easy to fancy that I looked down upon an arctic scene, with dark, bare, granitic ridges—swept free of snow by fierce icy gales—rising above level snow fields. The blanket of low-lying cloud mist stretched away to the north and northwest until it merged imperceptibly into the purple-tinted stratus clouds that lay on the vastly distant horizon. This mantle of mist might lie unbroken until seven or eight o'clock in the morning, when it would lift and gather into long, fleecy-edged banks, each stretching many miles from east to west with dark bands of forest showing between them. Now the diurnal breeze, setting up the mountainsides, would drive the cloud banks toward us, and some time between nine and eleven o'clock, the chill, gray mist would reach and envelop us. Thus, our fine sunny mornings came to an end, and afternoons were usually dark or rainy. But all too often the day broke darkly, to remain bleak and dismal until nightfall.

Often, when at daybreak the greater portion of the lowland was covered by an unbroken blanket of mist, a narrow belt lying along the base of the mountains would be quite clear, the dark forest contrasting strongly with the white mantle beyond. This was because the cool mountain air, increasing in temperature and decreasing in relative humidity as it drained down the slopes during the night, had blown the condensing vapors farther back upon the plain. Similarly, while I lived in Rivas, the valley of the Río Buena Vista, down which cold air from the heights flowed strongly on most nights, was almost never mist-shrouded at dawn, while white mists often covered those parts of the broad basin of El General that were more distant from the mountains. In tropical lowlands, it is best to dwell at the foot of high mountains, where nights are cooler, and there is less disagreeable, chilling mist at dawn.

Through September and October, the weather continued bad, with rain almost every afternoon and often also in the morning. My collecting went slowly; if I made a long excursion, I was almost certain to receive a cold drenching. In mid-November, I sought sunshine, fresh scenes, and different kinds of birds in the lowlands of Guanacaste, where the dry season was already beginning. Returning to Montaña Azul early in December, I found the interior of the cottage and my bed wet with the rain that the wind had driven through the walls during the storms of the preceding weeks. The weather was still dark and bleak, with a chill in the damp air that penetrated my heaviest clothing. Hugging the fire in the little wood stove in the drafty hall, I could keep only one side warm. While I sat gazing gloomily out on those gray clouds which drifted in endlessly from the north to envelop me, the odds against finding a Quetzal's nest next March or April began to appear about a thousand to one. Since the long rainstorm of the preceding July, I had seen scarcely any of these birds. For a while, I thought that they had departed the region, like the Three-wattled Bellbirds.

It was impossible to accomplish anything with either birds or plants in such weather. Alone in the chill, moisture-soaked dwelling, my thoughts took on the dun complexion of the skies. How attractive those drier forests of the Pacific side appeared to me now! After a week I fled again, returned to Rivas for my horse, and with him made a long trip through the forests to Buenos Aires de Osa, where the visiting *padre*, resident in San Isidro, had kindly given me permission to occupy the priest's empty house next to the church. It stood in the midst of an attractive garden, tightly fenced to keep out the pigs that wandered at large through the village. Here I found sunshine, an abundance of delicious oranges, and multitudes of birds. A great flock of graceful Fork-tailed Flycatchers roosted nightly in the orange trees beside the porch; in the daytime, they spread over the neighboring savannas, catching insects in company with wintering Myrtle Warblers. Ruddy Ground-Doves and many wintering Baltimore Orioles slept among the broad red leaves of the dracaena trees in front of the little wooden church. During the heat of the afternoon, I read the compact volume of Tennyson's poems that I carried in my saddlebags; henceforth, the *Idylls of the King* and *Maud* will always call up visions of oranges, orioles, Fork-tailed Flycatchers, and sunshine.

In these visits to climatically different regions, I was impressed by the diverse physiognomy of the forests. In Guanacaste, where the dry season is long and severe, the woodland was open, and the largest trees (except those lofty ones growing in areas where the ground water was abundant and unfailing) were notable for their beautiful, wide-spreading crowns rather than for impressive height. In southern Pacific Costa Rica, where the rainfall is greater and the dry season shorter and less severe, the noble forests averaged about twice as high, and the dominant trees tended to have full, wide-spreading crowns. In regions like Vara Blanca, where the rainfall is extremely high and the woods are much of the time shrouded in mist, the trees are lofty but, as a rule, have meager, open crowns which do not form a continuous canopy but allow much sky to be seen through them. Many of the taller trees appear sickly and poorly developed. In such excessively wet climates, tremendous masses of mosses, ferns, orchids, bromeliads, shrubby and even arborescent epiphytes burden the boughs and appear to prevent the fullest development of the tree. Wide-spreading, ample branches might be broken off by the excessive weight of the aerial vegetation, hence few such are found. One tree at Vara Blanca, the yos, tall and shapely with its full, broad crown of glossy foliage, was at first sight an exception to this rule, but in reality confirmed it, for its smooth, close, gray bark discouraged the attachment of epiphytes. Finally, on lofty ridges approaching timber line, the trees have a very different aspect, with dense, compact crowns of sombre foliage.

By mid-January, I was back again at Montaña Azul, where the weather was almost as gloomy as it had been a month earlier. Determined now to stay, for the season of profitable field work was approaching, I read, played checkers with Fernando, Faustino's boy who helped me in the field, and waited. When the weather lifted for a few days, we began to collect with energy. The old stumps in the pastures higher up the mountain, each resembling a gigantic mushroom with the wide-spreading crown of flowering shrubs, ferns, orchids, and vines that flourished atop it rooted in the decaying wood, proved a rich collecting ground. Here grew those lovely ornaments of the mountain forests of tropical America, the Cavendishias, delightful to behold when their glossy foliage is overspread by waxy blossoms in compact, pink heads. Related to the heathers and the huckleberries, they grow chiefly on moss-covered trunks and boughs, but in the Pastaza Valley of Ecuador, I saw them forming tall bushes rooted in the ground. Now, too, the climbing hydrangea, a thick woody vine that scrambled to the tops of tall forest trees, displayed broad inflorescences in which the deep pink sterile flowers masked the tiny fertile florets.

In February and March, we enjoyed some glorious days. Earth can have few regions more lovely than this, when a bright sun courses through a sky of tender blue, when myriad glossy leaves reflect the mild, caressing sunbeams, a multitude of blossoms glow in their purest colors, and the atmosphere seems to envelop one with benignity. Doubtless, the very rareness of such days in this wet year increased their transcendent glory.

Now the Three-wattled Bellbirds, who like myself had sought refuge from the worst of the wet season at lower altitudes, some even descending to the coasts, returned to the heights. Each male took his stand in the top of a tall tree, where he was visible only from some elevation or clearing that enabled me to overlook the roof of the forest. Bright brown body and wings, gleaming white head and shoulders, with three long, dark, stringlike wattles dangling from the base of his black bill, this foot-long bird presented a striking figure against the sky—and his habits were no less remarkable than his appearance. Bending far forward and opening wide his mouth, revealing its cavernous black interior in sharp contrast to his white head, he emitted strange, far-carrying notes, in tone more like those of a wooden clapper than of a metallic bell. There was a deep, full note that sounded like *BUCK* and a sharper, higher note that I paraphrased as *wheat*. From two to six of these notes, in various combinations, came forth from the gaping mouth, with scarcely any movement of the mandibles; then the bird closed his bill and resumed a posture less strained. He never erected his dangling wattles, as he is too often depicted by artists. From March until July, each male bellbird was to be found daily in the same tree or cluster of neighboring trees, tirelessly sounding his dull wooden bell. I rarely saw the greenish, striped females; doubtless, like female blue cotingas, they built their unknown nests and raised their families all alone.

In March, I began to hear the beautiful, mellow calls of the Quetzals, fuller and deeper than the notes of other trogons, even as the Quetzal is more magnificent than they. Quetzals were much more numerous now—or was it only that their calls and greater activity made them appear so? Then at last, on April 4, my dream of years came true; my long wait amid the chilling cloud mists bore fruit. While following my favorite walk, the path that ran along the brow of the ridge with the forest on the lower side and the pasture above, I saw a female Quetzal, then her mate, cling upright for a few seconds each in front of a wide, round opening near the top of a tall, massive trunk at the forest's edge. Then they flew down into the woods. The height of fifty feet, together with the rottenness of the trunk, made this cavity inaccessible to us, but I could see from the ground that it had a single entrance. Now was a time for caution and restraint! I went away without showing too much interest in my discovery.

Quietly approaching the rotten trunk a few mornings later, I noticed two slender, green plumes projecting, to a length of six or eight inches, from the upper edge of the doorway and waving with every passing breeze. They resembled fronds of epiphytic ferns that were so abundant in these mountain forests. The male Quetzal was sitting on the eggs, and the two longest feathers of his train, bending upward against the rear wall of the deep cavity and then forward above his head to pass through the doorway, proclaimed his presence to every discerning passer-by. My predictions, based on studies of other members of the trogon family, were already confirmed: the nest had a single entrance, and the male took his turn at incubation. The details of their nesting remained to be worked out.

Although I could not see the eggs in this high nest, by long-continued watches I learned much about the manner of incubating them. The duller female attended the eggs every night, while the day was divided into three shifts of from two to more than four hours each. The female took the middle spell, the male the first and the last, which together occupied half or more of the daytime. The Quetzals' pattern of incubation differed from that of other trogons, in which, as in pigeons, the male takes one long session continuing through much of the day, while the female sits uninterruptedly from late afternoon until her mate returns next morning. On ending his matutinal session, the male Quetzal sometimes soared obliquely upward far above the treetops, where, circling through a wide arc, he shouted *very good, very good, very good*. Thus his exuberant vitality found expression after his long interval of confinement. Like Wordsworth's skylark, he was true to the kindred points of heaven and of home.

Although we enjoyed occasional drier spells, there was no real dry season this year, and the main trail passing through the region was rarely hard enough to be traversed without floundering through seas of mud. In April, May, and June, with the birds all nesting, the weather was foul. So, through the mist and the rain, with feet rarely dry and garments often wet and clinging, I learned the ways of the Quetzals and their neighbors of the highland forests: Blue-throated Toucanets, Prong-billed Barbets, Spotted-crowned Woodcreepers, Hairy Woodpeckers, Collared Redstarts, and many others.

The birds in this wild highland region were, on the whole, more confiding in man's goodness than I have ever found them elsewhere. It was not often necessary to conceal myself while watching their nests, which was fortunate, for sitting for long hours in a narrow blind of wet cloth is neither pleasant or healthful. Once, while I squatted in the pasture examining a wren's nest, a Collared Redstart alighted on my head! This fearless little yellow and black wood warbler is sometimes called *El Amigo del Hombre* (The Friend of Man).

Later, I found two more nests of the Quetzal. Since each of my three pairs raised two broods, I had six nests in all. These birds often raise both broods in the same cavity, which is apparently carved by themselves, although I was not fortunate enough to watch the process. All the first nestings were in high holes in rotten trunks, and to try to reach them would have been foolhardy—although I confess to have made a strenuous, but unsuccessful, effort to peep into the lowest of them from the very top of a twenty-three-foot ladder, while a visiting naturalist looked on and prophesied disaster. When, after the fledglings had flown, we pulled over the trunk that contained this lowest early nest to examine the cavity, it fell into a formless heap of rotten wood, and I realized how close I had come to a bad fall.

The pair of Quetzals who had the nest that we pulled down for inspection obligingly laid their second set of eggs in another hole made the preceding year or earlier, only fifteen feet above the ground in a rotting stub which stood in a pasture shaded by scattered, epiphyte-burdened trees. This nest was not too high to be reached from a stepladder, and here, at last, I could see the two light-blue eggs and watch the development of the naked nestlings that hatched from them. They were nourished with a variety of large caterpillars, winged insects, frogs, small lizards, and, as they grew older, a great quantity of the hard, large-seeded, green fruits of certain trees of the laurel family. One day I saw their mother bring them a beetle that appeared to be made of the purest gold. At first, both parents took nearly equal parts in feeding and brooding, but toward the end, the female, for some unknown reason, seemed to tire, and the male alone faithfully attended the nestlings during their last week in the hole. At nests of the Black-throated and the White-tailed Trogons, too, I have known the female to lose interest before the young fledged. As other trogons, the Quetzals failed to clean their nest, and as the nestlings grew they rested higher and higher on the mass of waste matter, including many regurgitated seeds, that filled the bottom of the nursery.

This male Quetzal's glittering, iridescent plumage suffered even more than that of most of his neighbors; both of the longest plumes of his train were broken off short by bending and friction on his innumerable passages in and out of the cavity. True symbol of the artist who sacrifices youth and strength in the creation of beauty, he had worn away his chief ornaments in the multiplication of his own lovely kind. But unlike the human artist, in a short while the bird would renew his plumage in all its pristine splendor.

These nestlings of the second brood did not take wing until August, when they were twenty-three days old. In staying to witness their departure, my sojourn among the clouds at Montaña Azul was prolonged to thirteen months. By this time, I had become almost as thoroughly acclimatized to this humid region as the Quetzals themselves or as the rosy-cheeked mountaineer children, who braved the bleakest days in thin cotton garments and would not admit that they felt cold. I myself no longer suffered from the chilling mists as I had done when I first arrived after a long residence in a milder climate, and I was reluctant to depart.

The superlative beauty of the Quetzal grew upon me during those long months of close association with it and amply repaid every sacrifice I had made to cultivate its acquaintance. The drenchings, the wet feet, the chills, and the rheumatism that I suffered while studying its home life left no lasting ill effects, and it is not unpleasant to recall that I could bear these discomforts. But the recollection of intimate contacts with so magnificent a creature will remain bright and vivifying as long as memory itself endures.

9

Winding Creek

WHEN I FINISHED my study of the Quetzal at Montaña Azul in August, 1938, I wished to visit my parents in Baltimore, whom I had not seen for well over four years. Passage on the ships from Puerto Limón to New York had been booked so far in advance that I had to wait five weeks for a berth. I passed this interval most agreeably at Las Cóncavas, a large coffee farm near Cartago. After a beautiful autumn in Maryland, I returned to Costa Rica in December. On the ship going south, I met Dean Rounds, a college student on his way to the tropics to collect insects for his professor. He decided to join me, and together we went to Rivas for my horse, which Juan Schroeder had been keeping for me. Bayon neighed the moment I came in sight of the pasture where he grazed; I was glad that he had not forgotten me after a year's absence and was in excellent condition. Rounds bought a horse, and together we set out to find a place to live and work.

In my natural history work over the years, finding living quarters in a

Headpiece: The beach at Dominical.

locality still unspoiled has been half the battle, and sometimes it has been lost. In the wilder parts of the earth, accommodations are not easy to find, especially if one seeks a modicum of cleanliness and privacy. Today, when throughout tropical America highways are being built into the wilderness, the ideal solution would be to have a trailer or housecar which one could park in the newly opened wilderness before its inevitable spoliation by land-hungry settlers. Thirty years ago, there were fewer motor roads penetrating the wild country, and, besides, a car with living accommodations would have been beyond my means.

After looking around the Térraba Valley for a while, Rounds and I decided to try our luck on the other side of El Cerro de la Muerte. For the rocky trail over the mountains, our horses needed shoes, which were unnecessary on the soft roads of the valley. The blacksmith in San Isidro had horseshoes but had run out of farrier's nails. I ordered some from San José by radiogram, and, while awaiting their arrival by air, I continued to poke around the valley.

In a most indirect fashion, I discovered an unoccupied cabin standing on a hillside above La Quebrada de las Vueltas—so-called from the many sharp turns in the lower part of its course—near its confluence with the Río Pedregoso. The rustic dwelling had been built a few years before by a young man engaged to be married; at the last minute, he had been jilted by his fiancée, and the house remained unoccupied or was used only as a granary and storehouse. It had a tile roof and three small rooms enclosed by rough boards, with the usual wide chinks between them. Its site in the midst of a pasture of tall, ragged tussock grass was not attractive, but it looked over the winding course of the creek, beyond which was a level field carpeted with the soft green of ripening rice. In the background was a long, forest-crowned ridge, and in the farther distance rose the lofty summits of the Cordillera de Talamanca.

Of the many places where I had sojourned in the tropics, the Valley of El General was where I had dwelt longest and most contentedly, and it had called me most persuasively to return. When the young man unfortunate in love agreed to furnish his cottage and lease it to us for six months, we jumped at the opportunity. Two unvarnished tables, a pair of folding cots, a clay-covered platform for cooking, and shelves for books and specimens were made by a carpenter in San Isidro and quickly installed. On the last night of the year 1938, we moved in, eager to begin field work.

Before long, other tenants arrived; a swarm of the big, black wasps called *Guittarróns* settled on a pillar at a corner of our narrow front porch and began to build their nest. They looked formidable.

"What ugly wasps!" remarked my entomological companion.

"There is an attractive iridescence on their wings," I pointed out.

"Gun-metal finish!" was his laconic retort.

He and I and Efraim, the boy who cooked for us and carried my plant press, held a council of war, and, despite their gun-metal finish, suggestive of automatic rifles and other murderous weapons that had lately come into such unhappy prominence, we resolved to permit the big wasps to live on our front porch as long as they kept the peace and refrained from stinging us. In our moments of leisure, we watched them tirelessly bringing little brown pellets in their jaws and building up the walls of their new dwelling. When completed, their nest was an oblong structure about two feet long, covered with grayish brown paper with strong transverse corrugations to give it rigidity. It was entered through a single, narrow, round orifice at the upper end. Within this envelope, the hexagonal brood cells were attached to the surface of the post in a single continuous sheet.

It seemed miraculous that, beginning to build out the enclosing walls from diagonally opposite beveled corners of the square post, then curving them sharply inward, the wasps brought them together in the middle in perfect alignment, as accurately as though they had been laid down according to a blueprint, with ruler and calipers. The substance of the wall, composed of fibers from decaying wood cemented together by some unidentified material, became rigid as soon as it dried; there was no question of flexing the sides to bring them into contact; it was masonry laid true to course. But the instinct of these black wasps is not infallible, and sometimes they err. I have seen them build out one side of the envelope farther than the other; when the two sides failed to join in the center, they continued to extend the edges of the walls until they overlapped broadly, making a misshapen nest.

In ten days, the outer envelope of the vespiary was closed and cemented together in the middle. Those February nights were clear and cool, for the chilled air that flowed down from the high summits settled in this hollow. At dawn, when the thermometer registered 58 or 60 degrees Fahrenheit, the wasps would be torpid with cold and unable to fly. If they lost their hold on the nest, they fell to the ground and lay there helpless until warmed by the rising sun. As the temperature rose, our wasps became more active. If we hammered on the post that supported their nest or on neighboring beams, those within would vibrate the corrugated shell with a sonorous whir of many wings, a warning sound that we always heeded, for, if the stroke were repeated, they would come sallying forth to defend their citadel. But at dawn, some of those that crawled slowly out in response to our knocks would fall to the ground when they attempted to fly and lie ignominiously in the dust until the air grew warmer. In April, after the wet season broke, the first sharp peals of a thunderstorm would bring them swarming out of their single doorway, to fly about seeking the cause of the disturbance, and we would prudently retire from their vicinity.

During the five months while we were such close neighbors, our wasps never broke the peace; we suffered not a single sting. We even came to feel some affection for our tenants with the gun-metal finish; one night I discovered Efraim carefully returning to the nest one that had fallen into the dishwater. When we vacated the cabin at the expiration of our lease in June, it was with regret that their nest must soon be destroyed, for, mild-tempered as we had found them, they doubtless would not tamely allow the carpenter to make the improvements projected by the owner, and their sting is said to be formidable. I think it was chiefly to save our vespiary from demolition that I objected to having these improvements made during the period of our tenancy.

Here by La Quebrada de las Vueltas, we were surrounded by many wintering birds from the United States and Canada, while others, including great flocks of Barn Swallows and Cliff Swallows, passed over us on their northward migration during the spring months. In January, flocks of Dickcissels foraged in the field of ripening rice in front of our cabin. Toward the end of February, they began to sing, at first in whispers, then more loudly; soon they were repeating their modest verses over and over in the cool, bright mornings. Often several black-throated males would sing while perching close together in the same bush; there was still no rivalry between them. They sang more and more during March, but after April 3, we saw them no longer.

At that time, most of our published information on the habits of tropical birds was written by collectors so busy plying their trade that they could spare little time to study the creatures they were shooting. The reports of these bird collectors contain the statement that migratory birds are songless in their winter homes—a glaring falsehood. Each year, I add names to the long list of migrants from the North that I have heard sing in tropical America, but, while some kinds sing only rarely, others are habitually tuneful. From March to early May, wintering Olive-backed or Swainson's Thrushes raise their liquid spirals of song in the forests of El General, repeating them so often that at this season they contribute more melody to the woodland than any other bird. This song, so different from that of any purely tropical thrush that I know, so suggestive of spruce and hemlock in the far north, seems strangely out of place among the notes of trogons, toucans, and antbirds. It was also surprising to find Olive-backed Thrushes foraging on the outskirts of the swarms of army ants, along with antbirds, woodcreepers, and ant-tanagers. Those who have not watched migratory birds in their winter homes have seen only half of their lives.

In the lowlands that drain into the Gulf of Honduras, where they winter in great numbers, Orchard Orioles are songful after their arrival in late July or August and again for two months before their departure in April. Young males in transitional plumage sing even more than those in fully adult attire, as though eager to try their newly acquired vocal powers. In January, on the Pacific slope of Guatemala, I found Blue-headed or Solitary Vireos singing freely among the shade trees of the great coffee plantations. Birds such as the Summer Tanager, the Yellow Warbler, and the Black and White Warbler, which maintain a "territory" in their winter homes and resent the intrusion of others of their kind, are stimulated to sing by the excitement of driving away a trespassing rival. As the date of their long, northward journey draws nigh, many male birds who have long been silent begin to sing more or less freely. Cheerfully they face the perils and fatigue of their voyage through pathless, nocturnal skies. Similar facts have been recorded for Old World migrants in tropical Africa.

In the surrounding woods were two kinds of squirrels. The larger one, about the size of the familiar Gray Squirrel of the North, grayish above and tawny below, often entered clearings with scattered trees to hunt for food. The little, dark brown Pygmy Squirrel, no bigger than a Chipmunk, seldom left the heavy forest. One morning, I saw one of these diminutive squirrels carrying a youngster almost as large as herself. The young squirrel formed a compact ball beneath its mother's neck and chest, with its tail wrapped around her shoulders, its head indistinguishable. The little mother climbed up and down slender trunks with her heavy burden, apparently seeking a safe place to deposit it. Finally, becoming tired, she forcibly disengaged it from herself and set it down on a log. She scampered off a short way, twitching her upright tail and voicing short, sharp notes that were evidently calls for the youngster to follow; but it remained where she had left it. In the end, she was obliged to return to it, and, with much coaxing, persuaded it to walk to the end of the log, from which it climbed up the base of a slender tree. From here the mother wished it to jump to a neighboring sapling, and several times she demonstrated the long leaps that she desired her offspring to take. But evidently it was not capable of the feat, and finally it vanished into the undergrowth, using less spectacular modes of locomotion.

The first quarter of the year was very dry in El General, and during three months scarcely any rain fell on the lower side of the basin. By March, the pastures were brown, and few plants were in flower in the neighborhood of La Quebrada de las Vueltas. Few birds had begun to sing and nest so early, and the days were, on the whole, monotonous and dusty. My entomological companion had already departed for what he hoped would prove to be richer fields.

I decided to make a journey to the Pacific coast at Dominical as a means of augmenting my collection and breaking the monotony of those bright, warm days. At dawn, Efraim and I set forth on horseback with food for two days in our saddlebags and a light collecting press. We forded the Río San Isidro, crossed a high ridge, then forded the Pedregoso and the Pacuar, all of which streams had shrunken currents. Near the foot of the abrupt coastal range we dismounted for the ascent of the too-steep path, which, instead of winding to overcome its adversary by gentle insinuations in the manner of a well-planned trail, charged the slope bullishly by bold frontal attack. Bayon, who had unpleasant memories of the deer flies in the forest on the summit, was recalcitrant and more than once attempted to double back and return to the valley. I should have remembered that the last time he refused to cross a mountain, three years earlier, I later had occasion to approve his behavior.

But at length, after a sharp climb of fifteen hundred feet, we reached the summit, whence we beheld the Pacific spread out vastly, thirty-five hundred feet below us. Here on the mountaintop, exposed to the moist sea breezes, the forest trees were densely burdened with moss, orchids, and a great variety of other epiphytes; the undergrowth was heavy and impenetrable. Here I found a new kind of begonia, a pretty species with pinkish blossoms. Even after descending five hundred feet, or at only three thousand feet above sea level, we heard the sweet strains of the Black-faced Solitaire, which I had never found any lower than four thousand feet above sea level, on the more protected southern slopes of the main cordillera. Here, also, we heard Howling Monkeys, which, inexplicably, I never found in the basin of El General, even while great forests remained to support them.

While riding down through the forest toward the ocean, we watched a pair of Swallow-tailed Kites, soaring gracefully around with twiglets that they had broken from treetops with their feet and were trying to transfer to their bills, not always an easy task for them. Without doubt, they were building a nest high above the ground, but we could not stop to look for it. Swallow-tailed Kites always snatch dead twigs from high, exposed branches as they soar past, a trick that evidently requires acute discrimination, for were they to grasp too strongly a piece that failed to yield to them, they might be jerked out of the air with disastrous results to their long wings. To alight upon the growing nest, they must hold their material in their bills. Like the Plumbeous Kite, they catch insects, even small ones, in their feet as they soar about high in the air, then bend down their heads to pluck off the wings and swallow their prey. Although these kites have departed widely from other raptors in their mode of hunting and the nature of their diet, they follow the family tradition of seizing victims in their talons rather than in the bill, like most flycatching birds. Swallow-tailed Kites present a curious appearance as they soar overhead, sometimes in company with much smaller swifts and swallows, striking with their feet at insects invisible from the ground. They vary their diet with tree snakes and nestlings plucked from exposed nests, thereby earning the enmity of the larger flycatchers, which pursue them with great spirit.

The way was steep and rough, worked into deep corrugations by the hoofs of beasts of burden always stepping in the same places. In the wet season, it must have been a terror, but fortunately we found it everywhere dry and hard. For hours, we wound slowly down the southern slope of the range, along this narrow track through forest broken only at long intervals by small clearings, each with a solitary dwelling. Halfway down, we reached El Platanillo, a large opening with perhaps half a dozen thatched cabins. From a tall tree standing isolated in this clearing, the long, neatly woven pouches of the Chestnut-headed Oropéndola hung like huge exotic fruits. The presence of this small colony surprised me, as I have never seen either this species or the larger Montezuma Oropéndola in the Térraba Valley—an absence difficult to explain. Near the oropéndolas' tree, we noticed several of the parasitic Giant Cowbirds, which lay their eggs in oropéndolas' nests, leaving the hosts to hatch and rear their young. Continuing downward, we soon entered another long stretch of unbroken forest, in the midst of which we passed a train of pack animals bound for San Isidro with salt from the coast. Before the advent of the airplane, most of the merchandise for El General came from Puntarenas by this difficult route.

In the middle of the afternoon, we forded the Río Barú. The stream was hemmed in by low, abrupt hills, and the trail was in places cut into the side of a precipice far above the current. As we rode beneath huge flowering trees of Espavé and Guanacaste that grew along the banks, we heard the subdued roar of the distant surf. Efraim, who had never been to the coast, was puzzled by that increasingly loud booming. I envied his youth and the novel experience which awaited him as we approached the shore. I almost envied his fortune in having been raised in an isolated mountain valley, for so many things which for me had long since become commonplace remained to greet him with all the freshness and novelty of a first encounter. His only journey by a mechanical conveyance had been a short airplane flight.

Traversing dense thickets of slender, spiny palms, the trail ended abruptly on a wide beach of fine, dark sand. A wild scene spread before us: on one side, the broad expanse of the sea, with the long rollers curling and breaking far out from the strand, and the sun sinking low in the haze that filled the west. On the landward side, beyond a narrow strip of level, swampy ground, the foothills rose up abruptly in high, vine-draped precipices, along the tree-fringed summits of which a flock of gorgeous Scarlet Macaws flew laboriously two by two, their raucous shouts rising above the roar of the breakers. The only sign of human habitation was a solitary house situated near the end of a low, rocky promontory more than a mile distant. Toward this we directed our course, following hoofprints in the sand. As we proceeded along the beach, we encountered two solitary Whimbrels and a pair of American Oystercatchers, the first I ever saw. Three Brown Pelicans flew slowly and heavily just above the crests of the waves.

Bayon, who, like Efraim, had never been near any body of water larger than a fordable river, was afraid of the sea: whether intimidated by its vast emptiness or frightened by the roar and surge of the breakers or disturbed by the strange smell of the shore or upset by the combination of the three, I could not decide. Since the dry sand high on the beach was loose and afforded poor footing, I tried to keep him on the more compact wet sand nearer the surf. But when I pulled his head seaward with the reins, he danced along sideways, as though he had heard the old saying about doing as Rome does, and, having arrived at the seashore, he deemed it proper to imitate the mode of locomotion of the crabs which scuttled along the sand ahead of us and suddenly plunged into narrow holes.

We slept that night on a pile of dry banana leaves in a shed behind the solitary house on the point. Early next morning we set forth, planning to make the return journey in two days instead of one, collecting along the way. The tide was rising, and all the beach was wet from the rain that had fallen in the night. Bayon had discovered that the salty sand tasted good and licked it up whenever I relaxed the reins, which was frequently, for many things claimed my attention. As I rode along, musing upon the queer, elongate shape of the coconuts on the tall palms that fringed the beach, a wave suddenly higher than any of its predecessors washed over the sand around us. Now sober, sure-footed Bayon, who had many a time carried me through impetuous mountain torrents, breast deep, where a misstep might have proved fatal, was terrified by the sudden appearance beneath himself of a few inches of flowing salt water, where a moment before there had been only moist sand. Instead of bolting for the land, the frightened horse, looking only down at his feet, began to dance around in circles. Fearing that he was about to fall, in an ill-considered moment I jumped off with the intention of taking him by the head and leading him up the beach. I knew he would be calm if I held his head. But I slipped on the wet sand and went down beneath his hoofs.

The next thing I knew, I was lying in the surf with a terrific pain in my left shoulder. I rose up, feeling that the bones had been shattered, and staggered higher up the beach, to throw myself down again in agony. It was not until Efraim called my attention to it that I learned that my left ear and cheek were bloody; a hoof had scraped the entire side of my head before impinging upon the collarbone. Fortunately, the horse was not shod. Nevertheless, I marveled that I had suffered no more serious injury—a fractured skull, perhaps. I like to think that Bayon tried not to step on me. However that may be, he took it all calmly enough and, having fled to higher ground, began to lick the smooth sand.

The accident had befallen almost in front of the single hut along that lonely stretch of shore. The good woman who dwelt there came out and tied up Bayon to a coconut tree, while I lay on the sand; she said that horses newly arrived from the interior sometimes made themselves sick by licking up too much of the beach. Then she solicitously invited me to enter her hut for treatment, but knowing that there was little she could do and strongly suspecting that she would anoint me with grease of some kind, I politely declined. While I pulled myself together for the journey, she brought out for me a cup of black coffee, cold and very strong. I never learned my benefactress' name, but I have not forgotten the kindness this poor woman showed to a stranger in distress. What a contrast between her solicitude and the callous indifference often displayed by those nearest the victim of an accident in a teeming city! It seems that some of our noblest human sentiments are stifled by crowding.

My one impulse was to reach our cabin by Winding Creek before my shoulder grew stiff. I knew no nearer spot where I could find a couch soft, clean, and quiet, to lie down upon and recover from my injuries. Preparing for a rapid march over the mountain, I gave the plant press and extra equipment that I could spare to the woman who had befriended me. She surmised that it was a board for some sort of game that she had never heard of and said her little children would enjoy playing with it. At the first rivulet behind the shore, I paused to wash the blood and as much as possible of the sand from my head and to arrange a sling for my useless left arm. In checking over my property, I discovered to my dismay that corroding salt water had entered the binoculars and aneroid barometer, but here I was unable to open and dry these delicate instruments. With Efraim's aid, I mounted my horse to continue the journey.

As I rode up the valley of the Río Barú, the pain in my shoulder was intense. I tried to combat it by keeping before my mind's eye that beautiful, wild scene that had opened before us as we emerged upon the beach the preceding evening, with the Scarlet Macaws flying along the verdant summits of the cliffs, the oystercatchers running along the shore, and the pelicans gliding over the crests of the waves. My mind, whether from the sudden shock my body had received or from the stimulation of the strong coffee to which I was not accustomed, soon became more than ordinarily active. This pain, it occurred to me, was the price I was called upon to pay for that vision. Was it worth the price? Which would be more enduring, the memory of that vesper scene, the reality of which was before me for only a few minutes, or this racking pain, which was to be intensely real for many days?

Then I recalled how, since my earliest journeys to study nature, I had paid, in one way or another—and sometimes very dearly—for my experiences and adventures. Riding beneath the ferny cliffs along the Río Barú, I remembered other cliffs, no less lofty but of sterner aspect, on the rugged coast of Maine, where, while still an undergraduate, I had studied the seaweeds, multihued and multiform, that grew in wave-relinquished pools and on rocks exposed by the falling tide. Here I would sometimes watch a pair of Black Guillemots lightly rising and falling on the offshore waves. One day, I happened to see one of these birds enter a cranny halfway up a high cliff close by, where I surmised it had a nest, which I at once desired to examine.

Since it was impossible to reach that high cranny unaided, I enlisted another student in the project. We attached a rope to a tree at the head of the cliff: it was only a doubled clothesline, but youth is rash. I was the first to descend and, without mishap, lowered myself to the narrow ledge near which the nest was situated. As my companion followed, I called to him to be careful of a pile of loose rock fragments resting precariously on the shelf beneath the rope. My warning came too late. Touching the rocks with his feet, he upset the pile. One struck me sharply on the ankle before all dashed down into the sea. For many minutes, I lay in pain on that narrow ledge between sky and water, wondering how I would ever reach the land again. But, finally, the pain abating somewhat, I managed to clamber up to the top of the precipice and hobble back to the road, where our car was parked. The cranny that held the supposed guillemots' nest turned sharply to one side, so that we could not see what it held.

Thus, passing in retrospective review many another adventure and misadventure, I came to the point where the trail left the valley of the Río Barú to strike up the steep mountainside, and here my musing was dispelled by the difficulties of the ascent. Every jolt the horse made on that rough path, and there were many, caused a sharp pang in my wounded shoulder. Often it was necessary to dismount, either to pass beneath some fallen trunk that formed a low bridge over the track or to scramble up an incline too steep for riding. To dismount was painful, but mounting caused still more poignant twinges and could be accomplished only from some log or stump. For ten long hours, that seemingly interminable ride continued.

In one sense, I was grateful to that mishap for showing me of what my organism was capable. I went more steadily than I would ordinarily have done, with fewer halts for rest and refreshment, none for observation. The pain in my shoulder prevented awareness of fatigue, hunger, or thirst, which otherwise I should have felt as we toiled up that steeply inclined, narrow chasm between tall trees, into which the sun beat fiercely, with no breath of air to mitigate the heat. Our pampered, civilized bodies are malingerers, crying out for mercy, pleading faintness and exhaustion, while still far from the limit of their endurance. It is only when strongly belabored that they show us what they are capable of performing.

Darkness fell before we reached our solitary cabin, where I lay down, while Efraim kindled a fire and prepared a bit of supper. Next morning, I walked two miles to the newly opened emergency hospital in San Isidro, where the trained nurse, after feeling my shoulder, assured me that no bone was broken, although the contusion was severe. Not until a year later, when continuing pain caused me to have the shoulder X-rayed, did I learn that her diagnosis was wrong: the tip of the clavicle had been fractured.

Trusting her diagnosis and reluctant to interrupt my work by a visit to a doctor in the distant capital, I took to my cot, hoping to recover in a few days. Every movement of my torso brought a twinge; to sneeze was a sharp agony; to raise myself up a painful and tedious enterprise. Five days passed before I felt equal to creeping down to the creek to wash out the sand that had caked in my hair while I lay on the beach. After ten days, I could walk around again, holding up my binoculars with my right hand to watch the birds, which now, at the end of March, were building their nests everywhere in the thickets and forests surrounding our cabin.

How sweet and flattering are the sensations of returning health after a long illness, of recovering the use of a disabled limb! One might willingly suffer a fair amount of pain in order to experience them. Convalescence has much in common with adolescence: both are periods when we feel our powers daily waxing. Convalescence carries us back again to that time of youth when life was full of promise.

To me, in that spring beside La Quebrada de las Vueltas, the promise was of new discoveries in ornithology, and it was generously fulfilled. We found many new kinds of nests that I wished to study, and many fresh secrets of bird life were revealed to me. But interspersed with these joys was the pain of that slowly knitting shoulder, added to the usual sorrow of returning to rarely found nests only to learn that some predator had pillaged them since my last visit. Then there was the deep distress of watching my landlord's younger brother, a lad of twelve, waste slowly away and die horribly inch by inch, always in agony, from an infection that started in his thigh, despite all that could be done locally to relieve him. The blue threads of happiness and the red strands of pain are so tightly interwoven in life's fabric that, save possibly the Stoic sage, not even the wisest and best of us succeed in disentangling them.

When I left Winding Creek at the end of June, 1939, I sold to my landlord, at reduced prices, all our cooking utensils, enamelware table service, kerosene lamps, and other small household furnishings. Meanwhile, he had found another fiancée, and his marriage was only a few weeks distant. It was fortunate for both of us that we met. He provided for me a shelter and place to work in what turned out to be a favorable locality; I found him with an unfurnished house and left him with a dwelling well-equipped by local standards, the rental money with which to improve the building and begin housekeeping, and a bride.

10

The Hummingbirds' Brook

A WEEK AFTER leaving the Quebrada de las Vueltas, I embarked at Puntarenas for Guayaquil. I was eager to see the snow-crowned volcanoes, the forests rich in palms, and, above all, the marvelously varied and colorful bird life of Ecuador. But I went at the wrong season to find many nests for study, and, before the end of the year 1939, I returned to Costa Rica to take charge of the botanical section of the Museo Nacional, as I had agreed to do before leaving the country.

It was hard to stay within the thick walls of the old museum in San José during those clear, sunny months that started off the year. All around me in the herbarium were cases full of botanical specimens, long since dry and colorless, for which I had recently become responsible. They clamored, as well as such lifeless things can, for care and rearrangement. But the weather of the early *verano*, with its cold, starry nights and warm, sun-flooded days, was like some heady wine. Try as I might, I could not imprison my thoughts within those massive walls of puddled

Headpiece: Young Amazon Kingfishers.

clay, among the herbarium specimens. They persisted in floating out over the surrounding mountains whence, years before, Pittier and Tonduz and Brenes had gathered those same specimens. Through the deep-embrasured windows of the herbarium I could see nothing of those hills; only a little sunlit rectangle of courtyard where goldfish swam in a pond and a few orchids grew. But climbing the dusty, circling stairway of the old square tower at the end of the building, I could fill my eyes with the sight of the green hills that swept in a wide circle about the narrow plateau where the city stood, calling a naturalist in so many directions at once that his mind became a disordered whirl of enticing and mostly impracticable projects for exploration. In the northeast, seeming very close in the clear morning atmosphere, rose the immense bulk of Volcán Irazú, with a lofty column of smoke arising from its flat summit. Blown to the southwest by the trade wind, this eruptive material spread a fine layer of dust over the glass cases of the museum.

The call of those green hills was too strong to be resisted, especially by one who had so recently forsworn full liberty to roam them. Many a plant still unknown to science lurked among those forested mountains, so inviting in the distance, but on actual contact so rugged and forbidding, imposing such formidable obstacles to the progress of puny man. Would it not be well to collect, now in the good weather, samples of the flora of some still unexplored nook among the mountains? A few thousand new specimens, more or less, to arrange along with the old ones during the long, wet months that would follow could make no great difference. The sympathetic director of the museum readily agreed with these arguments. I was free to take to the hills!

My friend Juan Schroeder had recently bought a farm near the western end of the basin of El General, which I had not yet explored. He wrote to tell me that, on a neighboring farm, an unoccupied cabin was available. My horse Bayon was waiting in his pasture; Efraim, the boy who in past years had cooked for me and carried my plant press, was willing to help me again. The Ministry of Education provided a pass on the airplane, which set me down in San Isidro in time for breakfast. That same afternoon, Don Juan and I set forth on foot to visit his farm at Santa Rosa and the cabin he had rented for me. We went slowly, for those afternoons of late February, 1940, were warm, and the road was dry and dusty. We were ashamed to count how many times we paused to rest and chat with farmers, while we refreshed ourselves with the sweet, golden oranges that grew by the roadside. The narrow, winding cartway rose and fell, crossing many a ridge and many a clear stream in the valleys, passing among hillside pastures, strips of forest, and fields where the dry stalks of last year's maize were already nearly hidden by the springing weeds.

At length, as the sun fell lower, we came to the brow of a slope longer than any that we had left behind. Far below, the tree-bordered channel of the Río Pacuar meandered through verdant, shady pastures, amid which stood, here and there, low, rough farmhouses roofed with dull red tiles. Beyond the valley the coastal range rose up, summit behind summit, all clad in a dark green mantle of forest. The steep hills were notched by wooded gorges, whose cool, shadowed depths stood out in dark contrast to the intervening ridges aglow in the sunshine. In the north rose the rounded bosses of El Cerro de la Muerte, huge and grim and gray, and the other lofty summits of the Talamancan Cordillera. What a scene it made—the deep, narrow valley with its quiet dwellings set in the bright green of pastures and cultivation, like "a haunt of ancient peace" in the midst of those wild hills!

Near the foot of the long slope, we entered Don Juan's pasture, caught and saddled our horses, and resumed our journey on four feet instead of two. By a broad, shallow ford we rode across the Pacuar, passed over a level pasture, then forded the rocky bed of the Río San Antonio. On a shelf cut into the steep hillside above this stream stood the house I was to occupy. It was of the usual type and soon inspected: a narrow porch across the front; opening onto this, two small, square rooms to serve as living room and kitchen; two tiny, rectangular cubicles, under the sloping roof at the rear, to be used as bedrooms. In the kitchen were some shelves and a wooden platform covered with clay upon which to make a fire, the smoke escaping as best it might; in one of the bedrooms, a wooden bedstead with hard boards instead of springs; in the *sala*, or living room, a rickety table, a pair of stools without backs, and a great heap of maize ears piled up in a corner. The rough, unpainted walls of this room were partly covered with old newspapers, boldly announcing patented remedies for the most intimate maladies.

Not a palatial nor even a homelike dwelling, certainly; but with a few cooking utensils and a folding canvas cot—enough, with the collecting apparatus and some staple supplies, to fill an oxcart—it would make an exceptionally comfortable camp. If there were no pictures save the cartoons in the yellowing newspapers to relieve the drabness of the walls, it was only necessary to throw open the wooden shutters that closed the glassless windows to enjoy a diorama painted with master strokes on the grandest scale. In the foreground spread level pastures, shaded by slender, stately *ojoche* trees nearly fifty yards high. In the midst of the meadows, two lines of lower trees, converging into one line at the right, indicated the point of confluence of the Pacuar and San Antonio rivers. Beyond, the mountains rose up, crest above forested crest, to the bare, treeless summit of El Cerro de la Muerte and the long ridges of the continental divide, with their ever-changing masses of cloud, which closed off the prospect to the north.

Locking up the vacant cabin, we mounted our horses to ride up the ridge that rose sharply behind it. A hundred yards from the dwelling, the forest began like a wall, forty yards high. As we neared its edge, a small bird with spotless white plumage flew out from a treetop and swung in a long catenary curve across the valley to the hanging forest on the farther side. It was my first Yellow-billed Cotinga. I looked upon it as an augury for a prosperous season.

Two days later, we moved into our cabin. Efraim made the fire and put the beans and rice on to boil; Bayon grazed contentedly in the pasture at the side; I unpacked and set up the apparatus for drying the botanical specimens. In a day or so, we had settled down to a routine. Arising at daybreak, we breakfasted as the sun's first rays struck up the valley, dissolving the silvery mists that had gathered during the night. Almost every morning at sunrise, a flock of Little Blue Herons, four adults in slate-blue plumage and eleven young birds clad in purest white, winged deliberately up the river, following every winding of the tree-shaded channel and holding our gaze enthralled until they vanished around a curve. At sunset, they returned down the valley. Later I found where they roosted, on leafy boughs overhanging the channel.

While the sun was still low above the crests of the forest, we locked up the cabin and set forth on the day's excursion, with lunch in the knapsack and the plant press full of papers for the specimens. No matter where a man lives, he soon finds a favorite walk that attracts him beyond all others and of which he never tires. So it was with us. There were few roads or even clean paths in the immediate neighborhood, but the course of the Río San Antonio became our highway. We drank and bathed in its water, and it led us back among the hills into haunts of unsuspected beauty. It was an enchanting stream. Its current, filtered through scarcely broken forests, was always clear. Even when swollen with the heavy rains of May and June, it never became brown and turbid like the Pacuar, which flowed through a cleared and cultivated valley and when in flood formed a sharp contrast with the limpid tributary stream. During the nearly rainless months of February and March, both rivers were low and gentle, and the smaller San Antonio could at many points be crossed dry-shod on stepping stones.

First we explored the lower part of the stream, where it flowed through the pastures. Here and there it slipped over a rock to form a low, murmurous cascade, but there was no high waterfall. The channel was shaded by trees, chiefly gnarled Sotacaballos, whose long boughs reached far over the channel and in places completely overarched it, forming a dim, cool retreat never penetrated by the hot midday sun. Verdant masses of the River Cuphea, a shrubby relative of the humble clammy herb of northern fields, covered rocks that rose above the water, and on parts of these rocks recently exposed by the falling current, innumerable tiny brown seed pods of riverweeds, no bigger than moss capsules, stood up on short, threadlike stalks. Feathery green fronds of the same delicate water herbs—which include some of the very smallest of all flowering plants—waved in the flowing water, where they grew attached to rocks still submerged. At the end of February, a climber of the bignonia family spread a profusion of pretty pink trumpet blossoms over the lower branches of the Sotacaballo trees, and, later, another woody vine (*Securidaca*), an aspiring relative of the little northern milkwort, displayed in the treetops dense masses of small, two-winged, pealike blossoms, forming delightful expanses of pinkish lavender.

Where the twisted Sotacaballo trees cast the deepest shade over the water and were most heavily burdened with orchids, ferns, and other air plants, a slender log formed a footbridge from shore to shore. The slippery upper face of the log had been only slightly flattened with the axe, and one wearing shoes found it prudent to support himself with a long pole as he passed over. Beneath this rustic bridge, the current, which just above had rushed turbulently along a boulder-strewn reach of the channel, flowed smooth and deep over great, dark, flat rock strata of gentle inclination, locally called *lajas*. Later, when floodwater carried the log away, we could hardly leave our secluded camp except by fording the swollen current on horseback or else making a long and difficult detour down the river.

Above the still water by the footbridge, a Royal Flycatcher hung her yard-long nest of brown fibers. Here no boisterous wind could roll the two reddish brown eggs from the shallow niche in the middle of the tangled mass that resembled a hank of driftweed more than a bird's nest. Only on the rarest and most memorable of occasions did she or her mate spread fanwise their high, scarlet diadems, which transformed a pair of dull, olive-colored birds with low topknots into superb creatures of regal distinction. Here, too, lived a pair of Buff-rumped Warblers, perpetually wagging their dark-tipped, pale yellow tails as they hopped along the shore and over exposed rocks in the channel.

One morning in April, as we crossed the footbridge, a small animal clambered up the underside of the thick trunk of a great Sotacaballo tree. Climbing back-downward along the inclined trunk until it reached some erect branches, it easily scrambled up among the foliage, where it stopped in full view. It was a Kinkajou, about the size of its relatives, the raccoons, but more slender and shorter-legged and everywhere, including its long, gracefully curving tail, clothed with brownish gray fur that appeared thick and soft. Despite the low, flattened crown, its little face was attractive and appealing, with its short, blunt, black muzzle, large dark eyes, and little ears set far down on the sides of the head and expressively mobile. I have sometimes seen that puckish, somnolent face thrust sleepily from a hole in a trunk, when my tapping had aroused the beastie from its daylong slumber.

But this Kinkajou preferred, on a warm afternoon, to take its siesta among the open boughs. Disregarding two human spectators, the animal settled itself comfortably among the branches and started to wash its fur with a long, slender tongue. It seemed very sleepy, for it frequently interrupted its licking to yawn, extruding its pink tongue to an amazing length. It continued alternately to yawn and lazily lick its pelage until we grew tired of watching. Returning at intervals through the afternoon, I found the Kinkajou drowsing in various comfortable postures, once resting back-downward in a crotch, its head bent forward and resting on its abdomen, its arms loosely thrown over the surrounding branches for support, its feet in the air. When aroused, it yawned with sleepy indifference and promptly resumed its slumber.

An hour after nightfall, when day had dawned for it, I found the Kinkajou moving off through the uppermost boughs of the Sotacaballo tree, doubtless to breakfast on the fruits of neighboring trees. Its eyes shone with intense brilliance in the beam of my electric torch. I wished that I could follow as it moved away through the dusky foliage, to learn more about its ways. What a pity that so many of our fellow mammals are creatures of the night, carrying on their business of living under the cover of darkness and remaining stranger to us than the birds, which are not so close of kin! Even the crepuscular Pauraque that drowsed all day beneath the thicket at the edge of the pasture, venturing forth in the twilight to sound its clear, plaintive cries, was more companionable than most of the free four-footed animals among which we dwelt.

From the pastures, we gradually extended our explorations along the upper reaches of the river. The number of specimens to be gathered made it impossible to cover a great distance on any single day, but each day we penetrated a little farther into the mountain fastnesses. Now we were no longer able to walk easily over the meadows by the riverside and found it quickest to make our way along the bed of the stream itself, stepping or jumping laboriously from rock to rock or from ledge to ledge, often crossing from one side to the other to take advantage of the rocks closest together. But sometimes, where deep pools stretched from shore to shore, we were obliged to leave the channel and, with our long machetes, cut a path through the undergrowth at the forest's edge.

At most points, the slopes rose up steeply from the brink of the stream. They were covered with tall forest trees that met above the narrowing channel and cast a deep shade over its waters. In February, a tall shrub of the acanthus family, *Aphelandra tetragona*, displayed glowing masses of scarlet flowers in the more open glades along the river. But aside from this attractive shrub, which soon passed from bloom, there was, as usual, scarcely any color in the undergrowth of the forest.

The course of the stream itself was slightly more colorful. At times, during the brighter hours of the day, a wide-winged Morpho butterfly traced its swift, erratic course above the channel, flashing glints of the most intense azure. Other brilliant butterflies were not absent, and there were gigantic dragonflies, whose long wings were of glassy transparency and colorless, save for a small rectangle of deep blue at the tip of each.

Over the rocks in and beside the river and on the foliage along the banks rested bright-colored little frogs, seldom much over an inch in length, boldly marked with black and green and, on the larger specimens, red. They were sluggish creatures and, unlike many batrachians, most reluctant to remove themselves from beneath human feet. At best, they would creep slowly out of our way, so that often they owed their lives more to our own care in placing our steps than to any prudent efforts of their own. We forbore to touch these showy frogs (*Atelopus varius*), for they are known to be poisonous. Their excessive abundance and their indifference to concealment, in a region where even inconspicuous green and brown frogs are careful to hide themselves from the many frog-eating birds and reptiles, made me confident that here we had a genuine example of warning coloration.

The rocks along the stream were overgrown with delicate ferns of great beauty. A low herb with modest white flowers, *Spigelia humboldtiana*, blossomed on ledges where a little soil had accumulated. Great boulders, whose tops stood well above the water level, supported profuse overgrowths of plants, including a tall, glossy-leafed begonia with white flowers and Clusias with fleshy foliage and fragrant white blossoms. On an islet, we found a splendid shrubby *Columnea* with long, furry leaves, red over most of the underside, that were spread out fan-wise and completely sheltered the slender, tubular, red corollas. I had never before seen this beautiful plant of the gesneria family nor, apparently, had any other botanist, for in Washington it was declared to be a species new to science (*C. ornata*).

Through most of the day, a profound silence reigned along this forest watercourse: the only habitual sounds were the soft murmur of the falling water and the loud chirring of the big cicadas among the trees. These noises were so continuously in our ears that we soon lost consciousness of them; they formed the background against which less frequent sounds stood out. Among these were the loud, sweet songs of the Buff-rumped Warblers and, more rarely, the clear, ringing notes of the bay-backed Riverside Wrens, which dwelt here where the stream flowed through the forest as well as along the bushy margins of its course through the clearings. Now and again the short, compelling whistles of the Lowland Wood-Wrens rang out of the forest. Seldom, indeed, at this season, did we hear the voice of some other bird, such as the exquisitely modulated notes of the Great Tinamou. But on the morning when we frightened a pair of Crested Guans passing with half-grown young through the treetops, we had no lack of loud, excited calls, high-pitched and weak for such big, long-tailed fowl, the size of a hen turkey.

Continuing up the main stream, we reached a stretch of channel that was, if possible, even more beautiful than the part that we already knew. The river here followed the dip of the strata of the massive, dark gray rock of which these hills were largely built, but its descent was more gradual than the inclination of the rock layers. Thus each stratum exposed its edge to the erosive action of the stream. The softer layers had been worn away, leaving pools of water held back by the harder layers. Some of these pools were wide and deep, and each was brimful of the clearest water, which slipped over the lip to flow down a long, even incline to the pool below. In places there were abrupt falls, but there were also long reaches of nearly level channel, strewn with great, irregular rocks. Here and there low cliffs, draped with verdure, rose from the water's edge. Everywhere the great trees of the forest lined both banks and cast their shade over the hurrying, dancing waters. In the inmost recesses of this mountain forest, the world and its bustling activity seemed infinitely remote; yet at times even here our thoughts were abruptly recalled to it by the hum of an airplane passing unseen above the treetops, on its way between San Isidro and one of the little coastal towns.

As we laboriously worked our way up the rough, difficult watercourse, Efraim espied, on the rocks ahead, a bird such as neither of us had ever seen. It was a fairly big, stout-bodied fowl, with long legs, a long slender neck, and a sharp, straight bill of moderate length. In form it somewhat resembled a heron or bittern, but in coloration it was quite different from them, and its longer tail set it apart at a glance. Its colors were rather subdued: black on the head, brown on the neck, maroon brown on the breast, dark gray on the back and closed wings, white on the throat and abdomen, and nearly everywhere barred, spotted, or streaked with black and white. Its eyes were deep red, and its long legs, naked to well above the ankle joint, were bright orange.

Such was the appearance of the strange bird as it walked deliberately over the steeply inclined rock face between two pools, plucking certain small objects from the rocks washed by the smooth-flowing rapids. We had watched it for many minutes, attracted by its rareness rather than its beauty, when it slipped on the smooth, wet stone and, half opening its wings to balance itself, dazzled us with a glimpse of unsuspected splendor. As it flitted from boulder to boulder, it continued to reveal tantalizing flashes of hidden beauty. But only when the bird spread its wings broadly for a longer flight did it display their full magnificence. On each was a big, round shield of deep orange-chestnut, set in the midst of an area of much paler orange-buff—a sun darkly glowing in a sunset-tinted sky. When I saw those wings painted with the image of the sun, I had no doubt that I had my first Sunbittern before me. Like that other inhabitant of these forest waterways, the Royal Flycatcher, this rare bird kept its proudest ornament concealed most of the time.

Beside another wildly beautiful stream in the Térraba Valley, a few years later, I was shown the only nest of the Sunbittern that I have seen, a structure unlike any other bird's nest that I know. It was built twenty feet up in a small tree growing near the rocky shore. The tree was too weak to be climbed without jeopardizing the nest, but, from the top of a neighboring cliff, I could look down upon it. The dark, roughly globular mass, nearly a foot high and broad, was balanced rather precariously upon an ascending branch about two inches thick, at a point where I could detect no lateral twig to prevent its pivoting sideward. It was composed of decaying leaves, stems, and other vegetation, including a little green moss, and apparently also of mud. In the shallow depression in the top, two big, buffy eggs rested upon a few green leaves. While my guide and I watched from the brink of the cliff, the parent Sunbittern returned our gaze with big, red eyes. Finally, becoming alarmed, it jumped from the nest, spread its lovely wings, and glided down toward the river until lost to view amid the foliage.

The principal affluent of the Río San Antonio from the right was a rocky streamlet hemmed in by steep, forested slopes, so narrow that at many points we could leap from bank to bank. But it also had its picturesque cascades and shared the wild beauty of the river to which it delivered up its unsullied waters. Along this narrow watercourse, we discovered more birds' nests than along the broader stream. Here, in the still air, attached to the long, dangling, cordlike roots of epiphytic plants or to slender, pendant vines and shoots of climbing bamboo, hung the exquisite nests of the Oleaginous Pipromorpha, one of the most plainly clad of the small flycatchers. Each nest was a pear-shaped structure about a foot long, covered with green moss. A small, round doorway in the side gave access to a cozy chamber, well padded with vegetable fibers, where the two or three white eggs rested and the young were raised by their mother alone. In an even more conspicuous position above the channel, the Sulphur-rumped Myiobius, a brisk, little forest flycatcher, had constructed her nest, a thin-walled pocket of brown fibers, with a visorlike projection shielding the round doorway in the side. This flycatcher also builds its nest and raises its family with no help from a mate.

Most abundant along this watercourse, although most difficult to detect, were the nests of the Violet-headed Hummingbird, each a tiny chalice of green moss, softly lined with seed down of a light buffy color and fastened by spiders' silk to slender, usually drooping, leafy branches overhanging the channel at heights of from three to twelve feet above the water. Without making a thorough search, we found three of these nests along the Río San Antonio and five along the smaller affluent, making eight occupied nests along two or three miles of waterway. There were perhaps as many more empty nests, of which we kept no accurate count. Early March was the height of the breeding season, and the nests might contain anything from two minute, elongate, white eggs newly laid to feathered nestlings almost ready to fly. But there were never more than two eggs or nestlings in a nest. Because it is so unusual to find hummingbirds' nests in such abundance in lowland forest (I have rarely seen more than three or four in a year), we decided to name the stream above which they hung "The Hummingbirds' Brook."

After several hours of leisurely progress along the rocky bed of the brook, we halted for lunch in a spot of rare beauty. A steeply sloping ramp of naked gray rock rose in the stream bed before us, between low, vertical cliffs. Down this incline, the shrunken current of March flowed in two separate streams: one flowed against the base of the cliff to the right in a long, even trough; the other, with a low waterfall in its course, made a broken and precipitous descent on the left. At the foot of the twin cataracts, the waters were reunited in a broad pool, nearly square in outline, about forty feet on a side, and deep enough to swim in. But only a naiad could have entered its pellucid depths without seeming to defile them. We left them in unruffled serenity to mirror the broad, lacy fronds of a cluster of tree ferns that grew at the brink, surrounded by exuberant verdure and deeply shaded by the giants of the forest.

While climbing the tongue of rock between the cataracts, we found two more nests of the hummingbird, only forty feet apart. One, in a bush leaning over the falling water halfway up, held two eggs; the second, on a moss-covered, pendulous branch of a small tree at the head of the waterfall, cradled two feathered nestlings. It was surprising to find these two occupied nests of the same species of hummingbird so close together, but as we continued along the brook above the cataracts, we made a discovery still more astonishing. A richly branched shrub, leaning far out over the narrow channel, almost blocked our way. As we pushed past it, we detected another nest of the same kind, attached to a slender, pendent branch only thirty-nine inches above the water. This nest was unusually tall, as though it had been built atop an older one—as hummingbirds' nests sometimes are—and it held two eggs. Four feet away in the same bush and fifteen inches higher above the water was yet another nest, from which a well-feathered fledgling took flight as we approached. After a short pursuit, I captured the young fugitive and returned it beside its nest mate, where, rather unexpectedly, it was good enough to stay.

Hummingbirds are generally held to be unsociable. Certainly, they lack the true convivial spirit that inspires such flocking birds as parrots, crows, and cormorants; except in their courtship assemblies, where they exhibit a degree of community enterprise even in rivalry, it is every hummer for himself. The male and female form no lasting attachments, and the latter nearly always attends her nest and nestlings quite alone. Accordingly, the discovery of two hummingbirds' nests in the same small bush was a memorable event, calling for further study. But the day was already far spent, and since it would be folly to try to move along that broken stream bed in the black darkness that would prevail an hour after sunset, we hurried downward before daylight forsook us.

Next morning, I laboriously retraced my steps along the stream. I had already proved, at other nests, that if I sat quietly on a rock at no great distance, the hummingbirds would soon return to attend their eggs or nestlings. I seated myself on a rounded boulder, from which I commanded a good view of the two nests. The well-feathered nestlings in the one nearer me were bright, wide-awake, little sprites, who frequently preened their plumage and from time to time beat their wings into a haze, the while anchoring themselves to the bottom of the nest with their feet, lest they be carried away by these vigorous exercises. When an adult of their kind came within sight, they were all alertness, uttering clear little droplets of sound in anticipation of good things to eat. Apparently they were unable to distinguish their mother from her neighbor, for they called in the same fashion at the approach of either. But the incubating hummer, each time she arrived, went directly to sit upon her own eggs, paying no attention to the other's family. The two fledglings had the gray throat of their mother rather than the deep violet of the adult male, as did all others of their age that we found.

On returning from an excursion into the forest, the owners of these two nests would sometimes approach me closely, hovering only a yard or two from my face while they subjected me to close scrutiny. Then, apparently satisfied that this strange monster that spied upon them was not dangerous, they went to their nests. Or, again, after feeding her nestlings, the parent of the two would approach to look me over once more before darting off. At a nest farther downstream, a hummingbird flew up to feed her babies, apparently without having noticed that in her absence I had seated myself nearby. While she was in the midst of regurgitating food to them, my sudden movement in raising my field glasses for a closer view attracted her attention. Immediately interrupting the nestlings' meal, she darted up to examine her visitor in the usual fashion. Then she returned to plunge her sharp bill far down into a nestling's throat and continue the process of feeding, making me feel that I had created a favorable impression and my presence was not distasteful to her. These and many other examinations to which I have been subjected by hummingbirds of various kinds appeared to be purposeful acts, prompted in some instances by simple curiosity and in others by concern for the safety of their nests and offspring. They suggest that hummingbirds may be somewhat nearsighted, which is not surprising when one considers the minute size of the nests they build and of the insects they pluck from the vegetation or snatch from the air.

When approaching her nest, each hummingbird would alternately dart and hover, shooting a short distance now to this side and now to that, irregularly back and forth, at the end of each abrupt shift of position hanging stationary for an instant, on swiftly beating wings. Then, of a sudden, the diminutive bird would drop down upon her eggs with her wings already folded against her sides or alight upon the rim of the little cup to thrust her slender bill far down into a fledgling's crop and begin to pump nourishment into it. The hummingbird with eggs seemed a trifle fearful of her neighbor with nestlings, for on two occasions she suddenly flew away as the other came to attend them. Once she continued to sit while the young birds received their meal, only to dart away as her neighbor was leaving.

No male appeared on the scene; I never saw a single male Violet-headed Hummingbird anywhere along the stream. At this season, the more brilliant sex was to be found on sunny perches near the forest, each bird sounding his metallic little notes through all the long, bright day, and interrupting his animated but tuneless song only to moisten his throat at the inexhaustible fount of the flowers. Often four or five of these hummingbirds sang close together, each on his own perch to which he returned after each brief absence. So the males let the other sex know that they waited to woo them, but never did they aid in the care of a nest.

While sitting on the boulder watching the two nests above the forest stream, I was assailed by that uncomfortable feeling I sometimes experience in the woods, of being myself watched by unseen eyes. Suddenly, a long, black snake, mottled with yellow, glided down an oblique ledge on the cliff to my right. It advanced rapidly, without a pause, until it came to rest on a rock in midstream, almost beneath the two nestlings. There it lay motionless with its head raised high, looking up at the young hummingbirds and seeming to consider, in dull serpentine fashion, how it could reach them. Knowing from repeated unhappy experiences the Mica's insatiable appetite for eggs and nestlings, I resolved to remove all possibility of tragedy. A snake intent upon ravin appears to become insensible to everything else, at times even to mortal wounds. This one was no exception; it delayed immobile while I approached and delivered the stroke that sent it writhing madly into the water, where the current bore it slowly downstream to die.

Feeling that the hummingbirds were safe for the present, I continued upstream until I found my way blocked by a wall of rock ten feet high, stretching transversely across the channel. At this point the current was divided into two separate falls, like Niagara in miniature. That on the right dropped with a single leap into a deep, shady recess in the rock. The left branch babbled down among great, loose boulders, beneath a huge block of stone, which, wedged between the central pier and the high cliff that formed the left wall of the ravine, made a natural bridge over the cascade. Like most of the wider rocks above reach of the flood waters, this bridge was profusely overgrown with begonias, aroids, Clusias, and other plants. It was necessary to crawl beneath this verdant rock bridge in order to gain the top of the wall that obstructed the channel. Passing under the bridge, I almost brushed against a neat little nest that hung above the cascade. It was attached to a splinter beneath the butt of a huge, shattered trunk lying in the stream bed above. The nest was of pyriform shape with a round entrance in the side, shielded by a visorlike projection. Its walls were composed almost wholly of fibrous rootlets; the interior was amply lined with light-colored bast fibers finely shredded and some tufts of silky seed down. In this cozy retreat so excellently concealed rested a single pinfeathered nestling, who cried shrilly when I illuminated its nursery with a small electric bulb and looked in with a tiny mirror.

Unable even to guess who the maker and owner of this ingeniously hidden nest might be, I sat upon the central pier of rock to await her approach. After an hour, a tiny Slaty-capped Flycatcher, gray, olive-green, and pale yellow, arrived with a small green tree cricket in her bill. Nervous and shy, she approached and left her nest by darting beneath the bridge of rock, thereby making it still more difficult for hostile eyes to follow her movements. Yet she fed the nestling while I rested in plain view only ten feet away—three meals in as many hours.

Of a sudden, as I watched, I was startled by loud, shrill cries rising out of the deep recess to my right, into which more than half the flow of the stream leapt down in a single, unbroken fall. Leaning over the overhanging wall of rock, I peered into the obscurity of the chasm, without being able to discern more than rock and water—nothing that could emit such earsplitting cries. The shrill notes continued, so I descended by way of the gentler cascade on the other side, beneath the bridging stone, crept along the base of the abrupt wall, and peered into the recess from the front. There, on the wet, slippery, overhanging face of rock beneath the falling water, clung two big, black swifts with narrow, white collars. Crying loudly, at short intervals they fluttered from one point on the stone to another. Their hurried movements and sharp cries suggested great excitement. Suddenly they brushed past me, rose through the narrow chasm between the tree trunks that marked the course of the brook, and vanished into the illimitable vastness above. Nor did they return during the next hour.

Numberless times I had watched great flocks of these largest of Central American swifts wheeling with shrill cries far overhead, but never before had I come so close to them—nor to any other swift in tropical America. Suspecting that, like the Black Swift, White-collared Swifts might build their nests behind waterfalls, I removed shoes and stockings and waded into the alcove behind the falling water, not without a wetting. But I could find no indication of a nest nor any cranny that might have supported one. Probably these swifts were disappointed in their quest of a nest site, as I, on my return a fortnight later, was disappointed in my desire to learn something about their home life. In Mexico, White-collared Swifts have been found nesting in small colonies on ledges in caves behind waterfalls, where their shallow nests of mud and moss, each containing two white eggs, are kept constantly wet by the spray.

When I emerged from behind the cataract, the afternoon was more than half spent, and I turned homeward to make sure of reaching the clearing before nightfall. I was climbing down the long ramp of rock above the big pool, passing over a narrow, slippery ledge and thinking how unpleasant it would be to meet, in that insecure position, the huge snake that had left its slough upon the neighboring slope, when a creature of quite a different character appeared. A hummingbird flew out of the forest and clung to the inclined rock surface over which the water poured in a thin sheet, almost at my feet. First he appeared to drink, then bathed, pushing his head down into the flowing water, shaking his wings, and wetting himself all over. Large for a hummingbird, he had a long, straight, black bill and a deeply forked, black tail. His upper plumage was green, and I caught shifting glints of intense, metallic blue from his throat. He quite ignored my presence, even when I shifted my position to save myself from falling. Then he brushed past to perch in a low bush close behind me, shake the water from his plumage, and put it in order. Before I could maneuver myself into a position to view him favorably in the dim light, he was gone, unidentified in the terms of science, yet ever to be associated in memory with this beautiful cataract in the course of an enchanting sylvan stream. Thenceforth, the highest fall in the Hummingbirds' Brook was known as the "Hummingbird Cascades."

Spectacular Migrations

Our cabin overlooked the valley of the Río Pacuar, which stretches from northwest to southeast between the Cordillera de Talamanca and the coastal range and is an important flyway for migrating birds. In mid-April, the northward passage was at its height. Morning and evening, wave after wave of swallows streamed up the valley, flying low in a general westerly course. Barn Swallows and Cliff Swallows passed in tens of thousands, accompanied by less numerous Bank Swallows. In the middle of a bright day, we saw only a few of these swallows, who had evidently interrupted their journey to circle around with resident swifts, catching insects; but early one afternoon, during a sudden violent thunderstorm, great numbers filled the air. Apparently on clear days, between about eight o'clock in the morning and four in the afternoon, migrating swallows flew over us so high that they escaped detection, but rough weather forced them lower—as has been observed on the Gulf coast of the United States. In the evening, I sometimes watched great protean clouds of circling migratory swallows swing back and forth above the valley, dipping here and there toward the crown of an outstanding tree, as though seeking a roost for the night. But the cloud of birds always floated away, fading into the gathering dusk, and I never discovered where the swallows roosted.

Most of the small migrants evidently passed unseen in the night. Sometimes I became aware of these nocturnal voyagers after they had descended for the day: early one morning, while swallows in the thousands were streaming overhead, I noticed a flock of eight Olive-backed Thrushes in a small patch of woods on a ridge, where previously only single individuals had been seen.

Of all the migrants, the most spectacular were the Swainson's Hawks. At about four o'clock on the afternoon of April 15, a great host of these big raptors poured over the forested crest of the high ridge to the east of our cabin and slowly circled down to the hillside facing us. Many settled on the close-cropped pasture, others on stumps and logs, but the majority found perches on trees, either at the forest's edge or standing isolated in the pasture or bordering the rivers. Meanwhile, many more were descending behind the crest of the ridge, where they were soon hidden from view. It took about an hour for the huge multitude to drop easily and sedately out of the air.

Alarmed by this unprecedented invasion by great birds of prey, the resident flycatchers darted at them in needless frenzy, for neither they nor their nests were in danger. Although there was some shifting around as the day ended, many of the hawks stayed where they had first settled. Whether they rested on the ground or in the trees, they were well spaced out, usually each several feet from its nearest neighbors. I watched them as their light breasts faded in the gathering dusk. Many remained on the open ground, heedless of danger from prowling nocturnal mammals. All were quite silent from their arrival until nightfall.

As day broke, some of the hawks flew down from the edge of the forest to the open pasture. All lingered on the westward-facing slope where they had bivouacked, until they noticed the rays of the rising sun striking the crests of some tall trees on the brow of the opposite hill. Then, with alternate flapping and gliding, one or a few at a time rather than in a mass movement, they streamed across the Río Pacuar to the eastward-facing slope, where they alighted on the trees or the grassy slope below them, never crowding together. Here they rested, enjoying the earliest sunbeams for well over an hour, making as little attempt to find food as they had done in the evening and remaining as silent as when they first arrived.

At about half past seven, when currents of heated air were beginning to ascend from the sunward slope, the hawks started to leave. They took to the air with a little flapping of wings, but after rising about as high as the treetops, they ceased to exert themselves. Setting their widespread wings, they soared around and around, spiraling effortlessly upward on the thermal currents. Soon there was a column of circling birds several hundred feet high. As they reached the top of this vortex, the hawks detached themselves and glided westward, still without beating their wings. Now those that had passed the night beyond the high ridge where I could not see them were gliding across the valley in a steady stream. Above a long slope in the west, the two groups mingled in one great whirlpool of spiraling hawks. Alternately circling skyward on a thermal updraft and gliding forward with loss of altitude, the migrating host rose higher and higher as it advanced toward the lofty wooded summits in the west.

Soon the vanguard was shrinking to the vanishing point above distant ridges. Here and there in the intervening space were ascending columns of hawks, the topmost of whom were continually breaking away to glide onward and enter the bottom of the next feathered whirlpool to the west. On the hillside before me were many just beginning to flap upward. To the east were two revolving clouds of hawks rising above the ridge beyond which they had slept. It was fascinating to watch so many great birds in various stages of preparation for their long, effortless journey.

The early risers—in a very literal sense—had long since melted into the intense blue of this brilliant morning when, an hour after the departure began, the last two sluggards bestirred themselves for the journey. As one of these alternately flapped and soared to gain its initial altitude, it was pursued and buffeted by a Tropical Kingbird, who evidently made it the butt of all the ire that this vast raptorial host had stirred in his small breast. But his spirited onslaught hardly accelerated the pace of the great hawk, who continued to flap until it found an updraft, then easily soared to heights where the flycatcher did not care to follow.

After the disappearance of these laggards, I went to examine the hillside where the hawks had passed the night. The white droppings of so large a raptor would have been conspicuous on the close-cropped grass. But not a dropping could I find, not a casting from the mouth, not a single molted feather—that great host had passed onward without doing the slightest damage or leaving the smallest memento. My failure to discover any sign of excretion is in accord with my failure ever to see a Swainson's Hawk eat or hunt, as year after year I have watched these big birds pass northward over Costa Rica. Indeed, if they needed food on the journey, they could hardly travel in such huge flocks; they would have to spread out widely in order to find enough prey. Unlike those other diurnal migrants, the swallows and the Eastern Kingbirds, the Swainson's Hawks do not snatch meals along the way.

However, there are exceptions. After all the rest of the vast flock had passed from view over the distant hills, a lone Swainson's Hawk glided down from the forest on the ridge and flew low over the pastures until it was beyond sight. Evidently, feeling the need to recuperate its strength, this individual would pass the day hunting instead of traveling onward. Paul Slud has seen Swainson's Hawks catch grasshoppers in northern Costa Rica.

These hawks are able to go so far without replenishing their reserves because they travel with so little muscular exertion, scarcely ever flapping their wings, but relying upon thermals to supply the energy for flight. Their outline as they soar upward is strikingly different from that as they glide forward, bartering altitude for distance. When spiraling upward, the wings are fully expanded, slightly convex on both the forward and trailing edges; the tips of the longest primaries visibly separated; and the tail somewhat spread. When gliding forward, the wings are partly closed; the forward edge is strongly convex; the joined tips of the outermost primaries point backward; the posterior margin becomes a double curve, strongly concave over most of its length, slightly convex near the body; the tail feathers are folded together.

Although I have in two years seen Swainson's Hawks migrating through El General as early as March 9, most of the great flocks pass between mid-March and late April. In addition to the vast companies that stretch across the sky from horizon to horizon and take an hour to pass, I have often watched smaller flocks in which Swainson's and Broad-winged Hawks intermingle. The latter winter in this valley; the former pass through on their way from their winter home in South America to their breeding ground in western North America. Although so many thousands of Swainson's Hawks migrate through El General in the spring, later in the year I have seen them only once, when a mere eleven flew southwestward over our house in early December. Evidently on their southward voyage during the rainy season, the hawks find conditions more favorable for their soaring and gliding progress on the Caribbean side of Costa Rica, where they have been seen migrating toward South America in October and November, as well as returning in March and April. Then they sometimes travel with almost equally impressive flights of Turkey Vultures, as told in chapter 22.

In late June, my young helper and I left the cabin by the Río San Antonio. This stream and the Pacuar were often so swollen by the torrential rains that we were largely isolated from the rest of El General, and food was difficult to procure. Although living had become hard, I regretted leaving so beautiful a spot. Soon after returning to San José to take up my duties in the Museo Nacional, I received a radiogram from Washington asking whether I would accompany, as botanist, a party that the United States Department of Agriculture was sending to northwestern South America to explore the possibilities of producing rubber there. The offer was too enticing to refuse; I resigned my post at the museum and in early August joined the other members of the party in the Canal Zone, whence we proceeded by steamship to Lima. During the next five months, we traveled incessantly, crossing the Peruvian Andes by air and by car and, for five weeks, exploring the upper Amazon and its great tributaries on a Peruvian gunboat of shallow draft. In Ecuador we ascended the Río Esmeraldas in a canoe poled by stalwart Negroes, and in Colombia we threaded the great mangrove swamps of the Pacific littoral in a dugout with an outboard motor. From Colombia we went to Washington to write our reports for the department.

I had now spent a dozen years moving from place to place in tropical

America, and I felt the need of a more permanent adobe, when I could build up a library, safely keep my growing mass of notes, and work them up for publication, while I continued to study tropical nature. Returning to Costa Rica by steamer in February, 1941, I began my search for a homesite, thereby opening a new epoch in my life.

Río Chirripó and Cerro Chirripó in El General. The Chirripó is one of the chief headwaters of the Río Térraba.

A grassy roadway in Rivas. Oxcarts were the only wheeled vehicles.

Rivas in 1936. The author's cabin is directly behind the newly finished church steeple. The school is in the right foreground.

Carboncillo Blanco (*Calliandra portoricensis*). One of the many flowers that brightened the valley of the Buena Vista as the rainy season ended.

The church and the forest's edge, Rivas, 1936. Before the steeple was added.

The author's residence at Montaña Azul, July 1937–August 1938. On a storm-lashed mountain, 5,500 feet above sea level.

A shrubby composite (*Eupatorium angulare*). In July and August, its ample panicles of lavender flowers brightened the side of the muddy road at Montaña Azul. It grew to be twenty feet high.

Volcán Poás from the east. Dairy farms occupy the foreground and lower slopes of the volcano.

A clearing in the forest at Montaña Azul. The isolated trees, living and dead, provided nest sites for a marvelous variety of birds.

A garden on a stump. A mushroom-shaped crown of ferns, aroids, orchids, heaths, and other epiphytes capped each old stump at Montaña Azul.

Giant aroids in a marshy spot in the woods at Montaña Azul.

Flowering Stachytarpheta. The purple florets, beloved of hummingbirds, are displayed in a wreath that daily moves upward along the slender green spike.

A colony of Chestnut-headed Oropéndolas. The neatly woven nests hang from the branches like gigantic gourds.

PART II

A Naturalist's Homestead

Headpiece: Finishing a bahareque wall. The wing was added in 1967. The wall has been filled in solidly with puddled clay, and the canes that enclose it are being covered with the same material. A coat of cement will follow.

11

A Farm in the Wilderness

IT IS NOT easy for a wanderer to settle down, even when satiated with wandering. He passes in mental review all the delightful spots he has visited and which, for a while, tempted him to shake the dust from his shoes and stay. Each had its peculiar beauties and attractions to be found nowhere else. But each, on longer acquaintance, turned out to be not without the discomforts and inconveniences inseparable from living, in whatever locality. The home-seeking wanderer hopes to find a spot which unites the advantages of all the most delightful places he knows, while excluding the disadvantages of each. Vain endeavor! The attractions of different localities are often mutually exclusive. We cannot have the salubrious atmosphere of the mountains along with the deeper and richer soil of the lowlands, a score of miles away. We cannot, in most parts of the world, have a good road and proximity to shops and a post office along with unspoiled wilderness. We cannot have magnificent rain

Headpiece: "Los Cusingos" and the unfinished house in 1941. Viewed from the opposite side of the Río Peña Blanca.

forests along with a dry climate. And everywhere there are plagues and annoyances, whether from the government, neighbors, rodents, snakes, insects, fungous parasites, or the weather.

When I felt the need of a permanent abode, I considered in turn all the most enchanting places that I had visited for a longer or shorter interval during a dozen years of travel in tropical America. In Guatemala, I had dwelt for a year in the high mountains amid noble forests of pine, oak, and cypress, with a marvelous variety of flowering shrubs and herbs and fascinating birds. But the rainy season was bleak and gloomy; the rapidly increasing Indian population was fast encroaching on the few remaining areas of unspoiled woodland; and the dictatorial government of that period was not to my liking. On the Pacific slope of the same country, I had visited coffee plantations with magnificent views, an agreeable climate, and cultured neighbors. But the land was so valuable that I could have bought only a small plot; little wilderness remained; and there was the same dictatorial government. In the eastern foothills of the Ecuadorian Andes, I knew a region of beautiful forests with an abundance of stately palms, a richly varied flora, colorful birds, and cheap land. But the rainfall was excessive and the soil unproductive. In eastern Peru, I had hastily visited lovely wooded valleys that I wished to explore at my leisure, but they were not as healthful as the interior of Central America, and to reach them cost more than I could spare.

After weighing all the points favorable and contrary, I chose Costa Rica as the country where I would settle, and, in Costa Rica, the Valley of El General promised best to satisfy my needs. During the two and a half years that I had already spent in this mountain-rimmed basin at the head of the Río Grande de Térraba, I had looked appraisingly at many a rough, backwoods farm and many a homesite on a hilltop with a wide view or beside a rushing mountain stream. But when I returned to the valley early in 1941, at last with enough money to buy some land and build a modest house, I was undecided just where to settle. Spots which promise the romantic wanderer fulfillment of his fondest dreams develop unexpected difficulties when viewed with the more critical and farther-seeing eye of the serious homeseeker.

When it became known about the valley that I was looking for a farm, offers of sale began to flow in. One afternoon, a man eager to sell his land took me to his farm near the summit of the coastal range. There was a remnant of good forest and a marvelous view across the wide basin of El General, with the high, rocky pinnacles of the Cordillera de Talamanca providing an impressive background in the north. But the land was steeply inclined and broken, serving chiefly for pasture, and the road leading up from the valley so long and steep that the vision of toiling up on horseback, beneath the usual afternoon downpour, warned me to look elsewhere. Other farms offered to me lacked woodland or good water or were on sterile land.

After a few days of land hunting about San Isidro, Juan Schroeder invited me to ride down the valley to visit a farm which he had bought while I was in South America. We set forth early one morning, he upon his big black mule, I upon my bay horse Bayon, each with a blanket tied behind his saddle, provisions and a change of clothes in his saddlebags. Our way led eastward over rolling country to the Río General, then down a long, level, grassy road through the pastures and small coffee groves of General Viejo.

In the middle of the morning, we forded the rocky channel of the Río Peña Blanca, then for hours we threaded the forest along a narrow trail, rough with the transverse corrugations made by horses stepping always in the same spots when the ground was soft with rain. The way fell and rose interminably, as it dipped to cross the numerous watercourses descending from the flanks of the Cordillera, then ascended to the low, intervening ridges. I did not hesitate to drink the sparkling water of these mountain streams flowing through unbroken forest, and I never had cause to regret these refreshing draughts. Between the noble trees, whose lofty boughs interlocked above the narrow trail, stood the slender gray columns of innumerable tall palms, including many chontas supported upon spiny, spreading prop roots. The silence that reigned in these woodland solitudes was broken at long intervals by the chatter of a flock of green parrots in the treetops or the barking and coughing of a restless band of White-faced Monkeys. Widely spaced along this rough forest path were new clearings with tiny thatched huts, pigs grunting and chickens cackling in the stump-studded dooryard, cattle grazing in new pastures littered with half-burned trunks. In the broader valleys were wider and older clearings with somewhat more substantial dwellings, more promising fields. At one of these valley settlements, called San Pedro, we paused for lunch.

Resuming our journey, we rode through forests of Ira Chiricano trees, with great columnar trunks of the hardest timber and wide-spreading crowns composed of leafy boughs that fitted together, like the tiles in a mosaic, to form the canopy of the forest. When a gentle breeze swayed the treetops, narrow bands of sky appeared momentarily between the foliage masses of contiguous boughs. I was grateful for my steady, dependable horse to whom I could give free rein while I leaned back in the saddle and gazed up into the crowns of the lordly trees above us.

In the middle of the afternoon, when we were approaching the big clearing of Volcán, we passed two rough wooden crosses set close beside the forest trail among planted shrubs with gaudy blossoms. They aroused memories of my previous visit to this part of the valley. Two years earlier, I had gone to Volcán with a young entomologist. We had difficulty finding a lodging for the night, and the policeman had kindly permitted us to sleep in his office, a rough construction which also served as a carpenter's shop. Rounds slept on the floor, while the carpenter's bench made me a hard and narrow bed. During the small hours of the morning, our sleep was disturbed by the sounds of hammering and sawing close by the building. We wondered what enterprising carpenter was plying his trade by lamplight, but were too weary to get up and investigate.

In the gray dawn, the mystery was cleared up, as four men carried in a corpse on a stretcher made with sacks slung between two poles. Above the dead man's abdomen was a great bulge tied up with sackcloth, where his entrails had oozed out through a deep wound. A number of small children followed to gaze wonderingly upon this gruesome spectacle. They were of a tender age to be thus exposed to some of life's harshest facts, but such is the realism of the wilderness! Two drunken Indians, of the vanishing local stock, had attacked each other with machetes during the night, and each had inflicted a mortal wound upon his adversary. Following a custom widespread in Latin America, crosses had been set by the wayside to mark the spot where they had been killed.

We spent two days on my friend's farm, resting from our journey, refreshing ourselves with the delicious oranges that burdened the trees, bathing in the river on warm afternoons, and examining the cattle. My companion had promised to return by a newly opened trail which he said would delight me exceedingly. We retraced our course up the valley to San Pedro, where we turned off the main trail to the right to follow a path that swung higher on the foothills, rising in places to three thousand feet above sea level. For miles, we rode along the soft woodland path through stately forest, which, save for this passageway freshly cut through the underwood, revealed scarcely any sign of man's destroying hand. Great Milk Trees towered up fifty yards above us, and there was a rich variety of palms. There was scarcely a clearing along the way until we crossed the Río Calientillo and entered a region of small, freshly made farms. Late in the afternoon, we unsaddled near the top of a high bluff overlooking the Río Peña Blanca. Here a tiny thatched shed, such as was used for storing maize, gave us shelter for the night. This locality was called El Quizarrá after the timber trees of this name that grew in the surrounding forests. My aneroid gave the elevation as twenty-five hundred feet above sea level.

We sat resting on the edge of the bluff, while the sun sank behind distant wooded ridges. Below us a wide mountain torrent rushed impetuously down a boulder-strewn channel. The narrow, somewhat level bottom of the valley was wooded with second-growth trees, readily distinguished from the ancient forest by the lighter green of their foliage. Beyond this was a long, steep ridge, still covered with the original forest, except at its northern end, where it had been felled to make a pasture so recently that the slope was littered with great blackened logs, lying between the charred stumps that thickly studded it. As this green slope descended toward the river, it flattened out to form a nearly level terrace perhaps fifty yards wide, then fell off abruptly to a lower terrace, also in grass, that bordered the river. On the upper terrace was an open stand of young Guava trees, between which the close-cropped sward gleamed emerald in the fading light. Here, I mused, was just the spot for the home of which I dreamed. A wide prospect, a clear river for water, a large tract of forest close by, a pasture for my horse, and rich bottom lands for sowing. Here, if I could acquire the land, I would end my wanderings and tarry for a while.

The farm across the river belonged to Francisco Mora, whom everybody called Don Chico, a restless spirit who could not remain long in one spot and made farms on unclaimed wilderness land, only to sell them after a few years. He had already intimated to Don Juan that he would consider an offer for this one. Next morning, while Juan rode back alone to San Isidro, I went to call on Don Chico, who dwelt with his woman, María, and their little fair-haired boy, Chico, in a low, earthen-floored, thatched hut set at the very edge of the terrace beside a high, wooded bluff that fell steeply to the shore of a creek tributary to the Peña Blanca. The advantages of this somewhat precarious site seemed to be proximity to water and the ease of disposing of trash by throwing it down the slope from the back door of the dwelling. Several great hogs, one the mother of piglets, slept in a shed hard by the hut, into which they had free entry.

At the northern end of the terrace, where it widened along the tributary stream, was a half acre of coffee already in production, with plantains and Inga trees as shade. Beyond this, the steep slopes above a smaller rivulet, tributary to the tributary, were planted with bananas. About the terrace was a scattering of fruit trees, including oranges, tangerines, avocados, a single mango tree, and a single clump of Pejibaye palms, all old enough to bear.

Don Chico was not at home to show me the farm, but I found a narrow cart road that led through a thicket to a two-acre field of sugarcane, beyond which was a rocky pasture of Calinguero grass, then resting bottom land where annual crops could be planted. After my round of inspection, I bathed in the cold, sparkling water of the Río Peña Blanca, then resumed my horseback journey to San Isidro, the nearest village and post office, eight or nine miles distant. The road was rough, very rocky on the level stretches and hilly elsewhere, and it was necessary to ford a broad river, which I foresaw would be troublesome when swollen by the afternoon downpours.

Three days later, I returned to Quizarrá to go over the boundaries of the farm with its owner, a wrinkled, barefoot, old man who was far hardier than he appeared. I was happy to learn that more than a third of the farm was still covered by unspoiled forest, chiefly on the ridges of red clay, much less productive than the dark, rich loam on the more level areas along the river. But I was pained to see that on one long slope the forest had been felled earlier in the year and burned so recently that some of the stumps still smoked.

Part of the western boundary of the farm was formed by a rivulet flowing through a deep, forested valley, rich in ferns and wild plantains with huge, broad leaves. As we walked down this vale, cutting our way through tangles of vines and climbing fern, one of the lean hounds that followed my guide began to bark at the mouth of a hollow log. After a rapid examination of the log, Don Chico cut a switch and, picking up his dog by the scruff of its neck, beat it mercilessly until the woodland resounded with its dismal howls. "I'll teach you to bark at *guatusos!*" exclaimed the irate old man. The dog's severe punishment was not inspired by pity for the Agouti that had taken refuge in the hollow log. It was merely that a good hunting hound should confine its attention to the *tepiscuinte* or Paca, another rodent whose flesh is more esteemed, and not waste its breath over the common and vulgar *guatuso*. I have sometimes found Agoutis that hunters had sealed up in logs where they had sought safety, leaving them to perish miserably by starvation.

"Thanks, old man!" I exclaimed to myself, as I watched the flagellation of the unlucky hound, "thanks for showing me how to be hard." The approaching negotiations would be my first business transaction of greater magnitude than the purchase of a suit of clothes, a steamship ticket, or a dilapidated automobile. I was a bit nervous, afraid that I would be too easygoing when we came to discuss terms. Although I pitied the dog, I was grateful for this reminder that the man with whom I was about to deal was not all softness and generosity but would get as much as he could for himself, so that it behooved me to look sharply to my own interests.

After making the rounds of the farm, we sat down by the roadside to discuss terms of sale. The farm had not been surveyed, but Don Chico estimated that it contained seventy hectares, or about one hundred and seventy-five acres. I now know that on such rough, forested land one is likely greatly to overestimate areas, but after the rather strenuous walk along the boundaries, I was inclined to agree with the owner's figure. By excluding from purchase the cattle, horses, and pigs, the annual crops for which the land had just been prepared, part of the barbed-wire fencing, and a small sugarcane press somewhat the worse for wear—by excluding, that is, most of the movable chattels—I was able to buy the land for five thousand colones, nearly a third of the capital which for years I had been scraping together by botanical explorations and plant collecting amidst the tropical forests.

A week later, on March 22, 1941, in the visiting lawyer's rough-walled, little office in San Isidro, we signed the contract of sale. The land was still untitled, and payment would not be made until the title was registered and transferred to me. Meanwhile, Don Chico could continue to live in his cabin on the farm for six months—a period later extended to twelve. That same week, the surveyor, a tall, blonde Swede born in Nicaragua, rode out with his theodolite to measure the land. When he had computed his readings, my seventy hectares shrank to fifty-three!

This abrupt shrinkage in the stated size of my holding hardly diminished my pride in it. On my hundred and thirty acres were crowded so many hills and vales, so many permanent streams and rainy-season watercourses, so many terraces and escarpments, and, above all, so many trees and rocks, that it seemed much bigger than the same area all on a level, and I spent many exciting days exploring it, feeling like Robinson Crusoe on his island. The very diversity of the terrain broken by escarpments and waterways, which was to make it the perpetual despair of the farmer, made it delightful to the naturalist. For a dozen years, I had wandered through the forests of tropical America, trying to uncover some of their well-guarded secrets, but always as a vagrant and a foreigner. Now, at last, a bit of this beloved forest was my own. I took it fondly under my protection, with all its monkeys, deer, coatimundis, and agoutis; all its parrots, toucans, trogons, tinamous, antbirds, and manakins; all its innumerable palms, creepers, tree ferns, aroids, and orchids; all its brilliant butterflies, dragonflies, leaf-cutting ants, and cicadas. Here I could study the forest life to my heart's content, without interruptions by another man's laborers, without feeling myself an intruder.

But I wished to do more than learn facts about the living things that surrounded me here; I wished to dwell in harmony with them. The concord that I desired intensely to achieve was more than ecological balance with my environment, which some people mistake for harmony. This ecological balance or stability, wonderful enough in its way, is in reality a balance of disharmonies, violence held within bounds. It is preserved by the merciless decimation, by predators and parasites and other natural checks, of any species that threatens to become so abundant that it will cause the deterioration of its environment by bearing too heavily upon its resources. Such ecological balance with our environment is indispensable for our survival as organisms, but it is too often achieved by means that distress an awakened conscience.

I yearned intensely to dwell at peace with all creatures, destroying no living thing. I was fully aware that the perfect realization of this ideal is incompatible with the preservation of life by animals whose needs are as large and varied as ours; but I was convinced that, by trying hard, I could come much nearer its fulfillment than people commonly do, and I wished to see how far I could go. Whatever I achieved in this endeavor would be highly satisfying to me. And while making this effort, I desired to do something even more difficult: to penetrate, as far as possible, to the secret springs of this multiplex phenomenon called life, to understand its significance in the whole vast drama of cosmic evolution. Here I hoped to have leisure to mature my thoughts on these baffling problems.

12

The House

As soon as a man feels his own land beneath his feet, he begins to think of a roof of his own above his head. The level terrace with the guava trees, which appealed so strongly to me as I gazed down on it in the evening twilight from the high bluff across the river, was near the northern end of the farm, and a more central location for my dwelling would have been in some ways more convenient. Near the center of the farm were higher terraces that gave an even wider outlook and offered a greater area of level ground for fruit trees, a garden, and the other adjuncts of a farmhouse. But their distance from a permanent stream would make water too difficult to procure in the dry season. Everything considered, my first choice of a house site, despite certain obvious disadvantages, was the best. Previous occupants of the farm had come to the same conclusion. Don Chico had built his hut at the edge of the same terrace, and the avocado and orange trees on and near this

Headpiece: Chico Mora and María. My unfinished house in the background.

terrace, already bearing fruit, indicated that still earlier cultivators had squatted in this part of the farm.

Even before the arrival of people of European ancestry, the aborigines had dwelt on or near this terrace. Close by the site that I chose for my house was a great, thick, roundish, flat stone, two and a half feet in diameter, with a shallow concavity in its upper side. This had probably been used by the Indians for breaking maize for their tortillas and, perhaps, for mashing cassava and other foods. The big spherical stone that rolled around in the hollow and crushed the grains was lost, and an edge had been broken from the flat stone. For all the abundance of rocks of all sizes and shapes on the farm, flat ones were hard to find, and this stone was eventually used as a step at the end of the front porch. Digging in the garden, I found shards of red, unglazed Indian pottery. Near the house was a huge rock with Indian carvings and, on top of the hill that rises steeply behind it, an ancient burial ground. But during the long period, apparently lasting several centuries, between the virtual disappearance of the Brunka Indians, who everywhere in El General left traces of a once dense and flourishing population, and the arrival of the recent settlers from central Costa Rica, mature forest had overgrown the region.

The tide of settlement was just beginning to flow into the lateral valley of the Río Peña Blanca. Those who first found productive lands here tried to discourage competition by spreading the report that the valley so teemed with venomous serpents that a man took his life into his hands when he went to work there. But it was soon discovered that snakes, although there were indeed some formidable ones, were no more abundant in this area than in other parts of El General. Settlers, always eager for fresh lands to clear and plant, began to pour in, and Quizarrá was talked about as a land of promise. By 1941, when I bought my farm, it was reached by a cart road, newly cut through the forest and rough with exposed roots. This made it possible to bring in building materials.

The tiny dwellings in the neighborhood were, with one or two exceptions, thatched with sugarcane leaves. Some had walls of sawn boards, unplaned and unpainted; others were of poles or split trunks. Some had wooden floors, but others, like Don Chico's, were floorless. I had lived for many months in thatched cabins and found them not uncomfortable. They cost relatively little to build but require constant repairs, for the thatch lasts only three or four years, according to how thickly it is applied, and the supporting posts, if set into the ground, are attacked by termites, which soon spread throughout the edifice. Such constructions are highly inflammable; a spark in the cane leaf in dry weather converts them into raging bonfires in a few minutes. My small capital had been so laboriously accumulated that I wished to invest it wisely and make it last. Accordingly, I decided to build with more durable materials. Besides, I wished to install my library, and, although my person might survive a leaky roof and termite-riddled walls, these would be fatal to books.

I recalled a house on a Guatemalan coffee plantation, where I had made several long, pleasant visits, and decided to build on the same model, although I did not need so large a dwelling and could not afford to finish it in the same style. The plantation house at "San Diego" was built in the form of an L, with a front veranda across the long arm, a back porch along the short arm, and an open passageway passing between the wings and joining the porches. Each room opened directly on a porch; each could have windows on at least two sides for good ventilation; and there was no enclosed hallway anywhere. This seemed a sensible type of construction for the tropics, especially in a region where screening would hardly be necessary.

Since boards that were nicely matched and finished were so difficult to procure, I would make the walls of clay rather than of wood. Of clay walls, two types were widely used in Latin America. In adobe construction, the clay is made into large bricks, which are dried in the sun and then built into walls without mortar. This kind of building is adequate for dry climates where there are no earthquakes. For the second type of construction, *bahareque*, a stout, wooden framework is first built, and the walls are covered with canes or laths nailed to both sides of the uprights, almost as for plastering. Then the space between the canes is filled with puddled clay, which is finally extended outward to cover and enclose these canes. When completed, one has a solid wall, six or seven inches thick, bound all into one piece with timbers and strong wild canes—a primitive version of reinforced concrete. On a visit to Callao in Peru in 1940, shortly after a disastrous earthquake, I had seen how adobe walls were shaken to pieces, while *bahareque*, although cracked, had withstood the shocks. In the tropics, where there are so many kinds of "vermin," double walls enclosing a dead air space are inconvenient; this was another reason for choosing solid walls of clay. So, disregarding warnings that *bahareque* construction is troublesome and time-consuming, I decided to have a house of this kind.

In a climate so damp, the house would have to stand above the ground, which is easily arranged with *bahareque*, more difficult with adobe. I would have liked supporting pillars of concrete, uniform in size and all on the same level at the top. But to transport a sack of cement by air and oxcart to Quizarrá cost twice as much as the cement itself in San José, where it had been brought by ship and railroad from Europe or the United States. The only alternative was to set the house on rough, irregular rocks from the fields or the stream beds. Although there were countless rocks of all sizes to choose from, it was not easy to find enough of the size we needed. It is exceedingly difficult to set rows of such poorly matched stones so that, after settling, their tops will be all on a level. Our failure to do so is still evident in the unevenness of our floors.

For the base beams of the house, we used timbers six inches square; for the upper horizontal frame, to support the heavy roof of tiles, they were five inches square. A local man undertook to prepare these timbers, cutting trees in the forest on the farm and squaring them with an adze. Like tropical rain forest everywhere, that on this farm contains a bewildering variety of trees with wood of the most diverse qualities. The wood of some of the noblest trees, such as the Milk Tree and the Candela, is so attractive to insects that even in a dry place it will be reduced to powder within a year or two, hence is useless for construction. Other timbers, like the Guayacán, the Comenegro, and the Cacique, will last for years even in contact with the ground. Some soft woods, especially those of the laurel family, are surprisingly durable; whereas some hard woods, such as that of the common Guava, decay readily.

Of some trees, the heartwood is more durable; of others, the sapwood. Thus the white outer wood of the Colorado is soon demolished by insects in a dry place and by fungi in a wet place; the pink inner wood, so fragrant and delicately tinted, is exceedingly resistant even in the ground. A fallen trunk of this tree is soon reduced to a solid cylinder of straight-grained, enduring heartwood. In the white-flowered Campana, however, the outside of the trunk is more resistant to decay than the inside; a fallen tree rapidly becomes a hollow cylinder in which an Agouti may take refuge.

To learn all the idiosyncrasies of the local timbers, years of experience are necessary. Although I had botanized extensively in the region and sent wood samples to northern museums, I could not have directed our woodcutter in the choice of trees. Yet without supervision, he prepared beams of a variety of kinds that were not only square and straight, but, with the exception of a single one that is often wet, have remained sound for nearly three decades. Carelessly chosen house beams may require replacement after only two or three years. I forget the woodcutter's name and would not recognize him if I saw him again, but I should like to tell him that I am grateful for a difficult job well done.

The boards and lighter timbers for the house were brought from small sawmills situated on the other side of San Isidro. Many of them came a dozen miles by oxcart. In the course of this hauling, one of the carters suffered a tragic accident. On each trip, he had to cross the Río General on a high wooden bridge without rail or parapet. On one crossing, an ox slipped over the edge of the bridge and hung in the air suspended by his horns from the yoke, which prevented his falling because it was also attached to the companion ox and the cart. Since there was no way of lifting the heavy animal back onto the planking of the bridge, and there was danger that he would pull the rest of the equipage after him, nothing could be done except to cut the yoke straps and let the poor creature fall five or six yards into the rocky stream bed, where he was so severely injured that he had to be killed.

Since the local sawmills were too poorly equipped to finish the boards, those used for floors, windows, doors, and other places where dressed lumber was required, had to be planed and given straight edges by hand —a time-consuming labor. One could never be sure what a board would be like until it was smoothed off, and some which looked fine and sound in the rough revealed ugly blemishes when the fur was planed off. Among the curiosities of the house were some boards with vines deeply embedded in the wood; the trunk from which they were cut had grown over and completely enclosed a liana that had twined around it. It was difficult to obtain any quantity of boards to match. One afternoon, when the house was nearing completion, a neighbor arrived under a drenching shower with a cartload of fine, broad, massive planks for the floor of the back porch. But there were not enough, and I bought them on the condition that he would bring me more of the same kind. They never arrived!

We found a farmer in General Viejo who had recently taken to tile-making, but he had little experience, and his tiles were irregular with many flaws. Better tiles were manufactured in San Isidro, but the distance was twice as great, and over those rough roads, with a fragile cargo, this was an important consideration. So with some misgivings, I bought three thousand of these inferior unglazed tiles at seventy colones per thousand. Nearly a quarter of them were broken on the four-mile haul and had to be replaced. The carter became so discouraged that he threatened to quit, but he was persuaded to persevere to the end. For years my dooryard contained a pile of broken tiles, which were gradually given to neighbors to reinforce the clay ovens beneath the cauldrons where they boiled their cane sap when making *dulce*.

Because of the poor quality of the tiles, the roof was given an unusually steep pitch. These rustic tiles could not be fastened to the boards that supported them but were held in place by friction alone. Soon after the house was built, a slight earthquake caused many of them to slip down, and it was necessary to relay them. Over the years, they have developed many leaks, but I learned how to take care of them. During heavy showers, I climbed into the attic and, by pulling tiles up from below or slipping thin sheets of metal beneath them, succeeded in stopping most of the drips. By these shifts, we have managed to keep fairly dry.

The clay for the walls was removed from the bank above the roadway that came obliquely down the steep hillside behind the house. We dug a broad, shallow pit, in which the red clay was mixed with water, then kneaded thoroughly by a horse, who, with a boy on his back, walked round and round for an hour or more, until the mass became as sticky as clay can be. When sufficiently puddled, the clay was piled up to drain, then pushed in between the Wild Canes which in double series covered the framework of the walls. As the clay dried and shrank, great fissures developed and were filled with fresh clay. When the inner space became sufficiently solid, the clay was built outward to cover and embed the canes. At this stage, chopped straw was mixed with the clay to serve as a binder. Then, in drying, more cracks appeared and called for more coats of clay. Meanwhile, the living Wild Canes sprouted and pushed roots through the wet clay, which served to bind canes and clay more firmly together.

When, after applying several coats of clay and waiting months for each successive application to dry, most of the fissures had been eliminated, we were ready for an operation of which I knew nothing when the house was begun and which might have deterred me from building in *bahareque*. The walls were smeared over, inside and out, with a thick coat of fresh cow dung! The man who did this, applying the soft, pasty mass with his hands, had been an ox driver and seemed not to be offended by the task. For a day or two, a great stench filled the rooms, but as soon as the paste dried, it became quite odorless. It produced a soft, gray, feltlike surface that was not unattractive and was admired by a visitor ignorant of its nature. For months, I slept and ate in rooms with dung-smeared walls, which reminded me that in other lands the droppings of herbivorous animals, rich in cellulose, are used as a cement for floors or as fuel for cooking. Finally, well over a year after the work was begun, the inside walls were finished with a thick coat of white lime, while the exterior walls were treated with a wash of light gray cement, which has stood up well over the years.

Much of the work of putting up ceilings, window frames, and other finishing touches I did with my own hands. On rainy afternoons, during my first year on the farm, I made most of the simple furniture: a big cabinet of Spanish cedar for books and papers, chests for clothes and storing grains, open bookshelves, tables, a kitchen cabinet, and a dresser for the dining room. One of the hardest parts of this undertaking was planing and giving straight edges to the boards, which came all rough from the sawmill. A small iron bedstead and two folding rocking chairs, which came by air from San José, were the only pieces of furniture that I bought. For cooking, there was a clay-covered platform, such as I had used in earlier, temporary habitations. The smoke went where it listed, into one's eyes or up through the cracks between the tiles. After the arrival of the highway, a small iron stove with a stovepipe was installed in the kitchen.

Two years after the foundations were laid, when the walls had been whitewashed and my books, which had come by sea and rail and air and oxcart, were lined up like old familiar faces on the shelves that I had made for them, my house began to feel like a home. At a cost of about six hundred dollars and much labor of my own of which I kept no account, I now had a substantial dwelling of five rooms: bedroom, dining room, kitchen, study, and storeroom. Across the front is a porch, whence I look across the valley of the Río Peña Blanca to wooded ridges in the east, which on many a drizzly afternoon of the wet season I view through the high arch of a splendid rainbow. To the northeast, a series of steep, forested foothills, rising ever higher, lead the eye up to a great, dome-like summit, which among people who take more interest in the landscape would surely be named, but here remains anonymous. Sometimes, when late on a rainy afternoon the sun shines forth again as it sinks in the west, its level rays cast a golden light of indescribable glory over the precipitous wooded flank of this great dome, which holds our eyes as though by a spell while it slowly fades through sombre purple into dusky gray. To the north, peeping above the summits of great intervening ridges, rise the craggy summits of Cerro Chirripó, where the Peña Blanca River is born. Even while I sit within the house, these mountains so rarely trodden by human feet seem close and friendly, for no window glass interposes a barrier between us.

For most of my first nine years in this house, I dwelt alone. For six months after the revolution of 1948, Darwin Norby, a young botanist, and his bride shared my home while studying with me, and occasional guests stayed a few days. Fifty yards from my house, I built a smaller one for a farmhand and his family, which usually included a daughter who came in the mornings to cook, clean the house, and wash clothes. Once, for three months, when I had trouble with labor, I lived with only the horses and birds for company, doing all the housework as well as looking after the farm. Finally, in 1950, I married Pamela, the youngest daughter of C. H. Lankester, one of Costa Rica's best-known and best-loved naturalists. Fortunately, she easily adapted herself to the simple life of a backwoods farm. After sixteen years of marriage, we adopted a boy who had grown up on our farm, the son of a man who had worked intermittently for me from the age of thirteen. When this man's family broke up, we took

Edwin into our home and gave him our name. He has been a good son, helpful on the farm and in my field work with the birds. With this addition to our family, we needed more room and added a second wing to our house, so that it occupied three sides of a quadrangle. At last, with highways leading to the capital, we had no lack of cement for this construction. After nearly thirty years, our house was almost finished. If I had not been vigilant, termites would have finished it long ago!

As my dwelling neared completion, I cast about for a name for my homestead. I should have preferred to call it for the jacamar, that brisk, dainty, glittering, gemlike bird that adorned my woodland and had long been a favorite with me. But this notable bird, like most of our feathered creatures, was nameless here, and none of my neighbors would pronounce the word "jacamar" as I do. So I called the farm "Los Cusingos," after the Fiery-billed Araçari, a small, slender toucan, whose great, red bill makes it too conspicuous to be overlooked by even the most unobservant peasant. These birds are among the species endemic to the region of heavy rain forests on the Pacific side of southern Costa Rica and adjacent Panama, and it is perhaps fitting that a bird-watcher's farm be named for them. But they are shameless brigands, who, in the nesting season, invade the shade trees around the house and pluck from the nests all the eggs and young birds they can find.

The year after I bought Don Chico's land, I acquired a larger, less developed farm that adjoined it to the south. After selling part of this tract, I had about a hundred hectares, about half of which was covered by a continuous stand of unspoiled forest, which I intended to keep intact, planting only on land that had already been cleared. I hoped that this would be large enough to preserve a good sample of the original flora and fauna, while I learned something about them.

13

The Garden and Its Birds

THE TERRACE that I chose for my homesite was part of the open pasture, which extended from the river back into the hills. When the house was well advanced, I fenced off the nearly level shelf of land on which it stood. This made a roughly quadrangular enclosure, about a hundred yards long by fifty broad. Although Sir Francis Bacon declared that a true princely garden should comprise no less than thirty acres, this area of roughly one acre was, as I later discovered, too large for the garden of a lone homesteader. But the terrace formed a natural unit, and the boundaries were determined by the terrain itself rather than by plans for a large and elegant garden. At the southern end, where narrowest, the enclosure adjoined the high forest; at the broader northern end, it was bounded by the roadway that led down into the pastures and fields. Behind the house, the grassy hillside rose steeply; in front, the land fell away by a high bank to the riverside pasture. The

Headpiece: A Flowering Melastome (*Miconia scorpioides*). For a few days in the dry season, the rounded crown is thickly covered with long panicles of small, fragrant, white flowers.

area that formed my garden had been in pasture for some years and was already covered by a close-cropped sward, so that it was not necessary to sow lawn grass.

About the new house were many young Guava trees that had sprung up spontaneously in the pasture, carried there by the horses and cattle that ate the fragrant fruit and passed the hard little seeds through their digestive tracts in a viable state. There were also several orange trees, a single avocado tree, a cashew tree that in this wet climate bore good fruit only in the drier years, and, along the top of the high bank, a number of young Calabash and Annatto trees. The former were more bizarre than graceful, with long, thick, stiff branches on which the leaves grew in clusters, and green trumpet flowers, pollinated by bats, that lurked inconspicuously among the foliage on the main stems. This position was necessary for the support of the great spherical fruits, six to nine inches in diameter, whose hard, woody shells formed durable vessels of a hundred uses. The thick branches of the Calabash trees, with their rough bark on which mosses and liverworts grew profusely, were useful also for forming aerial gardens of orchids and many other epiphytic growths.

The little Annatto trees, hardly more than tall shrubs, were attractive when, in July and August, they bore a profusion of big, pink blossoms, each of which lasted but a day. Later, when in fruit, they were equally colorful with their big clusters of dull red pods covered with long, soft bristles. These bristly pods reminded me of chestnut or chinquapin burrs, but the softness of their spines made them less forbidding. In the center of each hollow pod was a cluster of small seeds, each covered with a greasy substance much in demand for giving an orange color and a peculiar flavor to rice and other foods. In Ecuador, the Colorado Indians, who dwelt amid the forests of Esmeraldas, covered their whole bodies with a thick paste made from the Annatto seeds, doubtless to give them some protection from biting insects.

Although the Guava trees in the enclosure grew too close together, I decided to let most of them stand for the present and to remove them gradually as other things grew up to replace them. They yielded an abundance of aromatic fruits for making jelly and desserts. They also attracted many birds, and, so long as they flourished, my dooryard would not lack shade or songsters. Even the shy Chestnut-winged Chachalacas, big, long-tailed fowl of the guan family that preferred the secrecy of thick second growth to open fields and pastures, came now and then in noisy parties to eat the guavas in the tops of the trees close by my dwelling. Sometimes chattering bands of White-faced Monkeys would venture within fifty yards of the house to feast upon these fruits, the mothers carrying pert babies upon their backs. In the evenings, timid, tailless

Agoutis would steal out from the neighboring woodland to pick fallen guavas from the grass, and sometimes after dark my flashlight would reveal a small rabbit on the lawn. Rarely, the little reddish Forest Deer, as big as a three-month-old calf, would warily enter the garden to eat these fragrant fruits, while the chickens cackled excitedly at the unwonted visitor. The bucks had straight, slender, spikelike horns, as long as their big ears. How flexible is the deer's back, how lithe and supple his whole body, low-slung in front like that of the Agouti and, doubtless, for the same reason! Inserting its foreparts beneath bushes and vines, the animal pushes them up with its forward-sloping back to open a passage through the forest's tangled undergrowth.

After making the enclosure, I sought colorful plants to adorn it. In a region of perennial verdure, where few of the native trees displayed masses of bright blossoms to variegate the monotonous greens, the accent in my planting was on color. As I rode about the valley, I kept my eyes open for bright shrubbery. Even the humblest thatched hut was often prettily embowered amid flowering shrubs and vines. People who love flowers are, as a rule, glad to share them, freely giving seeds or cuttings; as those who love birds are nearly always happy to share their experiences with others. Whenever on these rides I noticed some attractive ornamental, I never hesitated to beg a bit of propagating material, and I was never refused—as I never turned away requests for seeds and cuttings after the plants in my own garden grew up. Thus the shrubs that now adorn our dooryard were little by little carried home in my saddlebags, sometimes as seeds but more often as twigs or stakes for rooting.

I planted much of the shrubby "dracaena," with ample red and green leaves colorful at all seasons. I found several kinds of hibiscus: one with great, brilliant, red, "double" blossoms; one with pale red, "single" flowers; and one with great pink pompons. Then I brought cuttings of the shrubby *Hibiscus mutabilis,* whose big "double" flowers are snow white in the morning when they first open, but as the hours pass they slowly turn pink, which color they preserve through the second day of their short life. The women call these inconstant blossoms *corazón de hombre* (man's heart), but the men, not to be outdone, retaliate by naming them "woman's heart." Another colorful plant of which I set out a number of cuttings was a shrubby Codiaeum with long, narrow leaves that, with increasing age, turn from bright green and yellow to red and, finally, deep bronze. Other red-flowered plants that I found for the garden were the Poró (of which more anon), a brilliant herbaceous lobelia, and a vigorous shrub of the acanthus family, which soon became a pest, it spread so rapidly from fragments of stem. Wet season and dry, I had no dearth of red and pink blossoms to brighten my surroundings.

For yellow I planted the Allamanda with great, golden, trumpet flowers and a shrubby Galphimia, which at all seasons bore a profusion of little, yellow blossoms. Before long, an elegant native shrub of the madder family, *Palicourea guianensis*, established itself in the garden from seeds carried by birds. Above its large, ovate, prominently veined leaves it displays, through much of the year, generous pyramids of small, bright yellow flowers on orange stalks. The flowers attract many hummingbirds, and the dark purple berries are sought by numerous tanagers, finches, manakins, and other birds.

For purple and lavender there were a shrubby Thunbergia, a Buddleia, and two kinds of Stachytarpheta. I fear that my planting ran too strongly to red to win the approval of connoisseurs in these matters, but this effect was largely unpremeditated. I took plants that I found in the neighborhood and were easy to propagate, for I had in those first years little time to nurse along delicate and dilatory ornamentals, and many of the seeds and cuttings that I stuck too carelessly into the ground failed to grow. Evidently my informal color scheme reflected the local preference for plants that are bright even to the point of gaudiness and vigorous enough to thrive with little attention.

Don Chico brought me seeds of the Carao, a species of *Cassia* at home in the drier parts of Costa Rica, from which I grew two trees that hold the eyes with delight in the dry season when they are laden with masses of deep pink blossoms amidst the tender green of freshly expanding foliage. C. H. Lankester, dean of Costa Rican naturalists, sent me seeds of Flame-of-the-Forest from trees that he had introduced into the country from tropical Africa. These rather weedy trees with soft and brittle wood shot up rapidly in our wet climate, and after four or five years began to display their big trumpets, adding yet another red flower to my environs and carrying the brilliant hue far higher into the air. When ten years old, some of these trees were seventy-five feet high, and during most of the wet season their full, rounded crowns of dark foliage were covered with a profusion of bright red blossoms, a joyful sight whether viewed against the dark green of the distant wooded mountains or against the clear blue of the brilliant morning sky.

But at times the flaming color soared yet higher into the heavens, convincing me that my youthful dreams of the brilliance of vegetable and animal life in the tropics had not exceeded reality and filling the cup of sensuous delight. As the sun's earliest rays set aglow the flamboyant crowns of the Flame-of-the-Forest trees, flocks of great Scarlet Macaws came streaming out of the east, like gorgeous emissaries of returning Phoebus. Two by two they flew, with steady, laborious wingbeats, their scarlet under plumage aglow in the level beams of the rising sun. As though their color alone were not sufficient to arouse the sleepiest head, they heralded their approach with loud, raucous calls, making themselves as obnoxious to the ear as they were thrilling to the eye. In a flock of two or three dozen birds, composed of pairs which flew wing to wing but preserved a respectful distance from other couples, there were often one or two single macaws rudely attempting to break into mated pairs. Sometimes a few of these unbelievably brilliant parrots would settle to rest or feed in the tops of the trees at the forest's edge by the house, where from the rear windows we could admire the vivid yellow and blue of their wings contrasting with the scarlet of their bodies. After foraging all day on the fruits of the great trees in the woodland to our west, the brilliant macaws would return eastward in the late afternoon, often flying through rain beneath gloomy clouds that dimmed their splendor.

Sometimes arriving at the same time as the macaws, but always in separate flocks, were even larger parties of big, green Red-lored Parrots, who likewise flew in pairs, with now and then a distressed and disturbing odd individual. Sometimes with a favorable light I could detect the red on the forehead and wings of these noisy parrots, who flew with little mincing strokes, as though their wings were stiff. Neither the Scarlet Macaws nor the Red-lored Parrots nested in our neighborhood, but they came up from the lowlands in the second half of the year in search of ripening fruits. Sometimes a few of these big birds would appear in July or even June, but it was from September or October to December or early January that they came in greatest numbers.

In addition to ornamentals, I set out seedling trees of the avocado and the orange, the most advanced of which began to bear when eight years old. But I soon learned that it was unnecessary to plant oranges. Unlike some cultivated fruit trees, our local sweet oranges come true from seeds. Apparently this is because each seed contains several embryos, some of which are formed without fertilization by the proliferation of tissue within the ovule, and it is one of these apogamous embryos that germinates and gives rise to the new tree, genetically identical with the parent tree. When an old orange tree dies, there is often a crowd of hopeful seedlings pushing up beneath its drying boughs to replace it. Laborers cleaning the pastures often eat oranges and drop seeds, which germinate where they fall, and, without effort or expense, an excellent juicy orange spread over the farm.

Other citrus fruits behave differently. One day, before he sold the farm to me, Don Chico bought some tangerines in the market in San José. They were so delicious that he carefully preserved the seeds and brought them home to plant. They produced trees of unusually rapid growth for citrus, which in a few years bore big, juicy tangerines of a bright orange color. I can imagine the old farmer's surprise, disappointment, and actual physical pain, when he tasted the first of these deceptive fruits and found it intensely acid, the very antithesis of what a tangerine should be. The women found a use for these sour fruits for cleaning the bare, unpainted boards of their tables, shelves, and benches, which every self-respecting Costa Rican country housewife takes pride in keeping brightly scoured. When heavily sugared, these tangerines make a barely passable substitute for lemonade. Although they die at an age of six or eight years, the trees propagate themselves so freely, from both seeds and root suckers, that Don Chico's famous tangerine threatened to become one of the common, aggressive weeds of the district, and I tried to eradicate it from the farm. In the seeds which Don Chico brought home, it was evidently sexually produced rather than vegetatively formed embryos that sprouted, giving rise to trees so unlike those from which they came.

After we fenced the terrace to keep the cattle out, the grass grew tall. Since I lacked a lawn mower, I tried to keep it short with a machete. I have seen lawns so neatly trimmed with these long knives that one would have supposed that they had been mowed with a machine. But with my big enclosure, this laborious handwork proved too expensive. Finally, I decided to let the horses enter and crop the grass. They turned out to be efficient and inexpensive but somewhat capricious lawn mowers, in areas where they found the grass to their taste, keeping the sward short and smooth but in neighboring patches, especially in the shade, allowing it to grow tall and rank. Grazing animals possess marvelous powers of gustatory discrimination; when given the choice, they instinctively prefer those areas where the soil is richer and supports herbage better supplied with the nutritive elements essential to them. I found it necessary to guard the lower plants from injury by the horses' hoofs by setting stout stakes around them. But with the exception of some sorts of leguminous trees whose foliage attracted them, the horses rarely touched the fruit trees and shrubbery, in this contrasting with the cows, who, if they could surreptitiously intrude into the garden, tore at almost every plant they could reach. Almost anything green is grist for the ruminant bovine's mill.

To fence the garden we used wooden posts, which would last only a few years. They were intended to support the barbed wire only until we could replace them with living posts of Madera Negra (Black Wood) or Madre de Cacao (Mother of the Cacao), as it is called in Guatemala. This is a small leguminous tree, with pinnately compound foliage much resembling that of the Black Locust of the eastern United States. The end of the dry season, when the trees were nearly or quite leafless, was the time for cutting the long, straight branches to be planted for posts. They had to be so tall that the cattle could not browse on the fresh young sprouts that soon pushed forth at the top, while, at the buried end, roots grew out to anchor the pole firmly in the earth. The leafy shoots grew so vigorously that they would have weighed down the tall stakes had they not been cut back annually for several years, after which they were permitted to grow longer to provide new fence posts.

After a few years, my Madera Negra trees began to flower in the dry weather of February and March, when the leaves had fallen. The bare limbs laden with thyrses of pale pink, pealike blossoms brought memories of flowering peach trees, although the forms of tree and blossoms were different. They drew many insects and birds to add color and movement to an already lovely display. Everywhere in Central America, I have found these blossoms attractive to wintering Baltimore Orioles, the males rich orange, black, and white in plumage. Clinging beside the clustered flowers, the birds probe them with sharp bills, but whether to extract small insects or nectar, or both kinds of nourishment, I have not learned. The few Orchard Orioles that I have seen on this farm were visiting the Madera Negra flowers. They spend the winter chiefly in lower and warmer districts.

Purple-crowned Fairy Hummingbirds honor us with their presence chiefly when the Madera Negra is in blossom. With their long, slender form, glittering green upper plumage, and pure white under parts, they are even more graceful than most members of their charming family. Their short, straight, sharp bills seem specially fitted for probing the pealike blossoms, to which other hummingbirds pay little attention. Not only are our fence posts highly ornamental, whether in full foliage during the wet season or bright with flowers and birds in the dry months, but they also provide a delicacy for our table, for their blossoms, fried in a batter of eggs, make a tasty dish. Yet the seeds and roots are said to be poisonous to rodents, a fact—or fancy?—commemorated in the generic name *Gliricidia*.

The Stachytarpheta Hedge and Its Hummingbirds

The wire fence around the garden was necessary to keep out the cattle from the adjoining pasture, but without a hedge the garden lacked intimacy and definition; it seemed to lose itself in the surrounding expanses of grassland. On the Caribbean slope of Costa Rica near Turrialba, I had passed several pleasant weeks on a hospitable farm where there were long hedgerows of Stachytarpheta, a tall, straggling shrub of the verbena family. Its small purple florets, displayed in a little wreath that daily moves upward along a slender, whiplike, green spike, attracted one of the most colorful assemblages of hummingbirds that I had ever seen, along with many bright butterflies and moths. This was the only locality where I ever found the rare, diminutive, bronzy-purple Snowcap Hummingbird.

Riding home from San Isidro one day, I noticed some Stachytarpheta bushes along the road, and I begged cuttings of the old woman whose dooryard they adorned. She could not give me enough to complete my hedge, but I planted what I had and waited until they grew strong enough to supply more cuttings. The woody twigs struck root and grew rapidly, and by gradually extending my hedge as propagating material became available, I before long completed it about the back and sides of the garden. In front, along the top of the bank, I wanted a lower hedge that would not intercept the view, so I planted the common Privet.

For three years, my Stachytarpheta hedge was a source of joy. I spent countless hours watching the hummingbirds that in increasing numbers and variety flocked to the ever-greater display of purple florets. My eyes were held enthralled by their stationary hovering on wings vibrated into a haze, their rapid darts, their swift pursuits of rivals, often leading to inconsequential skirmishes; by the glinting of their glossy plumage in the rich sunshine; by the sudden gleams of unsuspected splendor—metallic violet or green or golden or blue—shot out from the gorget or crown as the tiny sprite assumed just the proper position in relation to the viewing eye, to pass as suddenly when this momentary orientation was altered.

First to discover the Stachytarpheta's earliest blossoms was the little Violet-headed Hummingbird, which brought vivid memories of The Hummingbirds' Brook, a dozen miles away. I first noticed this hummingbird when the hedge shrubs, ten months after planting, were reaching the upper strand of the wire fence and flowering profusely. Soon the Rufous-tailed Hummingbirds, which sang their odd little ditties in the trees about the house at dawn through most of the year, joined the Violet-headed Hummingbirds at the flower feast. Then came the minute White-crested Coquettes, first females, then males adorned with long ornamental tufts of green and white feathers on their heads and all delightfully fearless of me. In any plumage, the Coquettes could be recognized by the white band on their rumps, a rare marking in hummingbirds. Before the end of the second year, I had recorded at the hedge Blue-chested Hummingbirds, Snowy-breasted Hummingbirds, Blue-crowned Woodnymphs, Blue-throated Goldentails, Scaly-breasted Hummingbirds, and Long-tailed Hermits—designations that fail to convey the beauty of these living gems.

Later came Little Hermits, White-necked Jacobins exquisitely clad in green, blue, and white, and the rare, curiously attired Brown Violet-ear. One morning in dry February, my attention was attracted by the sound of a hummingbird's wingbeats louder and more insistent than that of any of the local species. I saw, in the direction of the high-pitched buzz, a splendid, male Ruby-throated Hummingbird sipping nectar from the purple blossoms. This rare winter visitant had come from the United States or southern Canada, perhaps flying across the broad expanse of the Gulf of Mexico to reach Central America.

For years I refrained from trimming this hedge, for I was reluctant to diminish, even temporarily, the profusion of the blossoms that delighted those who delighted me. The vigorous Stachytarpheta grew upward until it weighted down the boughs of the Madera Negra trees that stood above it and outward until it became an impassable barrier twenty feet thick, in the tangled depths of which the Scarlet-rumped Black Tanagers that flocked in the yard took shelter for the night. Finally, the hedge became so sprawling and unruly that I could no longer postpone a drastic pruning of the thick, gnarled main stems. The stumps sprouted forth and soon flowered again, but for some obscure reason the hummingbirds never swarmed about the blossoms as of yore. Then the plants began to die and were cut away to be replaced by a neater and more permanent, if more prosaic, Privet hedge. A few bushes of Stachytarpheta left in the garden never attracted the hummingbirds as formerly. Perhaps they had discovered greater bounty elsewhere.

The Poró Tree and Its Visitors

Behind the house stands another plant attractive to hummingbirds, the Poró. This tree and several others of the same kind that adorn the garden were started quite simply by setting long, freshly cut poles into the ground, in the manner of the Madera Negra. After nine years, they were about thirty feet high. Toward the end of the wet season, in October or November, the thorny branches begin to shed their trifoliolate leaves. Soon they start to flower, and in the sunny days of December and January, or sometimes earlier, the nearly leafless trees bear heavy clusters of vivid red blossoms. These papilionaceous flowers are so modified that only the standard, about three and a half inches in length, protrudes from the thick, tubular calyx. This long, fleshy standard is folded lengthwise, giving it much the shape of a machete or a sabre, and enclosing the stamens and pistil as well as the rudiments of the other petals. Not every bird can probe the depths of a blossom so tightly closed, and, of all the local hummingbirds, the only regular visitors to the Poró are the Long-billed Starthroat, an elegant creature with a magenta gorget, and the plain Scaly-breasted Hummingbird, an undistinguished member of a brilliant family. One hummingbird to one tree is the rule, to enforce which sharp clashes sometimes occur between competing nectar seekers.

Rarely a dainty Purple-crowned Fairy hovers beside the red Poró flowers, forcing its short, sharp bill through the two-millimeter-thick tissue of the calyx and, doubtless, managing to extract nectar through the fine slit it makes. The thickness of this calyx collar is evidently an adaptation to discourage the visits of birds and bees which cannot, like the Starthroat, reach the nectar from the front of the flower, thereby pollinating it in payment for the sweet drink, and which therefore might try to perforate the floral tissues to reach the coveted fluid. However, the Fairy's short and very sharp bill seems to be specialized for just this sort of plundering; it perforates a great variety of flowers, some much larger than itself, and it seems rarely to serve as a pollinator—a role ably performed by most kinds of hummingbirds. Sometimes the Scaly-breasted Hummingbird pierces the calyx of the Poró with its bill, which is long enough to reach the nectar through the length of the flower in the "legitimate" manner always followed by the Long-billed Starthroat.

Other nectar drinkers are more destructive to the Poró flowers. Wintering Baltimore Orioles pluck them with their bill, then hold them against a branch with either the right or left foot but always with the base inward beneath the body, while they push their sharp bill through the calyx and, forcefully separating their mandibles, split the thick tissue and extract the nectar. Orange-chinned Parakeets settle in garrulous flocks in the Poró trees, especially before sunrise. They pluck the swordshaped flowers with either a foot or the short, thick bill, bite through the calyx, then drop the flower. Soon the ground beneath the tree is strewn with hundreds of fresh blossoms, some with the calyx split by the orioles, more with a V-shaped perforation made by the mandible of a parakeet.

Although Orange-chinned Parakeets are widespread in the Central American lowlands, I did not see them in El General until January, 1965, when they came to our Poró trees. For several years they were present only in the dry season, when they visited both the common red Poró and a much taller species with orange flowers that are more open, so that the parakeets can extract the nectar without plucking the blossoms. In 1969, however, they remained with us into the wet season, long after the Porós had passed from bloom. Now they ate the small berries of arborescent melastomes and the seeds of the fat-boled Barrigón tree, embedded in the soft down that fills swollen green pods larger than the parakeets themselves. Their meal over, the pygmy parakeets perch two by two in the trees, mated pairs preening each other's plumage and sometimes joining in duets that rarely are almost melodious.

Before the red Poró puts out fresh young foliage with the return of the rains in March or April, the flowers have fallen, to be succeeded by pods of that peculiar form which botanists call "torose." The elongate pod is slender except where swollen about the widely separated seeds. As they ripen, these seeds attract the White-crowned Parrots, who settle in noisy flocks just outside an open window. Plucking a pod and holding it in a foot, the parrot deftly extracts the seeds, then drops the empty pod. Picking up these fallen pods for examination, I was surprised to find that the parrots had, in every instance, extracted the embryo from the still-soft seed coat, leaving the latter within the neatly opened swelling in the pod. So deft were those thick, seemingly clumsy bills; so dainty the birds in their eating!

Parrots remain paired throughout the year, and sometimes when feasting in the Poró tree, two White-crowns will approach and put their bills together, while with jerky movements of the head one regurgitates food into the other's mouth. Both are alike in appearance, so that there is no way of confirming my suspicion that the male gives and the female receives the food. The recipient, when about to be fed, bobs its head up and down and makes that loud, peculiar *da-a-a-dle da-a-a-dle* . . . which later in the year, when the young parrots are awing, sounds again and again from the trees near the house. Less brilliant than many members of their tribe, the small White-crowned Parrots are clad in dull shades of green and blue, but as they noisily take flight, they surprise and delight me with a display of rich blue on parts of the wing feathers that are concealed when the wing is folded and of vermilion-red beneath the tail.

It is obvious from these observations that parrots of two kinds exploit the Poró tree without making any return for the benefits they receive: the small Orange-chinned Parakeets drink the nectar without ever pollinating a flower; the larger White-crowned Parrots eat the seeds without spreading any of them abroad. And this seems to be, in general, the relation of New World parrots to the plants that nourish and protect them. Few families of birds are so exclusively vegetarian, and few that subsist on plants do so little for them. Soft-billed birds, like pigeons, that swallow whole seeds pass some of them undigested through their alimentary tract and so scatter them over the countryside, but by habitually extracting the embryo from the protecting seed coat, parrots preclude the possibility of voiding them in a viable state. Among the fruits that parrots bite open are the green pods of the mayo trees, full of winged seeds that without this interference would be effectively disseminated by wind. Yet there are a few exceptions to the generally one-sided relationship of parrots and plants. The pollen-eating, nectar-drinking, brush-tongued lories and lorikeets of the Australasian region are said to be important pollinators of the eucalyptus and other myrtaceous trees so abundant there, and the Gray Parrot of Africa is reported to disseminate the hard seeds of the Oil Palm.

Embryo eaters, like parrots and grosbeaks, are to the fruiting stage of plants what nectar stealers, like flower-piercers and Purple-crowned Fairy Hummingbirds, are to the flowering stage—thieves who give nothing for what they get. Fruit eaters, like tanagers and cotingas, correspond to nectar drinkers like the majority of the hummingbirds—they pay for their food by pollinating the flowers or disseminating the seeds.

The long Poró pods that escape the parrots split lengthwise about the time the rains begin, exposing the hard, glossy, red beans, one clinging persistently at each swelling. These brilliant seeds are a botanical puzzle. They hang there for months together, as though to attract birds or other animals that might spread them abroad. But if the bird digests the seed, the plant is not disseminated; if, as seems likely, the thick, impervious seed coat prevents digestion, the bird is not benefited by eating it. Once I watched a Yellow-throated Vireo, newly arrived from the North and doubtless without previous experience with this tree, swallow two of the hard seeds. Perhaps it mistook them for red berries, or for seeds enclosed in digestible red arils, of which the tropics afford many examples. I have never seen any other animal eat mature Poró seeds; even young domestic chickens disdain them. Dr. L. van der Pijl characterized these seeds as "premeditated deceit"; but however it may be in the Orient, where he chiefly worked, they seem not often to deceive our local birds. The seeds germinate freely where they fall to the ground, but men usually propagate the tree by its branches.

Edible Flowers

Often, after the orioles and parakeets have sipped their nectar and flown away, we gather from the ground the Poró flowers that they have dropped profusely and prepare them for the table, either boiling them or frying them in a batter, in the same manner as the flowers of the Madera Negra. Only the long corollas are edible and must be pulled out of the thick calyces. A third tree with edible flowers in our garden is the Itabo, *Yucca elephantipes*, whose specific name refers to the immensely swollen base of the thick trunk of old trees. Generous panicles of pure white blossoms adorn the summits of trees from fifteen to twenty-five feet high. It is difficult to reach these flowers at the ends of thick stems that bristle with long, stiff, bayonetlike leaves, but if one succeeds in bringing them down, they make a tasty dish, with just enough bitterness to serve as a relish. These flowers, known as *pichones de Itabo* (nestlings of the Itabo), are sold in Costa Rican markets, principally in the dry season. Since the flowers seem invariably to be sterile, the Itabo is always propagated by means of its thick branches; evidently, it has been domesticated since ancient times.

I had long been familiar with these three kinds of flowers as human food, when a correspondent in the distant state of Washington, who had read something I had published on the subject, called my attention to the edibility of squash flowers. We grow no squash on the farm, but going to the maize field, I gathered some of the great, yellow bells of the pumpkin, which when fried with egg are delicious. For this purpose, I chose only the staminate blossoms, which yield pollen but produce no fruit, leaving the pistillate flowers to give us pumpkins.

I have seen domestic chickens pick up from the ground and eat the red flowers of the Poró, the pink flowers of Madera Negra, the little purple flowers of Stachytarpheta, the white petals of the orange and the rose apple. Smaller birds seem to eat flowers only sparingly. Among our local birds, the Buff-throated Saltator, a thick-billed finch, consumes the large, succulent blossoms of legumes and other plants. In Hispaniola, the sociable Palm-Chats appear to eat corollas freely, sometimes plucking them as they fly past a flowering tree. In northern lands, small birds like House Sparrows, Mockingbirds, Cardinals, Marsh-Tits, and Woodpigeons have been seen eating the blossoms of apple, pear, cherry, plum, garden pea, and forsythia. Flowers appear to be an important component of the diet of some of the peculiar finches endemic to the Galápagos Islands. Even horses may eat a blossom as a rare delicacy; I have seen them devour the pink pompons of a hibiscus and the red Poró flowers.

Night-blooming flowers that depend upon bats for pollination may offer their fleshy corollas as an inducement to fruit-eating bats. These rare "bat-flowers," as Dr. van der Pijl has pointed out, are generally white or dingy in color and, to man, either deficient or unpleasant in scent, in contrast to the brilliant but frequently scentless blossoms that are pollinated by hummingbirds and the often richly fragrant as well as bright-colored flowers that attract butterflies, bees, and other insects. The colors and scents of flowers are adjusted to the sensory organs and manner of life of the creatures that visit them and transfer their pollen.

Petals and other floral parts that serve for advertisement are constructed on the principle of economy, with thin-walled cells poor in contents, other than water, and many air spaces. Usually they contain little nutriment and are of slight importance as food for animals. For plants to store starch or other foodstuffs in organs so evanescent as the majority of petals would not only be wasteful—it might greatly decrease the production of seeds if herbivorous creatures became habitual flower eaters, as some surely would if they found much nourishment in these organs. Indeed, as we have seen in the case of the Poró, even abundant nectar, whose function is to attract pollinators, may cause the flowers to be destroyed, before they can set seed, by birds that must pluck them to reach the coveted secretion. Yet even if flowers nourish us little, their use as food appeals to our esthetic sense and varies a diet which at certain seasons may become monotonous.

The Birds' Table

After I was settled in my new home, I attached a board to a guava tree beside the house as a table for the birds. Many people in northern lands feed the birds during the bleak winter months, when life is so difficult for them, and even throughout the year. But in the tropics I had, at that time, seen only two feeders. The first was that maintained at the biological station on forested Barro Colorado Island in the Panama Canal Zone by Frank M. Chapman. When I saw this table, it was attended only by a pair of Crimson-backed Tanagers, who nested in the clearing around the laboratory, and by "José," a clever Coatimundi who outwitted the distinguished ornithologist's efforts to reserve the board for winged visitors only by suspending it in mid-air on trolley wires; the agile quadruped used them as a bridge to reach the coveted food. The second feeding shelf that I saw was operated by a barefoot farmer, horny of hand and bent with toil, who dwelt in the Valley of El General, about a dozen miles from Los Cusingos.

At both of these tables, bananas were the chief, if not the only, food offered to the birds. This fragrant gift of the Old World to the New—a fair return for maize and potatoes—appeals to a greater variety of creatures than any other fruit that I know, from horses, cows, dogs, and pigs to opossums, raccoons, tapirs, and bats; from chickens and curassows to a host of brightly colored little songbirds; and even to lizards, one of which, a big, crested Basilisk, finally discovered my feeding shelf and caused much annoyance by pushing off the bananas with its clumsy mouth, ill-fitted for such a diet.

For several days, I displayed bananas on the shelf in the guava tree without drawing any visitors. Finally, the Scarlet-rumped Black Tanagers, so numerous in the garden, overcame their distrust of the strange object and alighted on the board, at first as gingerly as though coming down on top of a hot stove. These sociable birds were soon joined by songbirds of other kinds, as my avian restaurant grew in fame and popularity. By the end of the second year, the table had attracted fifteen kinds of birds as regular or occasional attendants. After three years, the table had been visited by twenty-two kinds of birds. In the twenty-seven years that the feeder has been in operation, it has had no less than thirty kinds of avian visitors, some of them regular attendants throughout the year, others wanderers who stopped to refresh themselves at my board, lingered a few days, then passed on, never to be seen again. Among the feathered attendants were eleven species of tanagers, five honeycreepers, five finches, two orioles, two woodpeckers, one wood warbler, one thrush, one flycatcher, one barbet, and one motmot. To this list I might add the Basilisk Lizard, who for a while came by day, and two kinds of marsupials, the tiny marmosa and the medium-sized Woolly Opossum, who often arrived in the dark to eat the fruit that the birds had left, their big eyes gleaming brightly in the flashlight beam that I cast upon them. By placing food daily on this table I fulfilled, in part, the beautiful old Hindu law of piety, which enjoined the faithful to make a daily offering to gods, ancestors, men, and animals, in addition to saying the daily prayers.

Although the birds' table serves visitors throughout the year, there is considerable fluctuation in attendance from month to month. One might expect attendance to be greatest from April to July, when the many birds then raising their families in the vicinity could take advantage of this readily available food supply. However, this is just when fewest bananas are eaten. The reason for this great decline in the number of visits to the table is doubtless the abundance of wild fruits and insects, at the season when nesting is at its peak. During the later months of the year, business is on the whole more brisk. But when in October or November or early December we have several days of continuously wet weather, the demand for bananas, or the ripe plantains that we sometimes substitute for them, is so great that it is difficult to keep the table continuously supplied; sometimes our stock of fruit is exhausted. Then there may be a dozen birds of five or six kinds crowding on a board only about fifteen inches square, with many others awaiting their turns on neighboring boughs.

What a colorful display they make! Red, orange, yellow, green, blue in many shades, even touches of violet, to say nothing of countless duller hues ranging from white and pale gray through olives, buffs, and browns to black—all these colors are mingled in constantly shifting patterns. The tanagers and honeycreepers are the chief contributors of color, with the woodpeckers and Baltimore Orioles making important additions to the display. One of the most brilliant of the visitors, the Red-headed Barbet, comes only late in the year. It is one of the most silent birds I know; the only note I have heard from it was a low, rasping complaint, uttered by a female when I kept her from the board while putting up another banana. These unsociable birds always arrive singly, never in pairs.

Not only does this assemblage of brilliant birds delight the eye; to the thoughtful mind, it affords what we might call a moral satisfaction that is hardly less pleasing. Here are scores, possibly hundreds, of birds of two dozen kinds, free and unregimented and obedient only to their inner impulses, consorting together, sharing the same food on the same narrow board, with scarcely any quarreling or friction among them. What native good manners most of them have! During the quarter century that I have operated this table, I have only at long intervals seen one visitor strike another and never any clash that appeared to injure either party. Rarely has any diner attempted to monopolize the table, and it was at most a momentary attitude, never a sustained policy. Frequently, the birds show, by opening the bill in a threatening posture and raising or depressing the head, that they resent being too closely crowded by other individuals, whether of their own or another species. A tiny tanager or honeycreeper may glare in this fashion across the banana at a finch or thrush several times its size, but soon they fall to eating together.

For a while, the Golden-naped Woodpeckers tried to drive away the Red-crowned Woodpeckers, who, however, continued to visit the table when their rivals were not looking. One Buff-throated Saltator would, as a rule, respectfully wait until its mate had finished eating before dropping down to the board for its share, but because of similarity in plumage, I could not tell whether the male or the female took precedence. A Black-striped Sparrow that nested nearby once struck a female Scarlet-rumped Black Tanager roundly on the breast with its feet, but I have seen no other attacks of this nature. The only visitor that always eats alone is the big Blue-diademed Motmot, which only recently began to visit the table. I have not seen it drive away other birds, but they maintain a respectful distance while it is on the board, which it occupies rather fully.

The most marked and constant antagonisms that I have witnessed at the table were among the winter visitors from the North, who are often intolerant of their own kind. The diminutive Tennessee Warblers are at times particularly quarrelsome, often chasing each other from the table; yet I have seen as many as eight eating bananas simultaneously, with no display of animosity. Among the Baltimore Orioles, one on the board at a time is the rule; later arrivals usually stand by awaiting their turn, although occasionally two eat together. Such conduct by the warblers and orioles, which travel in loose parties in the winter months, was unexpected. With Summer Tanagers, the attempt to monopolize the table is easier to understand. Each tanager selects an individual territory in which to live during its long sojourn in its winter home; I have watched protracted disputes between two of these migrants who could not agree on boundaries and for hours defied each other with calls or songs and inconsequential chasing, never coming to grips. Even of these unsociable tanagers, several might be in attendance at the same time, but they always took turns on the table instead of eating together, like the more convivial resident tanagers.

The fact that the most consistently selfish or mutually antagonistic of the visitors to the feeder have been migratory birds from the North is not without significance, for those who have operated feeding stations in northern lands have reported more unsocial behavior and attempts to monopolize the food supply than I have witnessed in Costa Rica. Apparently the less strenuous, less hurried life of birds that reside throughout the year in the same locality tends to develop more placid, easygoing dispositions, reflected also in the infrequency or mildness of territorial disputes of many species of the humid tropics. Yet, in spite of a few monopolists and rare clashes among the birds who attend the feast that I spread for them, the residual impression left by many years of observation is that amity and tolerance prevail among them. When I reflect that these birds are classified in different families and even orders, hence differ among themselves as greatly as men, squirrels, horses, and elephants, whereas men, who all of whatever race are classified as a single species, cannot occupy a planet without internecine strife—when I reflect on these things, I confess that the comparison is so unfavorable to my own kind that it puts me to shame.

A large proportion of the Costa Rican birds remain mated throughout the year, and these, as a rule, come to the table in pairs. These constantly mated birds, even the most brilliant of them, show little or no sexual differences in coloration, making it difficult to distinguish the males from the females. But I believe it is a fair assumption that it is generally the male who fills his bill with banana and with solemn gallantry passes it to his lady, who all the while has been helping herself freely from the same abundant source. This nuptial feeding is witnessed chiefly among the little, gemlike tanagers, especially the Speckled or Yellow-browed Tanager, the Silver-throated Tanager, and the larger Blue Tanagers and Palm Tanagers, never among the Scarlet-rumped Black Tanagers. It is most frequent as the breeding season approaches, although by no means confined to this period.

One morning, when our supply of ripe bananas ran short, I saw a cow devour a half-rotten orange, and later I watched some Scarlet-rumped Black Tanagers standing on the ground and pecking into a similar orange, eating the sounder parts of the flesh rather than worms, as far as I could tell by watching through field glasses. These observations gave me an idea. Selecting a ripe, juicy orange, I cut it in half transversely and placed it on the empty board. Hardly had I gone to the porch to watch before a male Scarlet-rumped Black Tanager, who had been looking on from the neighboring orange tree, flew down to the table and started to eat the orange and drink its juice. Soon he was joined by another male, and while the two tried to outstare each other, a female of their kind arrived to sample the orange. Next came some Blue or Red-legged Honeycreepers, then three Golden-masked Tanagers, then a Black-striped Sparrow, a male Green Honeycreeper, and little Tennessee Warblers. For the half hour after I placed the orange on the table, there was a constant succession of visitors, some of whom returned again and again. The shelf was almost as well attended when supplied with oranges as when bananas were available.

Not only did the birds' table provide many hours of entertainment, it greatly helped my effort to make comprehensive studies of the lives of various species of birds. By watching the table, I could trace the gradual change in the birds' appearance as they molted from the dull juvenal plumage to the brighter adult attire. This transformation was most striking in species of which the males are more brilliant than the females, as in the Scarlet-rumped Black Tanager and the Blue Honeycreeper. At the table, I obtained some of my earliest records of the arrival of migratory species from the North and some of my latest dates of their presence before their departure in the spring.

Even more important, the food and protection that the birds received in the garden caused some of them to lose much of their habitual shyness. One of these birds was that charming songster, the Black-striped Sparrow, which not only came to the feeder for bananas but, when I fed the chickens at daybreak, would hop over the lawn to pick up grains of corn. In bushy places I had found many of their roofed nests, containing nearly always two white eggs. But whenever I set up my blind or hid to watch from concealment the activities of the sparrows at these nests, the shy birds would stay away until the unfamiliar object was removed. I tried the usual ruses of setting the blind at a distance from the nest and gradually moving it closer and of screening it with leafy boughs, but in vain. I could make no progress with them, until at last I had Black-striped Sparrows building in the shrubbery close by the house, where I could set a blind on the lawn and, at my convenience, watch the birds attend their nest at a distance of a few yards from my eyes. Other rare birds built where I could watch their nests through the windows of the house. And many of these parents would later bring their young to receive billfuls of banana at the table, thereby enabling me to follow their development for weeks or months after they began to fly.

One of the most interesting observations that I made at the feeder was on the plumage changes of adult, male Blue Honeycreepers. These small, dainty birds have long, slender, slightly downcurved bills. The males are clad in deep blue and black, with turquoise crowns, black and yellow wings, and red legs. The females are olive-green with striped breasts. I had long suspected that, after the breeding season, the adult males molt into a greenish plumage resembling that of the females, but observations made in different parts of Central America were confusing: in the last quarter of the year, males in full nuptial plumage were abundant on the Pacific slope of Costa Rica but formed only a tiny fraction of the population on the Pacific slope of Guatemala. Proof that male Blue Honeycreepers do go into "eclipse" after the breeding season was provided by two individuals who, in different years, continued to become greener while they fed fledglings at the board. From about the end of June until mid-September, no males in perfect breeding plumage are seen in this region, although the adults in fullest eclipse usually bear a few flecks of blue or black on their greenish body plumage. They continue to wear their black and yellow wing feathers. Apparently the eclipse does not last long, for, after September, males in full nuptial attire become increasingly numerous. Some young males do not attain the full breeding plumage until March, but from then until late June, all the males, except those hatched in this interval, are in splendid nuptial dress.

Once we watched a male Blue Honeycreeper repeatedly give banana from the feeder to a fledgling Scarlet-rumped Black Tanager bigger than himself. Another Blue Honeycreeper gave a little food to a young Yellow-green Vireo.

Nearly all the land birds of the more humid parts of tropical America wear the same colors throughout the year. The only other species for which I have sufficient evidence of a pronounced seasonal change in coloration is the Blue-black Grassquit. Among the swarms of these tiny finches that I saw in weedy fields in northern Venezuela in April, May, and June, I noticed none in full nuptial attire. After the first of July, males in the shining breeding plumage became increasingly numerous.

A Census of the Birds

With so much food from nectar-bearing flowers and fruiting trees and a table specially spread for them, with the dense foliage of thorny orange trees to provide safety from their enemies and concealment for their nests, with no cats nor cruel boys with rubber catapults to persecute them, colorful, songful birds abounded in the garden. One December afternoon, while light showers fell, I listed all the birds that I could see through the windows or from the porch without setting foot on the ground. In the hour from three to four o'clock, I recorded thirty species, ranging in size from hummingbirds to parrots. It was hopeless to try to count the multitudinous, shifting individuals.

During the year from September 1, 1943, to August 31, 1944, I tried to find, record, and learn the outcome of all the birds' nests in the garden and the shady pasture in front, extending down to the banks of the creek and of the river into which the former flows almost in front of the house. The area of the census bordered in part on forest or old second-growth woodland, in part on lower thickets of more recent growth, but it did not include these heavy or dense types of tropical vegetation, where a substantial proportion of the birds' nests inevitably elude the most diligent search. Even in the scattered trees and shrubs of the area chosen for systematic searching, some of the smaller, less conspicuous nests doubtless escaped me, but I believe that they were few.

In this area of three and three-quarters acres I found, in the course of the twelve months, eighty-three nests, representing twenty-five species of birds, ranging from pigeons to finches. These nests were, as far as I could tell, attended by forty-nine pairs and two single females, of species in which the male takes no part in nesting. In addition, six male Rufous-tailed Hummingbirds had established their courtship stations in the area and sang every morning before sunrise, except at the height of the dry season. Thus the total breeding population consisted of one hundred and six birds of twenty-six species in three and three-quarters acres, at the remarkably high density of 28.2 breeding birds per acre.

Sixteen years later, I again tried to find all the nests in this same area, from September 1, 1960, to August 31, 1961. In this period, I recorded only forty-five nests of nineteen species. Since the censused area itself had changed little in the interval, I attribute the decline in the number of nesting birds to the deterioration of the wide surrounding region as a habitat, resulting from the rapid increase of the human population, the destruction of the forests, the sterilization of the soil, and the multiplication of boys with catapults.

Despite this decline in the total breeding population, I have continued over the years to find new kinds of birds nesting around our house. After twenty-eight years, the list of species breeding in the three and three-quarters acres has risen to sixty-six, including sixteen kinds of American flycatchers, nine tanagers, seven finches, seven hummingbirds, and three pigeons. The latest addition was the Long-billed Starthroat Hummingbird, whose nest I had sought fruitlessly for years.

I tried to learn how many of the nests in this area were successful. In the four years when I kept the most careful records, I knew the outcome of two hundred and eight nests of thirty-seven species. Eighty-five of these nests, or 41 per cent, produced at least one fledgling. This is a somewhat better record than that made by seven hundred and fifty-six nests of twenty-three species with open or roofed nests (not in holes) in clearings and second growth in various parts of Central America. Of these seven hundred and fifty-six nests, two hundred and seventy-seven, or 37 per cent, produced at least one fledged young. It is a far better record than was made by one hundred and thirty-six open or roofed nests in the forests of El General, of which only thirty-two, or 23.5 per cent, escaped destruction until the young were ready to leave.*

Orchids and Liverworts

To write about a tropical garden without mentioning orchids would seem to some readers like describing a visit to New York without alluding to the skyscrapers. I have so far remained immune to the orchid fever that smites so many residents in a country whose flora includes nearly a thousand described species in this prolific family. I find it hard to understand why a flower which it takes years and special precautions to produce should be considered intrinsically superior to some lovely, delicate blossom that opens within a month or two after the seeds are sown in ordinary garden soil. Although I have never attempted to nurse along slowly maturing orchids, I am always happy to meet them where they grow spontaneously as part of nature's bounty, just as I am delighted to see any other beautiful flower. The rough, moss-covered bark of the Calabash trees in our dooryard makes them excellent hosts for orchids, and a surprising number of the local species grow there spontaneously, along with bromeliads, ferns, and many other epiphytes.

Although many people think of orchids as large and gorgeous blossoms, the majority of the species in this cosmopolitan family have only moderately showy, or even quite inconspicuous, flowers. El General has fewer of the more elegant orchids of horticultural fame than are found in some other parts of Costa Rica. Nevertheless, there is a rich variety of the more modest species, many of which have established themselves in the trees around our house. Throughout the year, dry season and wet, there is a constant succession of orchid flowers.

Some of the more conspicuous orchids bloom in the drier months early in the year. This is the season when chiefly the epiphytic *lluvia de oro* or golden-spray orchids (*Oncidium* spp.) produce myriads of bright yellow flowers, of medium size, on inflorescences two or three yards long. Then, too, the related *Brassia gireoudiana* displays its spidery blossoms, with long, narrow, conspicuously mottled perianth divisions. *Epidendrum imatophyllum* catches the eye from afar with massed pink flowers, high on the arboreal ants' nests where alone I have noticed it in this locality. Two species of *Sobralia* with long, wiry stems and plicate leaves also flower in the dry weather: *S. pleiantha* with large, fragrant, cream-colored flowers and an unidentified species with still larger, mauve and purple blossoms that unfortunately is rare.

*More details are given in "A Breeding Bird Census and Nesting Success in Central America," *The Ibis* 108: 1–16 (1966).

The wet season is the time for the Stanhopeas, large, waxy, pendent blossoms with a pleasant spicy odor and curious hornlike appendages that earn for them the name *toritos* (little bulls). Then one of the showiest of the local orchids, *Pescatorea cerina*, sparingly displays its wide, flattish, waxy, yellow and white blossoms on shady trunks, usually in the woodland. If one looks closely, he can find, on the slender branches of hibiscus and other shrubs, in the wet season as well as in the dry, the charming little *Ionopsis utricularioides*, with lavender and purple florets.

Even during October's torrential rains, many orchids bloom. One October I found in our garden, all blossoming simultaneously, no less than seven native species of the genus *Maxillaria* alone: *neglecta*, with compact clusters of small, orange flowers on pensile, bulbiferous stems that may become four feet long; *oreocharis*, which has small whitish flowers with a deep crimson labellum tipped with dull white; *ctenostachys*, with larger, narrow-petaled, white flowers; the diminutive, white-flowered *vittariifolia*; two unidentified species with white flowers; and, most curious of all, an unnamed species with small brownish florets, of a shade much like that of *Stapelia* flowers. These flowers are carrion-scented like those of *Stapelia*, and, like that African succulent, they apparently depend upon carrion-seeking flies for pollination. This orchid has fanlike clusters of long, narrow leaves, which stand out almost horizontally from the trunks of trees. The inconspicuous, ill-scented flowers are borne beneath the fan, each on a short, slender pedicel that emerges from between the bases of the leaves.

The flowers of orchids lead my thoughts to the foliage of liverworts, which here in the tropics share the same trees with them, for both display some of the most bizarre of vegetable forms. On lank branches of the Calabash trees, as well as on shaded rocks in the pasture, grow great, dirty brown cushions of the liverwort *Frullania*. Beneath each of the dorsal leaves is a minute flask, which fills with water when it rains and retards the desiccation of the plant in dry weather. If one mounts a piece of the *Frullania* in water on a slide and examines it under a microscope, he will presently see a rotifer stick its foreparts out of the mouth of each flask and vibrate its flagella until they resemble two, rapidly revolving, spoked wheels, which set up currents that bear microscopic organisms to the animalcule's mouth. Other liverworts that I have found in the garden have dorsal leaves curiously coiled into bladderlike formations, doubtless also to increase the water-retaining capacity of these humble plants exposed to sun and air. On some of these curled leaves grow tiny multicellular gemmae that fall away and give rise to new plants.

But we must not delay too long in the garden. After all, the enclosure around the house is not my garden but only the annex to my garden.

The garden itself is the adjoining forest, with its bewildering variety of great trees, its tall and graceful palms, its flowering shrubs, its profuse displays of ferns and orchids, all growing in the spots most congenial to them, and, if unmolested by destructive man, maintaining themselves from century to century without laborious human assistance.

14

The Lives of Some Tropical Flowers

A FAMOUS and whimsical physicist once wrote a book on how to tell the birds from the flowers. They have much in common. They are among the fairest adornments of our gardens, as of the wild woodland and the fields, delighting our senses by their lovely forms, their colors, their voices, or their fragrance. Almost equally, they challenge the naturalist to uncover the often closely guarded secrets of their lives, for flowers, although but organs of plants, seem to have lives of their own, far shorter than those of the plants they serve and adorn.

The colors and scents of flowers serve a utilitarian purpose: to advertise to insects, birds, and other small creatures the presence of nectar or abundant pollen, so that these animals, coming to appease their hunger or to provision their hives, will incidentally transfer some of the pollen from flower to flower, thereby paying for their food. The advantage of cross-pollination is that it spreads favorable genes through a population

Headpiece: The orchid *Sobralia pleiantha*. The cream-colored flowers last a single morning.

of plants and that it yields new combinations of genes, which may improve the adaptation of a vegetable species to its habitat or prepare it to invade new habitats. Cross-pollination may promote the vigor of the resulting seedlings, as Charles Darwin demonstrated long ago.

To win the attention of the animal visitors that have these favorable effects, the flowers, one would suppose, need be no more esthetically satisfying than the billboard that blatantly proclaims the advantages of some commercial product. That bright and fragrant blossoms are pleasing to human beings, who are not natural pollinators, seems a fortuitous circumstance; yet flowers are the most universally satisfying of all things that are, or pretend to be, beautiful. People who regard each other's taste in painting, sculpture, or music as barbarous may delight in the same flowers. This fact might make us question some of the newest theories about art.

Natural selection favors the survival of those floral types that most promote the production of seed, especially cross-pollinated seed, and the propagation of the species. Man's selection of his horticultural favorites frequently results in "double" flowers incapable of producing seed, so that the plants must be multiplied vegetatively, as by cuttings, bulbs, or tubers. Yet it is for the sake of their flowers that these sterile plants are cherished and often spread more widely over the earth than any wild species, save perhaps a few aggressive weeds. So that it is still true to say that the survival of any floral type depends upon its success in propagating the species, whether directly, by the production of seed, or indirectly, by enticing men to multiply the plant vegetatively.

Short-lived Flowers

Those who know chiefly or only the flowers that florists sell may get an exaggerated notion of floral longevity. The florist's trade demands flowers that last rather than those that set abundant seed. The lives of most wild flowers are short. On several mornings in late January or early February, when the weather is dry and sunny, great masses of bright yellow adorn the edges of thickets and light woods on our farm, or the fringe of trees along the river. This golden display is provided by a slender, woody vine of the dillenia family, for which I know no name more poetic than its scientific designation, *Davilla kunthii*. It has large, stiff, rough leaves of a deep green color. Of the five sepals of each flower, the outer three are minute. The two inner sepals are much larger and strongly concave; fitting together like the valves of a mussel shell, they form a little hollow sphere, about a quarter of an inch in diameter, which contains the five yellow petals, the very numerous stamens, and the single pistil.

As day dawns, these inner sepals begin to separate, opening the spherical box and exposing the folded yellow petals. The expansion of the flowers is gradual and is hardly completed before eight o'clock, when the generous panicles are crowded with open blossoms. For two hours, the radiant floral mass exhales a delicate fragrance and attracts a murmurous throng of wild bees, busily filling the "baskets" on their hindlegs with pollen, and a variety of other insects. By ten o'clock, the petals are raining down in a golden shower. By half past ten or eleven, nearly all have fallen. Now the two inner sepals begin to close around the withered stamens and the pistil, which swells to a little seed-bearing pod within its furry spherical box.

Among the most ephemeral of flowers are those of certain palms. The inflorescences of the Pejibaye palm are borne at the top of the slender trunk, just below the spreading crown of plumy fronds. Each inflorescence develops within a tightly closed spathe which, like the trunk and leaves, bristles with long, sharp, black spines. Finally the boat-shaped spathe splits lengthwise, releasing a many-branched, white inflorescence or spadix. Mixed together on each cordlike branch are flowers of two kinds, male and female. The stigmas of the latter bear a slight secretion and seem to be receptive as soon as the spathe bursts. The far more numerous staminate flowers remain closed until late in the day. If the spadix escapes in the afternoon, these flowers do not open until the afternoon of the next day; if the inflorescence is released during the night or forenoon, they expand in the afternoon of the same day. Between 4:45 and 5:15 P.M., the three little, waxy-white petals separate, exposing six short stamens, which promptly shed their pollen, not too late in the day to attract multitudes of small, stingless bees, who busily collect the abundant pollen and seem to be the chief pollinators. The life of these male flowers is very short: about half an hour after anthesis, they are falling in a steady shower. Those that persist after dark are sometimes visited by many small beetles, who doubtless supplement the work of the bees as pollinators. Less than two hours after opening, the majority of the staminate flowers have fallen. By this time, the stigmas of the female flowers are discolored and seem no longer receptive.

The small staminate flowers are produced in vast numbers. From one inflorescence, I collected two quarts of them. The activity of this great floral mass generates much heat. A thermometer stuck into the midst of a spadix, just bursting out of its envelope in the evening, registered 97 degrees Fahrenheit, which was 20 degrees above the temperature of the surrounding air. On another evening, an expanding inflorescence was at 91 degrees, when the air temperature was 74 degrees. Plunged into a mass of newly fallen male flowers caught in a bag, the thermometer rose to 104 degrees, 30 degrees above the air temperature. Next morning, these flowers were still generating heat and were 18 degrees warmer than the air. The inflorescences of palms rival those of certain large terrestrial aroids as producers of heat. The Pejibaye palm flowers chiefly in April and May. A single trunk may bear up to a dozen inflorescences, which expand at intervals of a few days, sometimes two on the same day. The edible fruit ripens after three or four months, mostly in August and September.

Because the stigmas of the female Pejibaye flowers are receptive before the male flowers of the same inflorescence shed their pollen, the latter may be unable to fertilize the former. Once in March we found a large bunch of Pejibaye fruits—an out-of-season treat. Of normal size, these fruits were all seedless, although the main crop of the palm that bore them, produced in July and August, always consisted of fruits with seeds. At the time when this spadix flowered, toward the end of the preceding year, there were probably no other flowering Pejibaye palms nearby to provide pollen for it. Failing to be cross-pollinated, the female flowers proceeded to form seedless fruits—as the chief cultivated varieties of bananas regularly do.

Although male flowers of the Coconut do not last much longer than those of the Pejibaye, the opening of those in a single inflorescence is spread over a much longer interval. Beginning as soon as the branched spadix escapes its spathe, some of the yellowish or greenish staminate flowers expand daily for the next three or four weeks. About the time the last of these flowers drop, the much larger pistillate flowers scattered along the same spadix branches push their stigmas out from between the six perianth divisions that closely invest them, ready for pollination. At about the same time, from three weeks to a month after the escape of this spadix, another spadix on the same tree emerges, and its earliest male flowers release their pollen. This timing makes it possible for the pistillate flowers of one inflorescence to be pollinated by the staminate flowers of the next younger inflorescence of the same palm, although they are not likely to receive pollen from their own spadix. Both kinds of flowers secrete nectar, which attracts stingless bees and small wasps. The flowers of certain other palms attract insects by their exquisite fragrance, as Richard Spruce discovered along the Amazon and in the Andes long ago.

The flowers of the mallow family are noted for their short lives. A weed of northern fields is known as the Flower-of-an-Hour. The low, wiry broomweeds that abound in weedy tropical fields and furnish brooms for humble cabins also blossom briefly; the small, yellow flowers of one of them, *Sida acuta*, open around eleven o'clock on sunny days and close about three hours later.

Delicate herbs of the figwort family likewise have evanescent flowers. In lightly shaded pastures, the little white blossoms of *Stemodia verticillata* open between eight and ten o'clock, and most have closed by three in the afternoon, after five or six hours of full anthesis. The tiny, two-lipped, white flowers of *Vandellia diffusa*, which grows prostrate on our lawn, open slightly later in the forenoon and are mostly closed by the middle of the afternoon, after remaining expanded for about five hours. In the same family, *Bacopa salzmanni*, a slender, delicate herb that thrives in a marshy depression in a neighbor's pasture, displays its pale violet flowers for less than four hours on sunny mornings.

On the exposed hillside behind our house, the low herb *Sauvagesia erecta* (Ochnaceae) expands its pretty little flowers around daybreak; by midday it has shed nearly all its white petals, after five or six hours of full anthesis. These are only a few examples of the transitory flowers that surround us here in the tropics. One of the problems of the conscientious botanical collector is to dry his specimens before most of the flowers fall, as has already been told in the case of the Clusia that grew upon the fragrant mountaintop.

None of the short-lived flowers mentioned above open a second time. After their brief day of glory, the corollas fall or shrivel; or, if it fails to be pollinated, the whole flower may drop. Some flowers, however, expand repeatedly if they fail to be fertilized. A shrubby Cestrum, of the nightshade family, sprang up spontaneously in our garden. In late June, its slender branches were heavily laden with long, narrow, tubular flowers of a greenish yellow color. They began to open around sunset and continued slowly to expand while daylight faded. By seven o'clock, when it was quite dark, they were fully open and exhaled a rich perfume that attracted many moths. Throughout the night, they remained open and fragrant, but as it grew light, the short corolla lobes began to fold inward and upward, a slow process that was not completed until about eight o'clock in the morning.

For ten consecutive nights, this Cestrum diffused its delicate fragrance through our dooryard. Practically all of the myriad, crowded flower buds on the bush had opened on the first night. After a few days, some, evidently having been pollinated, began to fall, so that each successive night there were fewer flowers, but the remnant that survived longest opened and closed about ten times. This same shrub blossomed again in late October, when it bore a few white berries from the earlier flowering. Now the weather was extremely wet, and the corollas opened, in diminishing numbers, for only eight nights.

Orchids are noted for the durability of their flowers, which may last for weeks or even months if they are not pollinated. Some of the multitudinous species of orchids, however, have short-lived flowers. On trees and shaded rocks about our farm grow many plants of *Sobralia pleiantha*, each a compact cluster of thin, wiry stems about two feet high, sometimes as many as fifty together springing from a cushion of intricately entangled roots. In the dry days of late January and early February, these orchids display their cream-colored blossoms, about two inches across. These flowers begin to open at dawn or slightly earlier. By sunrise or soon after, they are fully expanded and shed a delicate perfume on the fresh morning air. In contrast to many other Sobralias, several flowers may open simultaneously on the same stem. By half past ten or eleven o'clock, they start to fold up, and soon after midday all have closed. Whether or not it is fertilized, each flower blooms but a few hours, and it never opens a second time.

On rocks in the same shady riverside pasture in front of our house grows another Sobralia, with thin grasslike stems, narrow plicate leaves, and slightly smaller flowers that are white, with a finely fringed, pale yellow lip. Sobralia is a genus troublesome to taxonomists; and in vain I have begged orchid specialists to name this species, which has a most interesting habit. Although *pleiantha* opens its blossoms daily over a period of several weeks, until the supply of buds is exhausted, this smaller Sobralia blooms only on special, widely separated days, when all the dozen or so clusters of plants that I had under observation opened their flowers simultaneously, generally one to a stem. In contrast to *pleiantha*, it blossoms in the rainy season, and the flowers open later in the morning; few are fully expanded before eight o'clock. They remain open, diffusing a delicate aroma, through the remainder of the day, even under the afternoon downpours, to fold up as night falls and never expand again.

In 1962, these orchids flowered on August 22, on an unrecorded date in early September, on September 29, October 22, November 5, November 25, and November 29. In November, the flowerings were sparse and some plants did not participate in them; but on the four days in August, September, and October practically all the plants in the area bloomed abundantly, and between these dates scarcely any flowers could be found. Such synchronized flowering has been recorded in a number of tropical trees and smaller plants. It is evidently controlled by changes in the weather, which in the case of my Sobralia were too subtle to detect without more meteorological data than were available to me.

The Color and Texture of Flowers

Flowers owe their beauty to their form, their color, and their texture. The forms of flowers, regular or at times bizarre, are depicted in many sumptuously illustrated books and described in minute detail in works on taxonomy and morphology. The colors of flowers, with their endless variety of shades, are produced by only a few fundamentally different pigments. Yellow, and at times orange, are caused by carotin and related lipochrome pigments. These yellow or yellowish pigments are commonly borne in chromoplasts, minute solid bodies that are usually roundish or somewhat elongated but occasionally are long and threadlike. Those of the latter form are relatively rare; of the many flowers that I have examined, I have found them only in the ray florets of the scrambling composite *Hidalgoa ternata*. Even in this plant, they are not found throughout the petals but only in the upper epidermis, where they occur in compact skeins; in deeper tissues of the same petals, the chromoplasts are rounded or slightly elongated, as in most flowers. The yellow pigments contained in chromoplasts are stable, resisting change by weak acids and bases, which alter or destroy most other floral colors.

These other floral colors, ranging from blue and violet of many shades to pink, red, orange, and sometimes even yellow, are due to anthocyan dissolved in the cell sap rather than concentrated in solid plastids. Anthocyan also imparts color, other than the green of chlorophyll, to many leaves, fruits, and other vegetable organs. This pigment is sensitive to acids and bases, which when weak change its shade in a striking manner and when slightly stronger destroy all color. When I mounted a fragment of the violet flower of *Thunbergia erecta* in lime water and placed it under a microscope, I watched it change to bright blue, then bright green, which soon faded to pale yellowish green. In the strongly acid juice of Don Chico's tangerine mentioned in chapter 13, the violet of the Thunbergia petal turned purplish or reddish; then slowly all color vanished. The bright red of a hibiscus petal changed to violet and then bright blue in lime water. When the same fragment of tissue was placed in acid juice, it regained its original redness.

When a fragment of the epidermis of a petal colored by anthocyan is mounted on a microscope slide and treated with an acid or base, the chemical penetrates into neighboring cells at different rates, producing striking and beautiful effects. In a purple or violet flower placed in lime water, purple, blue, green, and yellow, each in several shades, may sometimes be seen simultaneously in cells not far apart. A red petal may, by the same means, be converted into patches of purple, blue, bright green, and yellowish green. In a weak acid, such a petal may be made to display, at one time, shades of red, purple, and pink.

The majority of flowers contain only one kind of pigment, either a yellow or orange lipochrome or the more versatile anthocyan. But very many contain both kinds. They may occur in the same cells, jointly producing a color that neither could give alone, often a delightful shade of orange, as in the broad ray florets of *Hidalgoa ternata*. Or the two kinds of pigments may be situated in different regions of the corolla, which in consequence displays two, or rarely more, colors. This often occurs in trumpet-shaped flowers, in which the interior of the tube may be colored differently from the lobes; such flowers may be blue with a yellow throat or yellow with a dark "eye." Finally, there may be temporal changes in the amount of one of the pigments, causing the flower to change color with age. When this occurs, it seems usually to be the anthocyan that increases or decreases in amount or perhaps merely alters its shade in response to variations in the acidity of the tissue; the more stable lipochrome is less often involved in mutations of floral color.

An excellent example of such changes with age is provided by *Lantana camara*, a widespread, weedy, tropical shrub of the verbena family. The small florets are borne in flattish heads that are orange in the center, where the unopened buds are situated. Around this is a circle of bright yellow, containing freshly opened flowers with yellow chromoplasts in their cells. At the outside of the head is a zone of orange, composed of older florets. As the blossoms age, a reddish-purple soluble pigment appears in the epidermal cells and deepens the yellow to orange. The small tubular flowers of the shrub *Hamelia patens*, of the madder family, likewise contain both yellow chromoplasts and soluble anthocyan. Pale orange when they first expand, they deepen to red as the red anthocyan in their superficial tissues increases.

The beauty of flowers depends not only on their form and color but likewise on the texture of their surfaces—on what we might call their optical texture, which determines whether they will glitter like glass or enamel or glow softly and warmly like richly colored velvet or plush. Optical texture depends largely on structural features that escape the naked eye but are revealed by a good microscope. Finding hardly anything on this subject in botanical books that dealt at length with the forms, the pigments, and the modes of pollination of flowers, I decided to investigate it for myself.

Examined in cross section under a microscope, a petal somewhat resembles a foliage leaf, from which it was evidently derived in the course of evolution, but there are important differences. Both faces of the petal are covered by an epidermis, the outer wall of which is closely invested by the cuticle, which is waxy and relatively impervious to water. Without this thin protective pellicle, flowers would promptly wither in the morning sunshine. Without it they would also quickly absorb water or a colored solution.

In surface view, the epidermal cells of many corollas have irregular, wavy outlines; their lateral walls alternately project and recede, making embayments that are filled by the projecting arms of adjacent cells. Occasionally, as in the bright yellow petals of *Jussiaea suffruticosa* of the evening primrose family, the sinuses are not occupied by the lobes of neighboring cells but by air spaces that are separated from the outer air by the continuous cuticle. In other flowers, the epidermal cells have angular or zigzag rather than sinuous outlines. Their re-entrant angles may be continued inward as anticlinal flanges or plates, which project into the cell cavity and strengthen the cell. In yet other flowers, the epidermal cells are rectangular, polygonal, or somewhat rounded in surface view.

In many flowers, the epidermis lacks stomata or breathing pores, but others have them. In some species, the stomata of the corollas appear to be imperfectly developed and functionless, but in others they have chlorophyll in their guard cells and are apparently functional. The presence of chlorophyll in the guard cells is remarkable, as this pigment may not occur elsewhere in the same corollas. Stomata are not, as one might suppose, restricted to the more primitive types of flowers, for they occur in the corollas of certain orchids, plants of the madder family such as coffee, and even composites.

The corollas of flowers lack the palisade layer of close-set, elongate cells characteristic of foliage leaves; it would be useless to them, since they do not carry on photosynthesis. The whole tissue between the two epidermal layers of a typical petal is composed of large, thin-walled cells of extremely irregular outline, with many projecting arms that reach across air spaces to join similar projections from neighboring cells. The expanded tissues that display floral colors are built with the greatest economy of materials. The thinness of the walls of the cells of a corolla, their irregular form, and the great development of air spaces make a tissue of the utmost delicacy, capable of preserving its form so long as the component cells remain turgid with water but promptly collapsing when its task is done (Fig. 1).

The pigments which impart color to flowers, whether dissolved in the cell sap or in solid plastids, are contained chiefly, or in many instances wholly, in the epidermal cells, with smaller amounts sometimes present in the underlying tissues. Yellow chromoplasts often occur in the deeper layers of cells as well as in the epidermis.

The optical structure of flowers is evidently governed by two principles: the avoidance of superficial reflection or of highlights and the maximum penetration of light into the pigment-bearing cells. Since floral pigments are not situated on the surface, like the paint on a house, but are separated from the outside by a cell wall covered by a waxy cuticle, it is evident that light reflected from the surface of a petal will not be affected by its pigments; hence the two foregoing principles are complementary aspects of the same principle. The maximum penetration of light ensures the greatest richness or saturation of color that a given amount of pigment can produce. The avoidance of highlights or glossiness ensures maximum contrast with the foliage leaves among which flowers are usually displayed. These leaves often have a smooth, glossy upper surface that reflects much light. The light that is reflected, without penetration, from the surface of flowers and that of the surrounding green

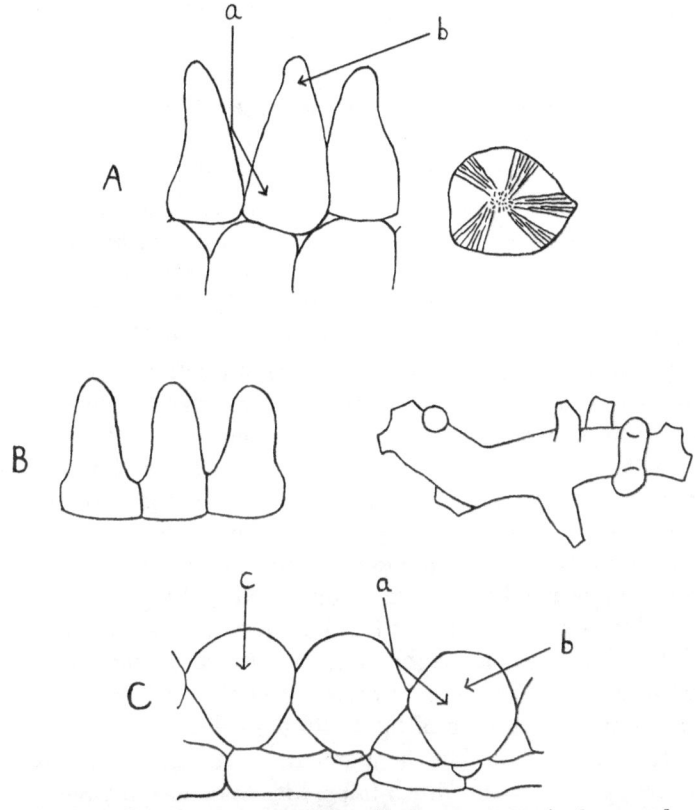

1. Details of corollas. A. Orange Poró (*Erythrina poeppigiana*): three epidermal cells of the standard in profile and, at right, a cell in surface view, showing the cuticular striations. B. Yellow Allamanda (*Allamanda cathartica*): three epidermal cells of a corolla lobe in profile and, at right, a cell from the central tissue, showing eleven arms that connect with projections from neighboring cells, leaving air spaces between them. C. Red Impatiens (*Impatiens sultani*): globular cells of the upper epidermis, filled with light red sap. In A and C, the arrows show how protruding epidermal cells act as light-traps. Very oblique rays (b), which would glance off the surface of a flat epidermis, enter the sides of the protruding cells. Perpendicular rays (a), reflected from the sides of a bulging cell, may penetrate a neighboring cell. If they strike the apex of a bulge, perpendicular rays (c) enter directly. All figures greatly enlarged.

leaves has much the same composition—that of the incident rays—for both are covered by a colorless cuticle.

Indeed, the highlights on all glossy objects, however they are colored, have much the same silvery aspect. If one holds before himself several round lead pencils of different colors—as red, yellow, and green—he will notice along the side of each a bright streak or highlight, situated on that part of the circumference that reflects the greatest amount of light to his eyes. The colors of the highlights of the several pencils do not contrast nearly as much as do the colors of the surrounding parts, which are deeper and richer.

Widely distributed among flowers are two modifications of the epidermis of corollas that strongly affect their optical properties, increasing the penetration of the light rays and diminishing highlights. The first of these features is the outward bulge of the epidermal cells. Although in some petals the outer walls of these cells are nearly flat, frequently they are more or less convex. In many flowers, they are hemispheric or dome-shaped; in some they are conical; and in yet others they project as long papillae. These convex or projecting outer walls of the epidermal cells act as light traps to increase the penetration of the incident rays. The influx of light from air into a body of higher refractive index is greatest when the incident beam is perpendicular to the surface; the more oblique the ray becomes, the greater the proportion of the light that is reflected without entering the body. (To demonstrate this, hold a mat black surface between your eyes and a source of light, so that the reflected rays strike the surface at grazing incidence; it no longer appears black.) But rays strongly oblique to the surface of a petal as a whole may be more or less perpendicular to the sloping sides of a projecting cell and so enter it. Moreover, rays that strike these projections obliquely may be reflected to, and enter, a neighboring projection, as shown in the accompanying diagram. In these ways, the strongly protuberant epidermal cells increase the penetration of light into the cells.

Of the sunlight that reaches the pigment, certain colors or wavelengths are absorbed, while others, which impart its color to the flower, are sent forth again. To attract the attention of an insect or bird that may pollinate the flower, or of a man, these re-emitted rays must find their way through the epidermal wall and the cuticle to the outer air. If they strike the outer surface of the petal too obliquely, they may be reflected inward again—the phenomenon of total internal reflection. But if this limiting surface projects strongly, as in a hemispheric or conical epidermal cell, the ray reflected from one side may impinge upon the opposite side at more nearly a right angle and so emerge into the outer air.

The second widespread feature of corollas that greatly modifies their optical properties is a striate cuticle. If a thin cross section of a petal is examined under high magnification, the outer walls of the epidermal cells are often seen to be covered with low ridges. In surface view of a preparation of a floral epidermis, with careful adjustment of the illumination, the courses of these ridges may be followed. When the outer walls of the epidermal cells are flat or bulge only slightly, the striations may be roughly parallel; they follow a nearly straight or irregularly sinuous course that is continuous from cell to cell. Many epidermal cells are both elevated and striate, and, in this case, the low ridges often radiate from the apex of the projection, forming a striking pattern. Cuticular striae are neither a universal nor an exclusive feature of corollas; many flowers lack them, and they not infrequently occur on vegetative organs, including the foliage and stems of many plants. But I have found such striations more common on corollas than on leaves. They help to make the surface optically rough and prevent highlights, and they may also increase the penetration of light to the pigment within the cells.

A primary source of light, such as a flame, diffuses its rays impartially in all directions, whereas a colored surface that is not self-luminous, especially if it be glossy, sends most of its borrowed light to the side opposite that from which it comes. By minimizing superficial reflection and maximizing the penetration of the incident rays, flowers simulate self-luminescence, diffusing their rich colors on every side, so that they may catch the eye of any pollen-bearing bird or insect that comes near. Their soft, velvety texture often contrasts with the glossiness of the foliage around them, increasing the loveliness of the plant as a whole.

In the deep shade of tropical forest, one sometimes finds leaves, especially those of young plants, which in richness of color and softness of texture approach, although they do not equal, the corollas of flowers. It is interesting to find that these velvety shade leaves often show the same modifications of the epidermal cells that are so frequent in flowers: strongly bulging outer walls, which may be either smooth or covered with striations. When the protruding walls are rounded and smooth, they act as lenses to focus the incident light deeper in the cell, as one may demonstrate beneath the microscope. Some botanists, including the German physiological anatomist G. Haberlandt, have concluded that these lens-like cells are sensory organs and that, guided by them, the leaf adjusts its position until the bright spot falls on the center of the inner wall of each of the cells of the upper epidermis, in which orientation the leaf receives the greatest amount of the available light. But in some of these velvety shade leaves, the protuberances are covered with diverging cuticular ridges, which diminish or destroy the lens effect. Probably the projecting epidermal cells simply serve as light traps to increase the penetration to the chlorophyll of the dim illumination that reaches these low plants through clouds of foliage high above them. I cannot explain why these shade leaves should be so richly colored with purple or red, unless the anthocyan pigment somehow increases the efficiency of photosynthesis in the weak light, as the red or brown complementary pigments of seaweeds that flourish at depths where light is dim are held to do.

Floral Behavior of the Aguacatillo

Naturalists have described many arrangements, which if thought out by human minds would be called "ingenious," to promote cross-pollination, or the fertilization of a flower by pollen from another plant. The most obvious of these is the separation of the sexes so that some plants of the species bear only staminate, pollen-producing flowers, while others bear only pistillate, seed-producing flowers. Such dioecious flowers are found in many species of the most diverse families. When, as frequently occurs, the flowers are monoecious, those of both kinds being borne on the same plant, their separation in space or in time of opening decreases the probability of close-pollination. Even when the flowers are bisexual or perfect, provision is often made to prevent self-pollination. The pollen may be shed before the stigma of the same flower becomes receptive, as happens in many composites, or else the stigma may mature before the anthers and wither before the pollen of the same flower escapes—the phenomenon known as dichogamy.

In yet other species with bisexual flowers, two varieties occur on different plants: on some the stamens are long and the pistil is short, whereas on others all the flowers have short stamens and long pistils. When a butterfly or bee gathers nectar in a field where the two kinds of plants of the same species grow mixed together, pollen will be deposited on different parts of its proboscis by the stamens of different lengths; thus it is likely to transfer the grains from the long stamens of one plant to the long pistil of another and from the short stamens of this second kind of flower to the short pistils of the first kind.

Of all the innumerable arrangements to promote cross-pollination, that exhibited by the avocado and related trees is among the most remarkable. Indeed, it is so improbable that it is difficult to believe. I first read about the floral behavior of the avocado in a paper by T. Ralph Robinson and E. M. Savage, while I worked at the United Fruit Company's experimental station near Almirante in western Panama. When I discussed the matter with the horticulturist in charge of the station, he doubted whether native avocado trees in the tropics exhibited the complex pattern that these authors had observed on named, vegetatively propagated varieties in Florida. His scepticism stimulated me to make observations on eight trees, apparently of seedling origin, growing on the grounds of the station, with the result that I found four that exhibited perfectly the double period of anthesis that had first been described by A. B. Stout, and four other trees that behaved erratically.

The avocado belongs to the laurel family, which is poorly represented in temperate North America (where its most familiar representative is the Sassafras) but in tropical America contains a bewildering variety of tall forest trees, some of which yield excellent timber. After my early observations in Panama, I was eager to learn whether any wild cousins of the avocado have the same complex floral behavior, but, unfortunately, most of them hold their flowers far beyond reach. Perhaps because of this circumstance, I have discovered only a single relative of the avocado whose flowers behave in much the same way. This is the Aguacatillo, a tree of medium size that often springs up in pastures and clearings, where it forms a shapely, rounded crown of glossy, ovate or elliptical leaves. There are a number of these trees on the hillside behind our house.

Here in El General, the leaves of the Aguacatillo or "Little Avocado" turn red and fall in the dry month of February. Soon the trees cover themselves anew with fresh foliage of vivid green, and then they begin to flower, usually in March. The dull yellowish flowers, much like those of the avocado in appearance and structure, are borne in loose panicles that spring from the axils of the full-grown new leaves. Each flower opens twice, on consecutive days. During the first opening, the simple stigma is receptive, standing up prominently in the center of the flower, while the nine stamens, their anthers still tightly closed, lie flat against the three small petals and three still smaller sepals (Fig. 2). On the second, the stamens stand up conspicuously, and the four anther sacs of each open by means of uplifted valves; the stigma is discolored and apparently no longer receptive. Thus at the first opening the flower is, functionally, purely pistillate or female, while at the second it is staminate or male.

If all the Aguacatillo trees in the neighborhood followed exactly the same schedule for their two openings, pollination would be difficult or impossible. But if one examines a number of Aguacatillo trees scattered about the same locality, he finds two classes that differ, as far as I can discover, only in the periodicity of their flowers. Class A comprises trees whose flowers open for the first time at dawn, remain expanded with receptive stigmas but closed anthers for four or five hours, then close late in the morning. Twenty-four hours later, these same flowers open for the second time and shed their pollen. They have, in many cases, already been fertilized during their first expansion. After remaining open for three or four hours, they close in the middle of the afternoon, never to open again.

On trees of class B, the flowers open for the first time late in the morning, while class A flowers are expanding for the second time and preparing to shed their pollen. In the afternoon, these class B flowers close, to open again early on the following day, ready to supply pollen to a

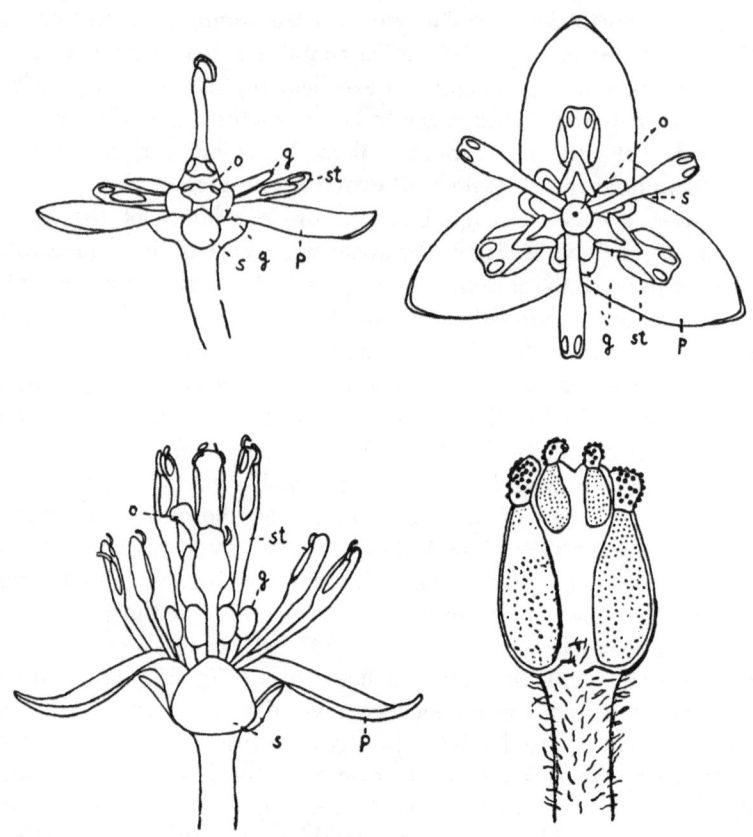

2. Flowers of the Aguacatillo (*Persea skutchii*). Above: a flower in the first opening, with anthers still closed, viewed from the side and, at right, from above (X5). Below: a flower in the second opening, with erected stamens and open anthers (X5); at right, an anther showing the four uplifted valves (greatly enlarged). g, nectar gland; o, pistil; p, petal; s, sepal; st, stamen.

new set of class A flowers. Thus the two classes of flowers reciprocate, class B providing pollen for class A in the early morning, class A yielding pollen for class B in the late forenoon and early afternoon. The many small insects that come to sip the nectar secreted by the large floral glands, and doubtless visit indiscriminately flowers of both classes in neighboring trees, carry the pollen from one to the other. Because all the flowers of the same tree open and close almost simultaneously, self- or close-pollination appears to be rare.

Although complicated, this system of cross-pollination is efficient; many fruits are set, to ripen in May and June. Hardly larger than a pea, each is a miniature avocado, with a single seed surrounded by thin, green flesh. Birds of many kinds swallow the glossy, leaden-gray fruits and spread their seeds far and wide over the open country. The Aguacatillo has been introduced into the United States for trial as a disease-resistant rootstock on which improved varieties of the avocado can be grafted.

Aquatic Flowers of Terrestrial Plants

Among the many curious flowers of the tropics are those which, although borne on terrestrial plants, develop bathed in water. One of the best-known examples is the Flame-of-the-Forest or African Tulip Tree, now widely planted in tropical America for its great, flamboyant trumpet flowers. The corolla, stamens, and pistil develop within a large, curved, brown, furry calyx, tightly closed and full of clear, secreted water, which squirts out if the bud is rudely pressed. Finally the calyx splits along one side to release the red corolla.

Here and there along the edges of the forest in this valley, a slender vine of the acanthus family, *Mendoncia lindavii*, forms a dense green

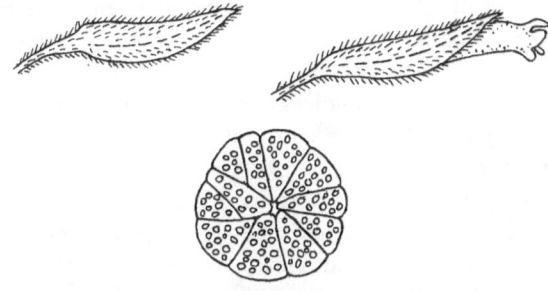

3. Water-filled flower buds of the vine *Mendoncia lindavii*. Above: a bud enclosed by two furry bracts tightly joined along their edges; at right, an open flower (X½). Below: a water-secreting gland from the inner side of a bract (greatly enlarged).

tapestry adorned with tubular red flowers, each peeping out from between two long, narrow, furry bracts. Before the bud opens, these bracts are joined along their edges, forming a tight vessel in which the flower develops, surrounded by clear, colorless, almost tasteless water. This fluid is secreted by mushroom-shaped, multicellular glands that are thickly scattered over the inner surface of the bracts (Fig. 3). The immersion of the flowers evidently prevents injurious premature visits by insects.

While the flowers of the Flame-of-the-Forest tree and the Mendoncia vine develop in tightly closed vessels, other kinds mature under water in open containers. An example of this is provided by *Tussacia friedrichsthaliana* of the gesneria family. This perennial herb thrives in rich soil with abundant humus, especially on rocky, lightly shaded banks; it does not grow in the deep shade of heavy forest but it is at home in our coffee plantation. From a depressed, globular corm that persists underground from year to year, a succulent green shoot springs up at the beginning of the rainy season. It reaches a height of a foot or two and bears pairs of large, lush, dentate leaves. The stem is crowned by a cluster of green, cuplike calyces that are nearly always full of clear, tasteless water.

Since this plant blooms when showers fall almost every afternoon, one might suppose that this is simply rain water that the upwardly directed cups have caught and held. However, if one shakes out all the water, then arranges a roof over the plant so that no rain can reach it, he will find the green cups full again after two or three days. This water is evidently secreted by the stalked glands that are abundant on the inner surface of the calyx, especially near the bottom. Bathed in this fluid, the inner organs of the flower develop, and, in due time, the pretty, inch-long, tubular corolla, deep yellow streaked with red, pushes up into the air. Each flower lasts two days. During the first morning, the anthers shed their pollen while the stigma remains small and apparently unreceptive. By the morning of the second day, the stigma has enlarged and opened, ready for pollination. On the third day, the corolla withers. The fruits develop within the water-filled calyces.

In a number of "tank" bromeliads, the whole inflorescence develops beneath the rain water that collects within the rosettes of closely appressed leaves. Another terrestrial plant with aquatic flowers is one of the most beautiful of the wild plantains, *Heliconia elongata*, or *H. bihai*, as it is often called. This giant herb thrives in abandoned clearings and along the banks of rivers and lagoons in the wet Caribbean lowlands of Central America. The blades of its great, gracefully arching, light green leaves attain ten feet in length by one in breadth. In the midst of them, at the top of the short false stem formed by their overlapping bases, stands the flattened, upright inflorescence. Its thick, fleshy bracts are strongly folded, and each of their exposed faces is highly colored, with a light red center that pales outwardly to orange, which in turn is narrowly bordered with green.

These cupped bracts retain the rain that falls into them and are nearly always well filled, forming little aerial pools in which the flower buds develop (Fig. 4). The mature flower is a slender, watertight tube about two and a half inches long. During the night before anthesis, it stretches up until its green tip stands above the water, while the white lower part remains submerged. Attracted by the bright inflorescence, long-billed hummingbirds, especially the big, brown Long-tailed Hermits, visit the flowers, plunging their bills down the narrow tubes to extract the nectar generously secreted below the water level within the base of each. In the absence of pollinating agents, the flowers are self-pollinated and set abundant seeds, as I proved by enclosing several inflorescences in bags in Guatemala.

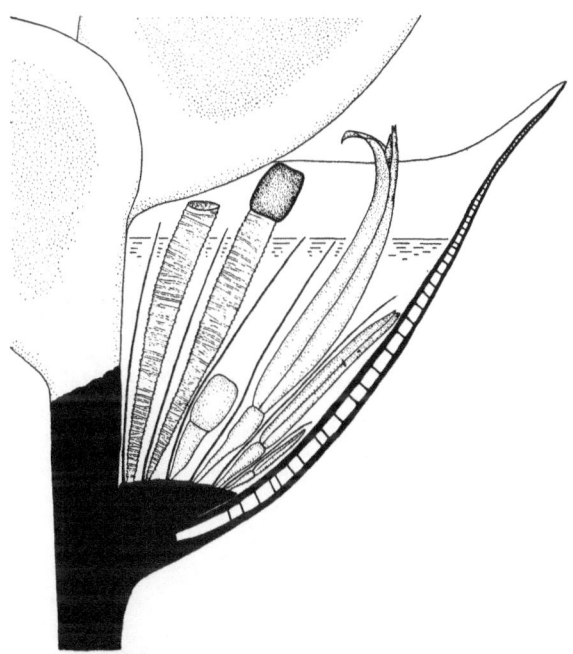

4. Aquatic flowers of a wild plantain (*Heliconia elongata*). A side of a primary bract has been cut away, revealing, from right to left, two submerged flower buds, an open flower with emergent tip, a submerged developing fruit, an exposed ripe fruit, and an elongated pedicel from which the fruit has fallen. Severed tissue is shown in black (X⅔).

The fruits, like the flowers, develop under the water, which is fouled by the decaying floral parts and soon swarms with small aquatic life, including many larvae of drone flies and mosquitos. As it matures, the white berry takes on a lavender tint, which deepens to rich cobalt blue as it is pushed upward into the air by the rapid stretching of the thick pedicel that supports it. The glossy blue berries, each containing three hard, rough seeds, are sought by a variety of birds, including Purple Gallinules. Not content to wait until the ripe berries are exposed for them by the elongation of their stalks, the gallinules tear apart the thick, fleshy bracts to reach those that are still submerged and perhaps also to capture the larvae that wriggle in the water. Along the banks of lagoons where gallinules live, the inflorescences of the Heliconia are often severely damaged by these birds. But what a lovely sight the Purple Gallinule makes, as with its long yellow toes it grasps the gaily colored bracts and tears them with its red bill, meanwhile exposing the white feathers beneath its short, uplifted tail!

15

The River

FORESTS are the living vestment of our mother earth, a utilitarian garment essential to her health and well-being—for when stripped of this attire her sensitive skin and flesh are chafed away by rain and wind—yet withal a splendid robe embroidered with the delicate tracery of foliage and the bright loveliness of flowers. The deep plutonic rocks are her skeleton, the soil her tender flesh, the ocean her vast heart, the rivers her veins through which circulates her precious lifeblood. But the little babbling rills and the clamorous mountain torrents are her tongues, which sing ceaselessly to her multitudinous children, assuring them that in spite of her immense burden of years she is not only alive and well but still young and vigorous, quite able to support her varied progeny. And as the physician gauges his patient's health by examining his tongue, so earth's liquid tongues reveal her condition: if they are pure and trans-

Headpiece: Río Peñas Blancas. Its cold waters rush down from Costa Rica's highest mountain.

parent, she is in a sound and flourishing state; if they are opaque with silt and debris, she is sick and wasting away.

In my travels about tropical America, I had traversed many miles of territory where the earth was sick, shorn of her protective garment of vegetation, her streams laden with mud that betrayed her impaired health. But at Los Cusingos I had found an area where she displayed all the symptoms of exuberant vitality. Her sylvan robe, although torn here and there by the clearings of the early settlers, was still sufficiently intact to protect her most vital parts. The Peña Blanca River that formed my eastern boundary ran clear and pure. Woodland and river together invited me to come and stay, to live healthily where the earth itself was healthy.

I was not greatly distressed by the countless rocks that littered all those lower and more fertile parts of the farm where the river had once flowed. If on land the stones were mute and lifeless encumbrances, deterrent to agriculture, in the river bed the boulders were too precious to be spared. They gave the stream its wild beauty, creating the rapids and the white foaming waters that revealed the current's vital force. They were the strings on which the rushing waters played their ceaseless tune, low and soothing when the stream was shrunken in the dry season, but when torrential rains fell on the hills, rising to a fierce insistent roaring, with overtones of deep rumbling as of distant thunder, caused by the rolling and shifting and striking together of the boulders in the channel.

The myriad rocks that littered the land and the river bed, giving the valley its rugged charm and its living voice, made it unfit to support an opulent human culture, expressing itself in art, literature, and science. But I am not one of those who assume that the fulfillment of the evolutionary process depends on a single species of animal, that earth is solicitous of the welfare of just one of her countless kinds of children. To me it was deeply satisfying to know that here, at least, the earth, our old mother, was still in her prime of health and vigor, strong to nourish and support her brood, even if those she chiefly favored in this particular valley were other than the human kind.

Those circumstances which are the constant accompaniment of our life, the ground and support of our being, seldom obtrude upon our consciousness save as they are altered in quality or intensity or as we are suddenly deprived of them. So it is with the air we breathe, so with those living associates most necessary to our happiness and well-being; and so, as days lengthened into months and months into years, it became with the voice of the river beside which I dwelt. Although the tympana of my ears constantly vibrated to its notes, for hours together I would remain unaware of this persistent undertone of my life. But a breeze that wafted the sound more strongly to my ears, a break in an absorbing occupation that held the mind away from its immediate environment, or the increasing volume of sound that accompanied the swelling of the stream beneath the heavy afternoon downpours—all these would revive my awareness of my cheerful companion, the river. I was always grateful for these reminders of its proximity. As I wandered in the forest, where its voice was muted by the crowded trunks and heavy foliage, it was easy to forget that it was close by. But when at length I returned to the clearing, the flood of sunshine and the river's voice united to greet me cheerfully, the voice indeed rushing forward to welcome me before I reached the brighter light.

Sometimes, as I lay in the darkness of the long nights of the rainy season, the sound of the swollen river fell upon my ears as a choir of many deep human voices hymning in solemn jubilation. But whether loud or low, whether soothing or insistent, I was happy to have that tireless voice always vibrating around me, a constant reminder that our old earth has not yet been wholly tamed and subjugated to the industrial uses of mankind.

To me, the river was more than an impersonal voice of wild nature; it was a friend and companion and comforter in distress. There were days when everything on the farm seemed to go wrong, when I imagined myself to be hated by my neighbors, scorned by my employees, and forgotten by distant friends. But no matter how gloomy my thoughts and depressed my vitality, the river could restore my drooping spirits. Its good humor was contagious; its abundant vitality communicated itself to me when I came near. As I walked beside its foaming, sparkling waters or sat on a mossy rock watching its dancing surges and listening to its vibrant voice, gloom and doubts would dissolve away, and before I was aware of the change, I would be humming a tune.

The river flowed down to us out of the rugged mountains to the north, where rose Chirripó Grande, the highest peak in the Talamancan Cordillera. Although not twenty miles away, the broken intervening terrain, the density of the trackless forests, made these summits seem far more remote. I never heard of anyone who had followed the river to its source. During my first years on the farm, I dreamed vaguely of tracing my river to its birthplace. But the expedition would have required a small party, with some to carry equipment and supplies for several days, while others cut a trail. Perhaps with a good companion, or a motive more impelling than curiosity, I would have made the journey. But every day there was so much to keep me busy on the farm itself! A naturalist who had spent the greater part of a long life in Costa Rica told me that he could never get anywhere in the country: there was always too much to engage his attention and delay his march in the first mile or two. Hence I never learned why our river is called the Peña Blanca; if there is a white cliff along its course, I have neither seen nor heard of it. From the hilltop behind our house, we can distinguish a whitish exposure of rock on a distant mountainside high above the Río San Pedro, the next fairly big stream to the east. Possibly this is the white cliff that gives our river its name. Some early settler might have seen it in the distance and, in the difficult forested terrain, become confused as to which river flowed below this conspicuous landmark.

The stretch of river that borders Los Cusingos offers no large pools for swimming. During most of the long wet season, the current is so strong that a swimmer is in danger of being dashed against one of the many rocks that encumber the channel. Moreover, the coldness of water that rushes down from chill mountain heights discourages long immersion. But in the dry season, when the stream is lower and less impetuous, there are a few pools deep and wide enough for swimming a few strokes, if one is heedful of submerged rocks that may give a painful bump. The water seems somewhat warmer then, and the sultry afternoons of February and March suggest a dip in the refreshing stream.

Although I did not often swim in the river, I washed in it regularly. As the house neared completion, we tried to dig a well behind it in order to have a convenient source of pure water not only for the kitchen but for bathing, when I came home too tired or too late in the evening to go down to the river or when the weather was unfavorable. The first well shaft that we sunk ran into a great rock at the depth of four yards. We filled it up and tried again nearby, this time going down six yards before we struck a boulder too big to be removed. So we resigned ourselves to hauling up water for the kitchen in buckets from a streamside spring some distance away and to bathing always in the river.

It was not difficult to be satisfied with such a bath, for no emperor of Rome, no opulent citizen of Sybaris, could have possessed one adorned more lavishly, yet in such exquisite taste. The walls were the greenwood trees, and especially the Sotacaballo or Riverwood, whose trunks were as gnarled as those of ancient olive trees, but more massive. With tough, sinewy roots tortuously inserted among the rocks that formed the shores, these aged, stubborn trees were braced to withstand the impact of the roaring flood waters and to lean far over the channel and join their crooked arms with those of neighbors on the opposite bank. The ceiling was formed by the interlacing, perpetually verdant boughs of these same spreading trees. The roof's design was no lifeless, frozen arabesque, but a living tracery capable of transforming itself with a garment of delicate blossoms. In November or December, or sometimes not until early February, the twigs and thinner branches would so indue themselves with faintly pink flowers, consisting largely of clustered stamens, that they appeared to be several times their actual thickness. Their heavy fragrance filled the air above the river and was wafted up to the house, chiefly in the late afternoon or during the night. Another change came during the dry months, when bronzy young leaves were added to the deep green of the persisting older foliage.

These were transient adornments, but at all seasons both the walls and the roof were profusely decorated with an incomparable vegetative display, for no tree of the region is more hospitable to epiphytic growths of all sorts than the rough-barked Sotacaballo. The long catalogue of floral adornments would prove tedious to all but the taxonomic botanist. Even to convey an impression of the wealth of forms and colors in these crowded aerial gardens is an overwhelming task. There are orchids great and small, some with dainty white flowers, some with bright orange florets, and some (*Elleanthus capitatus*) with heavy heads of small, purple blossoms embedded in glistening, colorless jelly. There are ferns in almost inexhaustible variety, with wide-spreading fronds intricately compounded, with tiny, lacy fronds, with stiff, entire fronds. There are bromeliads with strap-shaped leaves arranged in tight rosettes that hold little aerial pools of water, supporting an aquatic flora and fauna all their own. There are vinelike epiphytic heaths (*Satyria elongata*) with sprays of tubular red blossoms hanging above the rushing water. There are aroids with great thick leaves and stiff spikes of red or orange fruits. Although the verdant tapestry remains much the same throughout the year, the colorful minor decorations are constantly changing. I could never foretell with what delicate blossoms the unseen attendants of my sylvan bath would adorn its walls in anticipation of my next visit. With so much to enjoy and admire, no wonder my bath was often a protracted affair.

The floor of my bath was not covered with a mosaic of colored tiles in the Roman fashion. It was composed of rocks and boulders of all sizes and shapes, with here and there a small pocket of sand between them. I had to be careful not to stub a toe or skin a knee while bathing, but the need to exercise caution helped to keep me young and agile. The irregularity of the floor provided a wide choice of pools for my ablutions. In the dry weather when the stream was low, I often chose one in midchannel, where the water was deepest. During most of the rainy season, a spot beside the shore was safest and most convenient. But sometimes in October, when the water swirled angrily and threatened to overflow the banks, prudence counseled that I stand on a massive rock and pour water over myself with a calabash, as I learned to do long ago in Mexico.

The rocks in the stream bed are not unadorned. Those almost constantly submerged during the wet season bear curious growths belonging to the Podostemonaceae or riverweed family. The larger of these, *Marathrum schiedeanum*, has flat fronds, sometimes as much as eight inches long by three inches broad, that are twice-pinnately branched, with hairlike filaments springing in tufts from the ultimate divisions. Bright green in color, these fronds resemble an alga rather than a seed plant. The much smaller *Tristicha hypnoides* has flattened fleshy shoots that creep over the rocks like a liverwort and bear three ranks of tiny, rounded, green leaves, less than a millimeter long. All these riverweeds are rootless; their branches spring from fleshy cushions that cling to the rocks like the holdfasts of seaweeds.

As the river falls in December or January, little green buds appear on the fleshy basal portions of those plants first exposed to the air. Each bud is a simple sac or pouch enclosing a single flower, which bursts out from the top of its spathe and stands up on a slender, naked pedicel, sometimes as much as an inch and a half long in *Marathrum*, much shorter in *Tristicha*. The naked flower of the former, devoid of sepals and petals, consists of a pistil with two stigmas and from five to seven pinkish stamens closely surrounding the ovary. The minute flower of *Tristicha* has one pistil and one stamen, closely invested by three, or sometimes four, thin green perianth divisions, which leave only the three stigmas and the anther uncovered. As the water level falls, more and more plants are exposed to the air and rapidly flower, while those on higher parts of the rocks are already setting seed.

Once, in December, I removed from beneath the water and placed on the shore a stone bearing some plants of *Marathrum* that showed no trace of flower buds. After a week in the air, these plants had open flowers. But one unusually dry July, when the river fell so low that plants of this riverweed were exposed much of the time, I found no flowers; they were not deceived by this unseasonable low water that would not last long enough for them to mature their seeds in the air as they must do.

Riverweed flowers have no obvious devices for attracting insects and appear usually to be self-pollinated, as the anthers open close to, or in contact with, the stigmas. Cross-pollination may sometimes occur, for a slight shake, such as might be given by a breeze or a small insect accidentally alighting, sends forth from a ripe anther a little cloud of dusty pollen, which may settle on neighboring flowers. After pollination, the ribbed pods quickly mature and dry. When the telltale stamens fall, they resemble the spore capsules of mosses, especially those of *Tristicha*, which are smaller than the capsules of many a moss and sometimes deceive botanical collectors. While the seedpods are maturing, the exposed plants that bear them wither away in the hot sunshine, until the threadlike, brown stalks that support these pods appear to spring directly from the dry, naked rock. Soon splitting lengthwise, the capsules shed a multitude of minute seeds, which somehow become attached to the stones and germinate.

How these water plants survive the wild floods of the rainy season, which shift boulders in the river bed, grind them together, and scour them with sand, is cause for wonder. Yet enough of the fleshy holdfasts escape destruction to produce new shoots as the river becomes calmer after the heaviest rains have passed and to flower in the following dry season. One year, after disastrous floods that destroyed houses and bridges and changed the courses of rivers, I found both *Marathrum* and *Tristicha* growing in a newly formed channel to which they had evidently been transported as fragments of holdfasts attached to boulders rolled there by the raging torrent.

Two other species of riverweeds are known to occur in Costa Rica's swiftly flowing streams, and I have found both in the Río Térraba drainage system. In the Río Buena Vista at Rivas, the common species was *Apinagia myriophylla*, which has long, slender fronds consisting of a rachis bordered on each side by many bushy tufts of fine green filaments. At lower elevations grows *Marathrum utile*, a species of very different aspect, with flat, ribbonlike fronds like those of the sea lettuce, *Ulva*. While fording these warmer streams, my horse sometimes plucked them from submerged rocks. Paul Standley reported that in Guanacaste, in the rainless season when the pastures dry up, cattle feed extensively on water plants of this family.

For fellow bathers, I had the kingfishers and the cormorant and the otter. Of the halcyon tribe there were three kinds: the big Ringed Kingfisher, with slate-blue upper plumage and rich chestnut breast; the middle-sized Amazon Kingfisher, clad in deep green, white, and chestnut; and the dainty, little Green Kingfisher, a duodecimo edition of the Amazon. The Ringed Kingfisher I usually saw winging its deliberate way far overhead, voicing a stentorian *kleck* in measured time. But the two smaller kinds often flew close by me while I bathed, or they plunged into some deeper pool from rock or overhanging bough at no great distance from me. Their bath, of course, was usually incidental to their fishing. But at times the kingfishers performed deliberate ablutions. Along this rock-bound river were no banks of soft, sandy loam where these birds could easily dig the tunnels for their nests, and the ornithologist could conveniently study their domestic life, as years earlier I had done along placid lowland streams in Guatemala and Honduras. At Los Cusingos, the kingfishers had to seek pockets and veins of friable soil between the impacted boulders of the higher banks, and, doubtless, many a tunnel hopefully begun by a mated pair was prematurely blocked by an intractable rock, as had happened with the well shafts we dug by my house. In such circumstances, the kingfishers would be inclined to use a successful excavation year after year.

At least, this was true of the only kingfishers' burrow that I have found on this farm, one of the Amazon Kingfisher in a high, stony bank a short way below my favorite bathing place. Apparently, because of the rocks amid which the tunnel was excavated, the nursery had poor internal drainage and became foul with the liquid excreta of the nestlings, which in light, sandy soil is in large measure absorbed by the porous earth. After a visit to their nestlings in the filthy burrow, the parents would feel the need of a bath, and from a rock in mid-channel they plunged again and again into the river, after each partial immersion returning to the boulder to shake the glittering drops from their unwettable plumage. At times the female kingfisher took five plunges after a single visit to the nest. I had never before known New World kingfishers to behave in this wise, but, in Africa, R. E. Moreau saw Half-collared Kingfishers bathe in just this fashion, after emerging from their heavily fouled burrow.

Sometimes I found an Olivaceous Cormorant standing in a statuesque attitude on the rounded top of a great boulder in midstream. Or I would surprise one swimming in the rushing water where it fished. It would flap along the surface with a great splashing until it gained sufficient speed to rise into the air. Sometimes I would see one of these long-necked birds rise circling up far above the treetops, then fly off in a straight course, as though to reach some other river that it remembered or could see from its great altitude. Along the inland waterways of Costa Rica, I have not seen adult cormorants in black breeding plumage, but only immature or nonbreeding birds clad in brownish olive. Doubtless, these cormorants nest colonially in islands along the coast and wander inland along the waterways when not breeding. From about March until mid-June, they are absent from our river. During the remainder of the year, they are solitary birds, and I have rarely seen two together.

Another creature that I met chiefly when I went to bathe was the Nutria or Tropical Otter. Sometimes, while undressing, I watched one of these aquatic animals playing at some distant point along the opposite shore, but it was shy and melted away when it saw me. Once, when I rose from the water just above a big rock, I found myself staring into the squat, white-whiskered face of an otter who had simultaneously risen on the opposite side of the same rock. I hesitate to affirm which of us was more startled by this sudden encounter, but the smaller animal was more mobile, and in a trice it disappeared under water. When alarmed in this fashion, the otter could swim so far beneath the surface that when next it emerged for air it was out of sight.

Sometimes, on a morning of brilliant sunshine, I would find an otter stretched at ease on the top of a great boulder in the stream bed, with a broad trickle of water down the side revealing that it had just emerged all dripping from the cold river. How delightful to loll luxuriously in the warm sunshine after fishing in the chill water, to yawn, to lick one's sleek pelage, to lie full length on one's back with short legs and big paws sticking up into the air, or just to doze in the grateful warmth! Yet a creature of the wild can never afford to be quite forgetful of enemies. From time to time, eyes must be opened for a look around. Yet it is not the eyes but the nose that is most sensitive to danger. So long as the breeze drifts toward me from the river, I can stand immobile, watching the drowsy animal without arousing suspicion. But now the light, fitful wind shifts and carries human scent to those acute nostrils. The animal lifts its squat, bewhiskered head, sniffs the air, and, sensing my presence, slides off the rock to vanish in the foaming current. Only the wet spot on top and the trickle down the side reveal that he has been drowsing there.

Late one afternoon in August, while I sat writing in the house, my attention was aroused by a loud, staccato note repeated over and over. At first, I took it to be one of the calls of the brown Squirrel Cuckoo, but on listening attentively I perceived that it was too high in pitch and differed in quality. Dropping my pen, I followed the voice, which, continuing unabated, guided me to the creek in front of the house. As I came in sight of the stream bed, an otter slipped off a wet rock and disappeared into the water, and at the same time the sound ceased. But soon I heard the same sharp notes coming from a point downstream, and, approaching with greater caution, I saw the otter swimming around in irregular circles in a small pool of deeper water beside a rock.

Most of the time, the animal kept its head submerged and only its glistening, grayish brown back partly above the surface, but at intervals it stuck its head into the air and barked. It continued to call from various parts of the stream beside the pasture for the next quarter of an hour. The otter seemed to possess only a single note, which, I suppose, coming from a carnivore, might be called a bark, although at first I mistook it for the call of a bird, and later I recognized its great resemblance to the note of a frog that lives along the same stream, although it was louder and stronger.

One morning in July, I watched three otters disporting in the river, swimming under the shallow water, here and there raising their sleek heads to breathe, from time to time climbing up on a rock only to dive in again, and occasionally voicing the birdlike note. All seemed to be full-grown and on the friendliest terms. Accused of stealing chickens, the otter is persecuted by the local men and has latterly become rare.

The most winsome of all the creatures that kept me company while I bathed were the Torrent Flycatchers. These minute, chubby birdlings, whitish with dull black head, wings, and tail, are the elfin guardians of the rushing mountain streams of tropical America, from Costa Rica to Bolivia. They have no counterpart in the more northerly regions of the continent, and they promptly capture the affection of all who meet them. They seem too small and fragile to spend their days just beyond reach of the hungry surges of the most impetuous mountain torrents; yet the more boulders, the more white water, the more at home they appear to be. Like the sandpipers, waterthrushes, wagtails, dippers, and other birds of the inland watercourses, they are constantly flagging their short tails up and down. Flitting restlessly from rock to rock, they snatch some of their food from the air like other flycatchers, but much they pluck from the wet faces of the rocks, often darting down to seize some tiny larva or other creature left exposed by a receding wave, then bouncing lightly away just in time to escape the returning surge.

The male and female, who remain mated throughout the year, often stand together on some exposed rock and lift up their heads to sing a little duet of high, sharp notes. Their nest is a neat, open cup, covered on the outside with green moss and softly lined with downy feathers. As befits the nursery of a river sprite, this elegant structure is often attached to a leafy bough that reaches far out above the rushing current, and, appropriately, it may contain many wiry, brown capsule stalks of riverweeds. The male dutifully helps his mate to build, and often he comes to stand beside her on the rim of the nest while she incubates the two minute, pale buff eggs, keeping them warm in their mossy chalice so close above the cold surges of the restless mountain torrent.

Another attractive bird that I often watched while I bathed was the Riverside Wren. Rich chestnut above, narrowly barred with black and white over all the under plumage, this handsome wren forages by preference in tangles of vines along the riverbanks, although it may on occasion wander along the forest's edge up into the hills, and sometimes in wet weather it hunts among the shrubbery in our garden. Birds which frequent rushing mountain streams, and must make themselves heard above the incessant babble of the water, often have loud, ringing voices, sharper and more forceful than the notes of related species that dwell in more silent places. Often the clear, full notes of the Riverside Wrens carry up to the house above the roar of the river; *mil veces, mil veces* they sing, or *victory, victory*. Like many of the constantly mated tropical wrens, the male and female sing responsively.

Riverside Wrens balance their snug, globular nests upon a horizontal twig, often of a bough that projects above the water. On one side of the moss-covered structure is the chamber where the wren sleeps or attends its eggs and young; on the other, a vestibule or antechamber of almost equal size, entered through a wide doorway that faces downward and often also obliquely inward. Usually I have found a single wren roosting in one of these peculiar nests, but sometimes there are two. One evening I discovered three together, probably a mother with two grown young, since two is the usual number of eggs laid by this wren.

Once I bathed at sunset in another of El General's many mountain streams. As I emerged from the water, my eye caught a big, black snake, five or six feet long, lying on the rocks in the river bed just above me, with the forepart of its body held nearly erect, doubtless to watch me. When I chased the serpent away, it climbed into a tangle of bushes and vines overhanging the water. Just then a pair of Riverside Wrens came foraging through the streamside vegetation. Noticing the snake among the foliage, they scolded with harsh *churrs*. Then, approaching the creature so much bigger than themselves, they bit or pecked it twice on the tail, once near the middle of the body. After each attack by the birds, the snake moved slightly. The wrens, of course, retreated quickly after each swift assault. As far as I could see, the serpent did not strike at them. Soon the wrens went off, leaving the snake in the bushes; apparently, they had no nest nearby. I dressed and walked back to the village in the twilight, full of admiration for the courage of the little wrens.

Years later, I was reminded of this episode while studying Rufous-fronted Thornbirds in Venezuela. A black and yellow snake over six feet long, locally known as a *Tigra*, had climbed into a tree near the hanging, two-chambered nest of interlaced twigs in which a pair of these ovenbirds were feeding nestlings. When the snake stretched out, the brown, wrenlike thornbirds repeatedly pecked or bit its tail; when it coiled up, they approached very close but were not seen to touch it. The snake, whose subsequent behavior revealed that it would have pillaged the nest had I not intervened, did not bother the adult birds who came near it.

I have often watched a motley party of small birds flit with complaining cries about a small or large snake, "mobbing" it, without being caught by the serpent. Although I have seen snakes swallow eggs and nestlings more often than I care to recall, I have only once known a snake to catch an adult bird. One morning, while writing this book, I was aroused by shrill cries coming from the female Scarlet-rumped Black Tanager who was incubating an egg in a shrub beside the door of my study in the garden. Rushing out, I found the tanager hanging by one wing from the mouth of a green tree snake and struggling violently. Without waiting to learn the outcome of this situation, I seized a stick and rescued the tanager, who flew away apparently uninjured. Probably she had boldly attacked the reptile, as I have seen Scarlet-rumped Black Tanagers do to other snakes of about the same size, and, approaching too near, she had been seized. I doubt that the serpent could have swallowed the bird, for, although four feet long, it was hardly thicker than my middle finger. The reader will understand why I am sceptical of all tales of snakes "charming" or hypnotizing birds in order to devour them.

An alien among the birds along the Peña Blanca is the Spotted Sandpiper. One of the earliest migrants to come down from the North, it sometimes reaches our river by the middle of August. Here it hunts over exposed rocks and the few short reaches of sandy shore, much as on its northern breeding grounds. When sandpipers arrive in Central America, some still bear dark spots on their white breasts; some are in the process of losing them, while yet others are immaculate; but soon all wear the unmarked breast feathers of the winter plumage. Often staying with us until the second week of May, they fly northward with fresh black spots on their breasts. Waterthrushes, both the Northern and the Louisiana, sometimes walk deliberately along the banks of the river, flagging their tails much in the manner of the sandpiper. One February, I watched a Louisiana Waterthrush stand on a root jutting out from the shore and sing in a low voice—the only time I heard a waterthrush sing in its winter home, although other kinds of northern warblers often do so while in Central America.

Often, as I walked through the pasture toward the river, I met a big Basilisk Lizard sunning itself on a rock. Miniature dragons, the largest were about two feet long, grayish green or grayish brown in color, with a pale yellow stripe along each side. Each of the biggest ones wore on its hindhead a high, thin crest like the rudder of a boat; it had a long, elevated, frilled crest along the middle of its back and another on the basal half of its long tail. The small ones had rudiments of these ornaments or were quite smooth above. When alarmed by my approach, the wary Basilisks would invariably scuttle toward the river rather than back toward the woods. They ran swiftly on their strong hind feet alone, with their foreparts raised, their weak forelegs dangling uselessly, and their tail elevated to balance the foreparts of the body.

Often, too, I found these amiable monsters along the shore or resting on a rock or stranded log in midstream. If forced to take to the water, they ran nimbly over the river, using their hind legs alone, as on land. Their long, spreading, hind toes served to keep them above the surface, at least while they moved rapidly. But if they broke through the surface film and became submerged, they could swim like other lizards.

Largely vegetarian, the Basilisks eat ripe coffee berries, mistletoe berries, the sweet, white seed coats of Inga trees, and bananas. One big, crested saurian, with several inches missing from the end of his tail, formed the habit of visiting the birds' table and caused much annoyance by clumsily pushing the fruit off the board with his blunt jaws. When chased by me, the perverse lizard would run up a long branch of the tree that supported the table, only to return to the feast as soon as my back was turned. Once, when he glared insolently down at me from the end of a branch far beyond my reach, I shook the bough until he became alarmed and jumped into the shrubbery below. He scuttled off, apparently none the worse for his long fall, but never again did he come uninvited to the birds' table.

One evening, I watched several small fish beating around in a shallow pool among stones, often exposing their silvery bellies. Presently a big, crested Basilisk came and rested on a rock above the fish, at intervals shaking his head up and down in characteristic fashion. Suddenly he bent down, seized a fish in his mouth, and ran with it back into the bushes on the shore. I estimated the fish to be about three inches long. In northeastern Costa Rica, the basilisk lizards are bright green with a blue throat, instead of grayish, but otherwise they are similar to the western species.

When I first knew the Peña Blanca River, it contained fish of fair size, which somehow managed to escape being washed down to the ocean by the frequent raging floods that seemed to carry everything before them. The lads sometimes caught these fish with a baited hook. With their simple angler's equipment, they had most bites when the river was swollen and turbid from the afternoon downpours. When the water was clear, the wary fish eschewed gifts with a string visibly attached to them. As the human population increased and the practice of exploding bombs in the river to kill the fish became more frequent, the larger ones all but vanished. Although this wasteful method of fishing was illegal, no one seemed to respect the law. Chlorate for making the bombs and rolls of fuse for setting them off were part of the stock of many country stores.

Like many wicked practices, this one cut two ways; fatal to the fish, it was sometimes hardly less disastrous to those who bombed them. Fingers, hands, and even whole forearms were lost by premature explosions of the chlorate bombs. A little boy found a percussion cap that had been carelessly left on a rock by the river. The deceptively innocent toy suddenly exploded, seriously injuring the fingers of the boy's left hand—and as fate would have it, the poor child was left-handed! I did what I could to prevent the bombing of the river from my side, but it was a futile endeavor; the poachers merely crossed to the opposite shore to set off their explosives, and the result was precisely the same—depletion of the stock.

The reach of river bordering Los Cusingos contains several islands. The lowest of these is over a hundred yards in length, long and narrow, transected lengthwise by a rocky channel, along which in the dry season flows a mere trickle, which in the rainy months grows to be a considerable stream. One day when the water was low, Pamela and I bathed in the river above this island, then ate a picnic lunch on the rocks at its head. After our meal, we set out, machete in hand, to explore the double island, feeling like discoverers who first of all men set foot on some uncharted islet in mid-ocean. The trees were tall and heavy, the undergrowth of bushes, creepers, and great-leaved herbs so dense that it was often necessary to wield the machete to open a passage. I do not know whether this island belongs to us or to our neighbor across the river or to the government. As long as there remains a bit of unspoiled wilderness between the pastures and the cornfields, it does not matter who owns these small islands in our river.

There is another, much larger island, of recent formation, of which we definitely claim possession, as it is included in our title. Although I regard the river as a friend, it is not consistently amiable. Sometimes, swollen by heavy downpours, it goes on a frightful rampage. One of these occurred in October, 1955, when floods and hurricanes afflicted many of the more southerly parts of the North American continent, as far north as New England, and likewise the Lesser Antilles. During the night of October 13–14, the Peña Blanca carried away the roofed bridge that spanned it a short distance above us. It deposited along our shore, for half a mile, the huge squared beams and the sheets of heavy corrugated iron roofing, crumpled like pieces of paper that had been crushed into a ball.

The roaring current also tore all the beautiful ferns, aroids, orchids, bromeliads, begonias, and similar growths from the river banks, the tops of the higher rocks standing in the channel, and the trunks and lower branches of the Sotacaballo trees, in all of which places they had flourished undisturbed for years. Several Sotacaballo trees that had grown on the river banks were left standing, proudly triumphant, in the midst of the widened channel, all the vegetation, earth, and smaller stones having been washed from around them as the river tore into the shore behind them. Were I a poet, I would compose an ode to these sturdy trees, celebrating their stanchness and the might that saved all the lesser plants that perched on them above reach of the swollen current.

Yet even these stout trees sometimes yield to repeated pounding by the floodwaters and the logs they carry downward. I examined the roots of a fallen Sotacaballo. How grotesquely gnarled and twisted they were!

Here and there they expanded into great, irregular swellings, and often two roots fused together. Stones of all sizes, from pebbles to boulders heavier than I could lift, were too firmly clasped and embraced by these tough roots to be moved; some of the smaller ones were almost imbedded in the wood that had grown around them. I surmised that other stones were wholly enclosed in the wood, but I did not wish to ruin a machete or an axe by cutting into the mass of roots and rocks to prove the point. Now I understood better how the Sotacaballo resists the impact of tons of rushing water.

On the evening of May 9, 1960, rain began. Soon becoming harder, the downpour continued far into the night. The river roared loudly; at intervals we heard the rumble of boulders shifting in its bed and the dull thud of floating tree trunks striking against rocks. By daybreak the crest of the flood had passed, leaving signs that the river had risen as high as I had ever seen it before. As I walked down the familiar riverside path, I was suddenly halted by a swirling, muddy deluge, twenty yards wide, flowing where I had passed dry-shod many times before. The river had reopened an old channel that it had abandoned long before I came here, as was evident from the trees growing in this depression. Nearly half its current now flowed through Los Cusingos, making an island of five or six acres of our best bottom land. Here we had recently planted several acres of corn, a grove of bananas and plantains, a patch of cassava and taro, and a small vegetable garden; here was some of our best pasture and the best swimming pools. All this had suddenly become difficult to reach, and we had much trouble harvesting the corn. Since then, this land between the branches of the river has lain idle, becoming overgrown with dense thickets, amid which leaf-cutting ants have established some huge cities. After every freshet, I look hopefully to see whether the river has abandoned this channel in favor of others that it has been cutting farther to the left, as it gives indications that it will some day do. Its presence within our land makes a difficult farm even harder to operate.

16

Forest Trails

FIFTY YARDS from the house, the edge of the rain forest that covers nearly half of Los Cusingos rises like a high wall. To reach this woodland, I make a detour, passing through a narrow gate in front of the house and descending by a footpath cut into the steep bank to the horses' pasture that borders the river. This long, narrow, rocky pasture is pleasantly shaded by orange, guava, avocado, rose apple, and other trees that attract many birds. To scan the treetops for rare feathered visitors, to hear the cheerful bird songs, to rub Atalanta's velvety nose or stroke Rocalpe's sleek neck, are diversions that often delay my march to the forest.

When I came here in 1941, the trees along the edges of this pasture were draped with a scandent bamboo, a species of *Chusquea*, with thin, wiry stems and small, lanceolate leaves. I never noticed a flower on these bamboos until 1956, when in October and November many of them dis-

Headpiece: Rain forest in the Caribbean lowlands of Costa Rica. Small palms are the chief undergrowth.

played their inconspicuous green florets. By the following January, those plants which had flowered were dying, while those that had failed to flower continued to flourish. Most of the latter bloomed profusely in November of 1957, and after setting seed they likewise died. The few surviving bamboos flowered in November of the following year, and after they had set seed and died, none remained. Innumerable seedlings were now springing up beneath the old dead vines. Most of these succumbed, but those that survived continued to grow slowly and after a decade were scrambling high into the trees once more. But since 1958, I have seen no more flowers. The interval between successive efflorescences is certainly in excess of fifteen years, and it may be more than twice this long. Other bamboos have been reported to flower at intervals of over thirty years.

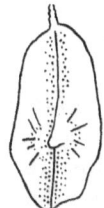 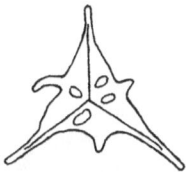

5. Fruits of the tall tree *Goethalsia meiantha*. At left, a whole fruit (X½); at right, in cross section (X1). It splits into three winged parts, each bearing a few small seeds at its center.

At the southwestern corner of the pasture, an unobtrusive opening amidst tall trees leads into the woodland. The roadway is soft, half covered with herbage, and rutted with vanishing cart tracks impressed there when the harvests were hauled out through the forest, a laborious detour made necessary by the extremely broken and rocky terrain along the river. I pass beneath the straight, slender trunks of second-growth trees of *Goethalsia meiantha*, forty yards high. They bring to mind the engineer who built the Panama Canal, to whom Henri Pittier, the Swiss-born geographer and botanist who long ago explored these forests of the Térraba Valley, dedicated this swiftly growing tree of the linden family. It displays panicles of pale yellow flowers in July and August. The curious, three-winged fruits are full-grown by October (Fig. 5). When sunnier weather begins in January, they dry and turn brown, but they persist on the trees until rains become frequent in April and May. When the fruit is at last shed, it splits into three parts, each consisting of a broad, oval wing with a few small seeds embedded in a hard swelling at its center. These seeds seem to require some special stimulus to germinate, and one looks in vain for seedlings in the woodland where thousands have fallen.

Beneath these tall trees grow Heliconias or wild plantains far taller than myself, with huge leaves resembling those of the banana, and heavy, pensile inflorescences with deep red, furry bracts, from beneath which peep tubular, yellow flowers—bizarre tropical growths unlike anything known in the temperate zones. Here I sometimes meet that rare, curious hummingbird, the White-tipped Sicklebill, whose strongly downcurved bill is just the shape for probing these strongly bent Heliconia flowers. The Sicklebill's feet and legs are stouter than those of most hummingbirds; it uses them to cling beside the flowers it visits, instead of hovering on wing in typical hummingbird fashion. Here also grows a lower, more delicate Heliconia, with upright inflorescences and bright yellow floral bracts prettily margined with red. Their nearly straight, yellow flowers are visited by hummingbirds with straighter bills. When the latter visit the sickle-shaped flowers of the red-bracted species, they pierce the corollas instead of probing them in the "legitimate" manner that effects pollination, as does the Sicklebill hummingbird.

To this low-lying woodland I often come in September and October to enjoy the beauty of two shrubs of the acanthus family: *Razisea spicata*, with long, tubular, brilliantly red blossoms, and *Poikilacanthus macranthus* with equally long, lavender flowers. Both are profusely generous with their bloom. Along the low bank bordering the little-used roadway, in the deep shade, tree ferns have grown up and spread their great, intricately divided fronds high above my head.

A short walk through this old second-growth woodland brings me to the taller, more massive trees, intermingled with noble palms, of the ancient forest. Sometimes as I enter it, I repeat those fine verses of Francis Thompson:

> This is the mansion built for me
> By the sweating centuries;
> Roofed with intertwined tree,
> Woofed with green for my princelier ease.

This, too, is my garden, which nature began to prepare for me ages before I was born—a garden such as no monarch, puissant though he be, could create for himself by royal command. Although for years my work took me almost daily into tropical rain forest, I rarely enter it without a feeling of awe, without a reverential, meditative pause, as though I passed through the portals of some magnificent temple, pervaded with delicate incense, illuminated by a dim, religious light. And is this not the fane that the mysterious Creative Energy has raised as its own monument, where in contemplative silence we come closest to it and perhaps achieve a fuller appreciation of its power and majesty, of its illimitable creativity, of the unfathomable enigmas it presents to finite human minds?

Perhaps, if I am fortunate, as I pass into this temple I meet its chief chorister, a big, brownish, stout-bodied bird that walks sedately over the forest floor or, if suddenly alarmed, takes the air with a loud burst of wingbeats that evince more strength than control and carry it swiftly through the underwood until it drops to earth again, well sheltered in the herbage, beyond sight and out of harm's way. This is the Great Tinamou, flute-voiced bird of ancient lineage. Often, as the day ends, we hear its vesper song, so powerful yet so mellow, so full of pathos yet of hope. These wild woodland notes seem to tell me that, although the tropical forest is yearly receding before the onslaughts of the most aggressive creature that has ever issued from nature's teeming womb, it will not wholly vanish from the earth, for it has that vitality, that patience, that limitless fecundity that will enable it to triumph at the last. When I reflect that the first brown-skinned men who penetrated these forests, thousands of years before Columbus sailed westward from Palos, heard these exquisite notes much as I hear them, that these brown men have vanished before alien invaders yet the tinamou holds its own, I have faith that the bird will live to carry its antique message to generations yet unborn, who may hear it more appreciatively and interpret it more clearly than we do.

One evening, while I stood quietly in the forest, in that sweet twilight interval when the big Chestnut-mandibled Toucans chant their *Dios te de* from the tops of tall trees kissed by the last rays of the setting sun, when the woodcreepers sound their varied notes from the trunks, and the Great Tinamous lift their mellow voices in the darkening underwood, one of the latter flew up into a small neighboring tree. It alighted on a nearly horizontal branch, a few inches thick and about twenty feet above the ground. Here the big bird stood upright and silent, just where it had first come to rest, while the toucans finished their vesper chorus and all the diurnal life of the woodland fell into quiet somnolence.

When I advanced through the dark undergrowth, the bird above me betrayed no alarm, so, becoming more confident, I threw the beam of my flashlight upon it. Its eyes shone brightly in the beam, returning a whitish reflection rather than the ruby glow of the crepuscular Pauraque. To judge by the intensity of this tapetal reflection, the tinamou enjoys fairly good nocturnal vision. After a good look at the bird above me, I extinguished the light and stole away, leaving it resting peacefully in the spot where it had first alighted.

Only on one other occasion have I seen a Great Tinamou rise to perch in a tree. This was in the late afternoon, and the bird, who had possibly been driven up from the ground by some prowling animal, did not remain until nightfall. Once, as night ended, I frightened up a Little Tinamou from dense herbage in a plantation, where apparently it had slept on the ground. Thus I confirmed in Costa Rica facts that William Beebe had earlier discovered with related birds in British Guiana. Now, when the melodious wail of the big tinamou reaches my drowsy ears in the dead of night, my mind's eye no longer pictures the bird as wandering bewildered over the ground in the pitchy blackness of the neighboring forest but as perching in comparative safety on some elevated bough, perhaps calling out in its dreams.

While wandering through this forest years ago, I found a "nest" of the Great Tinamou. The vivid blue of three big, glossy eggs, among the most beautiful of all birds' eggs, caught my eye from across a narrow rivulet in a wooded dell. The most conspicuous objects in the underwood, they were clearly visible at a distance of a hundred feet. I did not cross the rivulet nor go near where they lay on the ground at the base of a clump of tree ferns, inadequately screened by the heart-shaped leaves of a terrestrial aroid. But when I returned the following afternoon, only a few vivid fragments of intensely blue shell revealed that here had been a tinamou's nest. Their bright color had caught the eye of some marauding animal, as it had arrested mine. In later years, I found three more nests in this forest, each with three or four eggs. Here the Great Tinamou appears to breed chiefly in the early part of the rainy season, from April to July. In other regions, as many as twelve eggs have been found in a Great Tinamou's nest, although sets of more than six are unusual. Probably several females may lay in the same nest, as happens regularly with certain other tinamous.

Every Great Tinamou's nest that I have seen has been prematurely destroyed. Evidently, the safety of the conspicuous eggs depends on their being almost constantly covered by the parent bird, whose browns and grays blend well with the ground litter of the forest. One morning in August, as I passed along this stretch of roadway near the entrance to the forest, a parent tinamou with three half-grown chicks walked ahead of me, then veered aside into the undergrowth. Doubtless the parent was the father, who in the tinamou family incubates the eggs and attends the young, with little or no help from a mate.

A few paces after entering the old forest, the roadway climbs a short rise of ground and passes by the base of one of the noblest trees on the farm, a Milk Tree, locally known as *mastate* or *palo de leche*. The smooth, gray trunk is eleven feet in circumference above the spreading plank buttresses, and it rises clean and straight a full fifty feet to the first branch. The shapely, elongate crown of large, thick, oblong leaves stands above all its neighbors and is visible from afar. Although well over a hundred feet high, this particular Milk Tree is not the tallest or most massive of its kind; a large one exceeds one hundred and fifty feet in height. These trees shed all their foliage at some time between November and January, neighboring trees often in different months. After a short interval of nakedness, they cover themselves with bright green new leaves.

An incision in the smooth bark causes a thick, pure white latex to ooze copiously forth. This magnificent tree is closely similar to the cow tree that Alexander von Humboldt found in Venezuela, if not actually the same species. Few of the marvels of nature which that indefatigable and insatiably curious traveler met in the vast South American forests, then hardly explored by men of science, so aroused his wonder or inspired such glowing passages from his fecund pen. A tree from whose bark flowed freely an aromatic, nourishing milk seemed to confound the distinction between the animal and vegetable kingdoms, to afford a signal instance of nature's inexhaustible bounty. The enthusiastic explorer freely partook of the tree's milk "without feeling the least injurious effect"; he collected samples for various analyses and tests; he learned that plantation laborers in the Valley of Aragua moistened their bread of maize or cassava in this fluid and that the Negro slaves grew conspicuously fatter in the season when the tree yielded its white latex most freely for them.

Although oblique scars on my own Milk Trees reveal that their properties are not unknown to the local people, they scarcely ever use the milk. Nor do they beat out its fibrous inner bark into soft, thick fabrics and mats, as did the Indians before them. Along the Río Esmeraldas in Ecuador, our Negro boatmen, who did use mats from the bark of this tree, called it *El Rey de la Selva* (King of the Forest)—an apt designation. Yet the massive trunk of the Milk Tree is soft; riddled by insects, it rots away in a surprisingly short time after the tree has been felled. It is employed only for making forms for concrete and similar temporary uses. These impressive trees have been increasing in our forest, as trees of other kinds, especially the Campana, grow old and die.

A short distance beyond the big Milk Tree once stood another imposing tree, although less massive and tall, a Campana, which late in the year bore spreading white flowers with many stamens that showered down with profligate bounty upon the leaf-strewn roadway. One April, this fine tree was uprooted by a violent windstorm, which beyond the river laid flat several acres of heavy forest. The clay adhering to the Campana's roots formed a massive, vertical wall, higher than my head, standing up at the edge of the roadway. I mourned the fallen giant; but as the years passed, I became reconciled to its loss and even glad that the tree had been blown over.

The wall of clay bound together by roots afforded nest sites for three kinds of burrowing birds: a pair of lovely Blue-diademed Motmots with oddly trimmed, racquet-shaped central tail feathers; a pair of glittering, dainty Rufous-tailed Jacamars; and a pair of Scaly-throated Leaf-tossers, small, brown ovenbirds whose bright, vibrant songs often sounded from the neighboring undergrowth, where with short, black bills they assiduously flicked aside the ground litter in search of small creatures lurking beneath it. The motmots' burrow was destroyed by mischievous trespassers. The jacamars' first two nests likewise failed, but on their third attempt, in a later year, they fledged two sprightly youngsters. The leaf-tossers made most use of this root-bound bank, laying sets of two white eggs, in nests loosely constructed of leafstalks at the end of the burrow, in October, 1945, May, October, and December, 1946. Again in September, 1947, they began to dig a burrow that was abandoned unfinished. These dates reveal a breeding season most unusual for the birds of El General. In extensive level areas of forest, with few escarpments or high stream banks, uprooted trees of this sort must be of primary importance for birds that nest in burrows. Without such banks formed by great fallen trees, it is doubtful whether they could find suitable sites for digging their tunnels and raising their families.

Aside from an occasional Morpho butterfly flashing azure wings, there is little color in the underwood along this trail. Most of it is provided by shrubs of the madder family. The tall, smooth-leafed *Cephaelis elata* bears its white florets in a tight cluster surrounded by two bright red, roundish bracts. The lower, furry-leaved *Cephaelis tomentosa*, which prefers the more open spots, has pale yellow florets set amid similar red bracts. Both of these shrubs are much visited by hummingbirds, especially the lovely violet and green Blue-crowned Woodnymph, an inhabitant of dense forests. *Cephaelis pittieri*, which is more abundant at higher altitudes, has a compact floral head made conspicuous by many narrow, orange bracts. Looking down, I notice here and there along the roadway, never more than a foot above the ground, beautiful velvety leaves that are deep bronzy green with pinkish veins. Lifting one up, I notice that the under side is everywhere rich purple, which color, showing through the green of the overlying tissues, produces the bronzy tint. These handsome leaves belong to another rubiaceous shrub, a species of the large and confusing genus *Psychotria*. They are found only on young seedlings and on shoots which, after an injury, spring from the bases of older plants. Higher above the ground, this shrub bears only large, smooth, bright green leaves. Its open panicles of small, whitish flowers hardly attract attention.

Just beyond the site of the fallen Campana, I come to a hollow where the slender trees grow straight and tall, leading one's eyes upward and with them the spirit, grateful for the forest's majesty. Here grows the Chumico, a tree resembling the related guarumo or Cecropia. Its big, palmate leaves are covered on the upper side with short, spikelike hairs that make them harsh and abrasive, so that they are sought by the women as a substitute for sandpaper for scouring their bare woodwork and their pots. Here, too, stands the tall, dark-barked Cerillo, whose neat, glossy foliage is in August or September variegated with clusters of red flowers, which at a distance one might mistake for cherrylike fruits. In the Sarapiquí lowlands of northern Costa Rica, I found Cerillo trees flowering as saplings little more than head high, but here they grow much taller before they bloom. Both of these trees are, like the widespread Cecropias, supported by prop roots that spring from the trunk well above the surface of the ground.

These tall trees must compete for light with the most aggressive liana of the forest, the gigantic Entada, whose great swinging stems, like flexible trunks, are sometimes fifteen inches thick. They are irregularly furrowed and pitted; their dark, rough bark supports mosses, ferns, orchids, and other epiphytes like that of an erect tree. Far overhead, the thick, twisted branches of this pestilent vine swing in heavy loops from tree to tree, over the crowns of which it spreads a deadly profusion of twice-pinnate leaves, which smother the tree's own foliage if it does not break the supporting trunk or branches with its weight. The roots, when they extend from the forest onto the harder ground of an adjoining pasture or lawn, lie exposed like enormous cables on the surface, over which I have traced them for nearly two hundred feet before their thinner branches burrowed underground. Both the climbing stems and the roots are soft rather than woody, but they are difficult to cut with a machete, because the fibers in them foul the blade. The conducting strands, which include exceptionally wide vessels conspicuous to the naked eye, are scattered irregularly through the soft ground tissue.

The great, flat pods of this liana are a yard or two long by five or six inches broad. From the ground, I pick up the fallen beans, which may be as much as two and a half inches broad by an inch thick. They are roundish, with a hard, dark brown, lustrous seed coat. In regions frequented by tourists, souvenir makers remove the contents of the seed to make of its hard shell a little box with a tight-fitting lid in which coins or trinkets may be kept. In every way, this monstrous pantropical liana deserves the name *gigas* which Linnaeus gave to it. If I could eradicate this egregious weed from our forest, I would certainly do so.

In this low part of the forest thrives a vine of a very different kind, a fern that twines up the stems of saplings and slender trees, sometimes to a height of forty feet. It is the stipe of the frond rather than a true stem that climbs; its primary divisions, which those not initiated into the mysteries of the structure of ferns might call its "fronds," stand out from the supporting trunk like pinnately compound leaves. I still recall my delight when, as a young student of botany in another land, I was shown my first climbing fern and my enthusiasm for the greater variety of these curious growths that I met on my first expedition to tropical mountains. But I have lived to see the day when I called such ferns "accursed weeds" and a "plague." For *Salpichlaena volubilis* grows in great profusion in our forest, especially in low ground, and its wiry stipes, stretching from sapling to bush in an undergrowth already dense enough, trip my feet, hold me in a cordlike tangle, thwarting my efforts to stalk in silence some elusive bird that lurks amid this concealing vegetation.

Thus it was when, soon after I came to live at Los Cusingos, I heard, issuing from the densely tangled undergrowth of this little hollow in the forest, a bird voice unknown to me. The song was thin, plaintive, long-continued, almost a trill, so rapidly did the notes follow each other. Could this be a wood warbler, caroling in the underwood of tropical forest less than three thousand feet above sea level? In the high mountain forests where resident wood warblers are more numerous, this attribution of the song would have been more convincing. But if not a warbler's, to what bird could this appealing little lay belong?

Battling with the stubborn climbing ferns and other resisting vegetation, trying to advance without making enough noise to frighten away the bird whose voice I laboriously followed, I slowly made my way in the direction of the sound. After much peering about in the dimly lighted undergrowth, my eyes picked out their object—a hummingbird! A lone Band-tailed Barbthroat, one of the plainly clad "hermits," rested on a dead twig a yard above the ground, twitching his white-tipped tail up and down, sometimes through a wide arc, sometimes through a slight one. From time to time, he swelled out his dusky throat with song. His lay was more tuneful, more varied, suggestive of more intense feeling, than the utterances of most hummingbirds that I have heard. Each song was also longer, continuing for four or five seconds, but to compensate for these superior qualities, it was more sparingly given, with considerable intervals of silence between repetitions. The tiny songster was almost fearless of me, as I have nearly always found Band-tailed Barbthroats. Sometimes they hover close in front of me, as though examining the strange monster that has intruded into their thickets, and, while perching, they have permitted me to scrutinize them with my face less than a foot away.

For three consecutive years, I heard the barbthroat singing alone in the same spot. In the fourth year, he was back in the same location, but a second individual of his kind performed on a low perch not far away. In later years, three or four barbthroats formed a singing assembly in this part of the forest, in the manner of many other male hummingbirds in their breeding season. But the little songsters were not very sociable, and a hundred feet or more might separate their stations. They rarely perched more than five feet above the ground, and each was to be found day after day on his favorite twig. For ten years, I heard these quaint songs in just this part of the forest and nowhere else. They began after the rains had refreshed the vegetation, at the end of March in wet years, not until early May in very dry ones. In August or September, they ceased.

Beyond the fallen Campana tree, in the low ground where the barbthroats sang, the road forks, a branch running obliquely up each of the low ridges that enclose the hollow. The roadway to the left soon emerges from the forest into the planted fields and second-growth thickets. I choose the right branch, which ascends gently beneath noble chonta palms. Their tall, slender, smooth, gray trunks are curiously supported on a cluster of prop roots, each as thick as my wrist, the highest springing from old palms as much as three yards above the ground. Each wet season, more of these thick roots break forth amazingly from the dry, hard base of the columnar trunk to strike obliquely downward into the ground. When mature, the chonta's prop roots are studded with low, sharp spikes, which can inflict a painful wound upon one who carelessly rubs against them.

These stately palms grow slowly and evidently live to a great age, for the taller ones rise clean and lithe nearly a hundred feet to the spreading crown of great feather fronds, each composed of many divisions that expand from a narrow base to a broad apex, as in other "fishtail" palms. The center of the trunk is soft and soon decays when the palm is felled, but the outer shell is extremely hard and resistant. When pounded and flattened out, or split into long strips, it is most useful for rustic constructions.

On reaching the top of the incline, I turn northward along the ridge. Soon after I came to Los Cusingos, I cut several discreet little paths through the woodland, just wide enough for one to walk freely and watch the life around him without being detained by obtruding bushes or tripped by low vines. But when I found that my trails, intended only for those who cherish the forest and its inhabitants, served the purposes of trespassers who shot the animals and destroyed the palm trees, I abandoned my plan to form a whole network of them and even allowed some that I had already made to become choked with vegetation.

So at the crest of the ridge, where once I found a Kinkajou sleeping away the day in a hole carved in a dead tree by a big Pale-billed Woodpecker, I push through a fringe of bushes and make my way northward along an almost obliterated trail. Now and then I pause to eat a handful of the clustered berries of the canelillo, a head-high melastomaceous shrub very abundant in this woodland. The fruits are of about the size and color of the wild blueberry of the North, but more watery. A Ruddy Quail-Dove rises from the ground before me and skims away just above the undergrowth. A rapid, tinkling song draws my attention to the conspicuous black and white heads and bright beaks of a pair of Orange-billed Sparrows, lurking amidst the bushes. These finches are surprisingly brilliant for birds of the forest undergrowth, where browns and olives are the prevailing colors of avian plumage.

Here on the ridge there are scarcely fewer chonta palms than on the lower ground, but there used to be many more palmitos. These splendid palms are only a little lower than the chontas, the tallest rising at least seventy feet to the spreading crown but only six inches thick. They are easily distinguished by the absence of the long, spiny prop roots; such aerial roots as they have form a tight mass extending not more than a foot above the ground, and they are thornless. The divisions of the feathery fronds are much narrower, more ribbonlike, than those of the chonta. It is the palmito's misfortune that its embryonic tissues are not bitter like those of the chonta. Hence, they are much sought by the local people at all seasons, but especially at Easter, when the rivers are bombed and poisoned and the forest despoiled to furnish the fish and "palm-hearts" for the traditional festivities. Sorrowfully, I step over many a fine, columnar trunk that lies rotting athwart the path, cut by trespassers. The growth of a century, the most elegant adornment of the forest, has been ruthlessly sacrificed for as much food as might be grown in a few months on a square foot of garden soil.

When I first came here, I could not walk far through this woodland without being startled by a sudden, sharp noise like a loud human sneeze—a note so harsh and unexpected that it caused even one quite familiar with it to look up in momentary alarm. I would hear a rustling in the undergrowth, and, if fortunate, I would catch a fleeting glimpse of the golden-brown rump of an Agouti bounding away. These harmless, almost tailless, brown rodents, the size of a big domestic rabbit, were abundant in the forest, and little by little I gleaned some knowledge of their habits.

When alarmed, Agoutis hop like a hare, but when at ease they walk deliberately, often pausing with one foot raised while they look about. When puzzled by a strange object, such as the blind in which I sat watching the nest of some woodland bird, the Agouti may stand erect on its hindlegs, wrinkling its pink nose as it sniffs the air. During the wet season, the poor animals are accompanied by a swarm of ravenous mosquitos, which cause them constantly to shake their heads and twitch their short, round ears. Rarely I saw them swimming adeptly in the river, perhaps to escape some animal that had pressed them closely.

When Agoutis eat some hard fruit, like that of the Milk Tree, or open the tough green pods of the Inga to extract the green seeds enclosed in a soft, sweet, white coat, they sit on their haunches, back arched into a semicircle, and hold their food in both little hands, like a squirrel. They also devour the soft, white fruits of the Coronillo, a small melastomaceous tree of the second growth, and are fond of guavas, for which they venture forth from the forest into neighboring pastures but always in the shadows of dawn or eventide, never while the sun shines upon them, for these woodland creatures are averse to strong light. One that came into the garden on wet evenings would eat bananas that we threw to it from the porch, and in Panama a zoologist trained a free Agouti to take this fruit from his hand. A curious food that I sometimes saw them eat was decaying leaves picked up from the ground. This is also an occasional food of certain birds, such as the Gray-striped Brush-Finch, perhaps because such moldy leaves support a fungus of attractive flavor. Once while I sat in my tent, watching a nest of this bird of lighter woodlands, a female Agouti passed close by me, followed by a little one no bigger than a Guinea Pig, but a perfect miniature of its mother in form, color, and mode of progression. When pursued by trespassing dogs, Agoutis from the neighboring forest sometimes sought refuge beneath our house.

I now see and hear these attractive rodents far more rarely than formerly. The last that I glimpsed was fleeing for dear life before a couple of lean, mangy hounds, which came tearing through the forest, raising a hideous din. This loud baying is music to the ears of those neighbors who own such curs, feeding them barely enough to keep them alive, but to me it is the most distressing of sounds. It is a note alien to these forests, shattering their peace, wholly out of harmony with their natural sounds, such as the triple whistle of the Black-faced Antthrush, the flute notes of the Great Tinamou, and the Chestnut-mandibled Toucans' vesper chant. It is the death knell to all they contain of wildness and charm. The Jaguar, the Puma, and the Ocelot once dwelt in these forests amid a multitude of weaker creatures, on some of which they preyed yet which remained abundant in spite of this predation. But where man brings his hunting dogs—nasty, unprofitable beasts, that never lead their owner to enough meat to pay for what they consume—the equilibrium of the forest life is destroyed, and the free animals disappear. When I hear these canine trespassers raising their frightful clamor in my woods, my walk is spoiled; I try to call to mind all the sound maxims I have gleaned from Epictetus and Marcus Aurelius, lest I lose my equanimity.

From above me comes a medley of queer sounds that I can describe only as barks and coughs. I look up in time to see half a dozen White-faced Monkeys scurrying through the treetops. They are exceedingly wary, which explains why they persist in this forest from which all other diurnal mammals larger than a squirrel have nearly or quite vanished. I watch them flee by climbing up high branches, running lithely across slender vines that form swaying bridges from tree to tree, or taking tremendous leaps across gaps in the high canopy. Some are mothers with infants riding pickaback. Off in the forest are other members of the scattered troupe whom I hear but do not see.

In more remote forests where White-faces have had less experience of man's ability to send death from afar and are accordingly bolder, they sometimes deliberately break small dead branches from a treetop and try to drop them on the biped who stands beneath them, but they seem incapable of throwing as humans do.

On both slopes of Costa Rica, I have found White-faced Monkeys as high as fifty-five hundred feet above sea level, and I have wondered how these heat-loving animals endure the chilling rains so frequent on these heights. They are fond of guavas and other fruits, and they can wreak havoc in a cornfield that adjoins forest, while the maize is still in the milk. Although highly arboreal, they will on occasion run swiftly over the ground to reach tempting food. Insects and other invertebrates enter largely into their diet; once I watched one working along the branches of a towering tree, pulling off most of the epiphytes, including cushions of moss, clumps of orchids, and small bromeliads, and putting into his mouth unidentified objects that he found beneath them. Some of these growths were left dangling by a root or two, while many others fell to the ground. Such a cleaning is probably beneficial to trees, which in humid regions are sometimes overladen with foreign growths. White-faces are not above robbing birds' nests; once I saw one steal the eggs from a Green Heron's nest on the shore of Gatún Lake.

At the edge of a tract of forest in southern Costa Rica near the Panamanian border, I watched a company of White-faces eating the sweet seed coats of an Inga. Sometimes they opened one of the short, flat pods while it remained attached to the tree, but more often they plucked it and held it in their hands while they bit it open. Then they removed the seeds, one by one, and placed each in their mouth to suck off the soft, white coat, after which they spat out the green embryo, just as children eat these delicacies. While the simians were engaged in this feast, I heard a constant succession of low, whining notes, which I interpreted as little squeals of satisfaction. To reach the pods, they sometimes hung head downward, holding on with their hind limbs and tail. Meanwhile, other members of the group ransacked the epiphytes on a neighboring tree for insects, grubs, and similar tidbits.

Their hunger satisfied, these monkeys began what was evidently a game, an arboreal version of king-of-the-castle. One individual took possession of a particular point in the midst of a great tree's spreading crown. Here it was attacked by a constant succession of others, sometimes from above, sometimes from below. Each attack led to a wrestling match in which the assailant and the defender grappled each other closely and milled around, until I marveled that they did not fall to earth, a hundred feet below. After a while they separated, and one dropped to a lower bough. At times, half a dozen monkeys clustered around, waiting to take their turns at this strenuous sport. Interfering foliage prevented my following all the details of the game, and I could not tell whether the coveted central spot was always occupied by the same individual or whether each in turn was displaced by another, as seemed likely. For half an hour, this mock battle continued. Although the contestants seemed to use their mouths as well as their hands, I heard no cry of pain, and I saw no blood, which through field glasses would have been conspicuous on white chests and shoulders. As I watched, the hundred yards that separated me from these playful people of the treetops seemed to become millions of years: I was watching my own ancestors as they once were, smaller and more innocent than we have become and, doubtless, on the whole, more contented and happy.

The Coatimundi, a relative of the raccoons with a long, sensitive muzzle, and the Tayra, a sleek, black kinsman of the otters and the weasels—both of these mammals, half arboreal and half terrestrial, were once common in this woodland but have nearly vanished. Gone are the little red-brown Forest Deer. Of the larger birds, the Great Tinamou has maintained itself in the face of oppression far better than the big Crested Guan. Yet the tinamou feeds and nests on the ground, although it roosts by night in trees, while the guan spends most of its life well above the earth, eating berries and succulent foliage, nesting in trees. But when alarmed, the wary, coolheaded tinamou darts away like a kicked football, to return to earth amidst concealing vegetation. In the same circumstances, the excitable guan stands upon some lofty bough, usually with a mate, and gives vent to its feelings with an outburst of loud, high-pitched cries that one hardly expects from a bird of such noble bearing. The guan exposes itself gratuitously to the hunter's aim; the tinamou has darted out of sight before he can lift his rifle to his shoulder. The wary one remains; the foolish one has vanished from its ancient abode.

In this forest, I rarely notice a snake, and a year may pass without an encounter with a dangerous one. Yet I am constantly vigilant, for at least four kinds of the most venomous serpents lurk in this woods, and their bite, even when not fatal, has most unpleasant consequences. Most abundant is that scourge of tropical America, the Fer-de-lance, known in Costa Rica as the *Terciopelo* (Velvet) and in Honduras as the *Barba Amarilla* (Yellow Chin). Once a laborer on the farm was struck by one, but only a single fang passed through his loose trouser leg to the flesh, and he recovered after eight injections and four days in the hospital. Almost equally numerous is another species of *Bothrops*, the *Mano de Piedra*, so-called from the resemblance of its short, stout, nearly tailless body to the stone spindle or "hand" formerly much used by country women to grind maize for tortillas on the flat stone *metate*. This is said to be the only snake that can hurl itself free of the ground when striking. Once, while walking through the forest, I saw the man ahead of me step right over a *Mano de Piedra* without being struck, and the same thing happened with a Fer-de-lance. Apparently, much depends upon whether the snake is lazily sunning itself, as these two seemed to be doing, or is actively hunting. These two mottled brown snakes are largely or wholly terrestrial, although I have heard of the Fer-de-lance ascending a yard or two to rest or sun itself in the crotch of a bush.

The third member of the dreaded genus *Bothrops* in our forest is the Bocaracá or *Chinilla*. Those that I have seen were not much over a foot in length; they had irregular reddish blotches on a dull green ground. This snake, extremely variable in coloration, is distinguished by low excrescences or "horns" above its yellow eyes. I have twice surprised this arboreal serpent in the act of swallowing a small bird's egg. Deadliest of all is the Bushmaster, in Costa Rica called the *Cascabel Muda* or "Silent Rattler." Here I have seen only a single example, a six-foot monster with fangs an inch long, which at midnight I shot as it passed beneath a corner of our porch. The brilliant coral snakes are found more often in light secondary vegetation and plantations than in the forest. Although their venom is fatal, their small fangs are far back in the mouth and they are not likely to bite anybody who does not step on them with bare feet or foolishly try to pick them up, as happens from time to time.

I continue northward along the ridge, musing upon the vicissitudes of the forest, until the increasing brightness between the trunks ahead warns me that its edge is not far off. The transition from the forest depths to the clearing is like passing from the crowded center of a city to open country, without passing through any suburbs. Pushing through the dense marginal vegetation, I stand in full sunshine on the hilltop behind the house. When I bought the farm, this northern end of the ridge was bare and treeless, littered with great, half-consumed trunks lying helter-skelter between charred stumps. From the back of the house, the naked, unbroken skyline was bleak and forbidding. To relieve the drabness, I planted a few trees, but chiefly I permitted spontaneously sprouting seedlings to grow up. Soon there were hundreds of flourishing young Guava trees, from seeds distributed in the droppings of the cattle and horses. They were convenient horn scratchers for the pair of black oxen I then owned, and many were broken by the rough treatment they received. Still, they were growing much too thickly. Little by little, the less shapely ones were cut out, until I had an open grove of fruiting Guava trees, which graced our western skyline and provided nourishing food for the cattle and ourselves and the best wood for the kitchen stove.

Before descending the steep slope to the house, I pause to feast my eyes once more on the grand panorama visible from this isolated ridge. Before me stretches the Talamancan Cordillera, from the huge, sprawling, gray mass of El Cerro de la Muerte in the northwest to the rocky summits of Chirripó in the north. Beyond Chirripó, toward the east, rises the great, nameless, rounded dome upon which we look from our front porch; then wooded summit beyond wooded summit lead the eye into the purple distance toward Panama. Below me spreads the narrow valley of the Río Peña Blanca, whose murmur rises to my ears.

At all seasons, the prevailing color of this wide panorama is green, darker on the high, precipitous slopes, where I am pleased to see that many square miles of ancient forest still lie untouched by the axe, lighter in the foreground, which is covered with coffee plantations, cane fields, pastures, and resting fields overgrown with dense thickets. Scattered amidst this greenery are scarcely visible habitations, mostly rude cabins devoid of paint. Over the years, as the influence of the outer world has grown, I have watched the yellowish brown of cane-leaf thatch give way to the silvery glint of metal roofing, and this turn brown with rust, since nearly everyone bought the cheapest grade of galvanized iron. To the northeast, almost hidden by foliage, rises the low, square steeple, crowned with a cross, of the Quizarrá church. In March, patches of charred ground tell where maize will be planted; in August, brown expanses reveal the drying grain.

As the seasons change, scattered trees lend touches of color to the verdant landscape. At the beginning of the dry season in January, the chief adornments of the valley, as of the whole Pacific slope of southern Costa Rica up to at least four thousand feet above sea level, are the buríos. These swiftly growing trees of the linden family have wood as soft and light as that of the better-known balsa and tough, fibrous bark, much used for cordage. The small, pale yellow flowers, borne in generous panicles often a hundred feet in the air, hardly attract notice. They are succeeded by masses of flat achenes, each surrounded by short, soft rays like a miniature sun (from whence comes the poetic generic name *Heliocarpus*, the sun fruit), which take on the loveliest soft shade of red as they ripen—a glory that passes all too soon.

In late February or March, after the sun fruits have turned brown and been carried afar by the wind, the Gallinazo, a kind of jacaranda, comes into bloom in the dry weather and continues until April to cover its still-leafy crown with large panicles of lavender flowers. When growing in the forest, this tree becomes very tall and displays its glorious inflorescence above the heads of its neighbors. Like the buríos, it is a rapidly growing tree that often springs up in cleared lands. Here it shoots straight upward, slender and polelike, frequently remaining unbranched until it is fifty feet or more high. Instead of branches, the main stem bears huge, fernlike, pinnately twice-compound leaves, which sometimes attain six or seven feet in length and have over a thousand small leaflets. When these fronds fall, they leave great, conspicuous scars on the smooth, gray trunk. Their hard, sticklike rachises, from which the lateral divisions have dropped, are picked up by children, who call them *caballitos* and ride them as play horses, pretending that the thick basal pulvinus is the steed's head.

The strategy of these trees seems clear: by producing no branches until they stand above their competitors, but only leaves that drop, they give little hold to the aggressive vines of these second-growth thickets, which, nevertheless, sometimes overwhelm them, bending over or snapping off the weak, overstrained trunks. If they escape this hazard, the Gallinazo trees form narrow, symmetric, low-convex crowns. Their life is all too short for their admirers, and their soft, white wood is of little value. Their winged seeds, produced in great numbers in flattish woody pods that split into two valves, are carried far and wide by the breezes.

As the jacaranda trees shed their last blossoms in late March or April, two other splendid trees come into flower. They are species of *Vochysia*, a large South American genus, belonging to a family of the same name, that is poorly represented north of Panama. Both are very handsome when in full bloom, with their rounded crowns in fullest foliage, thickly covered with yellow flowers in long, compact panicles that stand up above the leaves at the top of the trees. The Mayo may be distinguished at a distance of half a mile from its relative the Mayo Colorado or Recino by the brighter hue of its golden blossoms and its shinier leaves. Its glossy, light green foliage, of a more vivid emerald than that of most tropical trees, provides a delightful background to the pure golden thyrses of flowers and sets off their splendor to the best advantage.

The more slender Mayo Colorado has rustier leaves as well as slightly darker flowers. It is often heavily infested by the *Psittacanthus*, a kind of mistletoe that, strangely enough, rarely attacks the closely related Mayo. The parasite, a heavy, profusely branched bush with green leaves, opens its long, slender flowers at the same time that its host blooms. Deep orange-red at the base, paling to yellow toward the tip, they contrast prettily with the old gold of the blossoms of the supporting tree. But sometimes the parasite so drains the strength of the Mayo Colorado that it cannot flower; it upholds on its slender, lofty stem only the colorful blossoms of its despoiler.

The spurred flowers of the two mayos are much visited by the Snowy-breasted Hummingbird, usually one to a tree, but other hummingbirds seldom come to them. The chief pollinators in this locality are bees, especially large, shiny, black ones that swarm over them when the sun shines. The winged seeds are carried by wind into new clearings, where the Mayo Colorado thrives better than its more massive congener. In June, when both mayos have passed from bloom in the valley, those in the more continuous woodland on the surrounding mountain slopes are in full flower. From the hilltop, I survey a broad belt in which the dark green of the forest is diversified by vivid patches of yellow. The tide of efflorescence has flowed over us, flooding the valleys, then casting its golden drift on higher shores.

Sometimes, before leaving the hilltop, I visit the old Indian burial ground. Despite promises of golden ornaments, I have never permitted anyone to excavate these graves, for I believe that we should treat the burials of alien races with the same respect that we desire for our own. Sometimes, in a meditative mood, I ask myself whether, from the moral standpoint, my title to this land is as valid as that of the men whose dust lies here beneath the red clay. Perhaps the only answer to this perplexing question is that he most deserves to have the land who makes the best use of it. If my love of the mountains and rivers and forests is greater than theirs; if these things speak more meaningfully to me and I am more keenly appreciative of their beauty; if I strive harder to preserve this natural setting in its pristine splendor and to conserve the soil's fertility—then, perhaps, I can justify my possession of this land that once belonged to them. If I fall short of the aborigines in these respects, then I—and the whole line of too-aggressive palefaces who transmitted to me what was once theirs—are but piratical intruders, whose right to this land would be hard to defend.

Enlarging on this theme, it seems to me that, unless evolution miscarries, the ultimate possessor of the earth will be the race that most appreciates its grandeur and beauty and cherishes it most carefully, that rules it as a generous and compassionate lord instead of raping it like a greedy tyrant, as men have all too commonly done.

My spirit filled with this spacious panorama and uplifted by this hopeful forecast, I end my walk by descending the grassy slope toward the red-brown tiles that I glimpse amid the trees on the terrace below me.

17

A Last Home of Mystery

THE FOREST on which I look from my study window was not long ago an integral part of the dark green mantle that covers so much of the warmer regions of the American continents. Beginning along the southern shores of the Gulf of Mexico, this tropical rain forest stretches over the Usumacinta Valley and the great northern plains of Guatemala to the Caribbean littoral of Central America, over which, a few decades ago, it was practically continuous for all the thousand-mile length of this great isthmus. Most of the Pacific side of Central America is too dry for the rain forest, but it is splendidly developed on the lower slopes of the mountains in western Guatemala and again in northern Costa Rica, while here in rainy southern Costa Rica it extends down to the seacoast.

In South America, the verdant mantle of forest is divided into three unequal parts. The smallest part stretches from Darién down the ex-

Headpiece: Heavy forest in the Térraba Valley. A new clearing beside the trail from El General to Volcán.

tremely wet Pacific coast of Colombia to the Río Esmeraldas in northern Ecuador. South of this point, the garment frays out into the arid scrub that covers much of the Ecuadorian littoral, then the last thin shreds disappear in the coastal deserts of Peru. In northernmost South America east of the Andes, the Caribbean coast is arid, and the green mantle clings precariously to the windward slopes of the mountains and the courses of great rivers, until in the Guianas it extends magnificently over much of the land. Thence it stretches on to the immense Amazonian basin, where it spreads out vastly into the greatest continuous expanse of tropical forest on the face of our planet. Over the western affluents of the Amazon the dark robe lies thick and flat, so that even from an airplane the skyline is as level and circular as the horizon of a seascape. Along the southern tributaries of the Amazon and the eastern foothills of the Andes in Bolivia, the last fringes of this sylvan robe reach into more arid types of woodland. Along the coast of Brazil, from about fifteen to twenty-five degrees of southern latitude, stretches a long, narrow, isolated band of the same luxuriant rain forest.

With its outer margin following the irregularities of the strand, the dark green mantle lies flat over the level coastlands, then rises in innumerable creases and folds over the broken foothills to the lower slopes of the mountains. Just where it stops short on the mountainsides is difficult to determine. Its fabric is so deftly interwoven with the threads of the forest cloak of a different texture that covers the higher flanks of the mountains that no one can say, "At this point the lowland rain forest ends and montane forest begins." At twenty-five hundred feet above sea level, the forest has, in many regions, much the same aspect as on well-drained lowlands; a large proportion of its component threads—trees, shrubs, vines, and herbs—are the same as at sea level; but already the practiced eye detects the downward-trailing ends of the strands of the highland mantle, cunningly woven into the cloth. Here in El General, for example, the first oak trees appear at about twenty-five hundred feet. At five thousand feet, the forest takes on a different aspect: bright-flowered shrubs and epiphytes are more in evidence; the highland element in the flora is more prominent; but many strands from the lowland fabric extend this high, and even higher. The lowland rain forest ascends higher at its equatorial center than at its northern or southern margins, and everywhere the zone of transition is pushed up or down according to local topography, climate, and exposure.

Until the present century, this immense mantle of forest lay over the American continents in almost unbroken glory and splendor. Fate had been kinder to it than to the great temperate-zone forests to the north, for while men had already torn these to scarcely recognizable tatters and shreds, the tropical selva still spread in primitive majesty over most of the lands it had covered in ancient times. To be sure, it had been rent here and there by human hands, as in the Caribbean region by the great banana plantations, and nearly everywhere at its upper edges, where the land was not too abruptly steep and broken, by the advancing frontier of a more indigenous and permanent culture centering in the highlands. But at its heart, the great Amazonian plain, the little settlements clung timidly to the banks of the navigable streams, and the clearings of the natives had barely frayed the riverward margins of the vast forest that mantled all the land. Now, in the third quarter of the twentieth century, this noble forest is being destroyed at such a rate that almost any estimate of its extent that one makes will be dated before it appears in print.

With similar conditions of soil and drainage, this thousand-league-broad mantle of forest is of surprisingly uniform aspect from end to end. The tall, slender trunks of the dominant trees, rising straight and branchless into the leafy canopy far overhead; the long, slim stems of the suppressed youthful trees of the middle story, standing crowded, spare and trim, while year after year they patiently await an opening in the verdant roof above them so that they may shoot up into the sunlight and mature; the low palms and shrubs of the underwood; the scattered ferns and herbs of the ground cover; the carpet of moldering fallen leaves, flowers, and twigs; the great swinging lianas, hanging in long catenaries below the boughs; the ample heart- or arrow-shaped foliage of aroids clinging here and there to the columnar trunks; the long cords of aerial roots dangling from epiphytes far above; the bromeliads with their watertight rosettes of strap-shaped leaves, forming miniature ponds of gathered rain water where they perch on boughs high above the ground; here and there, far above, a glimpse of the white or yellow or mauve blossoms of an orchid—these are universal features of the American rain forest, whether in southern Mexico or in Brazil. I have photographs of the high forest taken in Honduras, in Panama, and in Peru, and I do not believe that there is a man alive who could tell in what part of tropical America they were taken. Some of the wider-ranging species of trees spread from end to end of the American tropics. Yet everywhere are plants and birds and insects peculiar to the locality, so that their presence might reveal his geographic situation to a naturalist set down blindfolded in the midst of the forest. Yet very few know enough to tell where they are by such local signs.

This immense area of forest is one of the last strongholds of mystery, one of the major regions of our planet that has most stubbornly withheld its secrets from the prying gaze of men. In no other part of the earth directly or indirectly accessible to man do more prime discoveries await the diligent investigator, save possibly in the depths of the ocean. The arctic regions, of course, have been explored less than the tropical forests, but the tropics with their teeming life hold a thousand secrets for every one in the nearly lifeless polar caps.

I dwell here surrounded by mysteries. The forest that begins fifty yards from my door obstinately guards its secrets. Some of the puzzles that most obviously thrust themselves upon my attention are the most difficult to solve. As I write on this sunny morning in early March, a clear whistle, rapidly twice or thrice repeated, is borne to my ears from the neighboring forest. I know it to be the song of the Green Shrike-Vireo; for the next few months, I shall hear these notes innumerable times each day; I shall scan the lofty treetops until my neck aches for a sight of the elusive bird, and most probably in vain, so well does it remain concealed amid the masses of foliage a hundred feet above the ground that almost match its plumage in color. Year after year, I hear these same wild wood notes; yet for more than three decades, I have searched fruitlessly for this bird's nest, which to my knowledge has never been described.

It is not only the voices of the treetop birds that baffle. Another of the characteristic notes of these forests is a calm, beautiful whistle, sliding up the scale in three parts, the middle shortest. This lovely, moving utterance sounds through the woodland from January until July; yet it took me uncounted hours of patient scrutiny to ascertain its authorship. For the whistle is so ventriloquial that, at whatever point one imagines the whistling bird to be, there he can persuade himself is the source of the sound. It happened that the first bird of the kind that I glimpsed, unsatisfactorily, while he called was well above my head; and thus I formed the habit of peering into the trees above me for a sight of the whistler, while nearly always the retiring brown bird lurked amid the undergrowth, rarely shoulder high. Now that I am familiar with the Thrush-like Manakin, have found its nests and studied its ways, and can watch it sing without much trouble, I am touched with shame when I recall how long it remained merely the mysterious, unsubstantial "Voice of the Forest."

The call of the Streaked-chested Antpitta—seven or eight loud, mellow whistles delivered in a peculiar, hollow, melancholy tone—is another woodland sound that I was long in tracing to its source. So secretive is the stout, long-legged, stubby-tailed bird that I never succeeded in seeing it as it called until I found a puzzling nest, quite different from any that I had seen. By concealing myself nearby, I was able to watch the antpitta approach; he hopped rapidly over the ground, now and then flicking aside fallen leaves with a vigorous sideways sweep of its bill. While sitting on the shallow bowl of dead leaves, warming the two mottled eggs, it delivered the unmistakable whistles that I had heard so many times before without associating them with any bird I knew—and another of the mysterious sounds of the forest ceased to be a mystery. But even some of the diurnal sounds remain in this category, in spite of all my efforts to classify them. If the voices heard by day can be so baffling, what is to be said of those that sound only in the night?

The difficulty of seeing many of these sylvan birds, even when they so loudly and persistently proclaim themselves, suggests how hard it is to find their nests, which they hide away with all their skill and cunning and approach with hesitant caution. Who would look for birds' eggs in a wasps' nest, a termites' nest, or the heart of a decaying palm stump? Even some of the nests built with long-continued effort, in plain view, are so different from a conventional bird's nest that the newcomer in the tropical forests may see them without recognizing what they are. I recall how for many minutes I had within my visual field my first nest of the Royal Flycatcher, without suspecting that I was in the presence of one of the most amazing examples of avian architecture, until the continued interest of the crested builder focused my attention upon it. It looked more like a yard-long tangle of dead vegetation caught on a branch above a forest stream than any bird's nest I had hitherto known.

The nests of many of the common and widespread birds of the tropical forest remain unknown to ornithologists, and some that have been described in scientific publications are attributed to species that almost certainly did not build them. Even when one knows, from having seen the parents repeatedly arrive with food, that they have a nest in a certain tree, its actual discovery may be a baffling undertaking. While I lived in Rivas, a Scarlet-thighed Dacnis, a tiny bird of the treetops, built her nest in a tall Muñeco tree that grew isolated by the roadside within view of my cabin. As the nestlings grew older, the arrival of a parent with food was greeted by shrill cries that reached me sixty yards away. I had no doubt that there was a nest with young in that tree, but to find it was another matter. Long and careful scrutiny of the dense crown through field glasses failed to disclose a trace of a nest. Coming with food, the parents promptly vanished amid the dark, glossy foliage and helped not at all to guide me to their secret.

Twice I climbed up and searched through the crown of the tree, carefully scanning the foliage from every bough that would bear my weight, without sight of the coveted structure. But on my second visit, after I had been in the treetop an hour, the nestlings, becoming very hungry because my presence kept their parents away, began to call loudly from a point close beside me. Their voices issued from a dense tangle of a green parasitic vine draped over the leafy outer boughs, and here I glimpsed, or thought I glimpsed, a nest. But I could distinguish nothing of its form or occupants. So I waited a few days, until I no longer heard the nestlings' cries, then cut down the limb to collect the vacant nest.

It was one of the slightest and frailest of birds' nests that I had ever seen, a birdlings' cradle held to the irreducible minimum. The cup, or rather hammock, was supported between two, parallel, slender twigs. Constructed of coarse, wiry, fibrous rootlets and tendrils, it measured only two inches in diameter by three-quarters of an inch in depth. It fitted snugly in the cupped palm of my hand. As though the slight hammock were not sufficiently difficult to detect because of its small size and the density of the foliage amid which it was hung, forty feet above the ground, its bottom had been covered with pieces of green fern frond, some wider than itself, which made it, when viewed from below, indistinguishable from the screening leafage. What chance has anyone of finding such a nest when built in the crown of some forest giant, instead of in a much lower and more easily climbed tree at the edge of a naturalist's yard? Yet many another nest, no bigger nor more readily located, awaits discovery in that vast, scarcely explored sea of verdure, the canopy of the tropical forest.

Most of the nests that I have seen in the tropical rain forest and neighboring clearings have held only two eggs; less often there have been three, but rarely more. Some of these nests belonged to hummingbirds and pigeons which, regardless of where they breed, do not normally lay more than two eggs in a set or, for a great many species of pigeons, only a single egg. But many other nests with only two eggs belonged to American flycatchers, wrens, wood warblers, tanagers, and finches; and in these families, species that breed in the temperate zones or the subarctic produce sets of eggs that are often two or three times as great. Why do tropical birds raise broods so much smaller than those of the most closely related species at high latitudes?

Several explanations of this enigma have been advanced. One school of thought holds that all animals everywhere produce as many offspring as they can, simply because strains that multiply more rapidly will eventually supplant the less prolific strains of the same species. In birds, the factor that limits the rate of reproduction is likely to be the food available for forming eggs or nourishing the young. Tropical birds, these theorists hold, raise small families because they cannot supply food rapidly enough to adequately nourish larger ones. For one thing, in regions near the equator they have a shorter working day than do birds at high latitudes in summer, when days are long and nights short.

Differences in the hours available for finding food cannot be the sole explanation of the larger broods of birds at high latitudes, which often raise two or three times as many young as their tropical cousins, although they certainly do not enjoy two or three times as much daylight. It is also necessary to assume that food is actually scarcer, or harder to find, in the tropics than in northern woods and fields in summertime. Another difficulty with this theory is that the size of the broods of tropical birds is largely independent of the number of adults attending the nest. In hummingbirds and manakins, as likewise in many species of flycatchers, cotingas, woodcreepers, icterids or New World orioles, and others, the female alone attends the young; yet in these groups broods tend to be as large as in those many other species in which both parents feed the nestlings. If ability to supply food is the limiting factor, lone females should, on the average, raise only half as many young as do both parents working together. Moreover, it has been demonstrated, by placing extra nestlings in a nest or by keeping the parents away until the young have become very hungry, that in case of need the parents can bring food much more rapidly than they ordinarily do.

Evidently the view that the size of bird families in the humid tropics is limited by the availability of food, attractive because of its simplicity, is too naïve. More probably, the size of the brood has been adjusted, over the ages, to the maintenance of a stable population in a stable environment. Just how this has been effected is more difficult to understand than it is to visualize how a more prolific race might replace one that reproduces slowly; but we do know that animals that overpopulate their habitat may suffer severely from starvation and disease; apparently the rates of reproduction of tropical birds have, in a long course of evolution, been limited to avoid this danger. The brood size of tropical birds seems to have been adjusted, over the centuries, to the average annual mortality of each species.

The small size of bird families in the humid tropics is just one aspect of their more leisurely schedule of reproduction. Tropical birds not only lay fewer eggs; as a rule, they take longer to build their nests, allow a longer interval to elapse between the completion of the structure and the start of laying, have longer incubation and nestling periods, and feed their fledged young for a longer period than do closely related birds in the temperate zones, which must hurry to rear enough young to compensate for losses in bleak winters or, if they avoid the inclement season, on long and hazardous migrations.

The recognition that animals can hold their rate of reproduction below the maximum that is possible for them throws fresh light upon that most hideous blot on the fair face of nature, predation, the killing and devouring of one creature by another. It is well known that if predators are suddenly removed, the animals on which they preyed may become so numerous that they exhaust their food supply, with tragic consequences not only to themselves but to other associated animals. This is particularly striking in the case of large herbivores which, in the absence of checks upon their increase, may so overbrowse or overgraze their range that, even after their removal, it takes years to recover. Hence predation is frequently regarded as a blessing in disguise, necessary to preserve the health and balance of a natural community. But if animals can adjust their reproduction to the mortality of their species, it follows that, if they were not subject to predation, they would breed more slowly. The predators themselves, by creating a need for more rapid multiplication, are responsible for the production of the individuals that they slaughter. If predation had never arisen, predators would not be necessary to prevent overpopulation. Predation, including its subtle form, parasitism, is a tragic miscarriage of evolution. It is responsible for some of the worst passions that afflict that long-time predator, man, and through them for a large share of the evils from which we suffer.*

We considered the birds first, for voice and movement make them the most obvious inhabitants of the forest. Without them, the high selva would appear silent and lifeless, like some mansion magnificently constructed and lavishly ornamented, with lofty vaulted halls that never resounded with music and laughter, nor the cheerful prattle of children. Because we can hardly avoid becoming aware of the birds, the wide gaps in our knowledge of their lives are more forcibly brought to our attention. But the very presence of most of the four-footed animals is shrouded in secrecy; they are shy and wary, and a large proportion of them hide away by day in hollow trunks, burrows, and caves, where we may pass close by them without suspecting their presence. Aside from such diurnal creatures as monkeys, squirrels, peccaries, sloths, Coatimundis, Agoutis, and Tayras, the mammals of the tropical forest lead their active lives in the deep obscurity of the woodland night. Their voices, which sound so weird and eerie through the leafy darkness, will long continue to perplex and mystify the naturalists.

The insect world, with its countless multitudes of kinds, is a vast and inexhaustible storehouse of mysteries. Although hundreds of thousands of species have been named and described, many more lurk in the tropi-

---

*I write in full awareness of the influence that the predatory habit in all its manifold forms, itself a product of evolution, has had upon subsequent evolution, speeding it up and increasing the diversity of living creatures, many of which are far from admirable. However, predation is only one of many selective agents, some of which, even if acting more slowly, might have had more benign effects. I like to think that on other planets, revolving around distant stars, gentler methods have brought life to fulfillment, and I would love to see the results.

cal forests, unknown to science. One can hardly expose a lamp at night without attracting insects still nameless to entomologists; the tiny moth that I inadvertently crush on my paper as I write may well represent an undescribed species. How all these creatures live, what they eat and how they reproduce, and how they interact with each other and with man, is a field of inquiry that ten thousand scientists could hardly exhaust in a century.

But the very blocks of which this wondrous sylvan edifice is built, the majestic trees themselves, are a source of endless perplexity to the botanist. I believe that any diligent amateur naturalist, equipped with the excellent guides now available for most extratropical regions, could learn the names of all the trees in a hundred acres of temperate-zone woodland in a single summer. But knowledge of the trees of the tropical forests is far more slowly and laboriously won. In the first place, the variety of trees in a given area is vastly greater, without a corresponding diversity of foliage. Fifty trees of the rain forest, all chosen at random, will show considerably less variety in the outlines of their leaves than the same number of northern trees, such as oaks, beeches, maples, sycamores, and birches. Even the leaves of the oaks of tropical mountains lose the stimulating diversity of shape familiar to us in the North and assume a monotonous rotundity of outline.

We depend in large measure on the flowers and fruits, bark and wood, for the identification of tropical trees. But the former are displayed high overhead, screened by clouds of foliage, where only the monkeys and birds can reach them. We smell a delicious fragrance of flowers in the tropical forest and crane our necks in vain to discover its source. We pick up a bright fallen blossom, which obviously came from somewhere above us, yet straining our eyes upward into the brighter light, we discern only brown branches and green leaves; we cannot be sure whether our flower fell from a tree or from some vine draped over its topmost boughs. The fallen fruits similarly puzzle us.

With great labor, and not without a feeling of guilt for the destruction we are causing, we cut through the trunk of some forest giant to bring its flowery crown within reach, and we shall be fortunate if it does not lodge against a neighboring tree, the coveted specimens still far above our puny grasp, and their acquisition now attended by greater danger. The plant collector of the tropical forest must be a fearless and skillful climber with a superb physique or else engage others to do the heavy work for him. In the East Indies, enterprising Dutch botanists trained monkeys to collect for them in the treetops. A wiry Guatemalan Indian who could throw and climb ropes was the best assistant I ever had for tree collecting. I constantly used field glasses to scan the crowns of tall trees and learn whether they bore flowers or fruits in the proper stage for making specimens.

An acre of tropical rain forest supports a greater variety of living things, vegetable and animal, macroscopic and microscopic, than an equal area of the earth's surface covered by any other type of vegetation. It is even doubtful whether man, by concentrating the productions of all the continents and all the islands in his botanic and zoölogical gardens, has ever succeeded in bringing so great a diversity of living organisms into a small area, as are found in the tropical forest. The spreading limbs of a single great tree may uphold a garden with a variety of shrubbery, flowers, and ferns that would be the envy of any gardener. There is even pond life in the little pools of water contained in the rosettes of the epiphytic bromeliads and in the close-set, fleshy, highly colored bracts that shield the flowers of some of the Heliconias. All these creatures exist in conditions that make their study a particularly arduous pursuit because of the excellent opportunities for the concealment of all small organisms, because so much of the activity of the forest is carried on by night, and, above all, because to man, the earth-bound, scarcely one-twentieth of the vertical depth of the forest is within easy reach.

And yet, despite its amazingly exuberant life, many people find the tropical forest monotonous. There is, indeed, a general sameness of aspect over large areas, and it has already been noticed that throughout their vast sweep, the forests of tropical America exhibit the same broad features under similar conditions of soil and rainfall. A gallery filled with the choicest paintings may soon become monotonous to one without knowledge of art or its history; and the halls of a great museum, so full of interest to one versed in the subjects they display, quickly become tedious to the mere wonder seeker. The fascination of the forest grows along with our foundation of knowledge and our skill in uncovering its well-guarded secrets.

To one who loves nature in her wild majesty, the aspect of the forest changes ceaselessly as he wanders through it. No two vistas are quite alike. Here is a fertile, sheltered dell where the trunks of the gigantic trees rise up with more than ordinary sweep and girth; here a ridge where the tall and slender columns of the palms cluster in more than usual profusion; here a ravine where tree ferns spread their broad filigree fronds in wondrous perfection; here an open glade where flowering shrubs make a display of bright color rare in the lowland forest. And just as the solitary wanderer is about to call the forest deserted and lifeless, he meets a troupe of monkeys chattering and gesticulating in the boughs above, displaying an interest in the earth-bound primate hardly less than he takes in the more typical arboreal members of the order to which he belongs; or a band of Collared Peccaries steal grunting away from him, leaving a strong scent of musk on the still air of the underwood; or a broad-winged Morpho butterfly floats rapidly past, holding his fascinated gaze with flashes of azure unbelievably intense; or he wanders into the midst of a swarming legion of army ants with its motley following of small birds, so varied in form, plumage, and voice, yet all fairly tolerant of each other, as each in its own fashion snatches up the insects, spiders, and other small creatures that rush out from concealment beneath the ground litter as the devouring horde of ants approaches—the whole forming one of the most animated displays that wild nature anywhere presents.

Such scenes of bloodless carnage as the wholesale destruction of roaches, spiders, woodlice, and centipedes by the army ants and their feathered camp followers are strikingly in contrast to the atmosphere of peace that generally prevails in the forest. Many of the most tranquil days of my life have been passed deep in the forest, remote from the dwellings of men. The forest is a much safer place, for ourselves, than most strangers to it suppose. Perhaps the greatest risk is that of getting lost, if one wanders carelessly from the trail in unfamiliar territory. Next is the danger of being struck by falling trees and branches; during a windstorm, and at the beginning of the rainy season, when the weight of decaying trunks and limbs is greatly increased by the water they soak up, it is not prudent to delay beneath dead wood.

Venomous snakes are a peril; but if the forest wanderer sheathes his nether extremities in stout boots and puttees and avoids needless wandering about at night when poisonous snakes are most active, the danger from them is slight. Snakes in the forest are like fire in the house: as most of us pass our lives without having our dwellings burn down, yet we can never afford to relax our precautions to prevent fire; so few of those who live much in the forest are struck by snakes, yet the danger of such an attack is always at the back of their minds.

Snakes are far more abundant in lurid stories about the "jungle" than they are in the tropical forest itself, at least in America. On my return from an expedition to the lowlands of eastern Peru, I was shown a magazine article that told how the heroic members of our party forced their way through the mortiferous "jungle" brushing aside deadly snakes. Actually, in the several months that we spent in this region, we probably did not see half a dozen snakes longer than our forearms, and all were in a hurry to get out of our way. The forests of tropical America, unlike those of the Old World tropics, contain few quadrupeds dangerous to man. The solitary Jaguar—the *Tigre* of Spanish America—and the bands of White-lipped Peccaries are about the only mammals that man need fear, unless he goes out of his way to molest them. But few see these dangerous animals without hunting for them; and if, perchance, at rare intervals we meet a Jaguar or a herd of peccaries, the likelihood is that they will steal away, as nervous and as eager to avoid closer contact as we are.

Thus, we may saunter through the forest with a forgetfulness of the perils that beset all living things, that in the traffic of a busy city or even on a country lane where automobiles pass would soon involve us in disaster. And the peace in our hearts is reflected by everything around us. Rarely indeed do we witness violence in the forest. I have seldom seen a bird fall victim to a hawk or mammal in the forest and rarely even in the clearings among them where the outlook is wider. I have not seen one mammal attack another.

The quiet and changelessness of the forest are its outstanding characteristics. If man does not interfere in his usual violent manner, it appears much the same this year as last. The young trees in the dim light of the underwood grow very slowly; unless we use a measuring rod, we can hardly detect any change in them from year to year. The old decaying giant seems scarcely more decrepit than it was twelve months ago. The same epiphyte clings to the side of the same tree; the same thick liana twists about the same trunk, which is apparently none the worse for its long-continued constriction; the shrubs and herbs have altered little in aspect, save as the changing season elicits flowering or fruiting. In the rain forest there is no colorful season of general leaf fall, no bleak period of universal nakedness of boughs, no thrilling epoch of awakening and leaf renewal, as in temperate-zone forests. Each kind of tree renews its foliage, or flowers and fruits, at its own convenience, with the result that the aspect of the forest as a whole changes little from month to month.

Nearly all the forest birds reside in the same area throughout the year. The hummingbirds sing in the same spots; the brisk little manakins dance and snap their wings in the same places; the inconspicuous greenish flycatchers called pipromorphas call and flit their wings in the same saplings as last year and, presumably, are the same individuals. Only here and there in the forest is violent change evident, as where a dead or infirm tree has toppled over and wrought havoc on a small scale, creating a little light-flooded opening where vegetation shoots up with a rapidity never attained in the surrounding deep shade. But except in the rare event of a violent hurricane, only an exceedingly small proportion of the forest is so altered in the course of a single annual cycle.

This seeming peace of the forest is superficial and deceptive. Actually, the forest is pervaded by ceaseless, but only exceptionally violent, strife. The very diversity of organisms around us is proof of this. The forest is a vast laboratory in which new species are produced, tested, and eliminated if found defective. An important factor in species making is competition and the weeding out of the less fit—the struggle for existence. These crowded seedlings springing up so hopefully beneath their towering parent; these ranks of spare and lean, undernourished young saplings; these tall middle-aged trees, already nudging at the shoulders of the dominating old fellows above them, telling them quietly that it is time to make way for a newer and more progressive generation—all are silently, endlessly vying with each other for a place in the sun. This vine spiraling upward around the trunk of a tree must in the end either strangle it or be overgrown and buried in its expanding cylinder of wood; for all that, we may watch them month after month and notice as little change in the positions of the antagonists as we see in a marble statue of Laocoön and his sons entwined by serpents.

Although the birds appear carefree and happy and build their nests as though confident of success, their chances of rearing young to maturity are pitifully small. Doubtless it is to reduce the incidence of predation that many birds of the tropical forest have evolved a routine of incubating their eggs and feeding their nestlings which entails a minimum of parental visits, for such movements may disclose to hostile eyes the situation of a well-concealed nest. This is especially true of the antbirds, preeminently birds of tropical American forests, even the smallest of which may incubate continuously for hours and which bring their nestlings substantial meals at long intervals. Their infrequent visits to the nest contrast sharply with the bustling activity at the nests of many birds of the temperate zones.

Birds of the tropical forest typically approach their nests with the greatest circumspection, yet while hesitating to go to them, they may call loudly. This uncontrolled expression of excitement, especially evident in such forest birds as the Red-crowned Ant-Tanager and the Blue-black Grosbeak, seems inconsistent with the excessive wariness otherwise manifested in their approach; it might cancel all their caution if the principal enemies of their nests were led to them by auditory cues. The fact that natural selection has not sternly suppressed this volubility suggests that the chief predators are deficient in hearing. Most probably they are snakes, which are certainly the animals that I have most often surprised in the act of pillaging birds' nests. However, many other predators that operate more rapidly, or by night, usually escape detection. Despite the parents' skill in hiding their nests and their infrequent and circumspect approaches, hardly one out of five or six nests escapes destruction until the young are fledged.

The tremendous difficulty that the birds experience in rearing their broods, coupled with the small size of these broods, tells us plainly that the adults enjoy a fairly safe existence, for no species can long survive the combination of high adult mortality and slow reproduction. Just as those trees that survive the rigorous weeding out of seedlings and saplings and win a place for themselves in the forest canopy are likely to hold it for many years, so the birds that come safely through the dangerous period of nest life and reach maturity seem to lead, for birds, long and secure lives. This was demonstrated by the English ornithologist David Snow in a remarkable study of banded Black and White Manakins in the forest of Trinidad. He found that 89 per cent of the adult males, exceptionally conspicuous birds, survived through the year, which indicates a longevity greater than that of any small, temperate-zone bird whose survival rate is known. Often, when I have returned to a nest that I had been studying, only to find that it had been pillaged since my last visit, I have been consoled for the loss by the reflection that, if so few broods are successful, the adults must be long-lived.

Much of the more violent and sanguinary strife of the forest takes place under cover of darkness. It is chiefly then that tooth and claw and poison fang are at work. Rarely by day we come upon mute traces of the carnage: the hideously mangled remains of what was yesterday a beautiful creature enjoying its life, the scattered feathers, the forlornly empty nest. But unless we have keen and watchful eyes, we may wander far through the peaceful forest by day and meet few of these grim reminders of struggle and death.

Thus the tropical forest, the headquarters of terrestrial life on this planet, resembles human life, which is derived from it. We find there what we seek. If we seek beauty, it is there profusely. If we yearn for peace, it awaits us there. If, on the other hand, we gloat in strife and violence, it offers us that, too. If we search for some particular group of plants or animals, we find them, remaining oblivious of many wonderful things that are revealed to those who explore the forest with other interests. And if we enter the forest without any goals or interests, we find it a place of utter boredom. In all these ways, the forest presents an epitome of human life.

But in spite of beauty, tranquillity, and endless variety, the forest at last becomes oppressive. To stay too long in unbroken forest is apt to induce a mild case of claustrophobia. After all, a man in the forest is like a mouse in a cornfield, without that animal's agility in climbing the stalks. Our ancestors eons ago lost the freedom of the forest when they abandoned the arboreal in favor of the terrestrial life. Now we are no longer able to roam through the woodland as we see the White-faced Monkeys doing and long to do ourselves; we are pinned down in the lowest stratum, and, save by an effort too exhausting to be often repeated, we cannot rise above it. Fully 95 per cent of the lofty rain forest stands above our reach. This limitation at length becomes irksome and depressing; we feel a melancholy sense of frustration. We lose our proud pose as the lords of creation and come at last to feel what we actually are, small, bewildered creatures wandering timidly amid forces immeasurably more powerful and enduring than ourselves. This reminder of what we are is perhaps salutary, but so unflattering that we would dismiss it. When the forest has reduced us to submission, when our spirits are in a proper state to contemplate in all humility the vast, mysterious creative urge of which it is a visible expression, we hasten to escape from it.

Moreover, we need a broader outlook than we have in the midst of the forest and are most at ease when covered by a wider expanse of blue sky than we can glimpse through gaps in the high canopy of foliage. Were we birds, we might win these advantages by flying up to the treetops; but we are chained in the lowest galleries and can escape only by dragging our weight over the ground. How grateful is the wider stretch of earth and sky, the more vivid green, the freer air of the cleared lands, when we return to them after a long day amid the tree trunks; how soothing the sight of a dwelling nestling amid shrubbery and fruit trees, the scent of wood fire and perchance of cooking and roasting coffee, when we come back hungry and tired!

Scarcely anyone, no matter how much he loves the forest, chooses to dwell in its unbroken depth. He will prefer to live in a clearing with a wide view and the forest nearby, where he can really see it and enter it whenever he will. For it is true that in the midst of the forest we cannot see it for the trees. Only when we stand before its edge, as on the shore of a river or in a fresh cutting, can we survey the full majesty of its towering height; only when from an eminence we look over miles and miles of billowy treetops do we begin vaguely to grasp the vastness of its sweep. To know the forest, we must study it in all aspects, as birds soaring above its roof, as earth-bound bipeds creeping slowly over its roots.

18

The Coffee Grove

WHEN I BOUGHT Los Cusingos, it had about an acre of coffee already in production. I am not a coffee drinker, and the prospect of growing coffee for profit so far from a *beneficio* or processing mill was not encouraging. The care of a coffee plantation is laborious, and through the years I asked myself again and again whether the grove yielded enough income to justify its maintenance. But whenever I saw the little plantation in full bloom, I had no doubt that the bushes paid for the attention they received, if not with a cash return, at least with less tangible values. Coffee is a beautiful shrub, whether bedight with masses of fragrant white flowers or laden with glossy red berries or clad only in its dark, lustrous foliage. Were it not a plant of great commercial value, the economic foundation of many mountainous countries of the tropics, it might rank as a prized ornamental shrub in tropical gardens.

Headpiece: Coffee in flower. A transient glory of whiteness and fragrance.

Originally a woodland shrub, coffee is in many regions grown under light shade to simulate its natural habitat. In various countries, different shade trees are used, but leguminous trees are preferred because of the nodules of nitrogen-fixing bacteria that many species bear on their roots, by means of which they enrich the soil. In my little coffee grove, the shade was provided by tall, spreading, coarse-leaved Inga trees and by much lower plantains, which after a few years dwindled away.

The work of the coffee plantations begins with the return of drier weather in January. The crop has all been gathered, and the bushes enter a short period of comparative rest before flowering. This is the opportune moment for pruning. Like a number of other woody plants of the tropics, coffee has a peculiar system of branching, characterized by the functional specialization of the vegetative buds and of the branches that arise from them. In the axil of each of the opposite leaves of the upright main stem are two buds, one above the other. The upper bud usually produces a more or less horizontal branch, which bears the flowers and fruits in axillary clusters but mostly remains itself unbranched; with age it becomes a long, slender, whiplike, simple twig. The lower bud generally remains dormant, but it may be stimulated to grow into an upright shoot with the two kinds of buds. Flowers are never borne directly on these upright stems but only on the horizontal branches that spring from them. A healthy, uninjured young coffee bush has a single vertical stem surrounded by simple flowering branches.

A principal purpose of pruning is to increase the number of upright stems, which in turn can support a greater number of the twigs that bear the fruits. The simplest method of accomplishing this is to decapitate the main stem, which usually causes an upright branch to arise from the base of each of the opposite leaves of the highest remaining node. By cutting off the tops of these two uprights, after they have become stronger, four vertical stems may be produced. An alternative procedure, used in Guatemala, is to bend over the young sapling and pin its top to the ground: the curvature causes a number of upright stems to spring from the lower nodes. Certain experiments, disproving old beliefs, have demonstrated that, at least in their first years, coffee bushes yield more berries if permitted to grow naturally, without pruning. In any case, the pruning of coffee becomes necessary, as well as more complicated, as with increasing age the branching becomes more complex, and there are many old, effete branches and twigs to remove.

In those early years on the farm, I usually pruned the coffee myself during the first weeks of the new year, but sometimes a boy assisted. At about the same time, we cut back the limbs of the shade trees, which should not be permitted to cover more than half of the sky above the plantation. To reduce the shade just as the driest and sunniest days of the year approach seems inconsistent, yet it is approved practice.

In the bright days of January and February, the clustering, naked flower buds swell in the axils of the lateral twigs of the coffee bushes. They await the return of the rains to stimulate anthesis. A good soaking downpour, following a month or more of rainless weather, brings the coffee into flower after an interval of from eight to ten days, during which additional showers may fall. With us, this often occurs in March or even late February, but on the opposite side of the Valley of El General, where the dry season is longer and more severe, the coffee may blossom several weeks later.

The change in the weather brings the coffee shrubs into flower all at once, as though a fairy godmother had passed through the plantation with her magic wand, touching each expectant bush and clothing it in a snowy gown. And like the enchanted garment that, in the old tale, the good fairy gave the favored maiden for a single gala occasion, the full splendor of the coffee blossoms lasts only a single day. But what a glorious day! What a sanctuary of beauty the grove becomes, with the lovely shrubs standing in neat rows, all clad in snowy white and dark, glossy green! As I approach the plantation, I am greeted by an exquisitely delicate fragrance; yet once in the midst of the blossoming shrubs, I only at intervals become aware of it. Without doubt, the still air between the coffee bushes is saturated with this ethereal aroma; but my nose, coarse instrument that it is, cannot for many seconds remain attuned to so subtile a fragrance.

I carry out a book and a stool and sit amidst the coffee, in the still air pervaded with the most delicate aroma and murmurous with innumerable wings. But the book remains unread on my lap; there is so much to distract me from its pages. Now and again a hummingbird comes to poise upon vibrant wings before the snowy blossoms—a green Rufous-tailed Hummingbird or a brown Little Hermit. Or a Bananaquit, clinging to a twig, bends down to probe the white flowers with its sharp, curved, black bill. But there are far too few birds to pollinate the myriad flowers even in this little plantation. This task appears to be performed chiefly by pollen-gathering meliponine bees, which buzz through the grove in countless numbers and bewildering variety, some black, some amber, some as big as a horsefly, others not much larger than a gnat, but all stingless. By eight o'clock in the morning, the anthers are shedding pollen freely, and soon the busy harvesters have filled the baskets on their hindlegs. By afternoon, the dusty harvest has been gathered, and few bees are to be found in the plantation.

Our most enchanting experiences are the briefest; it would not do to have them become commonplace. By the following morning, the pure whiteness of the coffee flowers has become stained with brown, the discoloration beginning on the anthers and gradually spreading over the corollas. Soon the blossoms are badly stained and falling, as sorry a spectacle as soiled snow. Yet even on the second day, the discolored flowers are as fragrant as when newly opened. In more advanced stages of withering, they acquire a different but not unpleasant odor.

Usually there is some sporadic flowering before and after the great day of full anthesis; but where there is a sharp contrast between the dry season and the ensuing rains, the synchronization of blossoming over a wide area is indeed remarkable. If the dry season is interrupted by occasional showers, the flowering is less regular: some bushes come into bloom long before neighboring ones; and on a single plant different branches, and even different clusters of buds, may flower and set fruit independently of each other. Thus, there may be irregular flowering from December until April or May, and one enjoys the coffee blossoms for a longer period but with less intensity. If, because the open blossoms are drenched by a sudden shower, or for some other reason the first flowering fails to yield many swelling fruits, there may be another general blossoming several weeks later. When flowering is sporadic, the ripening of the berries is spread over a longer interval, and picking becomes more tedious and costly; here it may continue from June or July until November or December, with the peak of the harvest beneath the torrential rains of September and October. The coffee planter prefers a uniform flowering that results in bushes heavily laden with red berries ripening all together so that they are more easily gathered, and the pickers, who are paid by measure, earn more per day and work more contentedly.

The chief coffee-producing districts are well provided with *beneficios*— mills where, with complicated machinery and the use of much water for washing, the twin seeds are removed from the soft, sweetish pulp that surrounds them and, after thorough drying, divested of the thin, parchmentlike seed coat. Great plantations, which may contain thousands of acres of coffee, have their own *beneficios*; small growers sell their freshly picked coffee berries to *beneficios* that may or may not be on plantations. Until long after I came to Los Cusingos, the nearest *beneficio* was beyond the mountains, so we prepared a grade of coffee known to the trade as "unwashed." We simply spread the red berries on the sloping surface of a huge rock and left them exposed to sun and rain until the pulp decayed and dried around the resistant beans. After a bright, sunny morning, we gathered them up for a little more drying on the porch, then stored them. When my coffee-drinking employees needed coffee for roasting and grinding, the beans were pounded out of their dry shells in the same big, wooden mortar that we used for shelling rice. Now all this is changed, for three competing *beneficios* have receiving stations for the red berries half a mile from our gate.

The great rock where for years we dried the coffee is one of the wonders of the farm. Old Don Chico once told me that it was the farm's most valuable asset; as season after season we used it for drying coffee, rice, beans, and other things, I came to agree with him. Its northern face is a sheer wall twenty feet high, washed at the base by the clear water of the creek. Its more gently sloping sides bear a luxuriant garden of ferns, begonias, aroids, flowering shrubs, mosses, liverworts, and other epiphytic growths. The gently inclined top is roughly twelve yards in diameter. Incised into its weathering face are a number of cryptic designs, some still clear and others nearly obliterated, which, doubtless, were carved by the Indians who rest in deep graves on the hilltop behind our house.

The principal figure, repeated in several places on this same rock and on many another rock in El General as well as more distant parts of Central America, is a rather closely coiled spiral opening into a long, curving line. Such spirals are usually grouped in trios. Don Chico carefully explained to me that this design was a map of the Peña Blanca River. Archaeologists regard these spirals as symbols of the alligator. When they present a series of drawings showing a recognizable alligator, with its snout turned up and its tail bent down with a hook at the tip, followed by others with the reptile's body increasingly incurved, while it wastes away to a line and its limbs all but vanish, this attribution seems plausible. But in the absence of this careful reconstruction of a supposed historical process, the naïve person might contend that their explanation is even more fantastic than that advanced by Don Chico, who himself passed among his neighbors as an authority on Indian remains.

The shade trees of my little coffee grove, as of great plantations in other regions, offer exceptionally favorable conditions for watching small birds of the treetops. The wider spacing of the trees and their more open crowns make these restless, flitting creatures much more visible than in natural woodlands with more crowded trees and obstructing vegetation beneath them. The coffee grove is one of my favorite places for watching for the arrival of the bright little wood warblers, which, as days grow shorter and bleak weather approaches in the northern lands where they nest, pour in countless multitudes into Central America. In no other part of the farm have I seen so much of the Blackburnian Warblers, of which the adult males retain their glowing orange, white, and black nuptial plumage in their winter home. At times the crowns of the Inga trees swarm with Chestnut-sided Warblers in subdued winter plumage, Tennessee Warblers plain at all seasons, Philadelphia Vireos, and a variety of resident birds. The tall, gaunt Cecropia trees that grow along the edges of the coffee grove attract many birds both migratory and resident, who come to peck at the long, dangling, green, fruiting spikes. Although these seem a dry, harsh food, they are a mainstay of the frugivorous birds in the dry season, when more succulent fruits are scarce.

The coffee bushes themselves offer sites for the nests of small birds. The quiet, olive-green, female Orange-collared Manakins hang their slight hammocks in forks of the lower branches. Here they incubate their two eggs with no assistance from the brilliant, orange, black, and olive males, who dance noisily at their "courts" in neighboring woods. Later in the year, the female Variable Seedeaters build their almost equally frail cups in the tops of the coffee bushes. Unlike the solitary manakins, they are attended by tuneful, black and white mates, who help to nourish the nestlings with regurgitated grass seeds. Scarlet-rumped Black Tanagers, Buff-throated Saltators, Gray-striped Brush-Finches, Gray's Thrushes, Slaty Castlebuilders, Rufous-tailed Hummingbirds, Snowy-breasted Hummingbirds, Blue Ground-Doves, and other birds also place their nests in the coffee shrubs.

For a number of years, a pair of Gray-headed Tanagers nested in the coffee grove. These medium-sized tanagers, with bright olive-green upper plumage and clear saffron-yellow breasts, are forest dwellers. They regularly forage with the army ants, catching some of the insects and other small creatures that try to escape the voracious legions. Once, when hunting ants were evidently not available, I found a pair of these tanagers using chickens as substitutes. They perched close above several of the domestic fowls that were scratching at the forest's edge, from time to time seizing some of the insects stirred up by them. In this same dry season, evidently driven by unusual scarcity of food, the Gray-headed Tanagers began to come for the bananas on the birds' table, which for years they had neglected.

Even while nesting in the coffee plantation, these tanagers spent most of their free time, and seemed to find most of their food, in the forest nearly four hundred feet to the south. They preferred to travel between their nest and their foraging area by way of the garden with its many trees and shrubs, where they might seek refuge from the swift descent of a hawk, rather than across the open pasture, which was a slightly shorter route. Sometimes the male tanager would pause in the garden to sing his sweet, appealing song: *whichís whichís whicheery whichís wichú*— an exceptionally fine performance for a member of a family whose brilliance of plumage is seldom equalled by vocal capacity.

The Gray-headed Tanagers placed their frail, open nest in a coffee bush, at a height of about five feet. The male helped to build, and he often managed to pour forth a bright song while holding fibers or other material in his bill. Sometimes one of the partners, arriving with something for the nest, found the other sitting there, shaping the structure with breast, bill, and feet. Impatient to deposit its own contribution, the newcomer sometimes stood upon the other's back, making it fly suddenly away. The male never helped his mate to incubate the two pale blue-gray eggs, heavily mottled with shades of dark brown. But when they hatched, after fourteen or fifteen days of incubation, he brought many meals to the nestlings. The parents flew miles every day, bringing these meals from the distant forest. When only ten or eleven days old, the young, already feathered, flew from the nest, to lurk in neighboring thickets until strong enough to travel to the woodland, where Gray-headed Tanagers are most at home.

A number of forest birds build their nests in neighboring clearings, gardens, or plantations, where they are somewhat less exposed to predation by the snakes, toucans, mammals, and other nest robbers that make the rearing of a family of small birds in the rain forest so precarious an undertaking. But the opposite tendency, for birds that forage in the clearings or lighter vegetation to seek the heavy forest for nesting, is in my experience exceedingly rare.

Another forest bird that sometimes chooses the coffee plantation for its nest is the Blue-black Grosbeak. When we stored our maize in an open shed, these finches with grotesquely thick bills often came to pilfer grains, amply paying for their fare with full, rich song. Or, becoming bolder, they would venture close to the house to pick up stray grains that the chickens had overlooked, or disdained because they were decaying. It is not unusual for these grosbeaks to build their nest in a maize plant, a situation that has the advantage of proximity to food yet is precarious, for the supporting leaf is likely to dry and sink down, spilling out eggs or nestlings. Or the corn may be harvested before the young of these late nesters can fly.

Perhaps it was the pair of Blue-black Grosbeaks that stole corn from our granary who one year, in July, chose the sturdier support of a coffee plant for their cup-shaped nest. I set my little wigwam of brown cloth among the coffee bushes nearby, and hidden within it I spent tranquil hours watching the home life of this musical pair. The brown female had a song much like that of her blue-black mate; in a voice only slightly weaker than his, she would sing from her nest when she heard him caroling among the neighboring trees. Sometimes the two would sing responsively for minutes together—a charming performance. From time to time, he fed her while she sat warming her two eggs. After they hatched, he helped her to attend the young, patiently coaxing the blind, newly hatched nestlings to take their meals.

Just beyond the grosbeaks' nest, at the edge of the coffee plantation, rose a clump of tall Pejibaye palms. Their slender, gray trunks bristled from top to bottom with close-set, black spines, each longer and sharper than a woman's sewing needle. At the top of each palm trunk, just below the spreading crown of graceful, plumy fronds, hung great clusters of fruits, each of which was about an inch and a half in diameter, green or tinged with yellow or orange as it ripened. Leaf and spathe bore many more of the same formidable black spines. To gather these palm fruits hanging forty or fifty feet in the air on forbidding trunks, we climbed into the top of a neighboring avocado tree, where, with a hook attached to the end of the longest pole that we could wield, we pulled away a cluster and let it fall heavily to the ground. In its swift descent, it often struck against the bristling trunk, the spines of which entered and broke off in some of the fruits, so that we had to look sharply when we ate them.

Raw Pejibaye fruits sting the human mouth, much as raw Tiquisqui and Jack-in-the-Pulpit do. The tissues of these and many other plants that similarly sting contain compact bundles of long, thin, sharply pointed crystals of calcium oxalate. One might suppose that by pricking delicate membranes, these needlelike crystals or raphides cause the burning sensation. However, prolonged cooking, which removes the sting, leaves the crystals as microscopically sharp as ever. Evidently the crystals alone are not responsible for the pain, but they may, by piercing mucous membranes, make them more susceptible to the action of some caustic solute that is destroyed by boiling. When cooked and eaten with salt, the Pejibaye's solid, orange-colored flesh is delicious and highly nourishing. During their season, these fruits are sold on the streets and in the markets of Costa Rican towns. No other fruit that I know varies so much in size and quality, not only from tree to tree, but even on the same tree in different years, so that selection of propagating material hardly helps to stabilize the product.

To reach these nutritious fruits, squirrels climb over the spiny palms, while one who has experienced their painful pricks watches in wide-eyed amazement. Birds also enjoy these fruits, pecking into them while they hang on the tree, apparently without making their mouths sting. While I sat watching the Blue-black Grosbeaks' nest, Scarlet-rumped Black Tanagers, Blue Tanagers, Palm Tanagers, Red-crowned Woodpeckers, Golden-naped Woodpeckers, and other birds feasted in the palm trees in front of me. They knocked down both whole fruits and large fragments, which proved attractive to other birds that foraged on the ground.

Among these were the Gray-necked Wood-Rails, who lived in dense thickets along the neighboring stream, whence I often heard their loud, ringing *chirin-co-co-co-co, chirin-co-co* . . . , although I rarely glimpsed the retiring birds. From my hiding place in front of the grosbeaks' nest, I repeatedly saw one of these elusive wood-rails emerge from a neighboring thicket, pick a fragment of fruit from beneath the palm trees, then run with its morsel back amidst the sheltering bushes. But once the rail walked with its bill full along the edge of the plantation, between the coffee bushes, taking long strides and looking cautiously from side to side, then breaking into a run as it neared the bank above the stream, where it vanished into the dense shrubbery. I had never before enjoyed so satisfactory a view of a free Gray-necked Wood-Rail. What a bright bird it was, with its big red eyes, yellowish green bill, rich chestnut breast, and long red legs!

While I sat in my tent early in the morning, a wood-rail sang at the edge of the thicket in front of me, while another performed simultaneously along the bank of the stream to my right. The angular separation of the sources of the two songs left no doubt that they issued from separate throats and proved what I had long suspected from what I had myself heard and what I had read in books: that the *chirin-co-co* song is often a duet. The two rails, probably a mated pair, sang in unison, keeping such perfect time that, had they been closer together, the listener might have mistaken their performance for a solo. The voices of both birds sounded a trifle strained or "cracked"; and I recalled that Frank M. Chapman had compared the duetting wood-rails to "an aged couple singing in shaky, quavering voices a song of their youth." But in other pairs that I have heard, one voice was clear, smooth, and resonant, the accompanying voice weak and cracked, forming a bizarre contrast. The wood-rails' duet is sometimes continued for ten or fifteen minutes. It sounds best at a distance, which softens and mellows their notes. These songs often ring out in the stillness of the night, even when there is no moon.

I noticed that the rail carried pieces of the palm fruit back into the thicket, instead of devouring them on the spot. Could it have been taking these harsh, peppery morsels to its chicks? Twice I had found nests of the wood-rail amid the lush vegetation along the neighboring stream. Situated in dense tangles of vines beneath trees, at heights of six and ten feet, the nests were great, bulky masses of dead twigs and leaves, with a shallow depression in the foot-wide top of the high pile. Here rested the three big eggs, which were buffy white, sparsely spotted and blotched with rusty brown and pale lilac. I wished to make an intensive study of these wary birds, to learn which of the parents warmed the eggs and how they attended their young. But the nests were so well concealed that without removing some of the screening foliage I could see little of them. And the least disturbance either caused the suspicious rails to desert their nest or resulted in the betrayal of the eggs to some hungry animal.

Coffee wood, hard and resistant to decay, makes durable garden stakes. One morning in May, I was cutting stakes from coffee branches that had earlier been pruned away, my machete crashing loudly against the tough wood. At the edge of the plantation, on the brink of the high bluff that rose steeply above the creek, stood a tall, dying stub with a few small sprouts and in its side, high above the ground, a long, narrow opening giving access to a central cavity. After I had cut half a dozen stakes, I heard a shrill note, not unlike the call of the Sulphur-bellied Flycatcher, a bird not often found in this valley. Looking up, I espied a small animal climbing the blasted stub. Closer scrutiny revealed that the creature was a Kinkajou, a relative of the raccoons, distinguished by its long, slender body, short legs, dense, short, yellowish-tawny pelage, long, tapering tail, and squat, elfish face. In her mouth she carried a baby about as big as a squirrel.

The mother Kinkajou scrambled up the stub to the top, then climbed the slender sprout that stood upright at its truncate apex and appeared none too strong to bear her weight. Reaching beyond this, she seized the end of a thin twig of an Inga shade tree. Although this branch was not much thicker than a lead pencil, the Kinkajou carefully climbed across to it, much as a Howling Monkey might have done, the baby all the while dangling from her mouth. She climbed up to a thicker part of the bough and paused to look around. The clean-limbed Inga tree offered her neither cavity nor concealment; nor could she have passed, monkey-like, from this to another tree, without first descending to the perilous ground. After a minute of indecision, she returned to the top of her original stub, and seemed perplexed about her next move. At this point, I hurried back to the house for my field glasses. As I was returning, the Kinkajou climbed down the trunk headfirst and entered the opening in its side.

After the Kinkajou had vanished into the hollow, I resumed my task of cutting stakes. But before I could prepare another, she emerged from the trunk, the baby still in her mouth, and started to climb upward once more. I put up my machete and stood quietly watching: after ascending a few yards, the animal paused, then returned to the cavity. Whenever I made the sharp noise of cutting, she would emerge and climb to the top of the stub; whenever I stood quietly at a distance, she returned to her arboreal den.

As the Kinkajou climbed up or down, she kept the end of her long tail resting lightly on any convenient branch, with a half-turn to prevent its slipping off. I did not see her actually use her tail to support her weight. She held her baby in her mouth by its neck. When she climbed downward headforemost, its long body dangled limply, its four little, pink paws waving feebly in the air. When she came to an obstructing limb, the little one seemed greatly to impede her movements, and she dragged it rather clumsily over the obstacle. But whenever she found a crotch where she could support herself adequately with her hindlegs, she held her baby against her breast in both arms, like a human mother. The cub's long tail had a half turn at its end, like its dam's. I did not again hear the shrill whistle that had drawn my attention to the Kinkajou and am not certain that this animal was its author. In his *Mammals of Panamá*, Goldman ascribes to the Kinkajou "a squeaking noise" and "short, peculiar barks."

The large-eyed Kinkajou seems to be wholly nocturnal, but fear and maternal solicitude had driven her out into the brilliant morning sunshine. When I saw that my chopping invariably sent her forth in search of a safer refuge that she could not find, I carried away such stakes as I had and left her to drowse through the long hours of daylight. As far as I could learn, she passed all her days in the same hollow; I had only to go into the coffee grove and make a loud noise in order to see her. At first, the noise would send her up to the top of the stub; but after she became accustomed to my visits, she would merely look out through the opening. With her flat, short-eared, puckish head in the half-darkness of the cavity, she would stick out her long, slender, pink tongue as though to lick something or reveal her drowsiness by a series of tremendous yawns. Then, when all was quiet again, she vanished into the deep shadow of her narrow bedroom to resume her slumber with her little one.

Early in June, an urgent matter took me to the city for several days. Returning unannounced, I was descending the hillside toward the house when I heard voices and loud noises coming from the coffee plantation. Suspecting that something was amiss, I set down my handbag in the pasture and climbed through the fence into the coffee grove, only to find a group of men and boys in front of the Kinkajou's hole. They had driven the mother into the top of a neighboring tree, where she climbed along a slender bough with her baby dangling from her mouth. One of the men was aiming a gun at her. With a sudden word, I stopped the senseless slaughter in the nick of time. The faithful mother was accused of killing chickens, but the would-be executioner could present no evidence to convict her. As far as I know, Kinkajous never hunt by day, and at night the chickens roost in trees, the trunks of which are encircled by sheets of metal to keep down climbing animals. Moreover, Kinkajous subsist largely on wild fruits and insects; although it is not improbable that they occasionally rob a small bird's nest, I am not sure that they would attack a full-grown hen.

After I had sent the men off, the Kinkajou passed over to the trunk where she slept by day and climbed rapidly downward. But instead of returning to her hole, as I had expected, when halfway down the stub—which, it will be recalled, stood at the top of a high bluff—she made a great leap, which carried her across the narrow stream and into the much lower boughs of a tree on the opposite shore. It was a bold and hazardous jump that would have won applause for the most agile monkey. From these boughs overhanging the channel, she made her way inland and soon vanished with her cub.

A few days later, I was happy to learn that the Kinkajou had returned with her child to her old home in the tall stub. Now when I made a noise, the youngster sometimes looked out all by itself and voiced little peeping notes like a bird's. One evening, I tried to watch the Kinkajou set forth on her nocturnal outing. Arriving to begin my vigil, I clapped my hands in order to learn whether she was still at home. She looked out of her high doorway and yawned repeatedly, opening her mouth wide and sticking out her slender tongue for several inches. The sun was just setting; it was too early to get up, and she was still sleepy! I stepped behind some coffee bushes to watch, and, after a few minutes of yawning, the animal disappeared into the blackness of her hole, where she remained until the sky grew dark. Even an hour after sunset, the beam of my flashlight picked out her eyes glowing brightly in the opening of the hollow. Still, she had not gone to breakfast! Since it was now impossible to see anything without a light that might alter her routine, I stole away and left the sleepyhead to herself.

By early July the mother had vanished, and the hole was occupied by an immature Kinkajou. It seemed quite big to be the one that I had first seen as a babe-in-mouth only six weeks earlier, but possibly Kinkajous grow faster than I supposed.

To the north of the coffee plantation is a narrow, shady gully, through which, when in flood, the creek sends some of its current, avoiding the long loop of the main channel. Apparently this gully was an earlier stream bed, which the creek for some reason abandoned in favor of a curving course to the north, between which and the gully lies a high knob of ground covered by light second-growth trees. On the shady banks of the gully grows the splendid Costa Rican Skull-cap, a shrubby mint whose slender, tubular flowers, two inches long, are bright red with an orange lip. Over the steepest part of the bank hang the colorful umbels of a scandent *Centropogon*, a relative of the lobelias with long, tubular flowers that are red with yellow lobes. Often in the still, moist air of the little ravine I catch a strong odor as of Witch Hazel, which, after a moment, I can no longer detect. In various parts of Central America, I have tried for years to trace this elusive aroma to its source. Whatever this may be, it is not the true Witch Hazel, which does not grow so far south.

On the steeply sloping banks of this gully, beneath the colorful flowers, I have sometimes found, between April and June, the oven-shaped nests of the Buff-rumped Warbler. These substantial structures have a complete roof of straws and leaves and a round entrance facing down the slope. Unlike most wood warblers, the male and female Buff-rumped Warblers cooperate in the construction of the nest. Both wear the same dark olive plumage, with light yellowish buff on the rump and basal half of the tail. I can distinguish them only by their songs. The male sings a loud, jubilant crescendo, with that ringing quality so often found in the voices of birds that must make themselves heard above the sound of rushing water. A tireless songster, he is tuneful in every month but sings most freely while breeding. The female sings sparingly, but occasionally she answers her mate with an utterance wholly different from his, a sweet, full warble, indescribably beautiful. The contrast between the ringing crescendo and the soft, liquid warble makes one of the most enchanting vocal performances that I have heard from any bird. When two pairs engage in a territorial dispute and all four birds sing against each other, one is compelled to pause and listen.

Buff-rumped Warblers forage chiefly along the watercourses, both the narrow creek and the broader Peña Blanca River; but often in wet weather they come into the garden, and not infrequently I meet them hunting along a woodland road at no great distance from a stream. Unlike those denizens of northern watercourses, the waterthrushes, Buff-rumped Warblers progress over the ground and rocks chiefly by hopping and flitting rather than sedately walking.

Along the banks of the gully and on the knoll between this and the creek grow many clusters of small palms, ten or twelve feet high. Miniature Pejibayes, their stems, hardly thicker than a cane, bristle with similar, cruel, black thorns, which extend up the trunk to the pinnate fronds. Beneath the tapering tips of the broad fronds, the Little Hermit Hummingbirds fasten their downy nests; nowhere have I found so many of them as in this gully and on this knoll. If, in a playful mood, we compare the hummingbird family to the society of medieval Europe, the majority of these sprightly, glittering birds are elegantly attired, bejeweled lords and ladies; the modestly clad dwellers in the woodland shade are the contemplative hermits. The nest of the Little Hermit conforms in outline to the tapering apex of the arching leaf beneath which it is fastened, so that it is roughly conical, with the hollow base uppermost. Composed of plant down, fine fibers, deep chestnut scales from tree-fern fronds, and even small dry flowers, the soft nest is attached to the palm leaf by many strands of cobweb, which form a conspicuous light network over the dark back of the leaf tip. While building this nest, the diminutive hummingbird works largely upon the wing, often floating slowly around the apex of the frond, always facing it, to apply the essential cobweb.

Her nest completed, the hermit lays two of the tiniest, pure white eggs that I have ever seen. To incubate them, she sits with her breast toward the supporting leaf, her head and long, downcurved bill thrown so far up and back that her crown almost touches her long, light-tipped, uptilted tail. To sit doubled up in this fashion appears most uncomfortable, yet the hummingbird can rest motionless in this seemingly strained posture for from twenty minutes to over an hour at a stretch. To leave her eggs, she somehow sets her wings vibrating in that confined space and floats lightly upward and backward until clear of the nest, then deftly reverses her course and darts away. Returning, she never alights on the nest's rim, in the manner of heavier birds less adept on the wing; she flies right into the downy nest, and when her wings are folded she is already warming her eggs.

After fifteen or sixteen days of incubation, the eggs are replaced by nestlings so tiny and undeveloped that they appear embryonic. Obeying some mysterious instinct, within a day of hatching, the ugly, blind, nearly naked grubs wriggle around into precisely the same orientation that their mother assumes while sitting, heads toward the leaf, and they preserve this position until they fly away. To feed them after they are somewhat grown, the parent does not stand on the nest's rim but hovers in front of it on vibrating wings, while she reaches over the nestlings' backs to push her long bill far down into their throats, alternately, and pumps up food from her stomach; she feeds her young while hovering in the air, just as she probes the sweet depths of flowers. The nestlings' mouths are corollas that, instead of yielding nourishment, absorb it! At the age of three weeks, the young hummingbirds, who for several days have been well covered with plumage much like that of the adults, are strong enough to fly from the nest.

In all these arduous tasks, the female Little Hermit works alone. I never saw a male of her kind—nor indeed of any other kind of hummingbird—help at any stage of the nesting. The male Little Hermits spend their days in assemblies of their own, where each sits on his special low twig, a foot or two above the ground, in the deep shade beneath tangled second-growth woods, and all day long repeats his squeaky little chant, the while wagging his slender, light-tipped tail tirelessly up and down. But for this revealing movement, I might never detect the tiny brown minstrels, so well does their plumage blend with the brown dead leaves above which they perch. These assemblies are in session most of the year, except in the period of fewest flowers at the end of the dry season.

On rare occasions, I have watched one of the male hummingbirds perform his elaborate aerial dance above a perching individual of his kind, evidently a female. With head and tail bent strongly upward, the hermit reminded me of a miniature boat with a high prow and stern, floating upon an invisible fluid, as he oscillated gently back and forth, up and down, a few inches above his motionless companion. Every few seconds, he about-faced, and at longer intervals he rotated completely around or even turned through a circle and a half. He varied his performance by shooting swiftly back and forth for a distance of a foot or two, while his rapidly vibrating wings set up a louder, more insistent buzz. This fairy dance might continue for as long as ten minutes, while the watching hummingbird perched below, pointing her long bill straight up toward him and following his movements with her head.

19

Social Insects, Their Homes and Enemies

AMONG THE TEEMING insect life of the tropics, butterflies and beetles contribute most of the beauty, and the social hymenoptera provide most of the drama. With their endlessly varied nests, their aggressive habits, the fierce conflicts in which they sometimes engage, their interactions with other classes of living things, they command the attention of the naturalist in the tropics, whatever his major interest may be; even the layman is, often despite himself, driven to pay attention to them.

Ants, Pleasant and Unpleasant

In the warmer parts of the earth, the multitudinous ants are evidently the dominant form of animal life. In size they range from pale, scarcely visible mites that run crazily over the dinner table looking for something sweet, to inch-long, black ponerines that stalk sedately over the under-

Headpiece: A nest of Guitarrón Wasps on a Guava tree. The corrugated paper envelope of the upper section is still under construction and open along the middle.

growth of the forest, inflicting on the unwary a sting that is reputed to smart for twenty-four hours. Ants are everywhere, from underground to the treetops, not excluding the best-constructed of human dwellings. To keep them out of food is one of the major problems of the householder. But it is not only the larder that they defile; if they can find the smallest crevice, they invade the clothes chest and the desk drawer. Often, to my dismay, I have opened my most carefully made cabinet to find a colony of big, blackish ants installed within, in a nest composed of tiny fragments of my papers. The sanitary arrangements of these insidious ants are admirable: they set aside a special corner for a latrine. Unfortunately, this may be situated upon precious manuscripts or prized photographs, which will ever after bear ugly brown stains. In the dead of night, these vandals sally forth to patrol the house for dying insects or mice caught in traps. At times they establish themselves in bird houses, inflicting punishment on the nestling wrens.

More amiable are the spinning ants. *Camponotus senex* builds its nest amid the leaves of trees, preferring those with dense foliage, such as the orange, the mango, and the rose apple. About six to ten inches long, the nest is an irregular, angular structure composed of layer upon layer of a thin and delicate fabric, woven of fine, colorless strands like silk or cobweb, applied so thickly as to form a continuous, unbroken membrane. Between the sheets, among the leaves enclosed by them, are narrow, labyrinthine spaces in which the ants live. To preserve their privacy, they destroy the transparency of the silken fabric by covering it rather thickly with fine debris, such as particles of bark and fragments of moss. Here and there the outer wall is perforated by narrow, round doorways, through which the curious little inhabitants are continually passing in and out, at least during the daytime. About a quarter of an inch long, these ants have black bodies sprinkled with golden-brown hairs. These grow thickly on the abdomen, which is generally turned downward or even bent beneath the body, giving the ants an odd, hunchbacked aspect.

These spinning ants spend much time wandering over the leaves and branches of the tree that supports their nest, but it is difficult to learn what they find to eat. If their nest is shaken, one hears a noise as of many small seeds rattling in a dry pod. The ants make this sound in the following manner. Projecting from the walls of the nest are usually a number of leaves that have died and dried. There are almost always ants resting or running about on these leaves, and when the nest is disturbed, many swarm out to increase the number. By rapidly striking their hard abdomens against the resonant dry leaves, the ants make the rattle, which may warn or alarm their enemies.

If, after vigorously shaking the nest, one holds a hand close above it, the little spinning ants stand upright on their rear ends, supporting themselves in a comical attitude by their two posterior pairs of legs and waving around their forelegs in a threatening manner. If one touches the nest, some rush upon the hand and try to bite; but their jaws are so weak that they are hardly felt through the skin. They have no sting. Finding their attack ineffectual, the harmless little creatures scamper wildly over one's skin and clothing and are glad enough to run back on the foliage of their nest tree if the hand is placed in contact with it. By night, all the ants retire inside their nest, some keeping their heads in the narrow doorways, evidently acting as sentinels.

Adult ants cannot secrete thread. How, then, are these silken pavilions made? Sometimes one finds the ants adding to their house. Or if one is impatient to solve the mystery, he may cut a small hole in their wall. For several hours, this breach may be neglected, but finally the ants repair the damage. Then one will see them lined up inside the gap. In its mandibles each worker holds a long, slender, white larva, its body beneath the bearer's body, its head directed forward. The worker ant moves its burden slowly back and forth across the gap. Understanding by some marvelous instinct what is required of it, the sightless grub bends its attenuate foreparts outward and secretes a fine silken thread. By long and patient application, enough of these delicate filaments are laid down to form a continuous sheet.

The silken nests of this *Camponotus* are numerous in El General, and I have found them as high as four thousand feet on the surrounding slopes. Once I discovered a nest beneath a living banana leaf, attached along the midrib, and once I noticed one in a clay urn that had been deserted by the Banded Wasps that made it; but such sites are exceptional. I have watched small arboreal birds of a number of species take one of the spinning ants in its bill and rub it swiftly beneath its half-spread wing or its tail, in the puzzling activity known as "anting." Although northern birds commonly ant on the ground, tropical birds, in families ranging from woodcreepers to finches, in my experience always do so in trees or shrubs, using the many kinds of arboreal ants. There is some evidence that formic acid secreted by ants so rudely treated may help to control parasites in the bird's feathers, but the whole significance of this widespread avian habit is far from clear.

At least two kinds of gardener ants inhabit this valley. The first is the parasol or leaf-cutting ant, whose long columns of patient toilers, each carrying a little piece of green leaf over its back, are a familiar sight in tropical America and have often been described. Their subterranean nests are labyrinths of galleries and chambers beneath mounds of excavated earth that may become five or six yards across and are kept free of sprouting herbs. Here in the moist earth the ants cut the leaves into fine fragments to form the spongy mulch on which they grow the fungus that nourishes them. Propagating material of this fungus is carried from old colonies to new ones, so that the cultivated strain is never lost. These ants seem to waste much effort: one often finds the narrow trails, which they cut through the herbage from their nest to their harvesting area, strewn with innumerable pieces of green leaf that they have started to carry home and, for some obscure reason, dropped along the way. Then, too, one frequently notices, clinging to the piece of leaf that a middle-sized worker is taking to the nest, smaller workers who are doubtless trying to be helpful but are actually getting a free ride and increasing the bearer's burden.

The leaf cutters often attack and defoliate cultivated plants. Large coffee plantations sometimes employ a squad of men whose full-time job is to destroy their nests, fumigating them with poisonous gas or else digging them out, leaving holes big enough to bury an ox. Whether undertaken by ants or by men, agriculture without machinery involves grueling toil; as a fellow agriculturist, I cannot avoid a brotherly feeling toward the hard-working Atta ants, and I take measures against them only in extreme cases. Once when we planted a field with beans, we discovered a large nest at its edge. I resolved not to attack the ants unless they attacked the sprouting beans, which they hardly touched.

The second gardener ant is a tiny, dark, restless creature that often runs about with its abdomen bent oddly upward. It builds large, blackish, more or less globular nests composed chiefly of well-decayed vegetable fragments shot through with fungal filaments. In shape and the maze of galleries that fill them, these nests resemble arboreal termitaries. They are usually high in trees, especially the Sotacaballo trees along the rivers. Rooted in these aerial nests one almost invariably finds three species of plants, two of which, in this region, seem to grow nowhere else. The first is the orchid *Epidendrum imatophyllum*, which forms compact clusters of slender, erect stems, on vigorous specimens four or five feet high. It blooms through much of the dry season, even when terrestrial vegetation is languishing; its small pink flowers, massed at the top of the shoots, catch the eye from a distance of two hundred feet and are delightful to behold.

The second of these aerial plants is a fig with oblong, pointed leaves that grows to be a small tree but is often only a shrub, fruiting when a yard or two high. The fruits, borne singly in the axils of the leaves, are from one-half to three-quarters of an inch in diameter, green, dry, and tasteless. Eventually the roots creep down the trunk of the supporting tree to the ground. Older fig trees so rooted may grow without an ants' nest; but I believe that all examples of this species start on the nests, although some persist after the ant colony has decayed.

The third garden component is *Peperomia macrostachya*, which has fleshy, ovate leaves. The succulent stems hang limply below the nest and sometimes attain a length of ten feet. Unlike the orchid and the fig, this *Peperomia* often grows on trees and rocks without an ants' nest. The inflorescence is a long, slender spike solidly covered with minute, greenish flowers devoid of petals. Although the powdery seeds of the orchid are doubtless wafted to the ants' nests by wind and the seeds of the fig are probably dropped there by birds, the ants themselves carry the *Peperomia* fruits to their abode. Indeed, ants seem to be the principal distributors of the tiny, greenish fruits of most species of *Peperomia*, which attract these insects by the oil in the thin, soft tissue that covers the single seed. The oil in this particular species is faintly lemon-scented. If one places a *Peperomia* fruit, of this or some other kind, on a branch near the nest of these gardener ants, he will presently see some of the minuscule creatures gather around it, and soon one or several will drag it to the nest. Although hardly the size of a mustard seed, the *Peperomia* fruit is as big as, and heavier than, an ant; yet one is capable of bearing it. When two or more undertake the task, they seem to pull in different directions and impede the work. On some ants' nests, seedling Peperomias spring too thickly to have been planted there by chance. Their roots may help to bind the nest together.

Bees and Their Battles

Bees, like ants, are abundant in tropical America. In size they range from tiny "sweat bees," which annoy the overheated traveler in the bush by persistently alighting on his perspiring skin, to big, burly carpenter bees and bumblebees, as large as the end of a man's thumb. The most beautiful of the bees in this region are, unfortunately, the most exasperating. These are the euglossid bees, the size of a horsefly and clad in shining armor, which suddenly changes from the most brilliant metallic green to the most fiery copper as the hovering insect alters its orientation.

This woodland bee has taken kindly to the habitations of men, which it enters to build its brood cells in dry places, often among one's most cherished possessions. Any nook or cranny about the diameter of a lead pencil is chosen for their reception. A favored site is a space of this size that one has carelessly left among his books or magazines on an open shelf. When I used a long rubber raincoat with a shoulder cape for horseback riding, I would often, at the end of the dry season, find its folds firmly stuck together by these troublesome bees. Their brownish, oblong cells, placed singly or several together but in no regular pattern, are composed of the stickiest stuff imaginable, extremely difficult to remove from paper or rubber or wood, on which it leaves ugly, indelible traces. Each cell is provisioned with a whitish paste and contains a single egg or developing bee.

The aggressive ants, like the industrious bees, are ever eager to augment their supply of food, and it is not surprising that these two acquisitive tribes sometimes come into conflict. At the base of a towering fig tree standing beside a rivulet was a hive of small, black meliponine bees with amber-colored abdomens.* Stingless and most inoffensive, they never molested us when we crossed the stream close in front of their doorway, an inconspicuous opening between two of the projecting roots of the tree. Passing by the hive one day at the end of the rainless season when the watercourse was dry, I noticed that it was being attacked by medium-sized black ants with golden hairs on their abdomens. The assailants were larger and more powerful than the defenders, but the latter were much more numerous. Whenever an ant crossed the rim of the funnel-like entrance, it was attacked by a little bee, who very often would drop, maimed and helpless, from the formidable jaws of the intruder. But another and another bee would tackle the invader, grappling with it until ant and bees became a single, shapeless, struggling mass, which slowly sank deeper and deeper into the crowd of bees in the throat of the entrance tube and was finally lost from view.

The bees had two modes of defense. One was to fasten upon the intruders a tiny pellet of very sticky gum, which greatly impeded the movements of the ants. I saw one of these, as it crossed the doorway, receive a pellet square in the face and back away much discomfited, trying vainly with its legs to remove the adhesive stuff. Other ants were so plastered with the gum that they wandered about helpless and apparently blind. Two of these begummed ants, chancing to collide headfirst as they staggered aimlessly about, grappled together, as though each tried to punish the other for its miserable state. Another ant got a leg so securely attached to the gummy rim of the entrance that it dislocated the limb while pulling it away, and walked off with the injured member raised uselessly in the air.

The bees' second method of overcoming the ants was to attach their bodies inseparably to those of their adversaries. A bee would grapple a leg or antenna of an ant, only to be killed by the latter's mandibles. But the devoted insect died with its own jaws locked upon a limb of its enemy, who was doomed henceforth to walk about with the corpse fastened so firmly to a leg or an antenna that all its efforts to shake off the

---

*Probably *Trigona fulviventris*.

impediment proved ineffectual. Burdened with both the adhesive gum and the clinging bodies of the bees, many of the ants were soon in a pitiful plight.

While the struggle raged at the doorway, the majority of the bees went about the routine business of their day as though their citadel were in no danger, sallying out to fly away, and returning in a constant stream, some with golden masses of pollen or of wax attached to their hindlegs. One arrived with only a single hindleg, a condition rendered conspicuous by the load of pollen on one side only. Below this double current of bees going in and out, the maimed lay unregarded in their death struggles on the bottom of the entranceway, becoming enveloped in their own gum, which seemed to stick to them far less tenaciously than to the ants. The bees ignored my head as I watched close in front of their doorway.

When I left at noon, the battle still raged, but the uninjured ants were now so few that it was clear they could not win. Returning in the evening, I found that the attackers had retreated, leaving on the battlefield a few casualties more firmly stuck to the gummy rim of the bees' entrance than Br'er Rabbit to the Tar Baby. One of these feebly struggling ants still had a dead bee locked to its antenna. The victorious bees, having cleaned the wastage of battle from the mouth of their passageway, were flying in and out as usual.

Years later, I discovered a possible source of the sticky substance that bees use to construct their cells and the tubular entrances to their nests and employ so effectively against their enemies. The genus *Clusia*, a distant relative of the yellow-flowered St.-John's-worts of cooler regions, is represented in El General by a bewildering number of species. These plants start life as epiphytes, but some, sending roots down to the ground and thickening them into trunks, finally become self-supporting small trees. Some are dioecious, with male and female flowers on different trees. In the center of the staminate flower of certain species is a conspicuous mound, around the edge of which many minute anthers are situated (Fig. 6). The top of this glandular mound is thickly covered with an exceedingly sticky gum, on which a variety of small stingless bees alight to gather the stuff into little pellets that they attach to their hindlegs before flying off. On the female flowers of some species, the sterile stamens secrete a similar gum. The bees evidently have some special provision to prevent their becoming hopelessly glued to the flowers, for the gum is so adhesive that I had the utmost difficulty removing it from the razor that I used to cut sections of the gland for microscopic examination. Clusia is the only plant I know that entices its pollinators with gum rather than with nectar or excess pollen. Somewhat similar, however, is the case of a Brazilian orchid, *Maxillaria divaricata*, which attracts insect visitors with wax liberally secreted on its labellum, as reported by L. van der Pijl and C. H. Dodson in their book, *Orchid Flowers, their Pollination and Evolution*.

The stingless meliponine bees so abundant in the forest sometimes assail the hives of domestic bees imported from the Old World, stealing their honey. Different kinds of stingless bees also wage war against each other. Hanging in a thatched shed was a section of hollow log in which the previous owner of this farm had somehow established a colony of dark wild bees known as *jicotes*, which collect much honey. This pendent

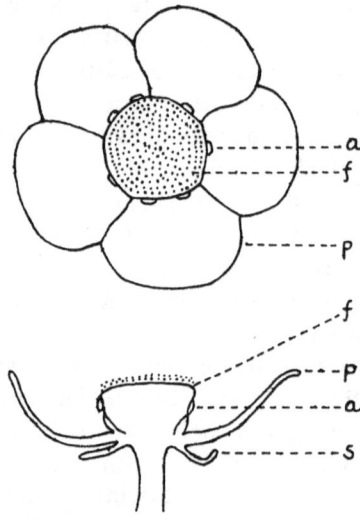

6. A source of gum for bees. A staminate flower of Clusia, viewed from the top and (below) in longitudinal section (X2). The center is occupied by a fleshy cushion (f), with tiny anthers (a) around its sides, and on top an extremely sticky gum (stippled). p, petal; s, sepal.

hive was repeatedly attacked by smaller black bees from the neighboring woodland. The *jicotes* defended their nest valiantly; the ground below was littered with the lifeless bodies of the assailants. Relatively few of the defenders lost their lives. Some of these casualties had the bodies of three or four of the smaller bees attached to them in a death grip, while from others one or more wings had been gnawed away. Despite their heavy losses, the little black bees gained possession of the hollow log and evidently carried off all the *jicotes'* honey—a point that I could not determine without ruining their nest. After the invaders withdrew, the *jicotes* returned to their hive and began to replenish it, only to suffer a repetition of the invasion a fortnight later.

The Homes and Family Life of Wasps

Wasps are hardly less abundant in Costa Rica than ants and bees. In size they range from innocuous mites smaller than house flies to the big, yellow and black tarantula killers, which I am careful not to disturb as they hunt along the pathways, ignoring the human presence. The architecture of their nests is hardly less varied than that of birds' nests and makes a fascinating study. The largest vespiaries of this region are the long, corrugated structures of the Guitarrón or Synoeca wasps, described in chapter 9. Only slightly smaller are the big, top-shaped nests of silvery gray paper attached to exposed branches in the treetops and visible from afar. With field glasses, one can watch the wasps flying in and out of the doorway at the pointed lower end. Smaller wasps attach their delicate papery nests beneath leaves. Some of these little wasps are quite timid; if one waves a hand over their home, the occupants may suddenly fly out in a swarm, as though seized by panic. Later they may return. When pruning trees and shrubs, I try not to disturb these pretty nests, which cost their small builders so much time and effort.

These paper nests are made largely of wood fibers; they have much the same composition as our own paper or cardboard manufactured from wood pulp, but they are more resistant to wetting. The clay walls of the pyriform nests that the Banded Wasp attaches to thin twigs are also treated somehow to make them impervious to water; despite their thinness, they resist tropical downpours for years.

Quite different from these nests of paper and clay are those of thickly felted vegetable hairs made by large wasps of the genus *Apoica*. Round or hexagonal in shape, five or six inches in diameter, these nests have the form of an umbrella without a handle or a stalkless mushroom. They need no stalk, as they are attached by the top to a twig, beneath which they hang, often a foot or less above the ground in a shady place. The flat underside of a large nest is covered with four or five hundred hexagonal cells arranged in regular rows, like those of a honeybee's comb.

By day these feltmakers hang nearly upright beneath their umbrella, often in several closely packed layers, those below clinging to those above. With their long, cylindrical, whitish or pale brown abdomens exposed, they look like overgrown, winged termites. A minority rest in various attitudes on top of the mushroom, but they take shelter beneath it in hard rain or when sunshine falls upon the nest. At nightfall they become active; they are the only nocturnal wasps that I know. Sometimes in the late afternoon, however, they fly wildly around in a loose, multitudinous swarm. They are probably prospecting for a new nest site, for between their erratic flights they rest in dense clusters on a leafy twig. Although they look so dangerous, I have more than once walked unharmed through the midst of these excited wasps. It was a different story, however, when I started to prune a shrub beneath which, unnoticed, a felted mushroom was attached. As I ran for my life, the angry wasps pursued me for a hundred feet. Fortunately, they tried to sting through my trousers and had little effect. Had they settled on my face and hands, I would have paid dearly for molesting them.

The walls and exposed beam-ends of our house are at times so plastered with vespiaries that they provide a museum exhibit of wasps' nests. The least attractive are the long, thick clay tubes of the mud daubers. Most fascinating are the homes of the Windowmakers, small, dull black wasps with beautifully iridescent wings. Their nests are of two kinds, although I can detect no difference in the builders. The more common variety is flattish, usually six to eight inches long by half as wide, with rough walls of gray or brownish paper. The other form of nest is paler gray, flat and circular in shape, with thin, irregular, papery wings projecting from the edge all around. In both types, the entrance is a short tube at the top. At first sight, the walls of these nests appear to be penetrated by many tiny, irregular holes, mostly less than an eighth of an inch in diameter. If one tries to pass a hair through these perforations, it will not go; each is closed by a thin, transparent pane that glitters like a flake of mica. The interior of the wasps' nest is illuminated by innumerable minute windows! Theirs is the only window glass on our house. To place glass in the windows of our rooms would be fatal to the birds that are continually trying to take short cuts through them, flying in one open window and out another, to reach trees that they can see through both. Even screening had to be removed because birds injured or killed themselves by flying into the hardware cloth.

The Windowmakers begin their nest by attaching a sheet of hexagonal cells directly to the flat supporting surface, often the wall of a house. While these cells are still quite shallow, they start the envelope, attaching it directly to the outermost cells all around. While building the papery covering, they leave many small gaps, which later they cover with transparent, cellophanelike material. Their paper is not made of wood fibers but of decaying vegetable tissues with short cells. A curious minor ingredient is the spore capsules of ferns! When a wasp arrives with a generous pellet of building material in its mandibles, it does not proceed immediately to add it to the nest but crawls around until another wasp takes part of its load. Each of the two wasps who now have this material may share it with another wasp, and it may again be subdivided, until the ultimate holders take small portions to a thin, growing edge of the nest, along which they carefully spread the plastic stuff with their mandibles. Foragers also arrive with a colorless fluid, doubtless nectar, which they regurgitate to nest mates who cluster eagerly around, and occasionally they bring a dead insect larva that they likewise share. Two weeks after a nest was started by a company nearly two hundred strong, it was completely enclosed by its translucent envelope. These wasps are wholly inoffensive and may be watched from within a few inches from their nest.

Although the Windowmakers start the envelope of their nest in contact with the outermost cells, either these peripheral cells are never completed or they are later removed. In a finished nest, a passageway about half an inch wide runs all around the structure, between the sheet of brood cells and the attachment of the covering with many windows. If undisturbed, one of these nests may be occupied continuously for years and grow gradually larger. The wasps tear away the envelope from one end or side, or more rarely all around, extend their sheet of hexagonal cells over the supporting surface, then cover the new cells with an envelope that they join to the remaining portion of the old covering. After retaining its original size for a long while, a nest attached beneath the top of a window frame of our house was in four months enlarged three times. It is now twenty-two inches long by nearly six inches broad and it has six round doorways—the largest nest of the Windowmakers that I have noticed. The wasps enlarge their nest at a time when they have few or no larvae to feed but many enclosed pupae.

Attached to our walls are also slender gray rods, sometimes over a foot in length but only an eighth of an inch thick, built by a little, long-waisted, black wasp narrowly banded with yellow. It attaches its tiny paper cells, single file, one below the other, thus forming the string or rod which is so light that it waves in a breeze. In contrast to the populous nests of the feltmakers and the windowmakers, these string nests are attended by only a few wasps.

Equally curious is the home of the tiny sticky-nest wasp, which is dull orange with a blackish thorax that is prettily marked with two narrow, longitudinal stripes of yellow. It forms a sort of flat blister on the wall of a house or the bark of a tree. The covering is a thick, tough, parchment-like material, pale gray in color, and finely wrinkled with innumerable transverse corrugations. Attached to the substratum by its edges, this envelope bulges out to form a low, flat dome above the hexagonal cells, which are fastened to the wall or bark in a single continuous sheet. An uninterrupted passageway encircles the nest between the brood cells and the attached edges of the covering. Roughly oval in outline, the nest may be six to ten inches high by three to five inches wide. The broad opening is at the lower end.

A most curious feature of this nest is the sticky substance that covers and surrounds it. All over the parchmentlike envelope, and in a zone from two to four inches broad completely surrounding the nest, are countless tiny stalks, of a similar composition, which stand straight out from the wall, each with a droplet of some sticky stuff at its tip. These protuberances remind me of the stalked glands of some insectivorous plant, such as the sundew or Drosera of northern bogs. The makers of these nests walk across the viscous surface with ease, but other small insects stick to it and can hardly move. This adhesive covering evidently serves to hold enemies aloof; how effective it is I did not learn until I watched the periodic invasions of the army ants.

At these closed vespiaries, it is hardly possible to follow the intimate life of the wasps and to learn how they raise their brood. But while I dwelt at Montaña Azul in the highlands, a Polistes wasp, dull black with dull red mandibles, built her open nest on the outside of the front door. Since she never lost her temper when I passed through nor seemed to be annoyed by changes in the position of the door, I permitted her to remain. Even when the door slammed in the wind, she did not lose her equanimity. As prisoners in solitary confinement become friendly with the spider or the mouse that shares their bleak cell, so I, living alone in a climate that often vetoed profitable outdoor work, took a friendly interest in my closest neighbor.

The nest, made of thin, gray paper, was a single, exposed, horizontal comb or sheet of prismatic hexagonal cells, opening downward. When finished, it contained seventeen of these cells. A single short, thin stalk attached the group of cells to the door. The exterior of the nest, the stalk, and the door at the point of attachment had been thinly smeared over with a black substance resembling hardened tar. At the upper or inner end of each cell was a single egg, or a white larva, in various stages of development.

I was impressed by the fastidiousness of this Polistes. Returning to her nest with food for her young, her first act was often to clean and preen herself. Then bouts of feeding might alternate with renewed attention to her toilet. Birds are unable to preen their own heads and necks and often depend upon their mate or some other companion to perform this friendly office, and we find it difficult to scratch or scrub between our shoulders; but this wasp, with her numerous appendages, could rub and cleanse every part of herself in the most thorough fashion. She cleaned each antenna by passing it between the corresponding front leg and a short spine that projected from its inner side. She cleaned her forelegs with her mandibles and mouth. She rubbed over all parts of her thorax and head with these same front legs. It was remarkable what flexibility and universal movement they possessed and how she could turn them upward and inward to reach the top of her thorax. Then, again, she passed her forelegs through her mandibles. Next, clinging to the nest with only three legs, she cleaned one of the free legs, of the middle or hind pairs, with the other two. Sometimes she dangled below the nest, holding on with her forelegs only, and rubbed all four of the free legs together in an intricate fashion. She used the middle and hind legs to clean her abdomen and wings. Placing one wing and then the other beneath her abdomen, which held it firmly, she rubbed their lower sides with her legs. She devoted many minutes to grooming herself, performing each of these movements over and over as though it gave her pleasure.

Even when the wasp came home dry, she often went through this elaborate cleansing process. When, as frequently happened, she flew in wet from the rain, her first act was to suck the droplets from her body. She dried her legs by passing them through her mandibles. Then she rubbed her legs over her back and wings, transferring the droplets to them, to be removed by her mouth as before. By these means, she dried herself thoroughly.

When wind-driven clouds deposited water on her nest, the wasp sucked it up. Once, to see what she would do, I sprinkled her and her nest with clean water. Instead of trying to punish me for this inconsiderate act, she straightway set about to dry up. First, she removed the water from her forelegs and antennae. Then, with droplets still glistening on the posterior parts of her body, she turned her attention to her nest. She sucked up the water from its top and sides, then from the door immediately above it, and finally from the interior of the cells. When she had imbibed all the fluid that she could hold, she hung over the nest's edge and ejected big, limpid drops from her mouth. I have watched a hummingbird dry her nest by sucking up water in similar fashion, but I did not see her disgorge it later.

When ready to feed a larva, the wasp placed her head at the entrance of the cell and tapped lightly on its inner wall by rapidly vibrating her antennae against it. At the same time, she might rub her abdomen sideways over the edges of the comb behind her. These noises or vibrations evidently stimulated the larva to take its meal. This consisted of clear, colorless droplets, probably of nectar, which she passed from her own mouth to the black mouth of the larva. Sometimes, after cleaning or drying herself, she fed a larva without first ejecting anything. I wondered whether any of the water or dirt from her body was given to the larva, just as I have wondered whether certain species of pigeons, which sometimes clean their nest immediately before proceeding to regurgitate to their nestlings, pass back their own excrements to them along with the "pigeon milk."

After some weeks, the solitary Polistes was joined by a companion, who helped to care for the larvae and, at night, slept beside her on top of the nest. By day, the two wasps spent much time resting idly upon it.

Ten weeks after an egg was laid, the larva that hatched from it had grown so big that it nearly filled its cell. Then it began to spin a lid over the open lower end, passing its fine, colorless, silken thread back and forth and across and across, until the many strands formed a continuous fabric, completely closing the cell. Then for forty-five days it rested unseen, while it transformed itself into a winged wasp. Finally, one hundred and fifteen days after the egg was laid, its metamorphosis was complete. Probably it took so long because of the coolness of this storm-lashed height. The young wasp bit through the silken lid along the edge, severing the attachment to the side walls until it could push back the covering and emerge, to spend several days crawling over the cells or clinging to the outside of the comb with the two older wasps. One of the latter finished cutting the lid from the empty cell, rolled it into a little pellet, and dropped it to the porch floor. Then a new egg was laid in this cell. Eggs, larvae in various stages of development, and enclosed pupae were often simultaneously present in this small nest.

In April, after we had lived together peaceably as neighbors for many months, the last surviving attendant of this nest blundered into the house and died before it was discovered there. The orphaned larvae survived for a surprisingly long while. Three were still living after thirty-eight days of fasting, and two were alive after sixty-one days without food, when they had visibly wasted away. One wasp, which had pupated before the last attendant died, emerged a month later and flew away.

Wasps and Birds

I have not known one kind of social wasp to attack the nest of another kind, as sometimes happens with bees. Nor have I noticed bees attempting to plunder wasps' nests, possibly because they as a rule contain little or no stored nectar to tempt these acquisitive insects. In my experience, the chief enemies of the social wasps are army ants and birds.

Birds make use of wasps in several ways: as guardians of their nests, as providers of nest sites, and as food. In the warmer parts of the Eastern and Western Hemispheres, birds of several kinds frequently build close to vespiaries, evidently for the protection against predators that stinging wasps can give their eggs and nestlings. The birds that choose wasps as a standing garrison are nearly all species that build domed nests with a side entrance or else pensile structures that are still better enclosed. In tropical America, the habit has been noticed in several kinds of flycatchers, including the Gray-capped Flycatcher and the Sulphury Flatbill, and in becards, which build bulky closed nests. In Australia, several species of warblers of the genus *Gerygone*, as likewise certain finches, often place their nests close to those of stinging wasps.

Birds with open nests rarely choose the vicinity of such fiery neighbors, which, if aroused by some large animal shaking their nest, may attack the birds or their nestlings as well as the intruder. When children tried to destroy a nest of large black wasps in a tree, one or more of the insects stung a well-grown nestling Scarlet-rumped Black Tanager, driving it prematurely from its nest two yards away. When, a few hours later, I discovered the victim hiding amid low herbage nearby, it had a bizarre aspect. Its neck had swollen to several times normal size, the crown of its head was greatly raised, and the skin was drawn backward from the eyes by the pressure of the swelling. To give the poor creature some relief, I punctured the transparent skin with a needle, expecting to see a watery fluid squirt out. To my amazement, only gas escaped as the neck rapidly shrank to normal size. I would like to know the chemistry of this occurrence.

Even parent birds may, in exceptional circumstances, pay dearly for their association with wasps. In *The Naturalist in Nicaragua*, Thomas Belt tells how a "yellow and brown flycatcher," flying from its domed nest in a thorny tree on the savannas as his party rode by, carelessly impaled itself on one of the sharp, curved prickles. Its struggles to escape resulted only in its greater entanglement; and meanwhile the wasps, aroused by its fluttering, stung it to death in less than a minute. They also punished the man who tried vainly to rescue the poor bird.

Usually, however, the wasps seem not to attack their avian neighbors, even while they are building the nest and are wholly exposed. A. H. Chisholm, an Australian naturalist, believed that birds seek the proximity of wasps chiefly for protection against reptiles, especially snakes, which prey so heavily upon eggs and nestlings. The only evidence on this point that I have gathered is an observation made long ago in Panama. When a black and yellow Mica invaded a small colony of nesting Yellow-rumped Caciques in a tree inhabited by many wasps and bees, the snake plundered the birds' nests by night, when most kinds of these insects are inactive, apparently hiding by day in one of the caciques' hanging pouches that it had already emptied. Yet, in other circumstances, Micas pillage birds' nests by day.

At least one kind of bird makes its nest in a vespiary, as numerous others do in termitaries, and at least one, the Rufous Woodpecker of India, in an active ants' nest. Early one morning in February, in the clearing on the mountainside above the valley of the Río Buena Vista where I spent so many hours watching the birds, I saw a pair of yellow-breasted Violaceous Trogons fly out of the forest and attack a large vespiary inhabited by blackish wasps of medium size. This structure, composed of silvery-gray paper, was top-shaped, attached by its broad upper end to an exposed outer branch of a noble *Stryphnodendron* tree, a hundred feet above the ground. The male and female trogons darted alternately up to the vespiary, where, hovering momentarily on wing as they do while plucking a berry, they tore at a small hole in the side, near the bottom. The gap grew slowly, as day after day the birds returned to their task, while the wasps were still sluggish and inactive in the cool morning air at three thousand feet above sea level.

Later, when the rising sun had warmed the mountainside and the inhabitants of the vespiary became active, the trogons perched nearby and made long, spectacular flights to catch them in mid-air or pluck them from the surface of their home. Apparently the birds ate the wasps, as I did not see the victims fall to the ground. When the gap in the side grew large enough for the trogons to cling to its lower edge while working, their spells of excavation grew longer, and soon they were digging into the brood combs. Doubtless they devoured the tender white larvae and pupae, but I could not see this, for the birds kept their heads inside. Occasionally a wasp attacked the despoilers of their nest, but, on the whole, they gave the trogons little trouble. After the birds had hollowed out a cavity among the brood combs, large enough to serve as their nest, the wasps deserted their hive.

Sometimes I have heard a Costa Rican peasant say, "*Nadie sabe para quien trabaja*" (Nobody knows whom he is working for). So it was with these trogons; although they did not know it, they were carving into the vespiary for a pair of Piratic Flycatchers, aberrant members of an industrious family, which never build a nest but capture covered structures made by a variety of other birds. Soon after the trogons finished their chamber, the Pirates gained possession of it, doubtless by their usual procedure of throwing out the eggs laid by the builder of a coveted nest. In later years, I found in El General half a dozen other nests of the Violaceous Trogon, all in vespiaries high in trees. In Panama, however, this species raises its young in cavities in decaying trunks or termitaries, which are more typical nest sites for trogons.

In October, when the migrants are coming down from the North, I sometimes hear a scratching on the outer wall of my study. If I look out carefully, I may see a Summer Tanager, newly arrived in the valley, attacking one of the wasps' nests attached to the building. After tearing off the envelope, the bird proceeds to extract the larvae and pupae from their cells and devour them—as the red tanager also does in its summer home in the United States. Many beautiful wasps' nests on our walls have been destroyed in this way. As far as I know, none of the many resident tanagers have this habit; but once, in Caribbean Costa Rica, I watched a Scarlet-rumped Cacique extracting food from a small wasps' nest attached to a hanging palm frond.

I have not seen the Summer Tanager attack nests of the big Guitarrón wasps. These are reserved for the Red-throated Caracara, a crow-sized black falcon with a white abdomen, yellow bill, leaden-blue cere, and bright orange-red legs. In the days when much forest remained in El General, I would sometimes see these caracaras fly overhead in noisy pairs or trios, calling raucously *cacáo ca ca ca cacáo*—whence their local name, *Cacao*. They appear to subsist largely on the larvae and pupae of wasps; I have watched one tear the bottom from the clay urn of the Banded Wasp, detach a comb and carry it up to some high bough, where, holding it beneath a foot, it pulled apart the structure to extract the tender immature wasps.

One afternoon in November, soon after I moved into my present abode, a caracara's hoarse cries called my attention to its presence at the forest's edge. Here it was attacking a large Guitarróns' nest fastened beneath an ascending limb of a Spanish plum tree. I expected these big wasps with barbed stings to defend their home with fury, but to my amazement they flew around in helpless consternation. Rarely the bird shook its head, scratched itself with a foot, or appeared to pluck one of the insects from its plumage, but, on the whole, they gave it little trouble. The caracara's chief problem was to make a breach in the citadel's wall, not to ward off its defenders. Resting on the thick supporting branch and bending far over, with difficulty it pecked two small perforations in the side of the nest. Clinging in these by its toes, white belly upward and partly spread black wings hanging in random attitudes, the bird proceeded to tear off the corrugated envelope from the top downward and to devour the contents of the brood cells. I marveled that paper so thin could sustain so large a bird in this fashion; yet the bird managed to hang on until it reached the bottom of the nest, where the material, being older and evidently weaker, broke under the load. The caracara fluttered down into the bushes on the slope below, but after a short rest it uttered its raucous battle cry and returned to the attack—only to flutter down into the bushes again. After seven attempts to cling below this weakest part of the nest, the bird became discouraged and flew down to the trees beside the river, leaving a few young wasps in the lowest cells. All the others were open and empty. A whole city of wasps had been devastated to supply one meal for a caracara!

Conflicts of Army Ants with Wasps and Other Ants

By refraining from attacking the plundering falcon, who, doubtless, was well protected by its feathers and would have nipped them fatally, practically all the adult Guitarrón wasps had saved their lives. After crawling dispiritedly over their ruined home for a while, they migrated about fifty yards to the front wall of my dining room, where they built a new nest. Here they prospered and increased so rapidly that after six weeks they started an annex to their structure. At this time, army ants from the neighboring forest made one of their periodic invasions of my house. All the smaller wasps prudently fled at the approach of the Eciton horde, making no attempt to save their progeny. I was eager to learn how the big Synoeca wasps would receive the pillaging ants.

After a while, several scouting ants, crawling obliquely down the wall, found the Guitarróns' nest, then turned back to convey the intelligence to the army, apparently by means of their long, constantly vibrating antennae. More and more ants came hurrying down; soon great hordes advanced toward the corrugated nest. All the wasps that had been working on the annex, in the open without protection, took wing and vanished as the myrmecine army drew nigh, but instead of fleeing as the smaller wasps did, those within the stout envelope remained to defend it. Without a skirmish, the attackers advanced to the single doorway, about an inch in diameter, at the top of the nest. Here they found their way blocked by the black heads of the wasps, who had lined up just within the sharp edge, as close side by side as they could crowd, with only their slender antennae projecting outward. Down inside, angry wasps were making the same rustling or rasping noise that one hears when he shakes their nest. Finding the gateway well guarded, the invaders lined up around the outside, a brown circle surrounding the black circle of wasp heads, ants' antennae vibrating almost in contact with wasps' antennae.

Standing in front of the house, I intently watched the attack through field glasses. From time to time, an ant ventured to cross the rim, which brought it upon the heads of the wasps, who with little effort pushed the smaller insect out again. The ant so repulsed was never seen to fall from the nest; as far as I could tell, neither the winged nor the wingless warriors were wounded in this battle. The two sides appeared to be about as evenly matched as the Achaeans and the Trojans, and the siege promised to be a long-drawn-out one. While the main troop of ants made a concerted attack on the doorway, scattered detachments tried to breach the corrugated wall. Whenever they succeeded in opening a tiny gap, too small for them to pass through, a wasp came to stand guard, its antennae sometimes slipping through the perforation. From time to time, wasps from outside approached the nest, but finding the ants surrounding the orifice, they tamely flew off without alighting. For three-quarters of an hour, while the siege of this vespid Troy was at its height, I saw neither ant nor wasp enter the beleaguered city, and no wasp leave. Then the main body of the besiegers withdrew, leaving a few ants still hopefully gnawing at the tiny gaps they had made in the walls.

Soon, however, the legion returned for a second mass attack, and this was followed by a third, but neither was more successful than the first. At last the assailants admitted defeat and withdrew; the city was saved, with only minor damage to its outermost defenses. It was the only one of the many vespiaries on the house that escaped destruction that exciting afternoon. From all the others, the pillagers were filing down the walls with soft white larvae and pupae in their mandibles. Some were so large that two or three ants carried them. Gaps between boards were bridged by ants that stood clinging to both sides, forming a living bridge over which the columns passed. They streamed down to the ground and vanished in the grass with their booty.

On the following morning, the Guitarrón wasps mended the holes in their nest. That afternoon they were attacked again, with the same outcome as before. Thereafter, for seven weeks, we enjoyed peace. The smaller wasps returned to lay new eggs in the cells that the ants had emptied without damaging the structures. The Guitarrón wasps, multiplying apace, finished their first annex and started another.

Then, one night in late February, a number of the big wasps flew into my lighted room—an unprecedented occurrence. Suspecting that they were in trouble, I hurried out to investigate. The ants had invaded their nest. On the surrounding wall I found a number of the poor wasps, each the nucleus of a seething mass of ants that had overpowered it. Later in the night, the invaders began carrying out the captured wasps and their young brood—just as all the citizens of an ancient city and their children were dragged away to servitude or death when the enemy overcame it. Each adult wasp, and each larger larva, was borne by as many ants as could attach themselves to it and moved along at a snail's pace. Despite the difficulty of transportation, the ants carried their plunder up the wall, across the top, and down the other side, stupidly retracing the course by which they had arrived, when they might have cut the distance in half. All night and all next morning in full sunshine, the toiling ants continued to drag the corpses from the fallen city. Although by day the large-eyed, diurnal wasps could easily defend their castle against the sightless army ants, at night the latter had the advantage and overpowered the community.

In encounters with such hereditary enemies as the caracara and the army ants, the Guitarrón wasps behave in what we might call a rational manner, defending their progeny when there is a good prospect of success, prudently withdrawing when defense is hopeless. In their dealings with man, however, these wasps display blind stupidity. Sometimes, when they have started a nest in an inconvenient situation, such as on a wall close to a door or on a tree that needs pruning, I have tried to persuade them to go elsewhere. But hanging leafy boughs over their chosen site, breaking down their structure as it is built, brushing off the wasps in a cool dawn when they are torpid, smoking them—all these means are without effect. The wasps stubbornly return again and again, and in the end we have always been driven, reluctantly, to use flame and utterly destroy a colony that we wished only to move farther off.

These and other experiences with insects lead me to believe that they are nearly or quite insensitive to pain. And why should they feel pain? The biological function of pain, which evidently promoted its evolution through natural selection, is to teach animals to avoid things and situations that are harmful to them—as the child learns to avoid the stove by burning his hand. But insects, guided as they are by those marvelous innate patterns of behavior that for brevity we call instincts, have slight capacity to learn. Accordingly, to feel pain would be of little service to them. But to postulate that they are free of pain is not to deny that they feel or that they enjoy life. Happy creatures, to know pleasure without pain! Indeed, I suspect that nothing whatsoever, down to the very protons and electrons, exists without some measure of feeling. For it seems absurd to suppose that anything should exist quite barrenly, with no satisfaction in its existence, or only for the benefit of some other being still far in the future. And if the stuff of which we are made is wholly insentient, how can we account for our own consciousness, except by the dualistic hypothesis, with all the baffling philosophical problems that it involves?

In later invasions by the army ants, I gave attention to the sticky wasps' nests on my walls. One day a thick column of the Ecitons streamed up and down a wall only a foot away from one of these nests. From time to time, a scout would leave the column and advance toward this vespiary. Reaching the sticky palisade surrounding the nest, it halted, struggled violently to detach itself from the gummy surface upon which it had blundered unaware, and withdrew as soon as it was able. Not a single ant crossed the protective zone. By way of experiment, I picked up an Eciton of medium size and set it down on the sticky palisade. After half an hour it was still hopelessly stuck, and I removed it so begummed that I doubted whether it would survive. An ant of the same size, set down upon the nest itself, remained there until it died. But when I made the experiment with one of the biggest soldiers, with huge, forcepslike jaws, the result was different. Struggling violently with its longer, stronger legs, it at last succeeded in dragging itself to the edge of the palisade and escaping.

On other invasions, however, the army ants, falling upon the sticky nests en masse, succeeded in reaching and pillaging them. So dense was the swarm of attacking ants that those in contact with the glandlike protuberances formed a pavement over which their comrades could pass without getting stuck. Apparently, the result was due in part to the fact that these plundered nests were older and the gum on the stalks not so fresh and adhesive. When finally the ants withdrew, none remained stuck to the palisade.

When the army ants came out of the forest, the feltmaker wasps fared no better than the wasps of various kinds that attached their nests to the house. One day I watched the Ecitons plunder a nest of the Apoicas in front of my study window. While the ants carried off their progeny, the wasps clung on nearby branches in three compact clusters. They did not even attack the chickens who approached to eat the Ecitons, pecking into the nest and ruining it in order to reach the ants and probably also the larvae and pupae that the invaders had not yet removed. The outcome of this invasion might be attributed to the fact that it came in the daytime, when the nocturnal feltmakers were at a disadvantage, just as the diurnal Guitarróns were in the face of an attack under cover of darkness. However, the feltmakers did not hesitate to attack me one day when I inadvertently stirred them up.

In tropical America, the most conspicuous myrmecine societies are those of the hunting Ecitons and the leaf-cutting Attas, each aggressive in its own way. What happens when the carnivorous hordes come into contact with the thronging vegetarians? At Rancho Grande in the coastal range of Venezuela, William Beebe, as he tells in *High Jungle,* watched columns of these two kinds of ants march past each other without conflict. Since army ants apparently do not use adult Attas as food, they had no incentive to attack them on this occasion.

The situation is quite different when foraging Ecitons encounter a leaf-cutters' nest. Not long ago, on the hill behind our house, I noticed a long, slender column of army ants stretched between one of the mouths of a leaf-cutters' subterranean nest and the neighboring thicket. The outward-bound Ecitons bore little white burdens, the larvae and pupae of the unfortunate Attas. Many small brown workers of the latter tried to save the immature ants by escaping with them through another exit and climbing up neighboring grass blades and weed stalks. Here the nurse ants remained, crawling slowly and disconsolately about with their precious burdens, until an exploring army ant bumped into them. One or two such contacts usually caused the frightened worker to drop her white load, which sooner or later was picked up and borne away by an Eciton. It was remarkable how close a blind army ant could come to an Atta bearing a larva, only to turn away without touching or seeming to notice her. After a while, however, one of the pillaging horde happened to pass a little closer to a nurse ant, upon whom it pounced, making her drop her burden, more from fear, it seemed, than by forceful compulsion.

I never saw an Eciton harm a worker Atta, considerably smaller than itself. After a brief examination, it would hurry away, leaving the little leaf cutter, perhaps one that had tried vainly to save a larva or pupa, wandering aimlessly about. With the big-headed Atta soldiers, twice as large as the army ants, the case was far otherwise. Sensing their danger, the spiny brown soldiers fled before the marauders far more rapidly than did their smaller sisters, the workers. A single army ant might bump into a soldier and hurry away, as though fearing to come to grips with the goliath. But if several Ecitons met it almost simultaneously, they grappled with it; soon it was the center of a seething, rolling mass of ants that did not release it until it was dead and perhaps torn asunder. The dead or dying soldier might be carried a short way toward the army's bivouac, but many of their mangled corpses were dropped along the trail. Evidently their hard, dry bodies were not considered good provender by the voracious horde, which spared the Atta workers that would have made easy victims and violently attacked the soldiers, only to abandon their corpses.

In my experience, the only social insects that escape the army ants' raids are the little, black, stingless Trigona bees that build, on trees and houses, large, dark carton nests that resemble arboreal termitaries. All the social wasps, including the largest and most fiercely stinging, and a great variety of other ants pay tribute to these relentless freebooters.

Yet the ferocity of the army ants has been ludicrously exaggerated by sensational writers, who have even represented them as dangerous to cattle! Their sting is less painful and lasting than that of the Fire Ants that in wet weather make many low mounds on the lawn and crawl up the legs of people who carelessly stand upon them, inflicting memorable punishment. But birds attending army ants sometimes stand calmly while the Ecitons crawl over their toes. I have also watched army ants wander over the nest where a small bird incubated, without harming or driving her away, and I have known both the large *Eciton* and the smaller *Labidus* to swarm over the mouths of puffbirds' burrows in the ground, without injuring the feathered nestlings within. When an antbird shot by a collector in Nicaragua fell into the midst of army ants, they passed on without even attacking the bare skin around its eyes, and they ignored a freshly killed snake that I once threw into the thick of a foraging horde. In contrast to my experience, T. C. Schneirla, a leading student of army ant behavior, has seen snakes, lizards, and nestling birds killed by them, and he believed that a larger vertebrate unable to escape would be killed by stinging or asphyxiation. But the Ecitons are unable to dismember or eat their occasional, more or less accidental, vertebrate victims. Their food consists largely, if not wholly, of insects, spiders, scorpions, sowbugs, and other invertebrates, and they are especially eager for the tender, immature stages of wasps and other ants. From all accounts, the even larger hordes of the African driver ants are much more dangerous to vertebrates than are their American relatives.

The Limits of Parental Devotion

Over the years I have, often unwillingly, watched animals of many kinds secure their prey. I have seen ants plunder the nests of wasps and of other species of ants; snakes pillage birds' nests; hawks capture snakes; and Tayras assault a Laughing Falcon's nest. Sometimes I have expected the victims to defend themselves or their progeny with fury, resulting in a fierce conflict of doubtful outcome; yet this has scarcely ever occurred. Predators commonly display an easy mastery over their habitual prey, rarely jeopardizing life or limb to secure it.

A little reflection will convince us that this is how it must be. A hawk that subsists mainly upon snakes, including venomous kinds, seems to live dangerously, often risking its life to procure its meal. Yet to nourish itself and its young, such a raptor must kill hundreds of serpents in the course of a year; if as much as one per cent of the encounters proved fatal to the hawks, these birds, with their slow rate of reproduction, would soon become extinct. The hawk must learn to restrict its attacks to snakes that it is certain to overpower. Such is the case with all other predators. Although young individuals may sometimes misjudge the strength of their intended victims, and no creature, however experienced, is infallible, mistakes cannot become frequent without jeopardizing the existence of the species. Prudence must govern the behavior of the predator in the presence of prey. Extreme hunger may, however, override this habitual prudence.

When we realize the prudence of predators, we will understand, and forgive, the often apparently pusillanimous behavior of their victims, and especially of the parents of helpless young. Birds seem terribly distressed when an enemy, real or apparent, approaches their nest: they cry out; they make feints of attack and sometimes even strike or peck an intruder many times their own size; and they drop to the ground and flutter over it as though crippled and unable to fly, trying thereby to lure the animal away from eggs or young with the promise of an easily captured meal. This ruse is sometimes successful, but if it fails in the face of an habitual predator, the nest is doomed. Despite all the show they sometimes make, birds rarely sacrifice their lives in defense of their progeny, so that one may suspect that the seemingly anguished parents are merely acting a part and have no real parental feeling.

Since the habitual predator must be master of the situation, it would be futile for the parents to jeopardize their lives in an effort to resist it. In view of the high incidence of predation on birds' nests, the adults must survive to try again and again to raise a brood. Birds and other animals that attend their offspring may serve the young to the limit of their strength, but they must not throw away their lives in a fruitless effort to protect the helpless progeny, which without them would perish anyway. This is the limit that natural selection sets to parental devotion; it would ruthlessly eliminate any race in which adults developed a strong tendency to sacrifice themselves in the defense of dependent young. The wasps that, offering no resistance, flee as army ants or caracaras approach to carry off their larvae and pupae are acting in the best interests of their species; they are needed to replenish the empty cells and rear another brood after the invaders have gone.

With social animals that are rather evenly matched, the situation is different. A hive of bees may sacrifice many of its members to capture the stores of another hive, yet obtain this honey more cheaply than by independent foraging, in which the lives of many workers are lost or worn away. And the hive under attack does well to defend its hard-won stores, even at the cost of numerous lives; if the defense is successful, the survivors will make good use of them and rear the tender brood. In a world pervaded by strife, the fiercest conflicts, the only warfare properly so-called, occurs among social animals and is intensified as they rise in the evolutionary scale.

20

Farming Without a Plow

IN THE FIRST THIRD of the present century, when the Valley of El General was remote and difficult to reach, Costa Rican peasants spoke of it as a land flowing with milk and honey. Doubtless its very inaccessibility added to its fame, for men generally think of paradise as a place hard to reach, and by a false logic a spot difficult of access is easily magnified into a paradise. The valley's fame rested upon a few narrow belts of rich bottom land, such as those along the General and Pacuar rivers; whereas by far the greater part of the area consisted of ridges and little plateaus of red clay of inferior value for agriculture. Nevertheless, El General was at that period a region where an enterprising, resolute man could, with scarcely any capital but much hard work, make a living for his family and look forward to an old age spent in self-respecting independence but hardly in luxury.

Headpiece: A milpa in a new clearing in the forest. In pioneer days, when thieves were fewer, the maize was often stored in the husk in thatched sheds like that in the foreground.

Few men of means were tempted by the agricultural potentialities of El General, even after the opening of the Inter-American Highway made it readily accessible. The few wealthy people who bought land in the valley were chiefly foreigners who had time and money for play, and most of these did not remain long. Of the prosperous Costa Rican landowning class who controlled the productive coffee estates in the Central Plateau, hardly any were lured by the fame of El General. These people knew good lands and were not to be deceived by rumor about them.

Although I did not come here primarily to farm, I needed to derive food and some income from my land in order to make ends meet. I began to farm with no illusions about the productivity of my fields. But the methods I should perforce use had a certain historical and economic interest, for they were hardly different from those employed by the aboriginal inhabitants of tropical America before the arrival of Europeans. And they were practically the same as those currently in use among millions of farmers on the rougher mountain lands, at lower elevations, throughout tropical America, from Mexico to Peru and Bolivia. Indeed, in El General we were better off than many of these peasants, for our land, if not intrinsically superior, was at least still new and fresh. If by farming here I could not become wealthy, I could at least acquire direct experience of some of the major agricultural problems of tropical America, such as few men with scientific training then possessed.

One of the first things that I noticed about the local men, especially those that I employed as farm hands, was their reluctance to dig into the ground. This was understandable on the dark loam of the riverside benches and *vegas*, which, although fairly rich, was so rocky that in many places it was difficult to dig a hole big enough to set a fence post or plant a fruit tree. But the reddish soil of the slopes and ridges, although of inferior fertility, was at least deep and nearly free of stones. Here and there a farmer had a plow and perhaps an acre or two of land sufficiently level and stoneless to be arable. But practically all the farm work was done with simple hand tools: the long, straight machete for cutting bush; the broad, scimitarlike machete for scraping weeds off the surface of the soil.

There are three chief methods of preparing the land for sowing. The most important of these is slashing and burning, but this, of course, is feasible only in the dry season, for crops that will be planted with the first rains in March and April. It is used chiefly for maize and rice, which are sown by dropping the grains by hand into narrow holes punched in the charred ground with a stick or an ironshod pole known as a *macana*. Less often is land burnt off for beans, which, if sown at this time, mature beneath the heavy rains of July, when germination in the pod is likely to spoil the crop. Each year we plant a few beans among the corn, as the Indians did of old, chiefly for the sake of the green pods to be used as vegetables. I soon learned that it does not pay to sow many beans in this fashion because of trouble in harvesting.

The second method of planting is to broadcast the seed through standing second-growth vegetation, then to cut down this growth and slash it up until it lies flat, forming a mulch over the ground, through which the young shoots find their way up to the light and air. This is employed chiefly during the rainy months when burning is impossible. A supplementary crop of maize is sometimes sown by this method in September. I have seen maize planted in this way beneath trees nearly a foot in diameter and perhaps sixty or seventy feet high, which were then felled over the seed. To move about in a field of corn growing up amidst the resulting tangle of trunks and boughs is slow and toilsome. Corn planted in this fashion yields possibly half as much per acre as the main crop on burned-over land. Sometimes we have broadcast a small patch of corn in September, in order to have some tender ears at the end of the year, when fruits and vegetables are scarce.

The principal bean crop is sown broadcast in late October or November, beneath the heaviest rains of the year. For best results, one looks for resting land on which the spontaneously springing vegetation has not become too tall and heavy, because beans cannot sprout up through a thickness of debris that might be penetrated by the taller and sturdier stalks of maize. I never cease to marvel that the men who do this work can scatter the seed rather uniformly when broadcasting in thickets well over head-high and so dense that they can neither move without cutting a path nor see three yards in front of their eyes. And, of course, it is impossible to learn how the seed lies until the rank growth has been slashed down and the bean seedlings peep up above the layer of dying leaves and stems. The crop ripens toward the end of January, when, as a rule, sunny weather permits the pods to dry in the field. Here a little booth is erected with sacks or blankets stretched between upright poles, which prevents the beans from flying widely when they are threshed out by beating the well-sunned vines and pods with a stick.

The third method of preparing the land is to scrape off all the vegetation at the surface with a broad machete, leaving the ground clean and bare. This procedure is possible only on land covered with light, weedy growth, and such land is likely to be insufficiently rested. For this reason, and another soon to be mentioned, yields tend to be low. In my first September on the farm, I planted a small patch of corn on scraped land, but Don Chico's prediction that I should harvest a mere handful proved to be correct. Nevertheless, this handful, in the form of green corn for the table, was greatly appreciated. Nor have I had satisfactory results with garden vegetables sown on land from which the vegetation was scraped aside, even when the ground was dug with a spade before the seeds were planted. My first rice, sown on a field that had been scraped clean, did yield generously; but rice is famed for what it will produce on impoverished soil. Upland rice will often produce a fair crop on a hillside too sterile for maize. Paddy rice is never planted in this valley.

The results of these various methods of planting are understandable in terms of the economy of the soil in a tropical region with over a hundred inches of rain each year and a growing season that is practically continuous. Soluble salts tend to be quickly leached from the upper layer of the ground. Nearly all of the chief mineral nutrients available within the depth freely penetrated by roots seem to be actually bound up in the tissues of the vigorous vegetation growing on this land. This is particularly true of mature forest, which has had time to come into equilibrium with the soil that supports it. It has been said of tropical rain forest that it lives on its fallen leaves and branches: some vegetation must die and release its mineral salts in order to provide nutriment for the growth of other plants. There may be slow increases of available minerals through the weathering of rocks or chemical changes in the soil, but the principal source of nourishment for the living vegetation is the dead tissues of plants.

When the vegetable covering is cut and burned, the more heat-resistant of the nutrient compounds are left in the ashes that cover the ground. The first light rains of the wet season wash the soluble salts from these ashes into the upper layers of the thirsty soil, making them available to the roots of the sprouting maize or rice plants. This fertilizing ash is of great importance in mountainous districts where the poverty of the farmers and difficult transportation prohibit the importation of chemical fertilizers, and the practice of keeping domestic animals always in open pastures prevents the accumulation of a manure pile. With the ash as fertilizer, maize grows tall and stout and yields gratifying crops.

When, instead of being burned, the vegetable covering of the land is slashed up and allowed to lie as a mulch over the sprouting seeds, the rapid decay of this organic matter releases nutrients to the soil, without the destruction of the less stable compounds by heat. But, with this procedure, the roots and rhizomes of the original vegetation are not destroyed; many remain alive to send up new shoots, so that they compete with the beans or the maize both above and below ground. Moreover, the litter covering the field so interferes with cultivation or cleaning of any sort that it is rarely attempted. These conditions decrease the yield of the crops, even when there is adequate nourishment for them. But when the spontaneous vegetation is scraped off and pushed aside in preparation for sowing, all the minerals that this vegetation contains are removed from the area so treated. Accordingly, if no other fertilizer is applied, yields will be low.

These primitive methods of farming are, on the better soils, not unproductive, so long as the ground is covered with vegetation of the sort that springs up in new clearings in the forest: with guarumo, burío, balsa, and Inga trees, with great-leafed herbs like Heliconias and shellflowers, with a tangle of native bushes and vines. But with the continued use of the land, this soft vegetation is gradually supplanted by a different kind of growth, consisting of rank grasses, wiry broomweeds (*Sida*), sedges, and other sun-loving plants of pastures and open ground. Some of these species form the usual covering of impoverished fields, but even before the soil is exhausted, they may intrude and cause trouble in the kind of land management we are considering.

To avoid the too-rapid deterioration of the soil, the too-swift influx of noxious grasses and weeds, the land should rest at least four or five years between successive burnings; a full decade is not too long. During this interval, it will be overgrown by a dense, woody vegetation, with guarumo, burío, or balsa trees forty to sixty feet high. Yet even with this conservative management, an increase of grasses and hard weeds is inevitable; they slip in each time the ground is exposed to the sun. Cleanings become more costly with each succeeding crop, and there is a gradual decline in productivity.

How the native woody vegetation restores the fertility of resting land is vividly illustrated by the hilltop behind our house. After being in pasture for a quarter of a century, this summit almost ceased to produce grass. Large patches of ground became bare or supported only depauperate weeds. We then stopped cleaning the pasture, permitting the native vegetation to re-establish itself. Flourishing shrubs and trees surrounding the bare patches indicate that only the superficial soil has been drained of essential minerals; deeper layers still contain them, and after a plant sends its roots down far enough, it finds what it needs for vigorous growth. With their fallen leaves and twigs, these woody plants are enriching the topmost stratum of soil with minerals brought up from deeper layers, as likewise with humus. In their shade, shallow-rooted herbs can again grow.

When a field is used only once in four or five years, one needs much land for a little farming. But as population increases and holdings are divided, each farmer has a smaller area and must plant it at shorter intervals. Because he reaps less from each acre, he must plant more acres each year to provide for his needs, and this also decreases the periods of rest that the land can receive. Hence a vicious circle, which rapidly wears out the soil. Some of the more enterprising of my neighbors, who came here as to a land of promise, have already sold out and gone to seek fresh fields, of which they boast mightily but which in another decade or two they will probably be ready to abandon for newer lands —if they can find them. Even though we have used the land more sparingly on this farm, our fields are becoming infested with stubborn grasses; and I sometimes wonder how much longer they will yield the heavy crops of maize to which we have become accustomed. It is distressing to see land that bore splendid forest reduced in a few decades to unproductive fields overgrown with grass and weeds, but if I had not come, the degradation of the soil on this farm would have been much more rapid.

The annual burning, indispensable if we are going to plant maize at a reasonable cost on our stony riverside fields, is most distasteful to me. The year after I bought the farm, I prepared a large field for maize in partnership with Don Chico, the previous owner, hoping to profit by his experience. Although the early months had been rainy, he insisted on delaying the burning, promising dry weather later. On the afternoon of March 6, when some neighbors burned large areas of recently felled forest, a heavy shower cooled the embers of their fires. On the next twelve days, a drenching shower fell every afternoon. Then followed two rainless days, after which I decided to burn beneath the midday sun. But the bushes and small trees that had been lying on the moist ground for more than a month were overgrown with green vines, which should have been carefully severed before the second-growth thicket was cut down. These not only retarded the drying of the fallen vegetation but they directly impeded the spread of the fire. Despite much nursing of the flames, they had crept over less than half of the field that we had prepared for burning when rain extinguished them, and with them our hope for a bountiful harvest.

Even the area where the fire had passed was poorly burned, covered with a litter of charred trunks and branches that would interfere with sowing and weeding; the rest represented so much lost labor. If misery loves company, we had plenty of it; other farmers who had waited too long for dry weather could not burn their clearings and, therefore, could not plant their corn. In the years before the airplane came to El General, a wet "dry season" that prevented burning and sowing brought hunger and hardship to the isolated settlers.

Since in that first year the fire had been so reluctant to cover even the area we had prepared for it, when next I burned for a milpa, I did so without a helper and without taking precautions to prevent the fire's spreading into the adjoining uncut thickets, which were still green and lush. The result was a runaway blaze that crept up a steep bank, through a tongue of deceptively green Calinguero grass, then with loud crackling rushed inexorably over several acres of the same mendacious herbage in an adjacent, neglected pasture. Far from exulting in the blaze as a spectacular natural phenomenon, as Thoreau did when he accidentally started a forest fire, I was profoundly distressed by it. Looking on helplessly, in anguish of spirit, I repented the carelessness that was causing the destruction of so many lizards, insects, and other harmless living things. To be responsible for an event but impotent to control it is a dreadfully harassing experience. It was terrifying and humiliating to be made aware, in so unequivocal a fashion, that our power often falls far short of our responsibility, that we cannot always stop what we start.

Since this unhappy experience, we have burned for twenty-five milpas without losing control of our fire. We never stint the hard work of making a wide, bare fire lane around the field to be burned. We set fire about the end of February, before, in a dry year, the surrounding uncut vegetation has become too dry and inflammable. If the weather has been rather wet, we ignite the brush beneath the midday sun so that it may foment the flames; if the weather has been dry, we wait until late in the afternoon so that falling temperature and increasing humidity may help us to control the conflagration. And we have enough hands to extinguish a blaze that jumps the fire lane.

Yet even when we keep our fire within bounds, I heartily dislike the burning. Many small creatures remain stubbornly among the drying vegetation and fail to escape the rushing flames. To a thoughtful man, it is painful to be responsible for the immolation of living things. I console myself with the reflection that plowing crushes countless small creatures or buries them alive—and not only field mice, the destruction of whose nests by the plow troubled the tender heart of Robert Burns. But unless we plow or burn, we cannot produce sufficient food to keep ourselves alive. This necessity to destroy in order to live is one of the most distressing aspects of life on a crowded planet. No one, not even the Jaina *saddhu*, who vows to harm not even the smallest living thing, really escapes from this curse.

Not only does the latter part of the dry season bring the hateful task of burning for the milpa; it brings the smoke-laden atmosphere, the hot and oppressive days, and the starless nights, of which I wrote in chapter 4. And after I became a landowner, it also brought anxiety about fire on my farm. Even when one keeps under control his own fires for clearing fields, he runs the risk of destructive fire from other sources. Sometimes careless burning on an adjoining farm results in a runaway blaze that crosses boundary lines. Occasionally, a fire is wantonly or spitefully set, perhaps to "pay back" a proprietor whose only offense was resisting some flagrant violation of his property. Among people of primitive mentality, the pressing of a just claim is too often regarded as an offense that calls for vengeance, and one of the most convenient ways of wreaking it is by starting a fire in the dry weather. Where is the witness who can prove how any particular fire was set when the whole countryside is burning? Three years after I came to Los Cusingos, several acres of pasture were burned and my cane field destroyed by a fire that either started from a brand that flew across the river or was deliberately set.

It is hard to judge the distance of a column of smoke rising beyond the treetops; one can rarely be sure, without going to investigate, whether his own farm is burning or another a mile away. Although racing crown fires, such as devastate vast areas of northern coniferous woods, are unknown in tropical rain forest, in the driest weather, ground fires spread slowly, destroying humus and low vegetation, scorching the bases of the great trees and opening them to the attacks of destructive insects and fungi. One who cares for his land and the vegetation upon it is immensely relieved when, in March or April, the rains return, ending the danger of fires, purifying the atmosphere, reviving drooping plants, and refreshing the earth. Soon the fields are green again; trees put on new foliage or bloom profusely; and the birds begin to sing and build their nests. The golden morning sunshine has now a special benignity; the limpid air seems to be impregnated with some subtle elixir that stimulates and nourishes all life. The beginning of the wet season rivals the outset of the dry season as a delightful time, and, for a naturalist, it is of even greater interest, for living things are now more active.

Costa Rica has long had on its statute books stringent laws to regulate burning. If they were rigidly enforced, little grain would be produced in this region, for the preparation of the land for sowing would prove too costly. This is another example of how too-drastic laws defeat the ends they were intended to accomplish. But let us not judge the backwoods farmers too severely. In the Palouse country of eastern Washington, I saw, just after World War II, thousands of acres of burning wheat stubble, miles of sagging and fallen wire fence where posts had been burned, and many charred service poles. These farmers could not contend that their deep, rich soils were not arable or that they lacked machinery for plowing them. But everywhere men are greedy and shortsighted. The excellent prices they were receiving for their wheat tempted them to sow annually lands which, because of meager rainfall, should, I was told, be left fallow in alternate years. Because of peculiar soil conditions, this destructive burning of the stubble on recently harvested fields was a necessary prelude to planting winter wheat in the same year.

The visitor to the ruins of Quiriguá in Guatemala, contemplating the elaborately carved monoliths standing in a grassy field bordered by heavy rain forest—as I saw them forty years ago—wonders what befell the brilliant civilization that produced them. Why did the Mayas abandon this fertile valley? Probably the people who set up these impressive monuments depended for their food upon agricultural practices such as we use in El General today, which O. F. Cook called the "milpa system of agriculture." To be sure, they had no rice, sugarcane, plantains and bananas, or coffee, all of which are of Old World origin and did not reach America until after Columbus; but they doubtless leaned heavily upon maize and beans, with perhaps pumpkins planted in the corn fields, just as we do here. It has been surmised that, with the passage of the years, the Mayas' productive lands became increasingly infested with grass and hard weeds, so that they were forced to go farther and farther from their centers of population to find ground suitable for planting. Finally, there came a time when their primitive modes of transportation, without wheels and beasts of burden, could no longer bring enough food from distant fields. Then the Mayas were obliged to abandon the cities of their Old Empire and migrate northward. But with the passage of centuries, their grass-infested fields were recaptured by the rain forest, which is the vegetation natural to this lower part of the Motagua Valley, and the forest at length restored the fertility of the land and made it suitable for the rich banana plantations of recent times.

Without much doubt, the Indians so managed their lands that they continued to yield good harvests longer than those in this valley; otherwise, they would hardly have had time to develop such elaborate cultures. I believe that this longer productive life of the land was possible because the American aborigines, except on the high Andes, did not combine grazing with agriculture. In this region, a principal cause of the degradation of the land is its invasion by coarse grasses introduced to make pastures, which, spreading widely, gradually invade the croplands, making them exceedingly difficult to work by the only available methods. Among the most aggressive and stubborn of these grasses are Calinguero or "Molasses Grass" and Guinea Grass, both natives of Africa, the home of many species of grazing animals. These and other introduced pasture grasses are more vigorous and tenacious than the native grasses of this originally forested valley and are chiefly responsible for the rapid, and often undesired, conversion of croplands into pastures—a process difficult to reverse. Without grazing animals, the Indians of Middle America had no occasion to make pastures. When cultures mix, incompatible elements are often introduced; the introduction of an Old World element into a native American system of agriculture is often disastrous to the latter.

Not only does the production of food present peculiar difficulties on rough tropical lands, its storage raises problems of a different sort. At high latitudes, low temperature favors the keeping of grains and other foods during the winter months. In the tropics, the difficulty can be solved, at least for grains, by high temperature—a temperature sufficiently above that of the air to dry the grain thoroughly and kill infesting insects. But bins equipped with heating devices are too costly for subsistence farmers to construct. Here we depend upon the husks of the maize and the chaff of the rice to enclose the nutritious grains and keep out insects. The heavy-yielding hybrid corn is not for us, for the cobs outgrow their clothes, permitting the heavy rains of July and August, along with weevils and other insects, to enter the ear at its exposed end. We prefer a smaller ear tightly enclosed in hard, purple husks that extend as a beak beyond the tip of the cob and exclude small pests, so that we may keep a supply of corn in our granary from one harvest to the next. Although shelled rice is soon infested with insects, the unhulled grains are long immune to their attacks. Beans are preserved by keeping them in the dust and fragments of vegetation that collect about them during the threshing. They are cleaned as needed by winnowing, tossing them into the air from a broad wooden tray. The use of dust to deter insects provides an enlightening commentary on the birds' widespread habit of "dust-bathing."

All the grains, except maize in the husks, require much sunning, especially if harvested in the rainy months. Sometimes, on a Sunday morning, I have seen one of the larger landowners, locally regarded as a "rich man," nursing a few bushels of beans or rice under a fitful sun, and I have wondered what the hourly earnings of such a man might amount to if he counted all the time he devoted to such necessary but unremunerative tasks.

Since my farm was not sufficiently big and productive to afford a foreman to keep the laborers active, nor could I supervise or work with them all morning without neglecting other things that I hoped to accomplish, I solved the difficulty by going into partnership on the annual crops with my hired man. With his own labor and a little cash, he paid for half of the work, and he received half of the harvest. Since he had a major interest at stake, and it was to his advantage to produce the grain as cheaply as possible, I could be fairly certain that he kept busy in the fields without being watched. And since in addition to applying half of his own time without salary he paid half the wages of any outside labor that we employed for these crops, I had little doubt that he would look for helpers who would give us an honest day's work. Moreover, there was an advantage in having a partner genuinely concerned to see that the cornfield was not invaded by wandering cattle, a neighbor's or our own. Except one year when at harvest time the partner I then had tried a maneuver of questionable honesty, this arrangement has worked satisfactorily.

It is distasteful to me to feel that those who assist me, men or animals, are working under compulsion. If my profits have been less than they might have been, had I paid all the expenses and taken all the crop, it was agreeable to have an associate with a personal interest in the enterprise, who labored for something more than a daily wage and so worked more eagerly and cheerfully. Moreover, every successful attempt at cooperation, with living beings of whatever species, is a moral triumph. Thereby I released many precious hours for my studies. Yet even with this arrangement, there was always a great deal for me to do, both in supervising and in attending to the innumerable odd jobs that arise on any farm where there are animals and fences and gates, fruit trees and garden plots and coffee bushes—little tasks for which the hired labor never seems to suffice. On some days, when everything seemed to demand attention at once, I would wearily ask myself whether I owned the farm or the farm owned me.

When the maize had tender milky grains and the animals came out of the neighboring woodland to feast on them, my partner and I would generally disagree. He would raise the cry, "Shoot the thieving monkeys! Kill the Coatimundis!" I would point out that they were here before us, and we had taken the land away from them; hence it was just that we pay a little rent to them. Or sometimes I would direct my partner to plant a few more rows for the free animals, so that there could be no complaints when they came to enjoy what had been provided for them. The chief of these maize-eaters were the squirrels, the Coatimundis with long, sensitive muzzles, and the White-faced Monkeys. When I saw what hard and tasteless fruits these animals were often reduced to eating in the dry season, I well understood their eagerness for the succulent corn, and I did not begrudge them. The only animals I have ever shot were snakes, which menace us with their venom or pillage birds' nests, and pigs. When the owners of trespassing pigs ignored repeated pleas to keep them at home, as good neighbors do, I killed the offending porkers to save our crops. This is the only legal method of getting rid of them.

If we insist on destroying every animal that touches our food plants or molests us in one way or another, there will eventually be no free creatures to give interest and charm to the country. Of course, if the depredations on our fields become too heavy, we shall be obliged to protect them somehow, or else starve; but we can well spare a little of our harvest for the birds and furry animals. Not only does a sentiment of charity or compassion or of natural justice toward those creatures whose land we have seized prompt us to allow them freely to take a small sample of its produce; there are other, more selfish reasons for adopting this course. Nearly everywhere, people spend a substantial part of their income on recreation and amusement. I derive entertainment, instruction, and esthetic delight from watching the free animals of the woodland. These values are cheaply bought with a few bushels of corn or some of the fruit from our trees. Few of our pleasures are at once so wholesome and so inexpensive.

Since the farm that I bought had a fair acreage of pasture and I like horses, I started off with the idea that I would raise them to sell. However, the first horse that I sold was so abused by the purchaser that I soon abandoned this project, and thereafter I raised only enough for the use of the farm. For many years, we kept a yoke of oxen for hauling, a few cows for milk, and chickens for eggs, never for slaughter. I tried to give all these domestic animals a happy life and regarded the work they did and the milk or eggs they furnished as but a fair return for the food and often laborious care that they received. My aim was to achieve a sort of mutually beneficial symbiosis with them.

The trouble was that the cows gave birth to too many bull calves, and the hens hatched out too many cockerels. To sell these superfluous males to people who might slaughter them was distasteful; to keep and feed them was expensive, and they often fought among themselves. While I was wrestling with this problem, a stranger approached me with an offer to buy my cows for stocking a new farm, and at the same time a neighbor sent a message that my cattle had damaged his sugarcane and he demanded compensation. The would-be purchaser had arrived at an opportune moment; I suddenly decided to sell the cows. Although it was painful to see him drive away the animals that for so many years I had attended faithfully, nursing their frequent wounds and disorders, I have never regretted their sale. Later, while we were away studying birds in other regions, most of our chickens disappeared and have not been replaced. We sell the corn that we formerly fed to the chickens and buy eggs and milk. We still have horses and our symbiosis with them has been very satisfactory; they pay for their keep with their labor rather than with products of their bodies, and we need raise no more than we want.

Although my experience with farm animals has convinced me that with thought and effort and some sacrifice of profits one may achieve a more humane and satisfying association with them than is commonly done, it would be better all around if we could live without them. Our animals fail to appreciate our intentions; they cannot understand the relation between what they receive and what they are required to give. They are often stubborn and annoying and sometimes destructive. To care for them without occasionally losing one's temper and abusing them, one needs a saint's patience; to raise them for maximum profits, one must stifle whatever finer feelings he may have. Dietetics and food processing have about reached the point where those who have access to well-stocked food stores can dispense with all animal products and live in perfect health and vigor on a wholly vegetable diet, as from ancient times and in many lands men of the most refined sentiments have aspired to do. Such a course has multiple advantages: we avoid the degrading violence and the cruelty inseparable from the exploitation of animals; we increase the amount of food for direct human consumption that the areas now devoted to farming can supply; and we correspondingly reduce the inroads upon the shrinking areas of wilderness, leaving them as sanctuaries where free animals can lead their natural lives without interference by meddling man.

Those who wrest a living from rough, broken lands like ours have received less than their share of technical assistance from governments and the scientific agriculturists. The reasons for this neglect are obvious. A principal one is the modern notion that to do things "scientifically" is to do them with complicated equipment and all the newest gadgets. As though it were beneath the dignity of applied science to show us how to use most effectively whatever poor means happen to be available for accomplishing the task before us! Is there not a "scientific" as well as an unscientific way of moving a stone with a stick? Do not the laws of the lever apply to any pole that we may cut in the woods, as well as to the most elaborate machine? Bacon, the great pioneer protagonist of the scientific method, held that the humblest task was not beneath the notice of science.

Even slash-and-burn farming may be susceptible to improvement by scientific experimentation. We deplore the necessity of burning the vegetation; but in many regions farmers must use fire to prepare for sowing or starve; and there are better and worse ways of burning, which will destroy less or more of the organic matter and microorganisms in the soil. We may recall that if much land has been impoverished by fire, perhaps even more has been ruined by the improper or excessive use of the plow, which has been so strongly indicted by Faulkner and others. Especially on steeply inclined lands washed by heavy tropical rains, breaking the surface with a plow may lead to disastrous erosion. Burning had advocates among the ancient Romans, who as farmers were far from contemptible. In Book I of the *Bucolics,* Vergil speculated on the subtle processes by which fire improved the soil: "Often likewise it is well to burn barren fields and consume the light stubble in crackling flame: whether that earth thence conceives secret strength and sustenance, or all her evil is melted away and her useless moisture sweats out in the fire; or that the heat opens more of these ducts and blind pores that carry her juices to the fresh herbage; or rather hardens and binds her gaping veins against fine rain or the fierce sun's mastery or the frostbite of the searching North."

Although scientific experimentation might improve an agricultural practice as ancient as that which we call the milpa system, such improvement will not be easily achieved. Long-established cultures have often, even in the absence of experimental science, worked out slowly through the generations the most efficient use of what is available to them. When we study these procedures in relation to the actual environment in which they arose, rather than some more favored region, we are led, at times almost in spite of ourselves, to respect the achievements of primitive or backward peoples. Although the rough methods of farming practiced here are not congenial to me, I confess that, despite much thought, I can see no ready way of radically altering them. Agricultural experimentation is generally too slow and costly to be undertaken by private individuals, especially by those who live by agriculture.

Meanwhile, throughout tropical America, populations soar while the land becomes impoverished. Hungry people are forced to bring under cultivation less favorable lands that deteriorate more rapidly. If one loves his fellow men or the natural world, he deplores the consequences. When men live too near the margin of starvation, there is a decline in the dignity and value of human life. A chronically deficient diet is as disastrous to morals as to intellectual and esthetic development. And it is painful to see millenial forests shorn from land that can hardly yield two good crops and to witness the decimation and perhaps eventual extermination of whole species of beautiful plants and animals, which nature has taken millions of years to produce and can never replace.

Undoubtedly, some improvement can be made by giving small farmers in the tropics better varieties of maize, beans, rice, and the other crops to which they are accustomed—better, that is, for their own peculiar conditions—and showing them how to produce these crops more efficiently. But if I were to undertake, with adequate resources, a long-term program for the improvement of tropical agriculture, I would choose a radically different approach. The yearlong growing season of the more humid tropics calls for perennial plants that will keep the soil permanently covered and take advantage of the almost continuously favorable temperature and moisture. How wasteful to sow maize, which in four or five months bears its single crop and dies, when something might be growing and producing and covering the soil throughout the twelve months! How much more wasteful when, after this single sowing, the land must rest for several years more, while fresh lands and more fresh lands are requisitioned for this extravagant grass!

Annual crops are well suited to semiarid regions with a short growing season, as likewise to extratropical countries where the growing season is followed by a long period of cold that puts an end to growth; but perennial crops are appropriate for the continuously verdant tropics. It is fitting that a country like Costa Rica should export the products of perennial plants like coffee, cacao, and bananas, and import from the North flour made from annual wheat. But the international market is often glutted with these products, and a country that is primarily agricultural should not be dependent upon imported foodstuffs. I would search the world for a constellation of perennial plants that together would yield a balanced diet, and I would spare no pains to adapt them and their products to the requirements of each of the major regions of tropical America.

This, to be sure, would involve not only the introduction of new methods of agriculture, but also the development of new dietary habits among the people—a difficult transformation, for men adhere to their dietary prejudices perhaps even more tenaciously than to their religious beliefs! It would mean the passing of the tortilla, that culinary oddity peculiar to the peoples of Mexico and Central America, for which so much maize is grown and so much forest destroyed. Whenever I watch our cook making tortillas, I am amazed that so many generations of women over so great an area should have submitted to a lifetime of such drudgery, that none has had the genius to invent a more easily prepared substitute. So much boiling of maize with ashes or lime to loosen the outer pellicle of the grain, so much washing to remove the lime or ash, such laborious turning of the little hand mill that grinds the corn, such endless pat-pat-patting by the hands to shape the great stack of thin wafers that a large family will consume in a day! Each of these tortillas must receive separate attention as it is roasted and turned on the *comal*. And the product of all this labor, delicious when fresh, rapidly loses its palatability. Imagine how difficult it would be to make bread if you started with whole grains of wheat instead of prepared flour, and you will have some conception of the effort involved in preparing tortillas from the hard maize, as is commonly done on Middle American farms. The emancipation of the Middle American woman, no less than the emancipation of the Middle American soil, calls for some readily prepared substitute for the tortilla, made with the product of a perennial plant.

There is a prevalent notion that the improvement of agriculture alone can raise the whole level of a people's life and elevate their culture. This too facile solution of the problem can lead only to disillusion. Agriculture is only one phase of culture, and it must be integrated with the whole culture of which it is a part. This has been the case in autochthonous cultures that developed in closest contact with their natural foundations. In such cultures, agriculture, along with all other aspects of man's relation to the natural world, was so closely bound to religion that they could hardly be separated. Agricultural practices were regulated by the same system of customs and beliefs that governed all the other vital activities of the community, whether in relation to the seen or the unseen world. The sowing and harvesting of the fields were attended by religious rites. Dietary regulations were adjusted to agricultural practices. With the spread of proselytical religions, along with urbanization, this close association of agriculture with the whole life of a people was profoundly disrupted.

Unless agriculture is again closely integrated with the whole culture of which it is the ground and support, improvements in agricultural practices will do little to elevate the spiritual level of that culture. A change in one element of a closely integrated pattern is necessarily followed by compensatory alterations in many of its other components, if that pattern is to preserve its close articulation and vital harmony. Such an integrated system of beliefs and practices, giving guidance to man's life viewed steadily and as a whole, is fundamentally a religion, whether or not it reaches out boldly toward a transcendent realm. Religion is primarily an effort to bring harmony into life. The chief cause of disharmony among living things is competition for nourishment, just as one of the principal causes of the failure of an individual to develop harmoniously is inadequate or improper food. Thus, religion cannot, without being unfaithful to its aims, become indifferent to what men eat and how this food is produced.

Religion and agriculture, then, should again walk hand in hand, as they did in the earlier stages of human culture. This is not to advocate a return to ancient fertility cults, which too often involved human sacrifices and sprinkling the fields with blood; both religion and agriculture have come a long way since those distant days of their groping infancy. Nor does this mean that agriculture should turn its back upon science; on the contrary, it cannot too closely embrace science. Science tells us by what procedures we can most readily obtain certain results to which numerical values can be assigned, but its competence does not extend to regions where values are not susceptible to instrumental measurement. Science can teach us methods, but we must look beyond science for the attitudes that guide us in the use of these methods.

Unless we view the problem of agriculture with the religious fervor that prompts men to discipline themselves, to forgo sensual satisfactions, and often also to change their dietary habits, for ideal ends, we shall be unprepared to meet squarely the vital issues that confront the contemporary world. Until a single, unified attitude pervades every department of our culture, ranging from its vital roots in agriculture to its highest branches and flowers in art and literature and spiritual aspirations, technical improvements will do little to advance us.

21

Butterflies and Moths

O<small>N N<small>OVEMBER</small></small> 20, 1948, the afternoon shower fell early and was lighter than usual in this rainy month. After it stopped, the sun, already low in the west, broke through the clouds. With this promise of a fair evening, I walked down through the pastures to search for pumpkins in the field from which the maize had been harvested in August. While forcing my way through the swiftly springing weeds, already head-high, I noticed a number of butterflies gathering in a tall, slender burío tree that stood at the edge of the field beside second-growth woods. Acraeines of medium size, they were settling on a dead branch at the very top of the tree, fully exposed to the sky. Many were already hanging, head upward, wings folded, in loose clusters at the ends of thin twigs, especially the slender divisions of some old, dry inflorescences. It was only a quarter to five o'clock—the hillside east of the river was still in full sunshine—but the butterflies were already going to rest.

Headpiece: The migratory moth *Urania fulgens*. The black wings are marked with golden green. Life size.

Sleeping Butterflies

For the next half-hour, more and more butterflies continued to arrive, singly rather than in groups. As restless as a flock of birds settling for the night in a communal roost, they were constantly fluttering their wings all together and shifting from place to place. The arrival of a late-comer or a change in position of one already present would stir up others and increase the confusion. The company at the roost seemed to be almost complete when the sinking sun, again sending its nearly level beams through a rift in the clouds, lighted up a magnificent rainbow in the east. The towering arch was perfect from its feet to its zenith, framing in its brilliant blended colors a long stretch of the steep, forest-crowned ridge across the Río Peña Blanca. There was a secondary rainbow outside the primary arch, and within the latter, in contact with its violet edge, were two or three fainter repetitions of the spectrum.

Soon the multihued glory faded behind an approaching shower. Before the rain arrived, I counted about seventy-five butterflies clustered in the top of the burío tree. A dozen or more of the butterflies clung to slender twiglets of a dead vine hanging from a dead tree in the midst of the weedy field. All were fully exposed to the elements and to the eyes of night-fliers.

At daybreak, I returned to learn whether the butterflies had passed the night where I left them and to watch them awake. The dead branch at the top of the burío tree was still crowded with roosting butterflies, motionless in the still, damp air. With their long wings folded together, dark and motionless against the brightening sky, they looked like small, dead leaves still clinging to the dead twigs. My count now gave only sixty-five, ten less than on the preceding evening; but they seemed to be more closely clustered and, being also immobile, were more difficult to distinguish from each other. Most were now clinging to the richly branched inflorescences in loose clusters of five to twelve; a few slept singly. Rain had fallen during the night, as on many nights at this season, but the hardy butterflies had weathered it without so much as a leaf to shelter them. Their survival in such a conspicuous situation was evidence that they were distasteful to bats and other nocturnal insect-eaters, as well as to diurnal birds seeking a late supper or an early breakfast. Such unpalatability is widespread in the Acraeinae.

I wished to see how long the butterflies would remain clinging to their roost; but a few minutes before six o'clock an inconsiderate pair of Fiery-billed Araçaris, alighting one after the other on the dead burío bough, shook it violently and stirred up a cloud of fluttering wings. Nine butterflies, however, continued to hang motionless in the treetop. While I stood, cold and uncomfortable, among the wet weeds, watching the still quiescent butterflies, wave after wave of Red-lored Parrots in close pairs flew sunward high above me, shouting raucously and beating their wings mincingly, after the fashion of Amazonas. A pair of Scarlet Macaws crossed the valley in the opposite direction, making almost as much noise as the whole flock of smaller parrots. Then an orange and black Baltimore Oriole and a red Summer Tanager darted singly over the field. All these colorful, high-flying birds were brilliantly illuminated by the nearly level rays of the rising sun, while the nine butterflies and their watcher were still in chilly shadow.

It was not until 6:34, an hour after dawn, that the sun's beams slanted down across the eastern ridge to fall upon the nine butterflies who lingered motionless in the top of the burío tree. Six minutes later, I noticed the first signs of returning animation—one slowly opened and closed its wings. Twenty minutes after the warming rays reached them, eight of the nine had flown away. Although those on the dead vine in the midst of the field remained in shadow only a quarter of an hour longer than those in the burío tree, they were much slower in responding to the sunshine: eight were still on their roost half an hour after the sunshine fell upon them; three were present at the end of an hour.

Many of these butterflies were now flying over the weedy field, and I caught some in my hat for a closer examination, after which I released them. They varied considerably in size and intensity of coloration. They had a wingspread of about two and a half inches, and the body was about three-quarters of an inch long. Their forewings were pale yellow or brownish yellow, with dull black borders and a broad black band passing obliquely across them. The hindwings were dull orange with a wide, blackish posterior margin. Later, comparing these butterflies with the plates in the *Biologia Centrali-Americana*, I identified them as *Actinote anteas*. Avoiding the interior of the forest, they abound at certain seasons in weedy or bushy clearings. Even when not going to roost, they fly higher than most butterflies, sometimes above the treetops, doubtless relying upon their unpalatability to save them from aerial insect catchers.

That afternoon was almost rainless, and the butterflies continued to fly about later than on the preceding day. They did not approach the burío tree until five o'clock, when the field above which they had been flying lay in shadow. The first to go to the roost flew off again after a brief visit. A quarter of an hour later, they were coming in fast, and by twenty minutes to six, fifty were hanging motionless in the treetop. But on the following day, when rain fell during much of the afternoon, the butterflies retired much earlier. At a few minutes past four o'clock, I found twenty clinging in the treetop. They were joined by more and more, until by half past five the roost was crowded with about 115—the largest aggregation of sleeping butterflies that I have ever seen. Thereafter, the company began to dwindle. On November 23, there were 95; on December 4, 22; on December 12, only 7. By the end of the month, I could find no more of these butterflies anywhere.

For nearly two years, I noticed no *Actinote anteas*. Then, toward the end of 1950, they became abundant again. For nearly a decade after I first found them in 1948, they appeared in biennial waves in even years— 1950, 1952, 1954, and 1956. I would first become aware of them as the rainy season approached its end in November or December. They would rapidly become more abundant, and a month or so after their first appearance they would vanish, to be seen no more for nearly two years. In 1952, a few were flying about in August, but they soon disappeared, and no more were noticed until the advance guard of the main wave arrived about the end of October. In 1956, they came late, not attracting attention until the end of December, becoming abundant in January, 1957, and remaining with us until at least mid-February of that year. After this, their schedule changed. A few were present at the end of 1957; I failed to notice them in 1958; and they were fairly abundant from late December of 1959 into early January of 1960, having shifted the date of their first appearance from even years to odd years. My last record of their occurrence was in November and December of 1967.

In the seasons of their abundance, I have often found roosts of the Actinote butterflies, but no other as large as the first. These butterflies always slept hanging below the exposed dead tips of slender twigs of living trees, tall bushes, or vines, in clearings or at the woodland's edge, at heights of about twenty to seventy-five feet. Usually they were in loose or compact groups of from two to thirty individuals, but here and there a solitary sleeper could be found. On clear evenings, the occupants of the smaller roosts retired around sunset. They were not strongly attached to their sleeping places, and the number in any roost fluctuated from night to night.

Other butterflies choose more sheltered sleeping places. In October, 1949, a heliconian species became exceedingly abundant in bushy clearings and along woodland trails, up to at least three thousand feet above sea level. With a spread of about two and a quarter inches, their wings were predominantly orange-tawny, bordered and longitudinally streaked with black—a color pattern which, with minor variations, is widespread among the heliconians, making the species difficult to identify. These butterflies were particularly numerous in "Tree-fern Dell," as we called the hollow on the far side of the ridge that rises steeply behind our house. Here they were attracted, along with many other kinds of butterflies, to the tall, weedy composite *Eupatorium macrophyllum*, which grew profusely in this low, open ground.

In the evening, I watched these heliconians go to rest. As the sun sank low, they gradually flew into a neighboring thicket of tall second-growth bushes and low trees, threaded by cow paths. Here they settled on the lower ends of thin, hanging and drooping, dead twigs, by preference those which had fallen from higher branches and were loosely caught upon the lower vegetation. Each butterfly had its own roost; once one tried to join another on its twig, but only one remained. After they were all settled for the night, the closest were about a yard apart. Most of them were between six and fifteen feet above the ground. They clung upright beneath the ends of their twigs, sheltered by dense foliage from the downpours of this rainy season. By December, these butterflies had become rare.

Yet another species of the multitudinous heliconian tribe slept above the noisy river. The forewings of this rather large butterfly were velvety black conspicuously spotted with white, except near the base, where there was a small patch of orange. The hindwings were mostly orange or brownish orange. They roosted on a dead branch hanging beneath a massive, gnarled Sotacaballo tree. Clinging to slender, terminal twiglets with their four feet, they hung with the body horizontal, folded wings directed downward toward the rocky stream bed seven or eight feet below. On cloudy afternoons, I sometimes found them resting here, beneath the deep shade of the Sotaballo tree, as early as one o'clock. They would not move unless I shook them. Then, after fluttering around a little, they returned to the same twigs, where they stayed into the night. From April until July, these butterflies rested and slept in the same place, from three to six of them hanging close together.

The habit of gathering for the night in large or small groups is widespread among the heliconians which, unpalatable as they are to insectivorous animals, can afford to indulge in a practice that might be disastrous to unprotected butterflies. All the heliconians that I have found sleeping have hung beneath slender, dead twigs, either upright (the axis of the body vertical) or with body horizontal and wings downward, but their roosts have been in the most diverse situations.

One of the prettiest species in this valley is *Heliconius petiveranus*, a medium-sized butterfly whose wings are black, with a large red patch on the outer part of the forewing and a broad yellow streak, transverse to the body, on the hindwing. It inhabits second-growth thickets and brushy fields rather than woodland. One year, to reach the banana plantation beyond the creek, we cut a trail through second growth so tall and dense that our path was a tunnel roofed by tangled branches and vines.

On an evening in mid-July, I found these colorful butterflies going to roost here. By six o'clock, a number were already hanging, wings downward, from the ends of very thin twigs that projected into the clear space above the pathway. Late-comers, trying to find a place on the preferred branch, stirred up those already present, causing a flutter of red, yellow, and black wings that was a delightful display in the dim light. After the last butterfly had settled down in the dusk, there were eleven on the principal roost, a dead spray slightly over a foot long and broad that hung about four feet above the center of the path. Three other butterflies rested singly beside the path, the most distant of them about five yards from the main group. In the surrounding dense thicket slept a number of Scarlet-rumped Black Tanagers, Orange-billed Nightingale-Thrushes, and Chisel-billed Caciques, who with loud complaints had gone to roost while I watched the butterflies.

I often watched these red, yellow, and black heliconians go to rest in the evening. Some would arrive around four o'clock; but while the light was bright they were wary, and my presence would disturb them, as it also did when I approached as a new day brightened. But as daylight faded they became more tolerant of me, and while still plainly visible they would not budge when I passed a few inches from them hanging on their roost. Their number fluctuated from night to night; the largest gathering that I found was seventeen in early August. At the end of September, there were fifteen. After this, their number slowly declined. At the beginning of January of the following year, three were still present, but by February 9, only one remained. The highest sleeper that I ever saw at this roost was eight feet up.

In early March, I found another roost of this same species in a low Guava tree, overgrown with vines, that stood beside a small, grassy opening in a thicket. Here, clinging to the branching ends of slender twigs that hung beneath the canopy of vines, the butterflies slept in two close clusters of six, one compact group of five, a pair, and one solitary individual. The twenty butterflies were from three to six feet above the ground, and the most distant were about a yard apart. At the end of the following September, six of these butterflies still slept here.

In the dense thicket near the first roost of *Heliconius petiveranus* lived a smaller butterfly, a satyr, with a wingspread of about two inches. On the upper surface, the forewings were dark, ashy gray, the hindwings bright, iridescent blue, with a narrow, dark border. Below, all the wings were light gray. Near the anterior margin of each forewing, on both the upper and lower sides, was a large "eye-spot," bright blue or black and blue, bordered with yellow. I called these butterflies the "sleepy bluewings," because they rested most of the time beneath the horizontal leaves of a young wild plantain, in deep shade two feet from the ground. Here they held their wings spread out like moths rather than folded above their backs in the manner of typical butterflies. The gray forewings covered the blue hindwings, and, as I looked up from below, the big, blue eye-spots on the downwardly directed dorsal surface of the forewings were their most conspicuous feature. Although the brilliant heliconians were absent from their roost from morning until evening, at almost any hour of the day I could find from one to five of the "sleepy blue-wings" drowsing beneath their green roof. If disturbed, they would fly swiftly and erratically off through the undergrowth, keeping near the ground. Often they would return to their favorite spot within a few minutes. They seemed to have no regular time for activity but took brief excursions at various hours, after each returning to rest in the deep shade. Probably, in contrast to the heliconians, which were careless of concealment, these satyrs had reasons for keeping themselves well hidden.

Butterflies and Birds

Butterflies in the adult state are not only the most beautiful but also the most innocuous of insects. I have never known them to sting or otherwise annoy man or other animals, and they never mutilate the flowers that they pollinate while they sip the nectar, as bees so often do. Why are insects as abundant, large, and conspicuous as butterflies so seldom devoured by birds? I have watched flycatchers gathering insects in a field where butterflies of many kinds abounded, yet consistently ignoring them all. Some butterflies, including the heliconians that swarm in tropical America, are known to be unpalatable to birds, and other butterflies, not so protected, gain a certain immunity from predation by resembling these protected species—the phenomenon known as Batesian mimicry. The North American Monarch Butterfly is generally considered to be a protected species, and as such it is mimicked by the Viceroy. Yet F. A. Urquhart, in his book on the Monarch, testified that he had sampled this butterfly and found it tasteless. Nevertheless, it appears seldom to be taken by birds. Perhaps they, like ourselves, prefer tasty food!

Naturalists have detected certain protective devices on the wings of butterflies. Large eye-spots, especially if suddenly displayed by spreading the wings, may frighten away would-be avian captors. Smaller, marginal eye-spots may deflect a bird's aim from the head to the edge of a wing, a fragment of which remains in the assailant's bill, while the butterfly sails away slightly mutilated. And even the bright colors of a butterfly's wings may hold timid birds aloof. Examples of all these reactions are given in Niko Tinbergen's fascinating book, *Curious Naturalists*. Only a minority of butterflies depend upon cryptic coloration to escape their enemies.

Among the most famous of these are species of *Kallima* of the Oriental region. Brightly colored on the upper surface, they baffle pursuers when they suddenly alight and fold their wings, transforming themselves instantly into dead leaves complete in all details.

But I believe that, aside from bright coloration or alarming pattern, the butterflies' wide, stiff wings deter small birds from seizing them. Imagine how you would like to have flapping in your face wings as large relative to yourself as a middle-sized butterfly's wings are to a flycatcher! My belief that this mechanical effect is a powerful deterrent to birds is based upon observation of the few avian species that consume considerable numbers of butterflies. Chief among the butterfly eaters of tropical America are the jacamars, whose very long, often delicate, awl-like bills seem poorly adapted for their habitual aerial insect catching or for digging their burrows and nest chambers in the ground or in hard termitaries. But these slender forceps can reach past the butterfly's flailing wings and grasp the insect's body, where alone they can take firm hold, as the wings often break when seized. The long bill also provides leverage for the vigorous beating against a branch to which the jacamar subjects its victim to remove the wings before swallowing it. Likewise, and perhaps most important, the long bill holds the fluttering wings away from the bird's face and eyes while it removes them. I believe that the jacamar's bill is specialized for catching flying insects with wide, stiff wings, particularly butterflies and dragonflies, as that of the hummingbird is for probing flowers. Among the American flycatchers, the Royal, whose bill is considerably longer than that of most other flycatchers of its size, is more addicted to butterflies than are other members of this great family that I have watched. Some of the strong-billed motmots include large butterflies in their diet.

To remove a butterfly's stiff wings often requires so much hard knocking against a perch that jacamars finally give up and gulp down some or all of them along with the body, which seems an uncomfortable procedure. When small insects are abundant, a flycatching bird might capture and ingest several of them in the time it would need to prepare a single butterfly for swallowing. Evidently birds with short bills find it more pleasant and profitable to concentrate on insects with small wings when these are plentiful, eschewing butterflies that flap in their eyes wings troublesome to remove.

Even jacamars avoid heliconian butterflies, taking by preference members of more palatable groups. Considering the rarity of jacamars, with only fifteen species that seem everywhere to be among the rarer members of the avian community, one may question whether the selective pressure exerted by these principal butterfly eaters could be strong enough to have promoted the evolution of unpalatability in certain butterflies and of Batesian mimicry in many unprotected species. But in past ages jacamars may have been more abundant, in species and individuals, than they have since become; in any case, even a selective agent of slight potency may produce a wonderful effect if it continues to operate through long ages. In the Old World, where jacamars do not occur, other butterfly eaters must have been responsible for the evolution of unpalatability and mimicry. But perhaps the butterfly's broad, stiff, highly colored wings, which as organs of flight are no more efficient than the less eye-taking wings of many other insects, are its main evolutionary response to predation by birds. If they had not achieved a high degree of immunity from avian predation, butterflies could not remain the conspicuous, freely flying, diurnal insects that they are. To survive, they would need to become furtive, protectively colored creatures living obscurely amid vegetation. We should be grateful for the protective devices that make it possible for the two most beautiful classes of air-breathing animals, butterflies and birds, to live side by side with little mutual interference, adding immensely to the charm of woods and fields.

Curious Moths

The innumerable species of tropical moths are largely the province of the specialist, but over the years a few have interested me greatly. One night in early December, a large moth flew into our bedroom, attracted by the lamp that we had just lighted. It was everywhere brown, the color of a dead leaf. Each forewing, nearly three inches long, was marked with narrow, transverse stripes of a brighter brown. After fluttering around the room for a while, it clung to the white wall. We turned down the lamp and opened the window so that it might escape, but it remained in the same spot. When, to make it fly, I touched it lightly, it emitted a strong, skunklike odor and at the same time became rigid as though dead. It lay on a bed with its wings held upward above its back, not in contact with each other, and its abdomen curled strongly downward, completely exposed. Long, stout, prominently segmented, covered with stiff brown hairs, this abdomen resembled a large, hairy caterpillar of the stinging kind. Since the moth showed no inclination to move, after some minutes I laid it outside on the window sill, in the dark. Although I did not thenceforth touch or in any way disturb it, other than to flash a light on it from time to time, it remained motionless and rigid for at least half an hour. A quarter of an hour later, it had vanished.

This moth, the only one of its kind that I have noticed, had at least four attributes that might help it escape enemies: a protective resemblance to a dead leaf, making it harder to detect on an appropriate background; a fetid odor; deathlike rigidity when touched, which would make it unattractive to insectivorous animals that prefer living prey; and an abdomen that resembled a caterpillar covered with stinging hairs. The skunklike odor clung to my hands even after I washed them with soap.

One February afternoon, another peculiar moth rested on the porch floor, looking so much like a dead, wind-blown leaf that I ignored it until my sharp-eyed wife called my attention to it. In shape, it resembled the basal two inches of a large leaf that tapered to its petiole. The posterior ends of the wings were truncate, with irregular margins that suggested the torn edge of a leaf. The obscure markings on the brown forewings gave the impression of lateral veins. The mimicry was excellent.

When I picked up this moth for closer scrutiny, its eyes appeared to have pupils. I examined it with a low-power magnifying glass; it seemed to be returning my gaze with large, bulging, brown eyes, each equipped with a wide, round pupil of deeper brown. Whichever way I moved, these staring eyes followed me, turning in their sockets like human eyes. When I looked at the moth from directly in front, the big eyes converged upon me. A bit of the coiled proboscis projected between furry flaps. I seemed to be gazing into the eyes of an owl, with a short beak between wide, staring orbs. The effect was uncanny.

A lepidopteron with an eye containing an iris and a pupil, rotating in its socket, like that of a mammal! It was unbelievable! Under the magnifying glass, it was plain that each big eye was composed of many ocelli, in the usual insect pattern. Still, the impression that the eyes turned to follow me was too strong to be easily dispelled. I dropped a little powdered chalk on them. The particles remained stationary, and the "pupil" seemed to slide beneath them, as I turned the moth from side to side. The illusion of pupil and iris springs from variations in the amount of light reflected by the prismatic ocelli. One looks more deeply into the ocelli directed toward himself than into those turned more or less sideward, hence the former appear darker, a number together forming a round "pupil," surrounded by a zone of lighter ocelli, the "iris." I have noticed a similar effect in the compound eyes of various insects, but in none was it more striking than in this moth. Small birds often evince timidity when attacking large arthropods that they wish to eat, and I wondered whether the owl-like stare of the moth might hold aloof a bird that had not been deceived by its resemblance to a dead leaf.

The leaflike moth preserved deathlike immobility while I made these observations. Of a sudden, it raised its brown wings obliquely and vibrated them violently, as moths often do when disturbed. Then it unexpectedly shot out through the open window, depriving me of the opportunity to make further observations and drawings. May not this sudden flurry of the hitherto quiescent moth be its third trick to deceive or confuse an enemy? First its mimicry of a fragment of leaf; then its disconcerting, owl-like stare; and finally this sudden, vigorous coming to life, taking by surprise the small insect eater who seemed to have an immobile victim.

Large moths have a strange and puzzling effect upon small birds. From time to time, my attention has been drawn by a noisy commotion among the birds in the garden. Hurrying out to investigate, I have found, instead of the expected snake, a big moth, six inches or more across its spread wings, which were beautifully mottled with blended browns and grays. One of these moths had, in each wing, a wide, oval, transparent area or "window," through which I could see the foliage against which it rested. Usually the exciting moth, torpid or moribund after the deluge of the preceding afternoon, clung in a bush, motionless or perhaps slowly moving its wings at long intervals. Around it was gathered a motley crowd of birds—tanagers, finches, honeycreepers, wrens, flycatchers, antbirds, and hummingbirds—all nervously flitting about the poor bedraggled creature, each voicing its characteristic notes of complaint. Most of these birds remained at the respectful distance of a foot or more, except the hummingbirds, of which five or six individuals of several species might be present, sometimes hovering only a few inches from the insect larger than themselves. Although some of these birds were of kinds bold enough to peck a snake a yard or two long, I never saw any of them touch the moth that so aroused them. After many minutes, the feathered crowd would disperse, leaving the moth unharmed; but from time to time during the day, a passing bird would notice the moth, cry out in alarm, and draw a number of others to help protest its presence. Usually the excitable Scarlet-rumped Black Tanagers were the first to raise the hue and cry, and they were always most prominent in the gatherings around the moth.

The "mobbing" of owls, snakes, and other predatory animals by small birds occurs in many parts of the world and has long been known; an early description of this phenomenon is found in the famous twelfth discourse of the Stoic philosopher Dio Chrysostom, who compared the audience gathered about him at Olympia in the year 97 A.D. to birds around an owl. But aside from these moths, no instance of an insect "mobbed" by birds has come to my attention. Their strong reaction to such harmless creatures puzzles us, until we imagine how we might behave in the presence of a rarely seen insect bigger than ourselves. In one of these mobbing episodes, a male Buff-rumped Warbler rose higher than one ordinarily sees these birds, to join a number of tanagers, wrens, and honeycreepers flitting around a bedraggled moth twenty feet up in a bamboo.

The warbler stayed after all the other birds had drifted away, and when finally the insect fluttered to the leaf-strewn ground, he followed it down. Then for ten minutes he continued to hop around the big moth, singing repeatedly, but never venturing very close to it. Finally he flew away, leaving the moth to die in peace.

The Migrations of Urania

One of the most beautiful of the tropical American moths is *Urania fulgens*, which at first sight I took to be a butterfly, as it is active by day and is about the size and shape of a large *Papilio*, with long, attenuate "tails" on its hindwings. The upper surface of all the wings is black, adorned with bands and spots of glittering metallic green. I first became aware of this extraordinary moth at Montaña Azul, where I dwelt and made many of my studies of birds on the narrow back of a ridge that ran north and south, jutting out from the flank of the Cordillera Central and descending toward the northern lowlands. The crest of this ridge was in pasture, while forest covered its sides that fell away into deep ravines. In April and May, moth after moth passed northward along this ridge all day long. Their flight was strong, rapid, and direct, with only a slight waver. Some traveled low over the grass, others above the tops of the tall, scattered trees. Doubtless when they reached the unbroken forest down the mountainside, they flew above its roof, for neither here nor elsewhere have I seen these moths traversing dense woods.

About the first of June, I began to notice a significant number of these moths traveling southward up the ridge, toward the continental divide, and soon the great majority were headed in this direction. A small minority still flew northward, against the main stream of traffic, while a few aberrant individuals went in other directions. I never saw any pause to rest or feed. This southward stream of moths continued into August, thinning out toward the end of the month.

Observations continued over a quarter of a century, in various parts of Costa Rica, have convinced me that, like the Monarch Butterfly in the United States and many kinds of birds, *Urania fulgens* performs two-way migrations—northward early in the year, southward later. The time of these movements varies somewhat from year to year. In the Valley of El General, the vanguard of the northbound voyagers might appear in March or even February, and in 1959 the northward flight came chiefly from early January until mid-February. However, April and May were the months in which the largest and most sustained northward movements occurred, and sometimes they continued well into June or even early July. Usually, however, the majority of the moths were flying southward by June. Through July and much of August they continued to pass, and, exceptionally, the migration lasted into October. In 1944, I noticed a few Uranias in El General in December, but this was most unusual. In some years, the northward or the southward flight failed to appear, perhaps because the moths were taking other routes.

These migratory movements of *Urania fulgens* have been recorded as far north as the state of Veracruz in eastern Mexico. In Costa Rica the flights were country-wide: I have watched them on both the Pacific and the Caribbean slopes and in the Central Plateau. Others have seen the moths passing high up on the volcanoes. In El General, where most of my observations were made, the lay of the Cordillera de Talamanca, the coastal range, and the intervening valley of the Río Térraba, diverted many of the travelers from a straight north-south course. In spring, the northbound moths passed in various directions between north and west: if those going due north did not change their course, they would have passed over the high summits of the Cordillera. Correspondingly, the southbound travelers later in the year might be seen flying in any direction from south to east; a continued southerly course would have taken them over the coastal range into the Pacific Ocean. Day-flying migrants among the birds—swallows, Eastern Kingbirds, Swainson's Hawks, and Broad-winged Hawks—likewise deviate from the north-south line as they pass through this region, flying between north and west to reach Mexico and the United States in spring, between south and east as they return to South America in the fall.

The density of the flights of moths varied greatly from day to day and from year to year. Sometimes, even in the middle of the migratory season, one saw only a few moths pass in a day. At the other extreme, one August in the pasture behind our house, I counted a hundred passing overhead in three minutes. Usually, if one watched long enough, he would notice a few of the moths diverging from the mainstream, some going in random directions and others exactly contrary to the majority. It was hardly possible to follow these erratic individuals to learn whether they later corrected their course. But only in one year was I unable to decide where the main body of the moths was going, although I took compass bearings of individual flights. This was in 1940, when I lived from February to June beside the Río San Antonio near the head of the Térraba Valley, where the topography was possibly confusing to the winged voyagers.

Although the migrating moths do not go in definite flocks like many diurnal migrants among the birds, they sometimes pass in loose clouds that fill the air, between which few are seen. Often one closely follows another in all its twists and turns, as though in nuptial pursuit, and occasionally three individuals are involved in these chases, while they continue to migrate in the prevailing direction. The moths continue to pass even while rain falls hard. I have never seen a bird pay the least attention to a Urania.

Nearly always, the Uranias that I have seen in Costa Rica have seemed intent on reaching some far destination. However, if the leguminous Inga trees are flowering when they pass southward in August, September, or early October, many of the moths gather around their high crowns to sip nectar from the massed, white, "powder-puff" blossoms, in company with a variety of butterflies and hummingbirds. How the metallic golden green of their sable wings glitters in the morning sunshine! At the height of the migration in September, I found many Uranias fluttering over the Inga trees in the half-light of dawn, about the time the bats disappeared. This observation, repeated on several mornings, suggested that the moths had slept nearby, but I never discovered how they pass the night. All day, multitudes of Uranias continued to visit the Ingas, passing eastward from tree to tree of a coffee plantation shaded by them, finally leaving from the eastern end of the grove. As the flowers wilted, or as their nectar was exhausted, after the middle of the afternoon, the moths gradually deserted them. Their departure from the Inga trees at this time probably explains why, on some afternoons, I noticed unusually heavy eastward flights between three and four o'clock.

While so many Uranias were visiting the Inga flowers, a few settled on the tiny, yellowish florets of a lauraceous tree (*Ocotea* sp.) that was blooming profusely at the edge of the coffee plantation. But I never noticed a single one on several Candelillo trees that at the same time displayed great masses of yellow flowers, nor on the red trumpets that made neighboring Flame-of-the-Forest trees conspicuous from afar. During the northward migration in spring, I have seen Uranias gather around the white bloom of the Copalchí, a tree of the euphorbia family, but on no other kind of flower. Rarely they settle on wet mud.

I was impressed with the magnitude and extent of Urania's migrations when I traveled from Costa Rica to South America in 1940. On July 25, I noticed a substantial increase in the number of these moths, which since early in the month I had seen flying southward above the streets and buildings of San José. On the following day, as I traveled by rail from the capital city down to Puerto Limón, I saw countless moths all along the route. They were especially numerous between the continental divide and Cartago, where they flew in thin clouds over the open fields, a mile above sea level, that sloped down from the sprawling mass of Volcán Irazú. Many more were noticed as the train wound down the spectacular Reventazón Valley, and as we crossed the broad river on the iron bridge near Siquirres, at the edge of the coastal plain, Uranias were crossing the water, too. They were still with us as we sped through the level cacao and banana plantations toward the port. As far as it was possible to determine their direction from the moving train, all these moths, from the highlands to the lowlands, followed a generally southerly course.

At Limón that evening, I boarded the *Ulua* for Cristóbal. As she voyaged eastward off the coast during the night, many Uranias flew on board, attracted by the ship's lights.

Throughout the twelve days that I spent on the Isthmus of Panama, the great migration of moths continued undiminished. The broad stream of them covered the whole forty-mile stretch of land from the Caribbean to the Pacific, but they were particularly numerous on the Pacific side, as though massed together here by the prevailing winds or the northward curvature of the Isthmus. From the roof of my hotel, I watched multitudes of them fly over the city of Panama. All along the highway from the city to Summit, in the middle of the Isthmus, they were passing, and many were struck lifeless by the speeding cars. They were especially noticeable over the Canal itself, sometimes in open flocks, sometimes as scattered individuals. Here above the water, where there were no obstacles to deflect them from their course, I took their directions with a compass. The great majority were flying north-northeast, with some veering more to the northeast, others inclining more toward the north; but all were crossing the Canal from the North American to the South American side. Evidently the southward-bound moths that I had watched in Costa Rica had altered their course to follow the curvature of the continent and reach South America, instead of losing themselves in the Pacific Ocean, as would have happened if they had continued undeviatingly southward.

On the evening of August 8, in the channel opposite Balboa, I boarded the *Santa Lucia* to proceed down the west coast of South America. As the ship glided out of the mouth of the Canal in the failing light, a continuous swarm of the moths flew past, always crossing the water from North to South America. They seemed not to notice the ship—whose high vertical side blocked their passage like a long and lofty wall—until they nearly collided with it, when they fluttered up and over the barrier and continued onward toward the northeast. They were still flying past when we entered the open water of the Gulf of Panama, and many came aboard during the night. Next morning, the wire screens over the intakes of the ship's ventilators were covered with their crushed bodies and bright shattered wings. Many more lay dying upon the decks, where they readily fell into the hands of children delighted by their beauty. The trade winds blowing across the Isthmus must have carried many out to sea, to perish in the water.

Although in the coastal waters of both the Caribbean and the Pacific many Uranias flew aboard the ship in the night, apparently they had continued to travel in the dark only because nightfall found them over the sea. I watched from the roof of the hotel in Panama City and saw them continue to fly past until daylight waned, when their numbers gradually diminished. In the early part of the night, I noticed none in flight, although the lights of the city below me would doubtless have revealed them if they had continued their passage. Early next morning, they were flying by again.

During days spent at Buenaventura and Guayaquil on the southward voyage, I saw no Urania. From Lima we crossed the Andes to the forests of the Amazonian basin, where I made the acquaintance of *Urania leilus*, a species slightly larger than its northern congener and even more beautiful because of the greater amount of golden green on its dark wings. At the end of August, these moths were not migrating but flitting along the roadway and among the vegetation.

I next met the familiar *fulgens* in late November, when we ascended the beautiful Río Esmeraldas in northwestern Ecuador, in a dugout canoe laboriously poled against the swift current by black boatmen. Here the moths were not migrating but flitting among the luxuriant vegetation on the shores, resting on moist sand, or flying across the broad channel, as often in one direction as in the other. Their behavior here contrasted sharply with the purposeful journeying that I had always noticed in Central America. Many had frayed wings, as though they had come from afar. In this lovely land they seemed to have reached their journey's end and to be enjoying a well-earned rest. Indeed, they could hardly have gone much farther without changing their habitat, for here they were in a verdant cul-de-sac, with the widest of oceans on the west, bleak Andean summits on the east, and to the south the increasingly arid Pacific littoral. I wondered whether any of the Uranias that I saw here were the same that I had earlier seen migrating through Costa Rica or Panama. Perhaps some had come from distant Mexico.

Whether we observe it in birds, fishes, insects, or other creatures, the migration of animals is always a mysterious phenomenon, raising more questions than we can answer. How do these creatures without maps or instruments find their way over vast expanses of land or sea? How, especially in regions without strongly contrasting seasons, do they know when to start their long journeys? How, in each particular case, did the migratory habit grow up in the first place? In the case of these moths, what advantage has South America over Central America, or vice versa, to compensate for the high mortality that seems invariably to attend migration, whether of birds or of moths? Do the same individuals make the return journey—either from north to south or from south to north—and if so, how many times can they repeat it? These are questions to challenge the dedicated field naturalist and to give him an absorbing occupation for many years.

Unhappily, the opportunity to solve the riddles of the migrations of Urania appears to be passing. Like so many other beautiful things, these moths seem to be disappearing from a world overcrowded with unappreciative people. In most of the recent years, I have failed to see them passing through the Valley of El General in their former abundance, and in some years I have noticed none.

22

In the Caribbean Lowlands

AFTER TWENTY YEARS at Los Cusingos, there were still birds whose nesting I had not studied. Season after season, I had searched fruitlessly for nests of the Bare-crowned Antbird, Buff-throated Woodcreeper, Smoky-brown Woodpecker, Nightingale Wren, Green Shrike-Vireo, Shining Honeycreeper, and other resident birds that were not rare. Of some birds my studies were incomplete, because I had found only one or two nests, which too often had been prematurely lost. But I had reached the point where I was certain that I could contribute more to knowledge of tropical birds by working in localities where different species occur. Accordingly, we began to spend breeding seasons in other regions. One year we worked on the Barba massif in the Costa Rican highlands; another, at Cañas Gordas near the Panamanian border. A third expedition took us to Venezuela, to study the Rufous-fronted Thornbird, which builds large, hanging nests of interlaced sticks, containing several chambers. For two seasons, we studied birds at "La Selva" in

Headpiece: The house at La Selva.

the Caribbean lowlands of northern Costa Rica. Of all the localities that we visited, this has the richest avifauna and supports some of the most impressive trees.

After several days of preparation in San José, Pamela, Edwin, and I set forth for La Selva on April 10, 1967. The bus to Puerto Viejo was scheduled to leave Heredia at nine in the morning, but the dilapidated vehicle refused to start. Two hours dragged by before it was sufficiently patched up to take to the road. The driver, in a black humor after a hectic morning, made the ancient bus sway and rattle along the narrow highway that, with innumerable sharp turns, wound between coffee plantations and pastures up to the continental divide at Los Cartagos, in the saddle between Volcán Poás and the Barba massif. When I studied Quetzals at Montaña Azul thirty years earlier, the road beyond this point was a ribbon of mud along which I painfully trudged. Now it was paved, and, as we sped downward, I tried to pick out familiar scenes. Although the years had treated harshly the attractive cottage where I had dwelt, the ugly ruin was still inhabited, by people who obviously cared nothing for appearances. The surrounding forests, once the home of the Quetzal, the Three-wattled Bellbird, and the Black Guan, had been replaced by pastures where such widespread birds as the Rufous-collared Sparrow and the Yellow-faced Grassquit flourished. Repeating the pattern typical of our modern world, the drab and commonplace had supplanted the lovely and rare.

We continued downward with the gorge of the Río Sarapiquí on our right. Amid the lush vegetation on the roadside bank, the Higuera spread huge, roundish leaves, sometimes two yards across. At an altitude of about five thousand feet, we passed an open stand of *Wercklea insignis,* a tree mallow with lavender blossoms like large hibiscus flowers. As we rounded a curve, we glimpsed the great waterfall of the Río de la Paz, a tributary of the Sarapiquí, which plunges in a slender column hundreds of feet high into a profound ravine, where a perpetually saturated atmosphere encourages the most luxuriant tropical vegetation. Aware of the state of our conveyance and our driver's temper, I was far from happy as we ground too swiftly down a narrow road that hugged the brink of sheer precipices, over which from time to time a carelessly driven car plunged irretrievably. Passing through the villages of Cariblanco and San Miguel, we at last reached the lowlands, where the straight, level highway invited a velocity that was hardly reassuring.

It took us three hours to cover the sixty miles from Heredia to Puerto Viejo, mostly over winding mountain roads. Despite our driver's perilous attempt to make up for lost time, when we reached the boat landing on the Río Sarapiquí, a short way beyond the village, the operator of the ferry told us that the boat that was to meet us at midday had come and gone but would probably return for us later. As the sultry afternoon wore on, dark storm clouds massed in the sky and distant thunder pealed, making us fear that our baggage on the shore would be drenched.

At about four o'clock, a great flock of Turkey Vultures crossed the river from east to west, sailing low beneath the menacing clouds and sometimes circling on widespread wings to gain altitude. During the next half hour, wave after wave of the big, black birds passed over us, and with them were many Swainson's Hawks. For the next month, we were to see these vultures migrating northward, sometimes in huge flocks that stretched completely across the sky at a great height and took half an hour to pass. The last migratory wave, containing several hundred birds, was noticed on May 12. In the following year, when we reached La Selva in early March, the vultures continued to pass northward from March 25 until May 7. With them were often some Swainson's Hawks, and more rarely we saw the latter traveling in a great flock composed almost wholly of their own kind, with an admixture of Broad-winged Hawks. Although the spring migration of Swainson's Hawks is country-wide and one of the spectacular natural phenomena of the Pacific slope of Costa Rica, I have never noticed any obviously migratory movement of Turkey Vultures on that side of the country.

The afternoon was far spent when we heard the welcome sound of an outboard motor. Soon a large dugout canoe glided around a bend in the river, turned in a graceful arc, and pushed its bow up on the muddy shore beside us. With the help of Rafael Chavarría, the caretaker and boatman at La Selva, we piled our luggage aboard and embarked for the voyage upstream. In a few minutes, we reached the confluence of the Sarapiquí and the Puerto Viejo, two rivers of almost equal size. Veering to the left, we entered the latter and continued upstream between high banks lined with Sotacaballo trees, whose branches reached far out above the dark water. The current was gentle and so low that here and there Rafael had to pilot a course through shallows, but large uprooted trees, stranded in midstream, attested the force that it sometimes attained. The peaceful loveliness of the river soothed away the irritations of a frustrating day, and we felt rested when, rounding a bend, we beheld the house that we were to occupy, standing high above us on a narrow promontory between the Río Puerto Viejo and its tributary creek, the Surá. Landing in the deep shade of an ancient Sotacaballo tree, in the twilight we carried our numerous pieces of baggage up the long flight of wooden steps that wound up the steep, grassy slope to the building.

La Selva was then the property of Dr. Leslie Holdridge, a forester whose original classification of life zones has been used all over the world.

The two-story house was furnished as a weekend or holiday cottage, with folding canvas cots, rough tables, and kerosene stoves for cooking. When we arrived, several North American scientists were present with their families, but, after a few days, all left; through most of our sojourn, the three of us were there alone, with an occasional brief visit from a student and alternate weekends with Dr. and Mrs. Holdridge.

The dwelling stood close by the forest, facing the cacao plantation that occupied most of the level benchland along the river. The remnants of the primeval forest that had been left to shade the cacao included some magnificent trees. Most massive were the huge Ceibas or Silk-cotton Trees, their enormous boles, supported by wide-spreading plank buttresses, holding aloft horizontal branches as thick as most trunks. Most elegant were the towering Surá trees, which I estimated to be at least one hundred and seventy-five feet high. A splendid specimen rose in front of the house on the bank of the stream named for these trees. Others were visible from afar in the extensive pastures across the river, and many were scattered through the plantation, but they were absent from the well-drained ridges back from the river. The base of a large Surá is buttressed by thin planks of wood that often extend outward for ten feet from the trunk and upward for possibly twenty feet; it is difficult to decide just where they end upward, for the trunk itself is irregular rather than round. The spreading buttresses often cover a circle twenty feet in diameter. Even on the oldest trees, the pale gray, cinnamon-tinted bark is smooth. The crown is higher than wide, and the light green foliage is massed in irregular clouds, between which one beholds lengths of the clean gray trunk and branches and, on clear days, patches of blue sky. A tree that delights the eye, even while it makes us feel small and humble!

Behind the house, the forest reached unbroken to the high riverside bluff. In the opposite direction, it seemed to be continuous up to the slopes of the Cordillera Central, many miles to the south. Back from the river, it covered broken land, where sharp ridges alternated with deep hollows that were frequently poorly drained and swampy. In this upland forest, by far the most abundant tree was the leguminous Gavilán or Quebracho. Although not as impressive as the Ceiba and the Surá, it is a tall tree with a shapely, spreading crown. The massive trunk is very irregular at the base, with projecting ridges leading down to the roots, and between them grooves and depressions of all shapes, some of which provide snug nest chambers for such birds as the Wedge-billed Woodcreeper. In addition to more or less developed plank buttresses, occasional prop roots spring from the trunk a short distance above the ground. These buttressed trees give a false impression of stability. They are shallow-rooted, and the trunk often decays between the projections that lead down to the roots. Frequently they fall while still in full vigor, even in the midst of the forest where surrounding trees shield them from the full impact of the wind. Since the wood is hard and resistant to decay, the trunks remain lying on the ground for years. The abundance of these obstacles made walking through the forest toilsome whenever one left the narrow trails along the ridges.

The leaves of the Gavilán are twice-compound, with numerous small, acacialike leaflets. At night these leaves "sleep," folding up so tightly that each resembles a thin stick. The closing movement begins before sunset, and, as it proceeds in these trees that occupy such a large proportion of the forest canopy, it produces a curious effect. As the day ends, more and more sky becomes visible to one standing in the forest; for a while, the woodland seems to grow lighter rather than darker with the approach of night. A teleologist of the old school might have contended that this was a benign provision of nature, to give the belated wanderer more daylight while he finds his way out of the forest. In the morning, the folded leaves open slowly, permitting the light of the new day to penetrate to the depths of the woodland more rapidly than it does beneath a canopy of less mobile leaves. In May, the Gavilán trees flowered profusely. The long, cylindrical inflorescence, covered with myriad protruding white stamens, is curved; in shape it reminded me of a bent cattail spike. The long, flat, woody pods that follow these flowers burst open on dry days with a loud report.

Scattered among the abundant Gavilán trees stood gigantic Almendros that seemed solid and enduring as columns of granite. Large examples rose at least one hundred and fifty feet, with trunks eight feet in diameter above the high, widely spreading plank buttresses. On the downhill side of a tree growing on a slope were buttressing roots that formed curious, serpentine walls of wood a yard high and twenty-five feet long. The trunk and massive, ascending limbs were covered with slightly rough, grayish brown bark. In late April, these trees were in all stages of leaf renewal, some dropping their old foliage, others nearly naked, still others bedecked with bright green new leaves. Different branches of the same tree might present all these stages. The large, pinnately compound leaves were often badly eaten by insects before they matured. After leaf renewal, in late May and June, these huge trees adorned themselves lavishly with great panicles of pink flowers, of which the most conspicuous parts were the two enlarged, winglike calyx lobes. The woody seeds, larger than a walnut and somewhat flattened, are so hard that the edible kernel would seem inaccessible to any animal not equipped with a sledgehammer; but I have watched squirrels gnaw into them.

Conspicuous amid the verdure in the middle story of the forest were the long, bright red inflorescences of *Warszewiczia coccinea*, a slender tree of the madder family that attains a height of fifty or rarely sixty feet. The glowing color is provided by a single lobe of each calyx, which becomes two or three inches long. The yellow corolla is small and relatively inconspicuous. Flowering trees were already present in April, but they became more abundant in May and June. To me they brought memories of the Río Marañón in Peru, where what was evidently this same species made vivid splashes of red on riverside cliffs below the Pongo de Manseriche. I thought that these inflorescences, as brilliant as those of the poinsettia, would attract hummingbirds, honeycreepers, and other birds, but I watched for hours without seeing a single feathered visitor. Butterflies of many colors, along with smaller insects, seemed to be the chief pollinators.

Tall palms, soaring up into the canopy, were much less common in this forest than at Los Cusingos, but lower palms, from waist-high up to forty or fifty feet, were abundant. The undergrowth was composed chiefly of small palms, including species of *Geonoma* and *Chamaedora*. Some grew as clusters of slender, canelike stems crowned with small, pinnate fronds, and others had dwarf trunks surmounted by broad, bifid leaves. Scattered among these palms were vigorous plants of *Cyclanthus bipartitus*, a relative of the palms, whose big leaves, entire when they first expand, split lengthwise into two divisions at the slightest touch. Among the tall herbs were many terrestrial aroids, including species of *Spathiphyllum* with leaflike, green spathes and of *Dieffenbachia* with thick, fleshy stems that when severed emitted a strong odor of Skunk Cabbage. In the more open spots of the forest grew large-leafed members of the banana, arrowroot, and ginger families. The ground beneath all this heavy vegetation was rather bare, with few low herbs and hardly any litter of fallen leaves, for they decayed quickly in this exceedingly wet forest.

Abundant on the dimly lighted ground and on the lowest undergrowth was a tiny frog, *Dendrobates pumilo*, about three-quarters of an inch long, with a brilliant orange-red body and deep blue legs, all finely spotted with black. This little frog was almost as sluggish and reluctant to move as its red and green relative, a species of *Atelopus*, that lives on the rocks along the streams in El General, and doubtless for the same reason—because it is poisonous. Once I found one of these brilliant frogs climbing up a shrub with a tiny black tadpole on its back; the tadpoles are said to be transported by the males to aerial pools, such as those in tank bromeliads, where they develop. On wet days in May, these diminutive frogs puffed out their throats until they were bigger than their heads, while with vibrating abdomens they set up an insectlike buzz.

A decade before our visit, the ornithologist Paul Slud had spent a year at La Selva, studying the ecology of the birds. Including migrants and water birds as well as the permanent residents of the forest, he identified three hundred and thirty-one species—more than had been listed for any comparable area. Nevertheless, one who expected to find this forest swarming with birds would be disappointed. Many of the species were represented by sparse populations, and one might wander through the woodland for hours and see few birds. The lower levels, from waist-high up as far as one could readily see through the foliage—up to about twenty-five or thirty feet—often seemed almost devoid of birds, except for a few small vireos, flycatchers, and antbirds, such as the Tawny-crowned Greenlet, the Golden-crowned Spadebill, the Oleaginous Pipromorpha, the Eye-ringed Flatbill, and the Streaked-crowned Antvireo. I attributed the sparseness of bird life in the lower levels of the forest to the relative paucity of berry-bearing shrubs, particularly those of the melastome and madder families. The place that such shrubs occupy in other tropical forests, including those in El General, was here largely preempted by the multitudinous low palms, which provided less fruit for the birds, while their harsh foliage seemed to support fewer insects for them to catch.

The place to see birds at La Selva was not in the forest but from the house, which looked over the treetops, and above all in the cacao plantations. Although the cacao itself offered little food to birds and scarcely any nested among its coarse, open branches, the tall trees that shaded it attracted multitudes from the adjoining forest. On some afternoons, from three to five o'clock, these trees so swarmed with colorful birds that one did not know which way to look. Six kinds of woodpeckers, four kinds of woodcreepers, four parrots, seven species of cotingas including big Purple-throated Fruitcrows, three kinds of toucans, along with a variety of trogons, hummingbirds, flycatchers, honeycreepers, tanagers, oropéndolas, and many others—all found something to eat among these epiphyte-laden shade trees. The red-cheeked Cinnamon Woodpeckers had a special mode of feeding; I usually found them on the tall, slender Laurel trees, where, clinging to thin branches with one foot in front of the other, they pecked into the swollen nodes inhabited by ants, then rapidly gathered up the inhabitants, doubtless the larvae and pupae along with the adults. The much bigger Lineated Woodpeckers treated in similar fashion the Azteca ants that live in the hollow stems of the Cecropia tree.

While wandering through the cacao plantation one morning, I found a bird that I had long wished to see—the Great Jacamar. A pair of them were perching on a slender branch a few yards from a black termitary, fifty feet up on the trunk of a tall tree close by the forest. While I watched delightedly, admiring the metallic green upper plumage that glittered with blue and gold and bronze, one flew out, traced a long and tortuous course through the branches, and seized a large butterfly in its sharp, black bill. This was evidently the male, for the white patch on his throat was larger, the chestnut on his under parts slightly deeper, than on his companion. After beating the insect vigorously against his perch, he passed it to his mate, who continued the process until two of the bright, fluttering wings drifted earthward, then with difficulty gulped it down with two wings still attached. Next he flew to the termitary, stuck his foreparts into a round hole in the side, and after remaining for about a minute, rejoined his partner. Presently she went to the excavation and stayed for a quarter of an hour, her golden-green rump glittering in bright contrast to the black termitary, against which her frayed tail was pressed. I could not see what she did with her foreparts hidden in the cavity, but the tapping and crunching sounds that emanated from it were evidence that she pecked and tore at the hard plates of which the structure was composed.

For nearly two hours, the pair worked alternately at carving into the termitary, taking fairly equal turns that lasted from one to fourteen minutes. When not working, they caught insects on long aerial darts. Smaller ones were tossed about in the tip of the long bill before being eaten, larger ones beaten against the perch. Once the female caught a damsel fly, which she swallowed with the wings attached. Once again her mate fed her. In contrast to the smaller, more active and voluble Rufous-tailed Jacamars, these Great Jacamars were almost silent while they worked. The male voiced a high-pitched, clear note as he alighted beside his partner with an insect for her; she made a grating or rasping sound as she accepted his gift. They watched in stolid silence while two Collared Araçaris alighted near them; a third clung to the termitary.

On the following morning, the jacamars returned around ten o'clock to continue their task. As they approached and started to carve, they were more vocal than when I found them in the midst of their work, often repeating a soft mewing note, which became less frequent as the task proceeded. After this, we spent long hours vainly watching for the pair to continue their undertaking. Apparently they had struck an epiphytic cactus around which the termitary was built and could not cut through it to complete their nesting chamber.

While waiting fruitlessly for the jacamars to return, Edwin and I were rewarded by the sight of a pair of Yellow-eared Toucanets bathing. Their bathtub was a rain-filled hollow high in the side of a massive Gavilán trunk at the forest's edge. First the male toucanet bathed, while his mate waited patiently on a neighboring branch. Facing outward, he backed into the hollow, spilling water over the lip of the cavity as he immersed himself. After each wetting, he rested on the rim while he vigorously preened and scratched himself, revealing the orange tufts on his sides and the yellowish undersurface of his wings. When at last he left the niche, his deferential partner took her turn, bathing, preening, and scratching just as he had done. She continued for six minutes to wet and arrange her plumage, after which the pair rose higher into the trees for more scratching and preening. These pretty little toucans, one of the few species of the family in which the sexes differ in plumage, were rare at La Selva. The few that I saw were alone or in pairs, never in flocks. When disturbed, they uttered a hard, mechanical click or rattle while jerking their heads up and down through a wide arc. Although I have watched toucans of several kinds bathing in pools high in hollow trunks or branches, I have never seen them do so at ground level.

The rainiest parts of Costa Rica are its opposite corners, the Caribbean lowlands in the northeast and the southern part of the Pacific littoral, especially around the Golfo Dulce. In these regions the average annual rainfall exceeds one hundred and sixty inches, and the "Tropical Wet Forest" of the Holdridge classification flourishes. During our first season, our work was greatly impeded by excessive rain, which fell at any time of the day or night. In April it amounted to more than sixteen inches, and in May it was nearly twenty inches. In the following year, slightly more rain fell in these two months when nesting was at its height, but it tended to come in afternoon deluges, as on the Pacific slope; we enjoyed more clear mornings and accomplished more.

Despite the frequent rain and high humidity, the weather was rarely enervatingly sultry, as in some tropical lowlands. Often, when rain fell, it was cool enough to wear a jacket. Nights were pleasant; although we were only about four hundred feet above sea level, we nearly always slept under a blanket. Only in the early afternoon of a sunny day did we find it uncomfortably warm. Then, after a siesta, we swam in the Puerto Viejo River, which was always at a comfortable temperature. This stream, about fifty yards broad, was continually changing its level. After several rainless days, it would fall so low that, holding hands while we breasted the swift, clear current, we could walk across the nearly level bottom to the opposite shore. A day or two of steady rain might cause it to rise fifteen or twenty feet, bearing on its turbid bosom a constant procession of uprooted trees, decaying logs, branches, clusters of epiphytes torn from riverside trees, and other debris of the forest. When the river rose, the water backed far up into the tributary creeks, converting these usually shallow, clear streams into deep, muddy canals.

One afternoon, while we bathed, Edwin noticed a bird swimming along the opposite shore. Although herons, kingfishers, swallows, and other birds coursed above the river, I had never seen a bird alight on its surface, and I could not imagine what this small swimmer might be. Edwin ran up the long flight of steps for field glasses, which, focused on the distant bird, brought home the bold, black and white pattern of a Sungrebe's head and neck. The solitary bird continued to swim slowly downstream along the farther shore, where the current was slowest, now and again disappearing behind logs, piles of driftwood, or masses of foliage projecting from the high bank. Finally, it glided behind a stranded dead tree and vanished.

For the next month, we saw much of this Sungrebe and studied its habits while we bathed. It rested low in the water, its long tail hardly above the surface, and while swimming it waved its head forward and backward, like a walking pigeon. It never dived for its food but picked small objects, doubtless insects unidentifiable in the distance, from branches and foliage overhanging the stream and from decaying logs. Once it jumped almost clear of the water to pluck something from a branch above its head. It was always alone and silent. Before going to roost in the evening, it bathed, dipping its foreparts into the stream and splashing water over its back with its wings. After wetting its upper parts, it flew up to a low branch or a stranded log and spent many minutes preening and grooming its plumage. It might enter the water for a second wetting, to be followed by more preening, before it settled down for the night.

While there was still much daylight, the Sungrebe went to roost on a long, horizontal branch that projected well out from the bank. Here it was about four feet above the water, beneath abundant sheltering foliage. Only its white underparts were visible to the watchers across the river, and this light patch gradually faded into the shadows as dusk fell. One evening, after the Sungrebe had gone to roost, an otter swam beneath it, without causing it to move. Although the bird almost certainly saw the otter, the latter apparently failed to notice the bird. Likewise, the passage of a cayuco with a noisy outboard motor did not frighten it away. In the morning, the Sungrebe waited until the light was fairly bright before it jumped down into the water and started to swim upstream along the bank, picking its breakfast from overhanging vegetation. It continued to sleep on the same branch until this was submerged when the river rose in mid-May.

In the evening, after our swim, we often watched the river, the birds, and the sunset from the landing at the head of the outside steps to the upper story or the grassy clearing in front of the house. Parrots, toucans, oropéndolas, and Scarlet-rumped Caciques flew by, and woodcreepers called with loud, clear notes as they sought their dormitories in hollow trunks. Cattle Egrets, after foraging through the day at the heads of animals grazing in the pastures across the river, winged in small flocks toward the sunset, white against the darkening sky. It is surprising how rapidly these birds, recent immigrants from the Old World, have spread over the warmer parts of the Americas in the past two decades.

Among the many birds that flew by as the day ended was a pair of Red-lored Parrots. Over an interval of nearly a month, from mid-March until mid-April, we often saw one of these birds, doubtless the male, feed his mate. They would alight, one above the other, on an ascending dead branch at the very top of a tall tree, while the one above passed billful after billful to the one below. Before each transfer of food, the feeder alternately stretched and contracted his neck, to bring up the aliment, which the recipient took while loosely flapping her wings, especially the wing on the side toward her mate. These feedings were long-continued: one evening I counted forty-five installments; on another, forty-four; and on both occasions I had probably missed the very beginning of the process. My attention was usually drawn to the feedings by peculiar sharp notes that were evidently made by the recipient, for they continued while the donor was regurgitating food and could hardly have produced them. The feeding over, both birds called raucously in their usual fashion, then with mincing wingstrokes flew over the darkening pastures to the east. Probably the female was preparing to lay, or already incubating.

Sometimes, as I approached one of the swampy openings in the forest, a Green Ibis rose and flew over the tops of the surrounding trees, with loud, clear, high-pitched cries. At other times, I glimpsed ibises flying noisily over the roof of the forest or perching at the top of a tall tree, black against the sky. In May, we began to hear these ibises calling in the nearest swamp, a hundred yards from the house. In a loud, ringing voice, they sang *co co co co correct correct* or *co co co correct correct correct*. At a distance, the opening notes were confusingly similar to the *chirincoco* song of the Gray-necked Wood-Rail, but the *correct* was obviously from a different bird. Sometimes a song of the same form was delivered in a dry, cracked voice. When fairly close to a singing ibis, I heard low, hollow notes, as of air bubbling into a large glass bottle from which water is being poured, that conformed closely to the rhythm of the loud notes. It sounded as though the performer, or one of its companions, was beating time to the song on some resonant object, but probably the sound resulted from a peculiarity of the ibis's vocal organs. These birds sang most freely at dawn and in the early morning, again on a reduced scale in the evening, sporadically through the day, and occasionally in the depth of night.

It was not easy to watch these wary birds in the swamps, but, after several attempts, I succeeded. Pushing through flooded forest at the edge of a small swampy hollow, I stood for a hour among dwarf palms, in clear water up to my ankles, spying upon two of the big birds who rested side by side on a fallen tree. Although interfering foliage prevented a perfect view, I caught gleams of purple and green where the midday sunshine fell upon the lanceolate feathers at the back of their heads, and, at intervals, when they turned at a certain angle, a greenish sheen overspread their dark backs. The two ibises spent most of their time preening, both themselves and each other. Again and again, with the pointed tip of its long, dark, downcurved bill, one gently nibbled the feathers of its companion's head or neck, and presently the latter returned the favor. At times the two seemed to preen each other simultaneously. Occasionally they appeared to spar gently with their bills, but possibly they only had trouble deciding who was to preen whom. Sometimes the long feathers of their napes were raised into a low crest. One of the two, leaning far forward on the fallen tree, spread its broad wings above its back and fanned out its raised tail. Its head, bent low, was hidden by foliage, so that I could not see whether the crest was elevated in this display. After a while, I noticed a third ibis perching well up in a tree beside the swamp. Without disturbing them, I stole away.

After a night of torrential rain, I pushed into the swamp at daybreak to continue to watch the ibises. Before six o'clock, three came to stand upon the fallen tree, resting and at intervals preening languidly. They seemed to have already satisfied their hunger so early in the morning.

Helpers at the Nest

A principal reason for our visit to La Selva in 1967 was to fulfill a wish that had been born twenty-seven years earlier on the Río Yavarí, an Amazonian tributary that separates Peru from Brazil. At a tiny settlement that somebody had humorously named Islandia (Iceland), our party examined a young rubber tree while a small flock of blackish, starling-sized birds perched above us. They had bright orange bills and large, dark eyes, and they twitched their tails from side to side while they uttered soft, musical murmurs. These Black-fronted Nunbirds were the first representatives of their genus (*Monasa*) that I had ever seen, and this brief encounter convinced me that they had unusual social habits, which I wanted to study. Although for the next quarter century I was engaged in the study of tropical birds, I never happened to be located where nunbirds occur; they are absent from the Pacific side of Central America and the Panama Canal Zone, where I worked.

The species at La Selva is the White-fronted Nunbird, which has a wide but discontinuous range through humid lowland forests from eastern Honduras to Bolivia. A stout bird about eleven inches long, it is largely dark gray, with blackish wings and tail. At the base of the bright orange-red bill typical of its genus, it wears, on forehead, lores, and chin, a ruff of short, stiff, outstanding white feathers. The sexes are alike. In small parties of rarely more than half a dozen individuals, it straggles through the trees of the forest and nearby clearings; at La Selva, the cacao plantation was one of the best places to watch it. Nunbirds belong to the puffbird family, and, like other puffbirds, they perch motionless until they spy a suitable insect or other small creature, which they seize at the end of a sudden swift dart, without alighting. The distance at which they can detect a green caterpillar upon a green leaf demonstrates remarkably keen vision. They vary their diet with an occasional milliped, small frog, or lizard, but they seem never to eat fruit.

From late March until June, we often heard the unique chorus of the nunbirds. Alighting on a horizontal branch or length of vine stretched between trees, anywhere from about twenty-five to seventy-five feet above the ground, from three to ten nunbirds would line up in a row, a few inches apart. Then the dusky birds would tilt their heads upward and shout all together in loud, ringing, almost soprano voices, with such vehemence that their bodies shook. What they lacked in melody they made up in enthusiasm. At times, one of the performers nodded its head emphatically, as though in approval, or to encourage its companions to proceed with the "music." For fifteen or twenty minutes, the spirited chorus continued, swelling or waning in volume as more or fewer of the birds joined in. Then it would cease, and the performers dispersed through the forest in small groups or singly.

Three days after our arrival at La Selva, Dennis Paulson brought the exhilarating news that he had already found a nunbird's nest. While studying dragonflies in a grassy swamp, he saw three nunbirds fly across the open space from the neighboring cacao plantation. Noticing food in their bills, he followed them into the forest, where they led him to a burrow in a moderate slope, beneath tall trees. Since evening was approaching, we decided to postpone our visit until next day. After the morning rain abated, we went out to inspect the burrow, only to be greeted by a pile of freshly dug earth in front of a gaping hole. Some animal had destroyed the first nest of the White-fronted Nunbird ever, to my knowledge, to be found by a naturalist, even before it had been properly described. For the next two months, we searched through the dripping forest for another nunbird's nest, without success. In studying the lives of tropical birds, as in warfare and financial speculation, one who cannot become inured to such sudden reverses of fortune achieves little.

The following year, we had more favorable weather and better luck. After we had searched for nearly three weeks, Edwin found the first nunbird's nest on a fairly steep slope, where many small palms grew beneath the trees. This unusually short burrow descended into the hillside, with a slight inclination, for about forty inches. It was almost straight, so that, as we peered into it with a flashlight, we could see a nunbird bravely guarding three recently hatched nestlings in the face of our doubtless terrifying intrusion. The family rested in the expanded lower end of the burrow, which had been lined with dead leaves. Later I found two more burrows that had been dug into nearly level ground for fifty-five inches. Surrounding the mouth of each was a low collar composed of decaying sticks, petioles, and dead leaves, which reduced the size of the aperture and made it less conspicuous. These burrows also contained nestlings, but their length and slight curvature made it impossible to see to the end and learn how many. To have opened them for inspection would have jeopardized our studies.

Although many birds of the tropical forest are so shy at their nests that one must watch from a blind, these nunbirds were more confiding and would feed their young while we stood or sat ten or twelve yards from the burrow's mouth, with little or no concealment by the vegetation. It soon became evident that each of the burrows had more than the two attendants that one ordinarily finds at a bird's nest; at one of the burrows, at least three grown birds were bringing food, and at the other two at least four. All the attendants appeared to be equally mature, and with the exception of a few with broken tail feathers, they could not be distinguished from each other. At the shortest burrow, four birds were feeding three nestlings of the same age, which made it unlikely that more than one female had laid the eggs from which they hatched. Apparently the attendants included the two parents and helpers, hatched in the preceding year or earlier, who were not themselves ready to reproduce.

Flying up through the forest with food in its bill, the attendant nunbird would alight five or ten yards above the ground in a tree near the burrow. Delaying there, it repeated over and over a special call, a liquid ripple of sound, a churr, a soft purr, or even a rattle—there was much variation in this call, but it always had an undulatory quality. If suspicious, the nunbird might continue to call for many minutes, with each repetition elevating, then depressing, its tail, trogonlike. This delay gave us a good opportunity to see what it brought and, as the attendants accumulated, how many there were.

The vivid bill never held more than a single article of food, usually a mature or larval insect of substantial size, often a cicada, less frequently a spider or a small frog or lizard. Once, to my amazement, an attendant brought for half-grown nestlings a large, green caterpillar covered with branched, stinging spines, which I would not have picked up with my fingers for a hundred dollars, for I know no pain more acute and lasting than such caterpillars can cause. Yet Squirrel Cuckoos regularly eat such stinging caterpillars and give them to their nestlings, and the young nunbird that swallowed this one showed no ill effects after several hours.

Like many other nonpasserines, the nunbirds did not clean their nest, and, except when they intended to brood naked nestlings after feeding them, they never took food into the burrow. Even the youngest nestlings that we found, at most two or three days old, were fed at the entrance. After repeating the rippling approach call a number of times, the attendant flew down and stood on the ground in front of the burrow, where it waited until a nestling came for its meal. Past the attendant's dark body, we could sometimes see a pink, naked nestling run up the tunnel, bobbing its sightless head and waving its rudimentary wings. After seizing the meal from the adult's bill, it backed inward and was promptly lost from view in the dark burrow. At the longer burrows, the round trip from the brood chamber to the entrance and back again was eight or nine feet, which seemed a long pedestrian journey for a sightless birdling that crawled from beneath a brooding parent and then pushed back into its sheltering warmth. This method of delivering food continued unchanged until the nestlings flew. Except when taking their meals, the young nunbirds remained discreetly out of sight in the depth of their long burrow. In sharp contrast to such garrulous nestlings as those of the Rufous-tailed Jacamar, they rarely uttered a sound that was audible outside.

Returning to the shortest burrow eleven days after it was found, I was dismayed to see a heap of fresh earth in front of a yawning hole where the nest had been. The three nestlings had vanished. While I raked from the bottom of the hole a handful of fragments of dead leaves, finding many small white maggots among them, four attendants arrived with food in their bills. I withdrew a few yards and watched. One of the attendants soon disappeared, but the other three went, one by one, to stand in front of the ruined nest and call the vanished nestlings with sharp feeding notes—a pathetic spectacle! Finally, they flew off through the forest with the food they could not deliver. Even on the following morning, at least twenty-four hours after the nest had been pillaged, a nunbird alighted on the mound of freshly dug earth with food in its bill and called, at first in normal tones, which rose to almost frenzied intensity when they failed to win a response. I have seen birds of many kinds continue to bring food to a nest for hours or days after their young were lost. A pair of Golden-naped Woodpeckers did so for six days.

At the age of about thirty days, the young nunbirds left one of the long burrows and promptly rose into the treetops. Soon after emerging from the earth, young nunbirds were taking their meals in a spectacular manner, different from that of any other bird that I know. After catching an insect or some other edible creature, the attendant would beat it against a branch, then sit holding the food conspicuously in its bill until a juvenile flew up and, without alighting, snatched it away. Sometimes the young nunbird would fly, straight and swift, a hundred feet to grab a meal on the wing. In coming to the adult for food, rather than waiting until it was brought to them, the young were, in a way, continuing the habit they had formed as tender nestlings, when they came to the burrow's mouth for their meals. They were also getting excellent practice for snatching insects from leaf or bark at the end of a long aerial sally, as they would do when older. One might suppose that young birds with such well-controlled flight as this method of taking food from an adult's bill required would be quite capable of foraging for themselves, but apparently their skill on the wing developed more rapidly than their knowledge of what was edible—I saw one try to eat a flake of curled bark. Moreover, the adults seemed very indulgent.

The nunbird was not the only species at La Selva that had helpers at the nest. Another was the Black-faced Grosbeak, a yellow, olive, and gray finch with a black patch surrounding the base of its thick, dark bill. In April of our second season at La Selva, a pair of these grosbeaks built a nest in a cranny amid the epiphytes that burdened a small tree standing in the narrow clearing behind the house. Although both sexes built, they worked at such a leisurely pace that it took about a week to finish their slight, open structure, composed of dead leaves and the creeping rhizomes of a small epiphytic fern. It was not easy to discover the origin of the long, thin, tapering pieces that were coiled into the bowl as lining and remained green until the nestlings flew. I finally decided that they were the leaves of an epiphytic bromeliad, apparently a species of *Tillandsia,* an unusual constituent of birds' nests. All the materials were gathered from trees rather than the ground.

Twelve days after the nest was begun, the female laid the first of her three eggs, which were dull white, mottled and spotted all over with bright shades of brown. She alone incubated them, but her mate was most attentive, escorting her to the nest in a dashing fashion. As she flew down to it from a tree at the edge of the clearing, he accompanied her so closely that he seemed to be racing to reach the nest first; but while she alighted upon it, he swept past and turned his course upward into the trees on the other side, tracing a deep catenary loop between opposite edges of the forest.

Black-faced Grosbeaks are social birds, at all seasons wandering in loose flocks through the trees, searching for berries and insects. Sometimes one member of the flock feeds another adult. They show little territorial exclusiveness, and wandering grosbeaks that alighted close by the nest were not chased by the parents; at most, they were mildly threatened. Until after the eggs were laid, only two birds took an interest in this nest; but during the course of incubation, a third individual attached itself to the mated pair. Since in this species the sexes are alike, I could not tell whether this helper was a male or a female. However, it escorted the female back to the nest just as her mate did; now three birds raced down to the nest tree from the forest's edge, two shooting past it and one remaining. After a little over thirteen days of incubation, the eggs hatched, and then all three of the adults fed the three nestlings. After the female ceased to brood, they commonly came and went together. Occasionally, a wandering grosbeak would notice the nestlings and bring them food, but only these three continued as constant attendants until, at the age of twelve days, the young took wing. The adults promptly led them into the leafy mazes of the neighboring forest, where we lost track of them.

Another bird with unusual social habits was the Dusky-faced Tanager. Clad in yellowish olive green and grayish olive, these slender, yellow-eyed birds often reminded me more of jays than of tanagers. In flocks of six to ten, they hunted for insects and berries amid the densely tangled vegetation along the banks of streams, about the edges of the swampy openings in the forest, and in neighboring clearings rankly overgrown. Restless birds, they were so constantly on the move through concealing vegetation that it was difficult to become familiar with them. As they straggled through the low, dense growth, they kept in contact with each other by means of a constant chatter of sharp notes. I never heard them sing.

Despite much searching, I found only a single nest of this tanager, in a dense thicket beside a stream. The bulky open cup was composed almost wholly of the long, brown, threadlike pistillate inflorescences of *Myriocarpa*, a small tree of the nettle family that provides much of this material for nesting birds. Slung between two slender, upright stems, the peculiar structure had no support below. In it were two nestlings already becoming feathered. The density of the surrounding vegetation, which it was imprudent to disturb, made it difficult to study this nest; but watching from the higher opposite bank of the stream, Edwin and I convinced ourselves that at least three or four adults were bringing insects and placing them in the gaping red mouths, which we could see from our distant station whenever the nestlings stretched up to take their meals. The flock that often passed by this nest consisted of about seven birds, all of whom may well have been attending the young.

These three species—the nunbird, the grosbeak, and the tanager—were the only ones with helpers that we watched carefully at La Selva, but in six other species that occurred there, I had earlier found helpers elsewhere. One was the Collared Araçari, a widespread small toucan whose nests are rarely discovered. In Panama, I had watched five grown birds bring food to at least three nestlings in a hollow limb high in a forest tree, in which all the attendants slept with the young. The second was the Banded-backed Wren, one of the largest members of its family. At La Selva, these wrens hid their nests amid orchids or other epiphytes, at great heights on shade trees of the cacao plantation. At one nest, I watched four wrens building; in another, six slept; but otherwise it was impossible to learn much about their domestic arrangements. But in the Guatemalan highlands, where adaptable Banded-backed Wrens build their bulky, roofed nests in exposed sites in oak and pine trees, parents feeding young were assisted by one or more helpers, who were evidently nonbreeding yearlings. The third was the Golden-masked Tanager. I have repeatedly seen juveniles in transitional plumage helping their parents to feed their younger brothers and sisters of a later brood in the same season and also a trio of adults in full breeding plumage attending nestlings. The fourth species with helpers was the gray Plain-colored Tanager, an anomaly in a brilliant family. In Panama, I watched four grown birds bring food to two nestlings. The fifth was the big, boisterous White-tipped Brown Jay, rare at forested La Selva but more abundant on neighboring farms. In this species, parents feeding young are regularly assisted by from one to five yearlings, readily distinguished by their bills curiously pied with yellow and black.

In addition to these birds with helpers who apparently did not themselves breed, there was also at La Selva at least one species with mutual helpers, the Groove-billed Ani. Sometimes a pair of these black cuckoos nests alone; but frequently two, three, or rarely more, pairs join forces to build a bulky communal nest of sticks lined with freshly plucked green leaves, in which each female lays three or four chalky white eggs, all in a heap. All the cooperating birds of both sexes take turns incubating these eggs, and all feed and brood the young, but a single male is in charge of the nest each night.

The assistance given by nonbreeding birds to breeding pairs is one of the most pleasing aspects of bird life. In general, the reproductive activities of birds follow a stereotyped pattern, courtship leading to nest building, followed by egg laying, incubation, feeding and brooding the young, and finally, in many species, driving juveniles that have become self-supporting from the parental territory. In the absence of outside interference, stage follows stage with almost mechanical precision. But the helpers, in many instances still sexually immature, are not caught up in this fixed pattern; they break into the middle of it; their help seems to be freely given, rather than a biological necessity. These cooperating groups of birds are not comparable to social insects such as termites, ants, and honeybees, in which the production of young is indispensably a communal activity, since the females that lay the eggs become incapable of working, and the workers that attend the brood are incapable of laying. The parent birds that receive help are quite able to raise their families alone, and the immature individuals that assist them are not compelled to do so. Their voluntary help is a result of the close ties that continue to bind families together after the young become self-supporting.

I was puzzled by the greater prevalence of helpers at La Selva than in El General on the opposite side of the country, where many seasons of study of an almost equally rich avifauna had disclosed fewer species in which helpers are, or appear to be, customary. Here helpers are frequent in the Groove-billed Ani, the Smooth-billed Ani, and the Acorn Woodpecker, occasional in the Golden-masked Tanager, and exceptional in the Golden-naped Woodpecker and the Southern House Wren. Over the years, I have also noticed a few instances of birds feeding young of a different species: a male Blue Honeycreeper fed a Scarlet-rumped Black Tanager and a female fed a Yellow-green Vireo; a female Tropical Gnatcatcher attended a brood of Golden-masked Tanagers. But interspecific helpers are always rare and unpredictable, whereas intraspecific helpers occur regularly in certain species. What causes this difference between the birds of these two areas, both originally covered by rain forest?

I believe that one reason why helpers are not more widespread among birds is that the greater the number that attend a nest, the greater the probability that their activity will attract the notice of predators. Since two attendants, or even one, are adequate to raise the small broods of most tropical birds, in regions where predation is high natural selection will repress the tendency to assist mated pairs. Moreover, with high predation and low nesting success, birds should begin to breed at an early age in order to raise a greater number of young and maintain the population. But with low predation, high nesting success, and greater longevity, it might be advantageous, even for small birds, to defer breeding for one or more seasons after that in which they hatched in order to avoid overpopulation. The yearlings or two-year-olds who help breeding pairs, gain experience that will be valuable to them when finally they undertake to raise families of their own. Both of these considerations lead me to believe that helpers should become more abundant in the measure that predation and other sources of mortality decline. But I have no reason to believe that predation is lighter at La Selva than in El General; since I have noticed a tendency for it to decrease with altitude, the reverse may be true. Hence, I cannot explain this striking difference that we found, yet I am reluctant to conclude that it is due to "chance."

Birds and Arils

In both years, we stayed at La Selva until early June, when the majority of the birds had finished nesting. Toward the end of our first visit, I spent much time watching a fruiting tree of the spurge family, *Alchornea costaricensis*, that grew beside a stream in an open part of the forest and was a cynosure of the birds. Splitting open, each small green pod exposed two seeds, each of which was enclosed in a bright red aril. Within this thin fleshy covering, an outgrowth from the base of the seed and the only digestible part, was a hard seed coat that protected the embryo. Although these seeds provided so little nourishment, they were eagerly sought by birds so diverse as diminutive White-collared Manakins, who plucked the seeds by means of a short dart, and big Rainbow-billed Toucans, who seized a seed in the tip of the enormous bill and, with an upward toss of the head, threw it back into the throat. Among the twenty-four species of birds that I saw eat the little red seeds were also trogons, woodpeckers, cotingas, flycatchers, honeycreepers, tanagers, and finches.

At Los Cusingos, I had earlier listed the same number of birds, mostly of different species, eating the similar seeds of a related tree, *Alchornea latifolia*. Here, in April, the most abundant guests of the *Alchornea* were migrating Olive-backed Thrushes, who repeated their liquid *quit*, and even sang in an undertone, while rapidly gathering the red seeds, then flew swiftly back into the sheltering woods. Wintering Yellow-throated Vireos and Philadelphia Vireos also ate many of these seeds, and even Chestnut-sided Warblers, which are almost wholly insectivorous, nibbled at the thin red arils and occasionally swallowed fragments of them.

Plants that depend upon wind to scatter their seeds may grow wings, or other projections to catch the breeze, on their fruits—as in the ash, burío, and the dandelion—or on the seeds themselves—as in the jacaranda, the willow, and the milkweed. Occasionally even an associated vegetative organ, as the bract of the linden, serves as the sail. Similarly, those plants that entice animals to disperse their seeds may produce succulent flesh either in the fruit, on the seed, or, as in the apple and the cashew, in the receptacle or fruitstalk. When the seeds develop within a hard, inedible pod, which protects them until they mature and this receptacle splits open, they themselves must bear the nourishment for the animals that spread them abroad. In these cases, the edible tissue is usually in the form of an aril, a fleshy, sometimes oily, outgrowth from the base of the ovule that partly or wholly covers the seed. The embryo itself, especially when small, is usually enclosed in a hard coat to protect it from digestion while in the animal's alimentary tract.

In contrast to the immense variety of fleshy fruits esteemed by mankind, the list of arils appreciated by humans is short. It includes the edible portions of granadillas (fruits of certain passion flowers), the Mangosteen, the foul-smelling but delicious Durian of the East, and the Akee. A bursting Akee pod, with the white arils and the large black seeds that they partly cover peeping out between pale red valves, is a beautiful object. The pulpy arils are cooked as a vegetable, but great care must be taken in their selection and preparation, for they are a treacherous food that has been fatal to many people; years ago, after being nearly carried off by a dish of Akee, I vowed that I would never taste it again. The aril of the Nutmeg furnishes the aromatic spice known as mace, which is also a favored food of the large fruit pigeons of the East Indies; they regurgitate the seed after digesting away the branched aril. All of these arils eaten by man grow on tropical or subtropical plants. Among the few arils produced by the flora of the North Temperate Zone are those of the Strawberry Bush, the Climbing Bittersweet, and the Yew, beloved of European Blackbirds.

Because men make such slight use of arils, and so few kinds are found in the North, their importance as food for tropical birds and other animals has not been adequately appreciated. Whenever I find a tree liberally exposing arillate seeds, I expect a colorful display of bird life. Certain lagartillo trees (species of *Xanthoxylum* with spine-studded trunks) are hardly less attractive to birds than the Alchorneas. The small, oily capsules are borne in large panicles at the ends of the branches. Splitting into two valves, each capsule releases a single, shiny, black seed, about one-eighth of an inch in diameter, that stands above it on a short, threadlike stalk. The thin, black aril, rich in oil, covers a rough, hard seed coat. Birds as large as thrushes eagerly devour these tiny packets of nourishment, whose abundance and easy accessibility compensate for their smallness.

For certain small birds—including Blue Honeycreepers, Shining Honeycreepers, Green Honeycreepers, and the Oleaginous Pipromorpha among the flycatchers—arils rival, if they do not surpass, berries as sources of food. In addition to the arillate seeds of the Alchorneas and

Xanthoxylums, they are exceedingly fond of those of the multitudinous Clusias. The pods of these epiphytic trees, in size varying from that of a cherry to that of a plum, open at maturity like the petals of a flower, forming stars with few or many rays, according to the species. Their dehiscence exposes a multitude of small seeds enclosed in bright red or orange arils. Honeycreepers are so eager for these arils that, neglecting ripe bananas on a nearby feeder, they flit about impatiently, trying to extract them from pods that are just beginning to split. Strong-billed woodpeckers are more successful at removing the seeds prematurely, and I have seen Blue Honeycreepers try to intercept some of these tempting morsels that a Golden-naped Woodpecker was passing to his young. It is hard to understand why these and other arils attract birds so strongly, for those that I have sampled were either tasteless or disagreeable.

In the Costa Rican forests grow several species of trees of the nutmeg family whose olive-sized seeds, borne singly in two-valved pods, are covered with bright red arils. In *Virola*, the aril embraces the brown seed with a filigree network; in *Compsoneura*, it surrounds the seed like a sleeve. Far too large to be swallowed by any honeycreeper, these arillate seeds are eaten by toucans and the larger species of motmots and trogons. After digesting off the aril, these birds regurgitate and drop from the mouth the seeds, which accumulate, along with a variety of other kinds, on the bottom of their nest in a hole in a tree or a burrow in the ground.

23

Conclusion
Vicissitudes of a Valley

WHEN I FIRST SAW El General in 1935, it was still largely unspoiled. There were only about five thousand human inhabitants, a few hundred of whom were concentrated in the administrative and shopping center of San Isidro, while the remainder were scattered over the broad basin and the surrounding slopes on small or fairly large farms, many of which had been so recently carved from the forest that they were still littered with stumps and prostrate trunks. Between the clearings were tracts of forest, some of considerable extent. Indeed, on the very outskirts of the central village I found much woodland, and this is what first attracted me to the valley. Although the larger mammals, such as the Jaguar, the Puma, and the Tapir, had receded from the more settled districts, the more extensive tracts of forest among the clearings seemed otherwise to retain their original fauna. Surrounding this small, isolated agricultural community were vast areas of forest un-

Headpiece: In the Valley of the Río Peña Blanca at Quizarrá. Foothills of the Cordillera de Talamanca rise in the background.

touched by the axe, stretching in unbroken majesty from the seacoast up to the open páramos of the Cordillera de Talamanca. Could the valley have remained as I found it, it would be a shining example of how man can live in an unspoiled environment and an ideal locality for naturalists.

But this was not to be. The original inhabitants continued to multiply rapidly, and more settlers poured in from the densely populated center of the country. The population has increased more than tenfold. From a squalid hamlet, San Isidro has become a thriving commercial center on the only highway that leads from the United States and Mexico to Panama. Where a quarter of a century ago there was not a single motor vehicle, there are now many cars and filling stations. A bishop has his seat here, and an impressive cathedral, built of concrete in the modern style, fronts a central square that has been attractively planted with palms and other trees. A large, modern *jefatura* or town hall was recently completed. Among educational institutions are a *liceo* or high school, a large elementary school, a normal school, and a school conducted by nuns. A local radio broadcasting station is affiliated with the Church, and a relay station on El Cerro de la Muerte transmits to the valley programs from a central station in the capital. For amusement, there are three cinema theaters; for health, four pharmacies and a small hospital.

Traveling throughout the valley, one sees many neat cottages with metal roofs and painted walls, mostly small for the large families that inhabit them. But there are also hovels, swarming with children, dogs, pigs, and chickens, all happily intermingled. From nearly all these habitations, whether neatly finished or pitifully crude, the passer-by may hear, at almost any hour of the day, the blaring of a transistor radio, turned up to full volume and audible fifty yards away. Many of these homes are now served by community water systems. In 1968, such a system was installed for the neighboring communities of Quizarrá and Santa Elena, which lie above our farm, on opposite sides of the Peña Blanca River. Until the work began, I never believed that dwellings so poor and scattered would have the luxury of running water, but the International Development Bank, the United Nations, and the Costa Rican government helped to finance the project, along with many similar ones over the country, and the National Service of Aqueducts and Drains did the work. By laying two hundred yards of pipe, we connected with the pipeline that runs along the road beside our farm and brought to our house pure water from a spring more than three miles above us in the mountains. Gradually the road into Quizarrá and Santa Elena is being ballasted with rounded river stones to make it passable by cars throughout the wet season; now a bus comes thrice daily to the forking of the roads half a mile from our entrance.

These improvements, like improvements everywhere, have not been bought without a price—the spoliation of nature. Here and there, especially on the broader and flatter fields along the river bottoms, are farms that appear fairly prosperous. Large buildings for curing tobacco have in the past few years, since Cuba was excommunicated from the American family of nations, sprung up on many of them. Had the settlement of the valley been restricted to these darker and more fertile soils, all might have been well. The little farms on the red-clay hillsides do not prosper. There is no more disastrous fallacy than that soil that supports magnificent trees will, if cleared, yield a succession of rich crops, and these farms on land that two or three decades ago bore impressive forest now yield scarcely anything without heavy fertilization. Even when in pasture grass, which in some regions is used to restore exhausted soil, these slopes are so leached by the heavy rains that they furnish only miserable grazing, as has happened to the hilltop behind our house.

The salvation of the hillside farmers has been coffee, a perennial crop suited to a yearlong growing season. But with global overproduction, the price of coffee has fallen, and farmers are being urged to plant other things. Yet no satisfactory substitute for coffee in this region has been proposed, and my neighbors, far from abandoning it, continue to plant more. Some, to eke out a precarious livelihood, make moonshine liquor, hiding their crude stills away in the remaining patches of forest and keeping the fiscal guard busy ferreting them out. The petty theft of growing crops is so rife that we hid our new banana plantation in the woods.

The destruction of the forest, which is occurring at an accelerated pace all over Costa Rica and indeed throughout the tropics, has been particularly striking in this valley. Of the once magnificent wilderness, only shreds and patches remain in the valley and on the surrounding slopes below four or five thousand feet, and, in some places, as at the headwaters of the Río Buena Vista, deforestation had long ago proceeded much higher than this, resulting in long, desolate slopes—so steep that one wonders how laborers can cling to them—and more disastrous floods in the valleys. Only in the central fastnesses of the Cordillera de Talamanca, south of El Cerro de la Muerte, does the wilderness remain intact. This rugged region should be preserved as a national park.

One of the largest remaining tracts of forest in the valley is that of a hundred acres or so on this farm, which for nearly thirty years I have tried to preserve in its pristine state. What has happened to it will serve as an example of what has happened to the remnants of forest everywhere in the valley, for I am certain that none has fared better. The most obvious change is that thousands of tall palmitos have vanished—stolen. These elegant palms left enough seedlings to restore the stand, after many years, if they were permitted to grow undisturbed. But as soon as one becomes an inch thick, some trespasser comes along and slashes off its head for the few mouthfuls of food at its "heart" or growing point. With the exhaustion of the palmitos, thieves have begun to attack the even taller chonta palms, which formerly were neglected because their young tissues are bitter. Why not catch the thieves and get a judgment against them? One unfamiliar with heavy tropical forest can hardly imagine how difficult it is to learn what is happening a few hundred yards away. Two full-time watchmen would be required to properly guard even so small a tract as this. And who would watch the watchers?

It is widely held that mature tropical forest is a stable vegetable formation that remains essentially unchanged from century to century. Yet in this forest, which appeared mature when I first saw it, the largest trees have been dying faster than they are being replaced by younger trees. As was earlier mentioned, the tall Milk Tree is increasing while the old Campanas are dying out, but it has by no means compensated for the loss of other kinds of trees. The explanation of this puzzling phenomenon may be that this forest has not yet reached its climax but represents an advanced successional stage on lands cleared by the Indians and abandoned by them centuries ago. Or could it be that climatic changes, resulting from the destruction of the surrounding woodland, cause the large, old trees to die prematurely? The smoke-laden atmosphere of the latter part of the dry season must have some effect. Even the destruction of so many palms must alter the dynamics of the forest.

Of diurnal mammals larger than a squirrel, there remain only a wary troupe of White-faced Monkeys and a rare Agouti. The few survivors among these harmless rodents have become so elusive that I seldom see them, except when one runs through the dooryard or takes refuge under the house, trying desperately to escape a couple of madly yelping hounds. The brockets or Forest Deer, the Coatimundis, and the Tayras have been exterminated since I came here; the Tapirs, the peccaries, and the big cats had vanished before I arrived.

Of the birds, the big, noisy Crested Guans no longer make the forest ring with their protesting cries. It has been long since I saw an equally raucous Red-throated Caracara. Of the resident hawks, only the elusive little Barred Forest-Falcon remains, and it is so destructive of small birds that I would gladly see it go, too. Rarely we hear a wandering Laughing Falcon; with the virtual disappearance of this serpent eater, the arboreal snakes that prey upon eggs and nestlings seem to have become more numerous. The big Chestnut-mandibled Toucans, once abundant, have quite disappeared, although the smaller, more agile Fiery-billed Araçaris linger furtively in reduced numbers. The largest of our woodpeckers, the Pale-billed, is no longer seen here, and the slightly smaller Lineated Woodpecker has become rare. The glittering, ebullient Rufous-tailed Jacamar no longer graces our forest; but the four trogons, equally brilliant but more retiring, manage to hang on.

The largest arboreal bird that is still abundant is the thrush-sized, bright brown Rufous Piha that whistles sharply in response to any sudden noise, such as the crash of a falling branch, a shout, or the loud wing-beats of a startled Great Tinamou. This terrestrial bird has escaped destruction, as has the Marbled Wood-Quail. The latter, once common and so tame that I could watch them forage or preen each other a few feet from me, seemed for a while to have vanished. Now I know that they are still with us, because I sometimes hear their liquid, rolling duets floating out of the forest in the evening twilight; but they have become so wary that I scarcely ever glimpse one. Sunbitterns no longer forage along our river, and flocks of Scarlet Macaws no longer brighten our sky.

Happily, I have noticed no diminution in the numbers of the smaller passerine birds. While so many of the larger forest-dwelling birds have vanished, certain wide-ranging birds of open and cultivated country have invaded the valley. I have already mentioned the recent appearance of the Orange-chinned Parakeet. Long after I arrived here, I first heard the distinctive call of the Striped Cuckoo, a parasite which somehow slips its eggs into the well-enclosed stick nests of the castlebuilders. It has become abundant in the lower parts of the valley, and it will have more foster parents for its young, for only a few months ago I saw my first Pale-breasted Castlebuilder in El General. With the destruction of the intervening forest, this ovenbird, so widespread in South America, has made its way up the Térraba Valley from Buenos Aires de Osa, where it had long been known. Seven years ago, I saw for the first time Red-eyed Cowbirds in this valley—two in a neighboring pasture. I have not again noticed these parasites here, and I cannot say that I am sorry.

Although much has been lost, much also has been saved that would have vanished if I had made no effort to protect it. And of the things that have gone, some have been preserved, albeit imperfectly, in memory and in writings in which I have tried to convey to others their interest and beauty. Yet, as nature lovers have learned to their sorrow in many parts of the world, a small private sanctuary is at best an imperfect and precarious means of protecting a sample of the living community from neighbors too eager to exploit, to kill, and to destroy. Even the nature preserve on Barro Colorado Island in the Canal Zone, under the protection of government and isolated by the water of Gatún Lake, has for years been violated by poachers. And not even the great national parks will be able to preserve their integrity indefinitely—in the face of an ever denser and hungrier humanity—if they happen to be on land capable of producing a little food. Every nature preserve, be it a few privately owned acres or a great national park many square miles in extent, is but a temporary expedient to save something of the earth's pristine glory until the great fundamental problem is solved.

This problem is the stabilization of the human population of our planet within rational limits. This is the problem of problems, upon which the solution of nearly every other distressing problem that confronts us depends, for the whole possibility of satisfactorily carrying out any undertaking, whether it be making hats or educating a nation, depends in large measure upon the number of units involved. Until this matter of population control is settled, nothing will be satisfactorily settled.

Possibly, by a ruthless disregard of all other living things and the sacrifice of most natural beauty, the earth could support several times its present skyrocketing population; although I doubt not that in such crowded communities, in an environment poisoned by the pesticides that seem indispensable to agriculture on the scale necessary to support teeming millions, people would be even more subject to disorders of many kinds than they are today. But what sensitive man would care to live in a world so crowded that he could hardly move without bumping into his neighbors, in which every activity would necessarily be minutely regulated by government—in a world whose pristine beauty is preserved only in the writings of old authors and perhaps some dusty museum specimens, like the glory that was Greece and the grandeur that was Rome?

We should consider the possibility that throughout its entire existence, this planet can support only a certain total of human beings, so that the greater the number of the people who crowd it today, draining its resources, the fewer it will be able to support in future ages; just as, if a man has only a certain sum of money and no possibility of acquiring more, the more he spends today, the less he will be able to spend in the future. Every generous man cherishes the hope that future generations will be better and happier than the present one, which includes so many pitiful specimens of humanity living miserably. Would it not be preferable to keep the population low now, so that superior men may become more numerous in future ages? Likewise, the fewer the people we have to deal with, the sooner we should be able to solve the many pressing problems that confront humanity. A chief difficulty is that cities and nations have grown so huge that their problems defy our little minds and our limited resources.

This matter of population control is certainly not easily resolved. When all the physiological difficulties have been overcome, there remains the moral problem. Are our only alternatives a hideously overpopulated world, afflicted with famine, crime, ugliness, and disease, and a "contraceptive society," in which men, women, and children wallow, like pigs in mire, in sex divorced from its natural function of reproduction, which gives it dignity and makes it sacred?

Our salvation appears to depend upon discovering the true significance of human life and our proper relation to the vast whole of which we are parts. Ecologists have been insisting that man must achieve ecological balance with his natural environment or perish. It is certainly no less imperative for us to attain a correct spiritual relation to the natural world— to the whole universe, insofar as its influences reach us. Man bound up in himself is a pathetic creature, whether, by excessive concentration on humanity's long history of violence, terror, and frustration, he reaches the conclusion that human life is absurd; or whether, obsessed with his own body, he tries to make a purposeless life bearable by excessive indulgence in food and sex; or whether he excites his dull mind with scenes of violence and carnage, as in the Roman arena and the modern cinema.

Men who strive greatly to give significance to their lives have ever felt the necessity of reaching out beyond their individual selves and even the whole of humanity. The alternative points of orientation have been God and nature. But of God we know nothing; if a personal God exists, he has never condescended to reveal himself in a manner convincing to thoughtful men everywhere. The very religions that insist that he revealed himself in definite places at certain historical moments tacitly admit that he has made no universal revelation of himself; he neglected whole epochs and races that doubtless needed him as much and were as worthy of illumination by him as any people now alive. Hence, we cannot avoid the conclusion that if a personal God exists, he does not care to cultivate close relations with man. If he did, humanity could hardly be in the deplorable state in which we now find it.

There remains the natural world—which is just another name for the universe of which we are an integral part, conceived as one all-embracing system unfolding itself according to natural "laws"—to which we must orient ourselves, if we are to find dignity and significance in our lives. Some too-materialistic thinkers have held that man is of no more consequence to this system than an amoeba or a fly on a summer's day. I believe they were wrong. Consider some of humanity's greatest intellectual and artistic productions: the Greek tragedies, Plato's philosophy, Wordsworth's or Tennyson's poems, the great Renaissance masterpieces of painting, the imposing medieval cathedrals, Beethoven's symphonies, or what you will—would they have any value or significance at all if nobody ever heard or contemplated them with understanding and grateful appreciation, his life exalted and more meaningful by this experience?

So it is with the infinitely greater and more wonderful productions of the natural world, from the starry heavens to our planet with all its beautiful plants and animals, including those small creatures, such as the mosses and liverworts that incrust rocks and trunks, the protista that inhabit a drop of water, that we need a powerful microscope properly to see—would any of these things have any significance or value if they were not seen, appreciated, enjoyed, and at least partially understood? Doubtless every creature, however low in the scale of being, finds some satisfaction in its existence; but to man alone on this planet is it given, or so it appears, to survey the whole, in all its stupendous majesty, to find beauty throughout the natural world, and to strive to understand it all. Man is, on this planet, the organ wherewith the universe appreciates and tries to understand itself.

Since appreciation and understanding are necessary for the completion of the evolutionary process, to give it meaning, we may suppose that, from the beginning, the universe has been striving in this direction, gropingly and with many miscarriages to be sure, yet still with one unfolding purpose. Of late, astronomers have taken seriously the possibility that intelligent beings inhabit planets revolving around stars other than our sun, and they have even made sustained attempts to communicate with them by radio. We cannot imagine what these supposed beings look like or how they live, but we can hardly doubt that, as they come of age and discover meaning in their existence, they find this significance in the appreciative contemplation of the beauties of their planet and of the starry cosmos that surrounds it. Each planet must produce its own organs of appreciation.

Thus man, in the measure that he develops his powers of appreciation, love, understanding, and gratitude, imparts significance to the whole vast system of which he is a part, and in so doing he gives meaning and dignity to his own life. No one who understands this will ever agree with the Existentialists that human life is absurd; although, since in the end we must all take leave of that which we most love, he may conclude that life is tragic, which is a very different appraisal.

To feed and clothe and house ourselves and remain alive, we have destroyed stately trees and lovely flowers and driven beautiful animals of many kinds from their ancestral homes—this is our painful necessity. But to give our lives their highest significance, we must preserve as much as possible of the glories of the natural world, so that we may contemplate and enjoy them. To strike a proper balance between these two fundamental needs will require much wisdom and some long-term planning. Unfortunately, we shall never succeed in striking this balance unless we first learn to control our own numbers.

Puddling clay for the walls. Rocalpe's ears say plainly that he does not enjoy being led around and around in the clay pit.

The author's home since 1941.

The Red Poró (*Erythrina berteroana*). Leaf, flower buds, mature flowers, and a green pod.

The Itabo (*Yucca elephantipes*). To the little girl's left, an introduced cycad (*Cycas revoluta*).

The birds' table in a Guava tree. A Gray's Thrush is eating banana.

Golden-spray Orchids (*Oncidium* sp.).

White flowers of the orchid *Maxillaria ctenostachys*. It blooms beneath October's deluges.

The short-lived golden bloom of the vine *Davilla kunthii*.

A white-flowered Sobralia. All the plants bloom simultaneously at intervals of two or three weeks.

In the shady riverside pasture.

A Basilisk Lizard. Old males have higher crests along the back and tail.

The stilt roots of a Chonta Palm *Socratea durissima*. Instead of thickening, the slender base of the trunk decays, leaving the tall palm propped up on spiny stilts.

Pod and seed of the Giant Liana *Entada gigas*. The most aggressive vine in the forest.

Rain forest on the Caribbean foothills of Honduras.

Young Pejibaye Palms. Older plants form clumps from basal sprouts.

Edible fruits of the Pejibaye Palm. Delicious when freshly cooked; they sting the mouth when raw.

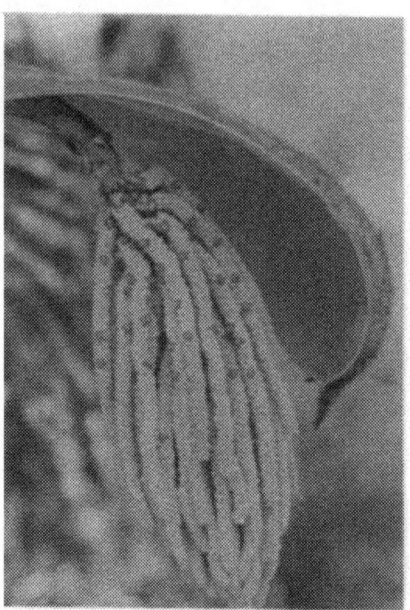

Open fruits of a large Clusia, from front and back. The thick valves expand like the petals of a flower, exposing many small seeds enclosed in bright red arils eagerly sought by birds.

An inflorescence of the Pejibaye Palm escaping from its spathe. The larger, darker female flowers are easily distinguished from the far more numerous buds of the male flowers.

Aguacatillo trees (*Persea skutchii*).

Tussacia friedrichsthaliana in flower. A perennial herb of the gesneria family with water-filled calyces.

A Wild Plantain (*Heliconia elongata*). The large, fleshy, water-holding primary bracts are pale red, light orange, and green.

The gnarled trunk of a Sotacaballo tree (*Pithecolobium longifolium*). In the midday heat, horses and cows seek its cool shade.

A nest of Spinning Ants. Many are visible as black dots on the silken fabric.

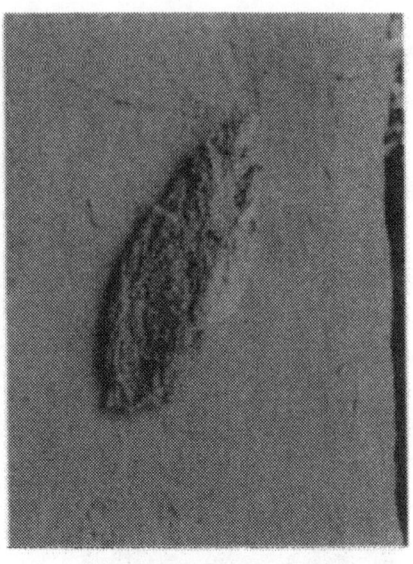

A nest of the Windowmaker Wasp (*Metapolybia aztecoides*). The thin paper envelope is full of tiny perforations closed with a transparent pellicle.

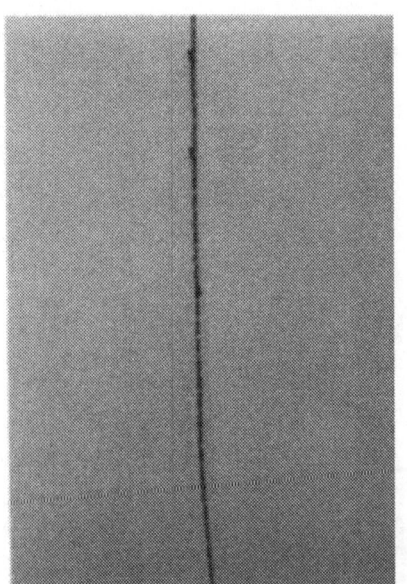

A stringlike wasps' nest. The tiny cells are built in single file.

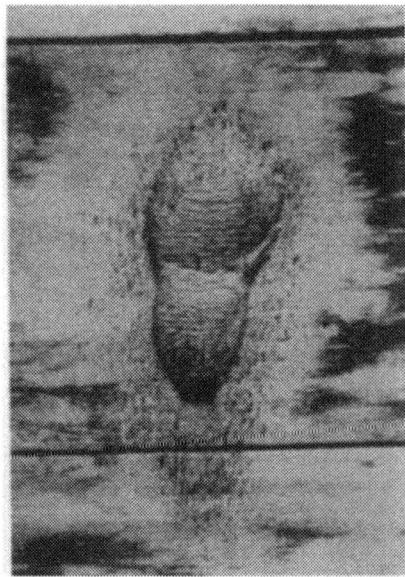

Home of the Sticky-nest Wasp (*Parachartergus championi*). The parchmentlike envelope and the wall surrounding it are densely studded with stalked, gum-covered bodies.

The Río Puerto Viejo at La Selva. Changes in level of fifteen or twenty feet are frequent.

Plank-buttresses of a Surá.

Entrance to a White-fronted Nunbird's burrow. The tunnel in the forest floor, about five feet long, leads to a chamber lined with dead leaves.

Surá trees (*Terminalia lucida*).

Appendix 1

Birds of Los Cusingos and the Valley of El General

This is an annotated list of the birds that I have identified, from 1941 to 1970, on the 100 hectares (247 acres) of Los Cusingos, 2,200 to 2,500 feet above sea level. To make this list more widely useful, I have added, between square brackets, the few species that I have, since 1935, seen in the Valley of El General but not on this farm. The area covered extends from the Río San Pedro on the east to approximately the 3,500-foot contour around the other sides of the basin, above which highland birds increasingly replace the tropical avifauna of the valley. All the birds listed here have been seen within the range of 2,000 to 3,500 feet above sea level.

An asterisk beside a species indicates that at least one of its nests has been found in El General, and two asterisks that a nest has been discovered within the boundaries of the farm. A dagger indicates a migrant that breeds in the North Temperate Zone, and a double dagger a "summer resident," that comes up from the south, or from lower altitudes in Costa Rica, to nest in the valley. Especially in the case of abundant migrants, the dates of arrival and departure in successive years tend to be clustered together, suggesting considerable year to year regularity in the migratory movements. For each migrant species, I have given the earliest of these clustered dates for arrival in the valley as a whole and the latest for departure, thereby indicating the interval when the species can be expected to be seen here. Unusual or isolated dates are given in parentheses.

The abundance of each species, in decreasing order, is roughly indicated by the adjectives "abundant," "common," and "rare."

In 29 years, 277 species of birds have been identified on Los Cusingos. Of these, 168 species might be classified as breeding residents, for they have been seen on the farm or in the vicinity at all seasons, and in most cases their nests have been found or they have been seen with dependent young; 6 species are summer residents; 51 species are migrants that nest in the North; and the remainder are of uncertain status or vagrants, chiefly from higher altitudes in Costa Rica. Nests of 133 species have been found on the farm. In the Valley of El General, as delimited above, I have identified 307 species and seen the nests of 157 species. In comparing these figures with those from other regions, it should be borne in mind that Los Cusingos has no aquatic habitat except a boulder-strewn mountain torrent, and the whole well-drained basin of El General contains only a few ponds and marshy areas of almost negligible size.

This list follows the classification of Eugene Eisenmann's *The Species of Middle American Birds* (Transactions of the Linnaean Society of New York, Vol. VII, 1955). In the few cases where I have used different names in my writings and still prefer them, I have given Eisenmann's names in parentheses.

Tinamous, Family Tinamidae

**Great Tinamou, *Tinamus major*. Terrestrial resident in forest, less common than formerly.

**Little Tinamou, *Crypturellus soui*. Common resident in low, dense vegetation outside forest.

Grebes, Family Colymbidae

[Least Grebe, *Colymbus dominicus*. Seen with young on small pond near Palmares.]

Cormorants, Family Phalacrocoracidae

Olivaceous Cormorant, *Phalacrocorax olivaceus*. Birds not in breeding plumage frequently rest singly or two together on rocks in rivers, except from March to mid-June.

Herons and Egrets, Family Ardeidae

†Great Blue Heron, *Ardea herodias*. Rare migrant. October 28–June 14.

[Green Heron, *Butorides virescens*. Rare; status uncertain.]
Little Blue Heron, *Florida caerulea*. Rare at Los Cusingos, more common in lower parts of valley; status uncertain.
Cattle Egret, *Bubulcus ibis*. First seen in the region in 1963; reached Los Cusingos in 1970.
Bare-throated Tiger-Heron, *Heterocnus mexicanus*. Rare vagrant.

American Vultures, Family Cathartidae

King Vulture, *Sarcoramphus papa*. Never abundant; not seen in recent years.
*Black Vulture, *Coragyps atratus*. Abundant resident.
Turkey Vulture, *Cathartes aura*. Common resident and rare spring migrant.

Hawks and Kites, Family Accipitridae

*‡Swallow-tailed Kite, *Elanoides forficatus*. Common summer resident. January 4–August 15.
Double-toothed Kite, *Harpagus bidentatus*. Rare; status uncertain.
[Plumbeous Kite, *Ictinia plumbea*. Seen once, February 15, 1942.]
Bicolored Hawk, *Accipiter bicolor*. Rare; status uncertain.
†Swainson's Hawk, *Buteo swainsoni*. Great, sky-spanning flocks pass overhead March 9–April 24; only one fall or winter record, 11 passed on December 4, 1963.
†Broad-winged Hawk, *Buteo platypterus*. Rare winter resident and abundant transient in spring. September 29–May 4.
Roadside Hawk, *Buteo magnirostris*. Rather rare resident in open country.
White Hawk, *Leucopternis albicollis*. Never common; not seen in recent years.
[Common Black Hawk, *Buteogallus anthracinus*. Rare; status uncertain.]
[Ornate Hawk-Eagle, *Spizaetus ornatus*. One seen June 16, 1939.]
Black Hawk-Eagle, *Spizaetus tyrannus*. Occasionally soars high overhead, calling melodiously.
†Marsh Hawk, *Circus cyaneus*. Rare migrant. February 7–May 2.

Ospreys, Family Pandionidae

†Osprey, *Pandion haliaetus*. Rare. September 14–April 16.

Falcons and Caracaras, Family Falconidae

*Laughing Falcon, *Herpetotheres cachinnans*. Formerly a common resident; a few remain.
Collared Forest-Falcon, *Micrastur semitorquatus*. Formerly rare; not noticed for years.
Barred Forest-Falcon, *Micrastur ruficollis*. The only hawk still resident in the forest at Los Cusingos.
Red-throated Caracara, *Daptrius americanus*. Never abundant, has disappeared from the valley.
Bat Falcon, *Falco albigularis*. Never abundant; not noticed recently.
†American Sparrow Hawk or American Kestrel, *Falco sparverius*. Formerly an abundant winter resident; has not been recorded at Los Cusingos since 1956. October 13–April 15; an immature female June 24–July 2, 1943.

Guans and Curassows, Family Cracidae

Great Curassow, *Crax rubra*. One seen January 19, 1947.
Crested Guan, *Penelope purpurascens*. Formerly a common resident in forest; has not been recorded since 1951.
**Chestnut-winged Chachalaca, *Ortalis garrula*. Persists in fair abundance in thickets with scattered trees, where not too severely persecuted.

Partridges and Pheasants, Family Phasianidae

**Marbled Wood-Quail, *Odontophorus gujanensis*. Formerly a common resident in forest and very tame; now exceedingly rare and shy.

Rails, Family Rallidae

Uniform Crake, *Amaurolimnas concolor*. One seen February 19, 1946.
**Gray-necked Wood-Rail, *Aramides cajanea*. A retiring resident in tall, moist thickets, avoiding heavy forest.
*White-throated Crake, *Laterallus albigularis*. Lurks in low, dense thickets.

Sunbitterns, Family Eurypygidae

*Sunbittern, *Eurypyga helias*. Formerly rare along streams; not recorded since 1954.

Plovers, Family Charadriidae

†[Killdeer, *Charadrius vociferus*. Rare migrant. December 16–April 18.]

Snipe, Sandpipers, and Allies, Family Scolopacidae

†[Solitary Sandpiper, *Tringa solitaria*. Rare spring transient. March 17–April 25, 1940.]
†Spotted Sandpiper, *Actitis macularia*. Common winter resident, along streams. August 1–May 23.
†[Common Snipe, *Capella gallinago*. Rare migrant.]

Pigeons and Doves, Family Columbidae

[Band-tailed Pigeon, *Columba fasciata*. Resident in highlands, rarely descending somewhat below 3,500 feet.]
**Scaled Pigeon, *Columba speciosa*. Common resident in forest and shady plantations.
**Short-billed Pigeon, *Columba nigrirostris*. Resident in forest, formerly more common.
[Mourning Dove, *Zenaidura macroura*. Rare; recorded in November, February, and March; status uncertain.]
**Ruddy Ground-Dove, *Columbigallina talpacoti*. Common resident in open and bushy country.
**Blue Ground-Dove, *Claravis pretiosa*. Common resident in open and bushy country.
**White-fronted Dove (White-tipped Dove), *Leptotila verreauxi*. Abundant resident in lightly shaded places.
**Rufous-naped Gray-chested Dove, *Leptotila cassinii rufinucha*. Abundant resident in woodland, taller thickets, and shady lawns.
**Ruddy Quail-Dove, *Geotrygon montana*. Common resident in forest.

Parrots, Family Psittacidae

Scarlet Macaw, *Ara macao*. Formerly conspicuous from June to January, not seen for many years.
Crimson-fronted Parakeet, *Aratinga finschi*. Rare vagrant.
Sulphur-winged Parakeet, *Pyrrhura hoffmanni*. Noisy flocks occasionally descend from higher altitudes.
Barred Parakeet, *Bolborhynchus lineola*. Large flocks occasionally descend from higher altitudes.
Orange-chinned Parakeet, *Brotogeris jugularis*. First noticed in the valley, at Los Cusingos, in 1965; now common through much of the year.
Brown-hooded Parrot, *Pionopsitta haematotis*. Common in forest and shady clearings.
**White-crowned Parrot, *Pionus senilis*. Common resident in clearings with scattered trees.
Red-lored Parrot, *Amazona autumnalis*. The great flocks that formerly came up the valley in the second half of the year (rarely as early as May) are now much reduced in size.

Cuckoos, Family Cuculidae

†Black-billed Cuckoo, *Coccyzus erythropthalmus*. Rare transient. April 4, 1948.

APPENDIX 1   347

**Squirrel Cuckoo, *Piaya cayana*. Common resident in shady plantations, thickets, and open parts of forest.
*Smooth-billed Ani, *Crotophaga ani*. An invader from Panama, first noticed in El General in 1940; now an abundant resident.
**Groove-billed Ani, *Crotophaga sulcirostris*. Although present sparingly in open country in El General at least as early as 1936, it has become much rarer than the preceding species.
Striped Cuckoo, *Tapera naevia*. Not found during my first decade in El General, this social parasite has become increasingly abundant; first seen at Los Cusingos in 1964.
Pheasant Cuckoo, *Dromococcyx phasianellus*. Seen at Los Cusingos only on May 14, 1946, and May 8, 1948; status uncertain.

Owls, Family Strigidae

Spectacled Owl, *Pulsatrix perspicillata*. In forest, rare.
Other owls have been heard but have never been seen by day and remain unidentified.

Potoos, Family Nyctibiidae

**Common Potoo, *Nyctibius griseus*. Rare; recorded by Underwood in El General in 1908, but neither heard nor seen in the valley by me until 1959; now resident.

Nightjars, Family Caprimulgidae

**Pauraque, *Nyctidromus albicollis*. Abundant resident in open and bushy places.

Swifts, Family Apodidae

White-collared Swift, *Streptoprocne zonaris*. Appears from time to time in large, noisy flocks.
Band-rumped Swift, *Chaetura spinicauda*. Occasional.
Lesser Swallow-tailed Swift, *Panyptila cayennensis*. Occasional.
Other swifts that circle high overhead have not been identified.

Hummingbirds, Family Trochilidae

**Bronzy Hermit, *Glaucis aenea*. Rare, first seen in July, 1967, when nesting.
**Band-tailed Barbthroat, *Threnetes ruckeri*. Rare to common resident in forest and lush secondary vegetation.
*Green Hermit, *Phaethornis guy*. Occasionally reaches Los Cusingos from higher altitudes.
**Long-tailed Hermit, *Phaethornis superciliosus*. Abundant resident, chiefly in forest.
**Little Hermit, *Phaethornis longuemareus*. Very abundant resident wherever it finds shade and flowers.
White-tipped Sicklebill, *Eutoxeres aquila*. Rare, chiefly among wild plantains (*Heliconia* sp.).
**Scaly-breasted Hummingbird, *Phaeochroa cuvierii*. Abundant resident in light, open woods, shady plantations, gardens, etc.
Violet Sabrewing, *Campylopterus hemileucurus*. Rare wanderer from higher altitudes.
White-necked Jacobin, *Florisuga mellivora*. Occurs sporadically at any season, sometimes abundant.
Brown Violet-ear, *Colibri delphinae*. Rare and sporadic.
[Green Violet-ear, *Colibri thalassinus*. Common in highlands, rarely descending to 3,000 feet.]
**Violet-headed Hummingbird, *Klais guimeti*. Common resident in woodland and flowery clearings.
**White-crested Coquette, *Paphosia adorabilis*. Sometimes common, it may disappear for long intervals.
**Blue-crowned Woodnymph, *Thalurania colombica*. Common resident in lower levels of forest, often visiting neighboring gardens.

**Blue-throated Goldentail, *Hylocharis eliciae*. Common resident, chiefly in light second-growth woods.

**Blue-chested Hummingbird, *Amazilia amabilis*. Chiefly in shady pastures and gardens. Sometimes common, like a number of other hummingbirds it disappears for long intervals.

**Snowy-breasted Hummingbird, *Amazilia edward*. Common resident of light, open woods, coffee plantations, shady roadsides, etc.

**Rufous-tailed Hummingbird, *Amazilia tzacatl*. Very abundant resident of deforested country and more open parts of forest.

White-tailed Emerald, *Elvira chionura*. Rare visitor from higher altitudes.

Green-crowned Brilliant, *Heliodoxa jacula*. Rare visitor from higher altitudes. A female and young male were present in the forest at Los Cusingos in late April and early May, 1948; an immature in the garden March 16, 1967.

*Purple-crowned Fairy, *Heliothrix barroti*. Common resident in semiopen country and gardens.

**Long-billed Starthroat, *Heliomaster longirostris*. Rare to common resident of semiopen country, gardens, and shady plantations.

†Ruby-throated Hummingbird, *Archilochus colubris*. Rare migrant. One seen February 25, 1945.

Trogons, Family Trogonidae

**Massena Trogon (Slaty-tailed Trogon), *Trogon massena*. Common resident in forest.

**White-tailed Trogon, *Trogon viridis*. Common resident in forest.

*[Collared Trogon (Bar-tailed Trogon), *Trogon collaris*. Common resident of forest from about 3,000 feet upward.]

**Black-throated Trogon, *Trogon rufus*. Common resident in lower levels of forest.

**Violaceous Trogon, *Trogon violaceus*. Common in upper levels of forest and clearings with scattered tall trees.

Kingfishers, Family Alcedinidae

Ringed Kingfisher, *Ceryle torquata*. Rare along the wider streams.

**Amazon Kingfisher, *Chloroceryle amazona*. Common resident along streams.

Green Kingfisher, *Chloroceryle americana*. Common resident along watercourses, including narrow woodland streams.

Motmots, Family Momotidae

**Blue-diademed Motmot (Blue-crowned Motmot), *Momotus momota*. Common resident in lighter woodland and semiopen country.

Jacamars, Family Galbulidae

**Rufous-tailed Jacamar, *Galbula ruficauda*. Formerly a fairly common resident in all types of woodland; now a rare visitor at Los Cusingos.

Puffbirds, Family Bucconidae

**White-whiskered Softwing (White-whiskered Puffbird), *Malacoptila panamensis*. Rare to common resident in forest.

Barbets, Family Capitonidae

Red-headed Barbet, *Eubucco bourcierii*. Visitor from higher altitudes, chiefly from October to March.

Toucans, Family Ramphastidae

Blue-throated Toucanet, *Aulacorhynchus caeruleogularis*. Visitor from higher altitudes, seen at Los Cusingos November 28, 1963.

*Fiery-billed Araçari, *Pteroglossus frantzii*. Formerly common; persists in reduced numbers in the shrinking forests.
Chestnut-mandibled Toucan, *Ramphastos swainsonii*. Formerly common resident in forests; has not been seen since 1962.

Woodpeckers, Family Picidae

**Olivaceous Piculet, *Picumnus olivaceus*. Common resident in light woodland and semiopen country.
Rufous-winged Woodpecker, *Piculus simplex*. A lowland species, first seen in El General, at Los Cusingos, June 6, 1950. Although rare, it now appears to be resident.
*Lineated Woodpecker, *Dryocopus lineatus*. Resident at forest's edge and among scattered trees; persists in reduced numbers.
[Acorn Woodpecker, *Melanerpes formicivorus*. Resident among oaks, chiefly above 3,000 feet.]
**Red-crowned Woodpecker, *Centurus rubricapillus*. Resident in semiopen country, the most abundant woodpecker.
**Golden-naped Woodpecker, *Tripsurus* (*Centurus*) *chrysauchen*. Common resident in forest and neighboring shady plantations.
†Yellow-bellied Sapsucker, *Sphyrapicus varius*. Winters chiefly above 3,000 feet. December 2–March 27; seen once at Los Cusingos, February 12, 1970.
Smoky-brown Woodpecker, *Veniliornis fumigatus*. Rare to common resident of forest and semiopen country.
**Pale-billed Woodpecker, *Phloeoceastes guatemalensis*. Resident in forest, formerly common but not seen recently.

Woodcreepers, Family Dendrocolaptidae

**Tawny-winged Dendrocincla (Tawny-winged Woodcreeper), *Dendrocincla anabatina*. Abundant in forest and neighboring shady plantations.
Ruddy Dendrocincla (Ruddy Woodcreeper), *Dendrocincla homochroa*. Rare to common in forest; status uncertain.
Long-tailed Woodcreeper, *Deconychura longicauda*. Rare in forest; status uncertain.
Olivaceous Woodcreeper, *Sittasomus griseicapillus*. Rare in forest at Los Cusingos, apparently a visitor from higher altitudes.
**Wedge-billed Woodcreeper, *Glyphorhynchus spirurus*. Common resident in forest.
Barred Woodcreeper, *Dendrocolaptes certhia*. In forest, rare.
[Black-banded Woodcreeper, *Dendrocolaptes picumnus*. Rare visitor to valley from higher slopes.]
Buff-throated Woodcreeper, *Xiphorhynchus guttatus*. Common resident in forest and neighboring lighter woods.
Black-striped Woodcreeper, *Xiphorhynchus lachrymosus*. Rare to common in forest.
Spotted Woodcreeper, *Xiphorhynchus erythropygius*. In forest, evidently a rare visitor from higher altitudes.
**Streaked-headed Woodcreeper, *Lepidocolaptes souleyetii*. Abundant resident in clearings with scattered trees and at forest's edge.
Brown-billed Scythebill, *Campylorhamphus pusillus*. In forest, formerly more common.

Ovenbirds and Allies, Family Furnariidae

**Slaty Castlebuilder (Slaty Spinetail), *Synallaxis brachyura*. Abundant resident in dense thickets.
[Pale-breasted Castlebuilder (Pale-breasted Spinetail), *Synallaxis albescens*. Long known in the middle of the Térraba Valley, it reached El General by 1969 and is now resident in bushy pastures adjoining Los Cusingos.]
**Buff-throated Automolus (Buff-throated Foliage-gleaner), *Automolus ochrolaemus*. Abundant resident in forest and taller second growth.

**Plain Xenops, *Xenops minutus*. Common resident in forest, taller second growth, and shady plantations.
**Scaly-throated Leaftosser (Scaly-throated Leafscraper), *Sclerurus guatemalensis*. Rare to common resident in forest.

Antbirds, Family Formicariidae
**Great Antshrike, *Taraba major*. In dense thickets, rare.
*Barred Antshrike, *Thamnophilus doliatus*. In thickets, rather rare, not seen recently at Los Cusingos.
**Black-hooded Antshrike, *Thamnophilus bridgesi*. Common resident in tall second growth and forest edge.
**Russet Antshrike, *Thamnistes anabatinus*. Rare to common resident in upper levels of forest.
**Plain Antvireo, *Dysithamnus mentalis*. Common resident in undergrowth of forest.
**Slaty Antwren, *Myrmotherula schisticolor*. Common resident in lower levels of forest.
**Velvety Antwren (Dot-winged Antwren), *Microrhopias quixensis*. It has increased over the years and is now an abundant resident in mid-levels of lighter forest and taller second growth.
**Tyrannine Antbird (Dusky Antbird), *Cercomacra tyrannina*. Common resident in tall, dense thickets and at forest edge.
Bare-crowned Antbird, *Gymnocichla nudiceps*. Rare to common resident in lush thickets.
**Chestnut-backed Antbird, *Myrmeciza exsul*. Common resident in luxuriant undergrowth of forest.
Immaculate Antbird, *Myrmeciza immaculata*. Rare visitor from higher altitudes; one seen at Los Cusingos September 6–21, 1958.
**Black-faced Antthrush, *Formicarius analis*. Common terrestrial resident in forest.
**Bicolored Antbird, *Gymnopithys leucaspis*. Common resident army ant follower in undergrowth of forest.
**Streaked-chested Antpitta, *Grallaria perspicillata*. Rare to common terrestrial resident in forest.

Manakins, Family Pipridae
**Blue-crowned Manakin, *Pipra coronata*. Abundant resident in lower levels of forest.
**Yellow-thighed Manakin (Red-capped Manakin), *Pipra mentalis*. Abundant resident in higher levels of forest.
White-ruffed Manakin, *Corapipo leucorrhoa*. Occurs sporadically in forest in any season, but seems to court and nest only at higher altitudes.
**Orange-collared Manakin, *Manacus aurantiacus*. Very abundant resident in tall, somewhat open thickets and at forest edge.
**Thrush-like Manakin, *Schiffornis turdinus*. Rare to common resident in forest undergrowth.

Cotingas, Family Cotingidae
**Turquoise Cotinga, *Cotinga ridgwayi*. Wanders widely; infrequently seen in treetops.
[Yellow-billed Cotinga, *Carpodectes antoniae*. Found only in Pacuar Valley in 1940.]
Bright-rumped Attila, *Attila spadiceus*. Rare resident in forest and neighboring shady plantations.
Rufous Mourner, *Rhytipterna holerythra*. Elusive resident in upper levels of forest.
**Rufous Piha, *Lipaugus unirufus*. The most abundant bird of its size, or larger, in the forest, where it usually remains high.
**White-winged Becard, *Pachyramphus polychopterus*. Common resident in clearings with scattered trees.

**Masked Tityra, *Tityra semifasciata*. Abundant resident in forest and clearings with scattered trees.
**Black-crowned Tityra, *Tityra inquisitor*. Rare to common resident in forest and clearings with scattered trees.
Three-wattled Bellbird, *Procnias tricarunculata*. Heard at Los Cusingos, calling loudly in forest treetops in every month, but not present throughout any year. Apparently it nests only at higher altitudes.

American or Tyrant Flycatchers, Family Tyrannidae

Black Phoebe, *Sayornis nigricans*. Rare vagrant along rivers.
[Fork-tailed Flycatcher, *Muscivora tyrannus*. Seen only at Los Chiles in February, 1955.]
†Eastern Kingbird, *Tyrannus tyrannus*. Transient in small or large flocks, chiefly in spring. April 6–May 15 and September 18–30.
**Tropical Kingbird, *Tyrannus melancholicus*. Abundant resident in open country.
**†Piratic Flycatcher, *Legatus leucophaius*. Abundant summer resident in open and semiopen country. January 20–October 12.
†Sulphur-bellied Flycatcher, *Myiodynastes luteiventris*. Rare transient in spring, breeding at higher altitudes in Costa Rica as well as farther north. March 13–May 11.
*†Streaked Flycatcher, *Myiodynastes maculatus*. Common summer resident in open and semiopen areas in lower parts of valley. (January 24) February 9–September 24.
**Boat-billed Flycatcher, *Megarhynchus pitangua*. Common resident in open country with scattered trees, often seen at top of forest.
**Vermilion-crowned Flycatcher (Social Flycatcher), *Myiozetetes similis*. Abundant resident in open country with scattered trees.
**Gray-capped Flycatcher, *Myiozetetes granadensis*. Abundant resident in open country with scattered trees.
†Great-crested Flycatcher, *Myiarchus crinitus*. Rare transient. November 6–9, 1942.
Brown-crested Flycatcher? *Myiarchus* (*tyrannulus*?). Rare visitor in dry season.
**Dusky-capped Flycatcher, *Myiarchus tuberculifer*. Common resident in light woods and semiopen country.
†Olive-sided Flycatcher, *Nuttallornis borealis*. Rather rare migrant, chiefly August 24–September 31 and March 15–May 18, with few midwinter records, mostly from upper edge of valley.
†Eastern Wood-Pewee, *Contopus virens*. See following species.
†Western Wood-Pewee, *Contopus richardsonii*. Both pewees have been identified by their voices, but when silent they are difficult to distinguish. They are common spring and fall transients. July 24–November 16 and April 14–May 19.
†Yellow-bellied Flycatcher, *Empidonax flaviventris*. Abundant winter resident in clearings and open woods. August 31–May 25.
**Ruddy-tailed Flycatcher, *Terenotriccus erythrurus*. Rare resident in woodland.
**Sulphur-rumped Flycatcher, *Myiobius sulphureipygius*. Abundant resident in woodland.
*Black-tailed Flycatcher, *Myiobius atricaudus*. Rare resident in thickets.
*Bran-colored Flycatcher, *Myiophobus fasciatus*. Rare visitor at Los Cusingos; abundant resident in bushy pastures at Rivas in 1936–37.
**Northern Royal Flycatcher, *Onychorhynchus coronatus*. Formerly common resident along shady streams in lower part of valley, rare at higher altitudes.
**Golden-crowned Spadebill, *Platyrinchus coronatus*. Common resident in lower levels of forest.
**Sulphury Flatbill (Yellow-olive Flycatcher), *Tolmomyias sulphurescens*. Abundant resident in open country with scattered trees and forest edge.
**Eye-ringed Flatbill, *Rhynchocyclus brevirostris*. Abundant resident in woodland.

**Black-fronted Tody-Flycatcher (Common Tody-Flycatcher), *Todirostrum cinereum*. Abundant resident in gardens, shady plantations, roadsides, etc.
**Slate-headed Tody-Flycatcher, *Todirostrum sylvia*. Common resident in dense thickets.
*Northern Bentbill, *Oncostoma cinereigulare*. Common resident in tall thickets and woodland edge.
Scaly-crested Pygmy-Flycatcher (Scale-crested Pygmy-Tyrant), *Lophotriccus pileatus*. Rare at Los Cusingos, more abundant upward, in forest.
**Yellow Flycatcher (Yellow Tyrannulet), *Capsiempis flaveola*. Common resident in scrubby fields.
**Torrent Flycatcher (Torrent Tyrannulet), *Serpophaga cinerea*. Common resident along mountain torrents.
**Yellow-bellied Elaenia, *Elaenia flavogaster*. Abundant resident in open country.
**†Bellicose Elaenia (Lesser Elaenia), *Elaenia chiriquensis*. Common summer resident in scrubby growth. November 21/January 16–September 3.
Greenish Elaenia, *Myiopagis viridicata*. Rare resident in woodland and neighboring shady plantations.
**Southern Beardless Flycatcher (Southern Beardless Tyrannulet), *Camptostoma obsoletum*. Common resident in light woodland and open places with scattered trees; has increased over the years.
**Paltry Tyranniscus (Paltry Tyrannulet), *Tyranniscus vilissimus*. Abundant resident in shady plantations and pastures.
*Slaty-capped Flycatcher, *Leptopogon superciliaris*. Rare visitor at Los Cusingos, more common at higher altitudes.
**Oleaginous Pipromorpha (Ochre-bellied Flycatcher), *Pipromorpha oleaginea*. Abundant resident in forest and taller second growth, entering gardens and shady plantations.

Swallows, Family Hirundinidae

**Gray-breasted Martin, *Progne chalybea*. Common resident in open country, many roosting on overhead wires in the center of San Isidro.
†Cliff Swallow, *Petrochelidon pyrrhonota*. Abundant transient in spring. March 30–May 21.
†Barn Swallow, *Hirundo rustica*. Abundant transient in fall and spring. September 4–November 25 and March 15–May 29; rarely seen in December and February.
**Rough-winged Swallow, *Stelgidopteryx ruficollis*. Abundant resident in open country.
**Blue-and-white Swallow, *Pygochelidon cyanoleuca*. Occurs sporadically; more abundant at higher altitudes.
†Bank Swallow, *Riparia riparia*. Transient in spring, migrating by day with Barn and Cliff Swallows, but less abundant. April 14–May 11.
Mangrove Swallow, *Iridoprocne albilinea*. Rare resident on broader rivers in lower parts of El General.

Dippers, Family Cinclidae

American Dipper, *Cinclus mexicanus*. Rare visitor, descending rivers from higher altitudes.

Wrens, Family Troglodytidae

**Chinchirigüí Wren (Plain Wren), *Thryothorus modestus*. Common resident in densely weedy fields.
**Riverside Wren, *Thryothorus semibadius*. Abundant resident in dense streamside vegetation and forest edge.
**Rufous-breasted Wren, *Thryothorus rutilus*. Abundant resident in tall, dense thickets, woodland edges, and shady gardens.

APPENDIX 1

**Southern House-Wren, *Troglodytes musculus*. Abundant resident in dooryards, clearings with stumps, and plantations.
**Lowland Wood-Wren (White-breasted Wood-Wren), *Henicorhina leucosticta*. Abundant resident in forest undergrowth.
Nightingale Wren, *Microcerculus philomela*. Common terrestrial resident in forest.

Thrushes, Family Turdidae
**White-throated Thrush (White-throated Robin), *Turdus assimilis*. First seen at Los Cusingos in 1947, it has increased in the forest. In other parts of the valley, it was present in 1936 and nested in shady plantations and thickets.
**Gray's Thrush (Clay-colored Robin), *Turdus grayi*. Very abundant in all cleared lands; enters forest to forage.
Black-faced Solitaire, *Myadestes melanops*. Rare visitor from higher altitudes, chiefly November–February.
†Wood Thrush, *Hylocichla mustelina*. Rare transient. November 29, 1969.
†Swainson's or Olive-backed Thrush, *Hylocichla ustulata*. Rare in autumn and winter, it becomes exceedingly abundant and songful everywhere during the spring migration. October 8–May 17.
†Gray-cheeked Thrush, *Hylocichla minima*. Rare transient. April 2–30.
**Orange-billed Nightingale-Thrush, *Catharus aurantiirostris*. A retiring resident in dense thickets that has increased greatly at Los Cusingos since 1941. Abundant at Rivas in 1936–37.

Kinglets, Gnatcatchers, and Old World Warblers, Family Sylviidae
**Tropical Gnatcatcher, *Polioptila plumbea*. Common resident in upper levels of woodland and scattered trees.
*Long-billed Gnatwren, *Ramphocaenus rufiventris*. Common resident in lower levels of woodland.

Waxwings, Family Bombycillidae
†[Cedar Waxwing, *Bombycilla cedrorum*. Occasional in small flocks in late winter and spring. February 23–May 7.]

Peppershrikes, Family Cyclarhidae
Rufous-browed Peppershrike, *Cyclarhis gujanensis*. Rare visitor at Los Cusingos from above 3,000 feet.

Shrike-Vireos, Family Vireolaniidae
Green Shrike-Vireo, *Smaragdolanius pulchellus*. Common (to judge by voice) in forest treetops.

Vireos, Family Vireonidae
†Yellow-throated Vireo, *Vireo flavifrons*. Abundant winter resident in upper levels of forest and shady plantations and gardens. October 12–April 24.
†Red-eyed Vireo, *Vireo olivaceus*. Common to abundant transient in spring and autumn. (September 3) September 12–October 18 (November 10) and March 31–May 17 (May 28).
**†Yellow-green Vireo, *Vireo flavoviridis*. Abundant summer resident among scattered trees. January 25–September 15.
†Philadelphia Vireo, *Vireo philadelphicus*. Common (in some years abundant) winter resident among scattered trees, arriving late. December 10–April 30 (May 12).
*Scrub Greenlet, *Hylophilus flavipes*. Rare, in open country.
**Tawny-crowned Greenlet, *Hylophilus ochraceiceps*. Common resident in lower levels of forest.
**Gray-headed Greenlet, *Hylophilus decurtatus*. Abundant resident of tree crowns everywhere.

Honeycreepers, Family Coerebidae

**Green Honeycreeper, *Chlorophanes spiza*. Abundant resident in forest, shady plantations, and gardens.

**Blue Honeycreeper (Red-legged Honeycreeper), *Cyanerpes cyaneus*. Abundant in shady plantations and gardens and upper levels of forest; a wanderer of somewhat sporadic occurrence.

**Shining Honeycreeper, *Cyanerpes lucidus*. Formerly rare, now an abundant resident in forest and neighboring shady gardens.

**Turquoise Dacnis (Blue Dacnis), *Dacnis cayana*. Rare to common resident in forest and shady gardens.

*Scarlet-thighed Dacnis, *Dacnis venusta*. Nests in higher parts of valley and at long intervals descends to Los Cusingos, sometimes abundantly.

**Bananaquit, *Coereba flaveola*. Very abundant resident among trees and tall shrubs outside forest.

Wood Warblers, Family Parulidae

†Black-and-white Warbler, *Mniotilta varia*. Rare to common winter resident. (August 17) September 9–April 6 (April 18).

†Worm-eating Warbler, *Helmintheros vermivorus*. Rare winter resident. October 16–March 19.

†Golden-winged Warbler, *Vermivora chrysoptera*. Fairly common winter resident. October 6–April 16.

†Tennessee Warbler, *Vermivora peregrina*. Very abundant winter resident in forest and shady plantations. September 27–May 1.

[Tropical Parula, *Parula pitiayumi*. Resident in forest in higher parts of valley.]

†Yellow Warbler, *Dendroica aestiva*. Winter resident in clearings, rare at Los Cusingos, more abundant in other parts of valley. September 8–May 7.

†Myrtle Warbler, *Dendroica coronata*. Winter resident in open fields and pastures, not noticed in most years. December 11–March 28.

†Black-throated Green Warbler, *Dendroica virens*. Winter resident in highlands, below 3,000 feet seen rarely, chiefly while migrating. October 21–April 2.

†Blackburnian Warbler, *Dendroica fusca*. Fairly common winter resident in shady plantations and upper levels of forest. September 10–April 25.

†Chestnut-sided Warbler, *Dendroica pensylvanica*. Very abundant winter resident in forest and shady plantations. (September 15) September 22–April 30.

†Ovenbird, *Seiurus aurocapillus*. Rather rare winter resident, on ground beneath taller and more open second growth. October 23–April 28 (May 14).

†Northern Waterthrush, *Seiurus noveboracensis*. Rather rare winter resident along streams. September 15–May 5.

†Louisiana Waterthrush, *Seiurus motacilla*. Rare migrant. (September 7) September 17–March 23.

†Kentucky Warbler, *Oporornis formosus*. Common winter resident in forest undergrowth. (September 15) September 22–April 19.

†Mourning Warbler, *Oporornis philadelphia*. Abundant winter resident in low, dense vegetation outside forest. September 21–May 14.

†MacGillivray's Warbler, *Oporornis tolmiei*. Rare transient in spring. April 21–May 4.

†[Common Yellowthroat, *Geothlypis trichas*. One male, May 2, 1940.]

[Gray-crowned Yellowthroat, *Chamaethlypis poliocephala*. Resident in weedy pastures adjoining Los Cusingos.]

†Pileolated or Black-capped Warbler, *Wilsonia pusilla*. Winter resident in bushy places, abundant at higher altitudes, rare at Los Cusingos. September 18–April 24.

†Canada Warbler, *Wilsonia canadensis*. Mainly a transient, more common in fall than spring, very rare winter resident. September 16–October 21 (November 25) and April 24–29; one immature in January.

†American Redstart, *Setophaga ruticilla*. Rare to common winter resident. August 23–April 6 (April 18).

[Golden-crowned Warbler, *Basileuterus culicivorus*. Resident in forest undergrowth from about 3,000 feet upward.]
**Chestnut-capped Warbler, *Basileuterus delattrii*. Rare to common resident in tall thickets and light woods.
**Buff-rumped Warbler, *Basileuterus fulvicauda*. Common terrestrial resident along watercourses, thence venturing to shady pastures, lawns, and along woodland roads.

American Orioles and Blackbirds, Family Icteridae
*Chisel-billed Cacique (Yellow-billed Cacique), *Amblycercus holosericeus*. Common resident in the densest thickets.
[Bronzed or Red-eyed Cowbird, *Tangavius aeneus*. Very rare; first seen in 1962.]
†Orchard Oriole, *Icterus spurius*. Rare migrant. November 2–April 10.
†Baltimore Oriole, *Icterus galbula*. Abundant winter resident in forest treetops and shady clearings. (September 10) September 26–April 28 (May 11).

Family Uncertain
*Queo (Rose-breasted Thrush-Tanager), *Rhodinocichla rosea*. Present at Rivas in 1936 but not noticed at Los Cusingos until 1959; since then resident in the densest thickets.

Tanagers, Family Thraupidae
Blue-hooded Euphonia, *Euphonia elegantissima*. A highland bird, descending to Los Cusingos in some dry seasons to eat mistletoe berries.
**White-vented Euphonia, *Euphonia minuta*. Rare to common in forest treetops and shady clearings. Like other euphonias, it appears to wander widely and may be absent for months.
**Yellow-crowned Euphonia, *Euphonia luteicapilla*. A wanderer, most often seen in deforested country.
**Tawny-bellied Euphonia (Spot-crowned Euphonia), *Euphonia imitans*. Common resident in forest, shady plantations, and gardens.
**Speckled Tanager, *Tangara chrysophrys*. Common resident in upper levels of forest, shady clearings, and gardens.
**Silver-throated Tanager, *Tanagra icterocephala*. Abundant resident in upper levels of forest, shady clearings, and gardens.
**Golden-masked Tanager, *Tanagra larvata*. Abundant resident in upper levels of forest, shady clearings, and gardens.
**Bay-headed Tanager, *Tanagra gyrola*. Abundant resident in upper levels of forest, shady clearings, and gardens.
**Blue Tanager (Blue-gray Tanager), *Thraupis episcopus*. Abundant resident wherever trees grow outside forest.
**Palm Tanager, *Thraupis palmarum*. Much less abundant than the preceding species; resident especially where palms grow outside forest.
**Scarlet-rumped Black Tanager, *Ramphocelus passerinii*. Very abundant in thickets, plantations, and gardens.
†Summer Tanager, *Piranga rubra*. Common to abundant winter resident in upper levels of forest, shady clearings, and gardens. September 26–April 18.
†Scarlet Tanager, *Piranga olivacea*. Rare spring transient. March 29–April 30.
[White-winged Tanager, *Piranga leucoptera*. Resident in forest above 3,000 feet.]
**Red-crowned Ant-Tanager, *Habia rubica*. Common resident in lower levels of forest.
[White-throated Shrike-Tanager, *Lanio leucothorax*. Seen only in forest on outer side of valley, at base of coastal range, at 2,500 feet.]
White-shouldered Tanager, *Tachyphonus luctuosus*. Occasional in upper levels of forest at Los Cusingos; status uncertain.
**Gray-headed Tanager, *Eucometis penicillata*. Common resident army ant follower in lower levels of forest and neighboring shady plantations.

Finches, Grosbeaks, and Buntings, Family Fringillidae
**Buff-throated Saltator, *Saltator maximus*. Very abundant resident in bushy clearings, shady plantations, and more open parts of forest.
**Streaked Saltator, *Saltator albicollis*. Abundant resident in bushy clearings and plantations.
†Rose-breasted Grosbeak, *Pheucticus ludovicianus*. Rare to common winter resident, outside forest. October 16–April 15.
**Blue-black Grosbeak, *Cyanocompsa cyanoides*. Common resident in lower levels of forest, maize fields, and shady plantations.
†Indigo Bunting, *Passerina cyanea*. Rare to common winter resident in coffee plantations and bushy places. November 9–April 16.
†[Painted Bunting, *Passerina ciris*. Rare migrant, not seen since 1946. January 21–March 13.]
**Yellow-faced Grassquit, *Tiaris olivacea*. Abundant resident in grassy places, gardens, and roadsides.
†Dickcissel, *Spiza americana*. Winter resident, more abundant formerly when more rice was grown in El General. September 8–April 23.
Slate-colored Seedeater, *Sporophila schistacea*. Rare; not seen recently.
**Variable Seedeater, *Sporophila aurita*. Very abundant resident in grassy places.
[White-collared Seedeater, *Sporophila torqueola*. Long resident at lower altitudes on the Pacific side of southern Costa Rica, it has recently been found in lower parts of El General, where it is much rarer than the preceding species.]
Yellow-bellied Seedeater, *Sporophila nigricollis*. Rare to common in grassy places, possibly a summer resident.
**†Thick-billed Seed-Finch, *Oryzoborus funereus*. Rare to moderate in grassy and bushy areas, recorded at Los Cusingos only from March 30 to November 3; possibly comes up from lower altitudes to nest.
*Blue-black Grassquit, *Volatinia jacarina*. Common resident in open fields.
*[Lesser or Dark-backed Goldfinch, *Spinus psaltria*. A wanderer, chiefly in bushy places above 3,000 feet.]
**Gray-striped Brush-Finch, *Atlapetes assimilis*. Common resident in tall, lush thickets and at forest edge.
**Orange-billed Sparrow, *Arremon aurantiirostris*. Abundant terrestrial resident in forest, now adapting itself to heavier second growth.
**Black-striped Sparrow (Green-backed Sparrow), *Arremonops conirostris*. Abundant resident in thickets, plantations, bushy pastures, and gardens.
[Rufous-collared Sparrow, *Zonotrichia capensis*. Rare vagrant from higher altitudes.]

Additions since 1970

Magnificent Frigatebird, *Fregata magnificens*. Rare wanderer. One, October 23, 1973.
[Black-shouldered (White-tailed) Kite, *Elanus caeruleus*. Rare. December 1978.]
Gray-headed Kite, *Leptodon cayanensis*. Rare. November 6, 1979.
Short-tailed Hawk, *Buteo brachyurus*. Rare. February 12, 1986, April 1, 1987.
Crested Caracara, *Polyborus plancus*. First seen April 15, 1982. Rare.
Yellow-headed Caracara, *Milvago chimachima*. Occasional since March 31, 1984; probably breeds.
†Yellow-billed Cuckoo, *Coccyzus americanus*. Rare transient. May 10, 1976.
Vermiculated Screech-Owl, *Otus guatemalae*. Rare. March 22, 1980.
†Chuck-will's-widow, *Caprimulgus carolinensis*. Rare transient. March 14, 1982.
Chestnut-collared Swift, *Cypseloides rutilus*. Occasional.
Fiery-throated Hummingbird, *Panterpe insignis*. Rare straggler from high altitudes. May 1977.
[Fork-tailed Emerald, *Chlorostilbon canivetii*. At lower altitudes since April 1973.]
[Great-tailed Grackle, *Quiscalus mexicanus*. Appeared in San Isidro in 1978, now abundant there; has not visited Los Cusingos.]

APPENDIX 1

Rose-throated Becard, *Pachyramphus aglaiae*. Rare straggler from farther north. April 1988.
[Great Kiskadee, *Pitangus sulphuratus*. Appeared in San Isidro in January 1979; not seen recently.]
Nutting's (Pale-throated) Flycatcher, *Myiarchus nuttingi*. Rare straggler from farther north. April 30, 1975.
Yellow-bellied Tyrannulet, *Ornithion semiflavum*. Rare straggler from lower altitudes. June 10, 1973.
Brown Jay, *Psilorhinus morio*. One, December 7, 1974.
†Gray Catbird, *Dumetella carolinensis*. One, April 20, 1976.
†Prothonotary Warbler, *Protonotaria citrea*. One or two, October 22, 1976.
†Bay-breasted Warbler, *Dendroica castanea*. Rare; first seen April 15, 1976.
†Hooded Warbler, *Wilsonia citrina*. One, March 30, 1973.
[Great-tailed Grackle, *Quiscalus mexicanus*. Appeared in San Isidro around 1970 and now abundant there; has not visited Los Cusingos.]
[Eastern Meadowlark, *Sturnella magna*. First seen in El General June 8, 1979.]
[House Sparrow, *Passer domesticus*. Established in San Isidro since about 1975.]

These additions bring the number of species recorded by the author at Los Cusingos to 295 and in the Valley of El General to 331.

Additional Nest Records for Los Cusingos

Black Vulture, *Coragyps atratus*
Laughing Falcon, *Herpetotheres cachinnans*
Orange-chinned Parakeet, *Brotogeris jugularis*
Lesser Swallow-tailed Swift, *Panyptila cayennensis*
Rufous-winged Woodpecker, *Piculus simplex*
Lineated Woodpecker, *Dryocopus lineatus*
Ruddy Dendrocincla (Ruddy Woodcreeper), *Dendrocincla homochroa*
Buff-throated Woodcreeper, *Xiphorhynchus guttatus*
Bright-rumped Attila, *Attila spadiceus*
Black-tailed Flycatcher, *Myiobius atricaudus*
Northern Bentbill, *Oncostoma cinereigulare*
Greenish Elaenia, *Myiopagis viridicata*
Long-billed Gnatwren, *Ramphocaenus melanurus* (formerly *rufiventris*)

These additions bring the number of species found nesting at Los Cusingos to 146.

Appendix 2

The Author's Published Writings

Books

1954. *Life Histories of Central American Birds*. With drawings by Don R. Eckelberry. Cooper Ornithological Society, Pacific Coast Avifauna, No. 31. 448 pp.
1956. *The Quest of the Divine*. Meador Publishing Company, Boston. 440 pp.
1960. *Life Histories of Central American Birds II*. With drawings by Don R. Eckelberry. Cooper Ornithological Society, Pacific Coast Avifauna, No. 34. 593 pp.
1967. *Life Histories of Central American Highland Birds*. Publications of the Nuttall Ornithological Club, No. 7. 213 pp.
1969. *Life Histories of Central American Birds III*. Cooper Ornithological Society, Pacific Coast Avifauna, No. 35. 580 pp.
1970. *The Golden Core of Religion*. George Allen and Unwin, London. 270 pp.

Articles*

1926. On the Habits and Ecology of the Tube-building Amphipod *Amphithöe rubricata* Montagu. Ecology 7:481–502.

*All references to *Nature* allude to *Nature Magazine*, now defunct.

1927. Anatomy of Leaf of Banana, *Musa sapientum* L. Botan. Gaz. 84:337–91.
1927. Peculiarities in the Structure of the Stem, Related to the Leaf-sheath, in *Hedyosmum*. Ann. Botany (London) 41:715–30.
1928. The Spinning Crustacean. Nature 12:103–5.
1928. Plant of Paradoxes. Nature 12:311–14.
1928. The Capture of Prey by the Bladderwort. New Phytologist 27:261–97.
1928. The Secret of the Bladderwort. Sci. Am., Dec. pp. 498–501.
1928. (With Duncan S. Johnson) Littoral Vegetation on a Headland of Mt. Desert Island, Maine. Ecology 9:188–215, 307–38, 429–48.
1928. (With Robert L. Burwell, Jr.) The Period of Anthesis in Hibiscus. Torreya 28:1–4.
1929. Early Stages of Plant Succession Following Forest Fires. Ecology 10:177–90.
1930. Unrolling of Leaves of *Musa sapientum* and Some Related Plants and their Reactions to Environmental Aridity. Botan. Gaz. 90:337–65.
1930. On the Development and Morphology of the Leaf of the Banana (*Musa sapientum* L.). Am. J. Botany 17:252–71.
1930. Repeated Fission of Stem and Root in *Mertensia maritima*—a Study in Ecological Anatomy. Ann. N.Y. Acad. Sci. 32:1–52, pls. I–IX.
1930. The Habits and Nesting Activities of the Northern Tody Flycatcher in Panama. Auk 47:313–22.
1931. Some Reactions of the Banana to Pressure, Gravity, and Darkness. Plant Physiology 6:73–102.
1931. The Life History of Rieffer's Hummingbird (*Amazilia tzacatl tzacatl*) in Panama and Honduras. Auk 48:481–500.
1932. The Pollination of the Palm *Archontophoenix Cunninghamii*. Torreya 32:29–37.
1932. Observations on the Flower Behavior of the Avocado in Panama. Torreya 32:85–94.
1932. Anatomy of the Axis of the Banana. Botan. Gaz. 93:233–58.
1933. The Aquatic Flowers of a Terrestrial Plant, *Heliconia bihai* L. Am. J. Botany 20:535–44.
1934. A Nesting of the Slaty Antshrike (*Thamnophilus punctatus*) on Barro Colorado Island. Auk 51:8–16.
1934. Familiar Birds in their Winter Homes. Bird-Lore 36:3–7.
1935. Helpers at the Nest. Auk 52:257–73.
1937. Life-history of the Black-chinned Jacamar. Auk 54:135–46.
1937. The Male Flicker's Part in Incubation. Bird-Lore 39:112–14.
1940. Social and Sleeping Habits of Central American Wrens. Auk 57:293–312.
1940. Some Aspects of Central American Bird-Life. Sci. Monthly 51:409–18, 500–511.
1940. Articles on Rieffer's Hummingbird and White-eared Hummingbird, notes on Smooth-billed Ani, Groove-billed Ani, Ringed Kingfisher, Texas Kingfisher, Merrill's Pauraque, Broad-tailed Hummingbird, and Heloise's Hummingbird, in *Life Histories of North American Cuckoos, Goatsuckers, Hummingbirds and their Allies*, by Arthur Cleveland Bent. Bull. U.S. Natl. Mus. 176.
1941. The Natural Resources of Costa Rica. Chronica Botanica, 6:399–402. Reprinted in *Plants and Plant Science in Latin America*, edited by Franz Verdoorn, pp. 281–84. Chronica Botanica, Waltham, Mass., 1945.
1942. Life History of the Mexican Trogon. Auk 59:341–63.
1942. Notes on Xanthus' Becard, Fork-tailed Flycatcher, Scissor-tailed Flycatcher, Arizona Sulphur-bellied Flycatcher, Rough-winged Swallow, etc. in *Life Histories of North American Flycatchers, Larks, Swallows and their Allies*, by Arthur Cleveland Bent. Bull. U.S. Natl. Mus. 179.
1943. The Family Life of Central American Woodpeckers. Sci. Monthly 56:358–64.
1944. The Life History of the Prong-billed Barbet. Auk 61:61–88.
1944. A Parable for Peacemakers. Sci. Monthly 58:253–60.

1944. Life History of the Blue-throated Toucanet. Wilson Bull. 56:133–51.
1944. Life History of the Quetzal. Condor 46:213–35.
1944. The Root of the Evil. Nature 37:466–68.
1945. The Most Hospitable Tree. Sci. Monthly 60:5–17.
1945. Incubation and Nestling Periods of Central American Birds. Auk 62:8–37.
1945. A Village in the Tree-top. Nature 38:125–28, 162.
1945. The Magnificent Quetzal. Nature 38:299–302, 330–31.
1945. Life History of the Allied Woodhewer. Condor 47:85–94.
1945. On the Habits and Nest of the Antthrush *Formicarius analis*. Wilson Bull. 57:122–28.
1945. The Naturalist's Dilemma. Sci. Monthly 61:361–71.
1945. Studies of Central American Redstarts. Wilson Bull. 57:217–42.
1945. Life History of the Blue-throated Green Motmot. Auk 62:489–517.
1945. A Natural Water-garden. Nature 38:404.
1945. Fern Collecting in Southern Costa Rica. Am. Fern J. 35:41–48.
1945. Born and Bred on Bananas. Nature 38:429–30.
1945. Tendrils. Nature 38:487–88.
1945. The Migration of Swainson's and Broad-winged Hawks through Costa Rica. Northwest Sci. 19:80–89.
1945. The Behavior of the Flowers of the Aguacatillo (*Persea caerulea*). Torreya 45:110–16.
1946. Ferns in Birds' Nests. Am. Fern J. 36:14–17.
1946. Life Histories of Two Panamanian Antbirds. Condor 48:16–28.
1946. Palm Forests. Nature 39:135–36.
1946. The Parental Devotion of Birds. Sci. Monthly 62:364–74.
1946. Life History of the Costa Rican Tityra. Auk 63:327–62.
1946. Back—or Forward—to Nature? Nature 39:457–60.
1946. The Catbird—at Home and Abroad. Fauna (Zool. Soc. Philadelphia) 8:87–89.
1946. The Hummingbirds' Brook. Sci. Monthly 63:447–57.
1946. A Compound Leaf with Annual Increments of Growth. Bull. Torrey Botan. Club 73:542–46.
1947. A Nesting of the Plumbeous Kite in Ecuador. Condor 49:25–31.
1947. The Castlebuilder. Nature 40:69–72, 106.
1947. A Nest of the Sun-bittern in Costa Rica. Wilson Bull. 59:38.
1947. Life History of the Turquoise-browed Motmot. Auk 64:201–17.
1947. The Balsa Tree. Nature 40:377–78.
1947. Life History of the Marbled Wood-Quail. Condor 49:217–32.
1947. Adventures with Sloths. Nature 40:521–24, 552.
1947. Life History of the Quetzal. Smithsonian Inst. Annual Report for 1946:265–93, pls. 1–4. (Reprinted from Condor, 1944.)
1948. Plants from Leaves. Nature 41:149–52, 164.
1948. In Fairness to Our Competitors. Audubon 50:76–79.
1948. Life History of the Golden-naped Woodpecker. Auk 65:225–60.
1948. Life's Greatest Evil. Sci. Monthly 66:514–18.
1948. Life History Notes on Puff-birds. Wilson Bull. 60:81–97.
1948. Anting by Some Costa Rican Birds. Wilson Bull. 60:115–16.
1948. A Naturalist Looks at Sin and Redemption. Aryan Path (Bombay, India) 19:248–52.
1948. Life History of the Olivaceous Piculet and Related Forms. Ibis 90:433–49.
1948. Life History of the Citreoline Trogon. Condor 50:137–47.
1948. The Isle of Boobies. Nature 41:358–60, 386.
1948. Earth and Man. Audubon 50:356–59.
1948. Life's Debt to Death. Aryan Path (Bombay, India) 19:530–33.
1949. A Conservationist's Philosophy. Audubon 51:12–18, 41. Reprinted in *English for Today*, by Martha Gray and Clarence W. Hach. J. B. Lippincott Company, Philadelphia, 1950, pp. 256–61.

APPENDIX 2

1949. Notes on Blue-gray Gnatcatcher, Russet-backed Thrush, and Wood Thrush in *Life Histories of North American Thrushes, Kinglets, and their Allies*, by Arthur Cleveland Bent. Bull. U.S. Natl. Mus. 196.
1949. Life History of the Yellow-thighed Manakin. Auk 66:1–24.
1949. Life History of the Ruddy Quail-Dove. Condor 51:3–19.
1949. Motmots—Dandies of the Bird World. Nature 42:69–72, 100.
1949. The Panama-hat Plant. Nature 42:173–75.
1949. Do Tropical Birds Rear as Many Young as They Can Nourish? Ibis 91:430–55.
1949. Northern Birds at a Costa Rican Feeding Station. Audubon 51:278–85.
1949. The Basilisk Lizard. Nature 42:436–37.
1950. A New Project for Human Happiness. Aryan Path (Bombay, India) 21:7–12.
1950. Life and Immortality from a Scientist's Viewpoint. Aryan Path (Bombay, India) 21:137–42.
1950. The Nesting Seasons of Central American Birds in Relation to Climate and Food Supply. Ibis 92:185–222.
1950. On the Naming of Birds. Wilson Bull. 62:95–99.
1950. Article on Yellow-green Vireo, notes on Blue-headed Vireo, Red-eyed Vireo, Yellow-throated Vireo, and Cedar Waxwing, in *Life Histories of North American Wagtails, Shrikes, Vireos, and their Allies*, by Arthur Cleveland Bent. Bull. U.S. Natl. Mus. 197.
1950. Problems in Milpa Agriculture. Turrialba: Revista Inter-americana de Ciencias Agrícolas 1:4–6.
1950. Life History of the White-breasted Blue Mockingbird. Condor 52:220–27.
1950. An Adventure with Toucans. Nature 43:411–13, 440.
1950. Outline for an Ecological Life History of a Bird, Based upon the Song Tanager *Ramphocelus passerinii costaricensis*. Ecology 31:464–69.
1951. Life History of the Boat-billed Flycatcher. Auk 68:30–49.
1951. Congeneric Species of Birds Nesting Together in Central America. Condor 53:3–15.
1951. Edible Flowers. Nature 44:92–93, 108.
1951. Ahimsa on the Farm. Aryan Path (Bombay, India) 22:135–42. Also published as Reprint No. 6 of the Indian Institute of Culture, Basavangudi, Bangalore.
1951. Life History of Longuemare's Hermit Hummingbird. Ibis 93:180–95.
1951. India's Conservationist Emperor. Nature 44:202–4, 218.
1952. On the Hour of Laying and Hatching of Birds' Eggs. Ibis 94:49–61.
1952. Animal Friends, Dependent and Free. Nature 45:134–36, 162.
1952. Life History of the Chestnut-tailed Automolus. Condor 54:93–100.
1952. The Royal Flycatcher. Audubon 54:226–31.
1952. Which Shall We Protect?—Thoughts on the Ethics of Our Treatment of Free Life. Aryan Path (Bombay, India) 23:382–86.
1952. Life History of the Blue and White Swallow. Auk 69:392–406.
1952. Kingfishers—Sovereigns of the Watercourses. Nature 45:461–64, 500.
1952. Scarlet Passion-flower. Nature 45:523–25, 550.
1952. Modern Esaus. Aryan Path (Bombay, India) 23:541–47.
1953. How the Male Bird Discovers the Nestlings. Ibis 95:1–37, 505–42.
1953. ¿Por qué No Enyugamos los Bueyes del Pescuezo? Revista de Agricultura (San José, Costa Rica), 25:60–62.
1953. The True Conservationist. Nature 46:258–61.
1953. Life History of the Southern House Wren. Condor 55:121–49.
1953. How the Male Bird Discovers the Nestlings. Animal Kingdom (N.Y. Zool. Soc.) 56:84–89.
1953. The White-throated Magpie-Jay. Wilson Bull. 65:68–74.
1953. Delayed Reproductive Maturity in Birds. Ibis 95:153–54.
1953. Notes on twenty-nine species in *Life Histories of North American Wood Warblers*, by Arthur Cleveland Bent. Bull. U.S. Natl. Mus. 203.

1953. (With Pamela Skutch) Two Costa Rican Begonias. The Begonian 20:193–94.
1953. Religion and the Conservation of Natural Resources. Aryan Path (Bombay, India) 24:426–30, 472–78.
1953. The Elusive Massena Trogon. Animal Kingdom 56:167–72.
1954. Divination by Birds. Aryan Path (Bombay, India) 25:147–53.
1954. Life History of the White-winged Becard. Auk 71:113–29.
1954. Our Difficult Choice. Nature 47:190–92, 215. Reprinted in Rosicrucian Digest 32:422–25.
1954. The Tangled Strands of Conservation. Nature 47:258–60, 276.
1954. Helpers at the Nest. Animal Kingdom 57:86–91.
1954. Nest Robber. Natural History (September) 306–9, 330.
1954. Life History of the Tropical Kingbird. Proc. Linnean Soc. N.Y. for 1951–53 (nos. 63–65), pp. 21–38.
1954. The Parental Stratagems of Birds. Ibis 96:544–64.
1955. The Parental Stratagems of Birds (continued). Ibis 97:118–42.
1955. The Hairy Woodpecker in Central America. Wilson Bull. 67:25–32.
1955. How Birds Handle their Population Problem. Animal Kingdom 58:72–77.
1956. Nature's Harshness and Man's Compassion. Nature 49:145–48.
1956. Religion and Technology. Aryan Path (Bombay, India) 27:222–28.
1956. Life History of the Ruddy Ground Dove. Condor 58:188–205.
1956. A Nesting of the Collared Trogon. Auk 73:354–66.
1956. Roosting and Nesting of the Golden-olive Woodpecker. Wilson Bull. 68:118–28.
1956. "Parental Care" and "Hides and Other Equipment" in *The Ornithologists' Guide*, edited by H. P. W. Hutson. British Ornithologists' Union, London.
1956. The Bird's Nest as a Dormitory. Animal Kingdom 59:50–55.
1956. Love for Our Earth. Rosicrucian Digest 34:292–96.
1957. Environment and Ethics. Rosicrucian Digest 35:88–91, 107–8.
1957. The Incubation Patterns of Birds. Ibis 99:69–93.
1957. The Friendly Bicolored Antbird. Animal Kingdom 60:75–79.
1957. The Convivial Ascetic. Aryan Path (Bombay, India) 28:302–6.
1957. Life History of the Amazon Kingfisher. Condor 59:217–29.
1957. The Naturalist's Progress. Nature 50:482–84.
1957. "Montezuma Oropéndola" in *The Bird Watcher's Anthology*, edited by Roger Tory Peterson. Harcourt, Brace and Company, New York.
1957. Eight articles in *The Warblers of America*, edited by Ludlow Griscom and Alexander Sprunt, Jr. The Devin-Adair Company, New York.
1958. Article on Boat-tailed Grackle and notes on nine other species in *Life Histories of North American Blackbirds, Orioles, Tanagers, and Allies*, by Arthur Cleveland Bent. Bull. U.S. Natl. Mus. 211.
1958. The Turquoise-browed Motmot. Animal Kingdom 61:6–11.
1958. Man as a Hunting Animal. Nature 51:96–99.
1958. Our Animal Heritage. Rosicrucian Digest, 36:97–101.
1958. Life History of the Violet-headed Hummingbird. Wilson Bull. 70:5–19.
1958. Life History of the White-whiskered Soft-wing *Malacoptila panamensis*. Ibis 100:209–31.
1958. Crítica del Humanismo (traducido por Ligia Herrera). Revista de Filosofía de la Universidad de Costa Rica 1:253–62.
1958. Roosting and Nesting of Araçari Toucans. Condor 60:201–19.
1958. Three-wattled Bellbird. Nature 51:345–47.
1958. Love and Lovability. Rosicrucian Digest 36:368–70.
1958. Are We Dissipating our Moral Patrimony? Aryan Path (Bombay, India) 29:449–54.
1958. The Stages in Spiritual Growth. Aryan Path (Bombay, India) 29:538–43.
1959. Ahinsa and its Practice. The Voice of Ahinsa (Aliganj, India) 9:10–13.

1959. The Scourge of the Wasps. Animal Kingdom 62:8–13.
1959. The Singing Wood-Rail. Audubon 61:20–21, 76–77.
1959. Life History of the Black-throated Trogon. Wilson Bull. 71:5–18.
1959. Life History of the Blue Ground Dove. Condor 61:65–74.
1959. Life History of the Groove-billed Ani. Auk 76:281–317.
1959. La Compasión (traducido por Hilda Chen Apuy). Revista de Filosofía de la Universidad de Costa Rica 2:43–54.
1959. Comments on "Ecological Indications of the Need for a New Approach to Tropical Land Use," by Leslie R. Holdridge. Symposia Interamericana (Turrialba, Costa Rica) 1:49–57.
1959. Trogons and Wasps' Nests. Nature 52:465–68, 500.
1959. The Great Tinamou of the Tropical Forest. Animal Kingdom 62:179–83.
1960. A Forest View of Kinkajous. Animal Kingdom 63:25–28.
1960. The Laughing Reptile Hunter of Tropical America. Animal Kingdom 63:115–19.
1960. Philosophy, Its Meaning. Rosicrucian Digest 38:334–38.
1960. One World—But How? Aryan Path (Bombay, India) 31:390–96.
1961. The Nest as a Dormitory. Ibis 103a:50–70.
1961. The Purple-capped Fairy Hummingbird. Audubon 63:8–9, 13.
1961. How Birds Leave the Nest. Animal Kingdom 64:50–54. Reprinted in Foreign Birds 27:250–56. 1961.
1961. Life History of the White-crested Coquette Hummingbird. Wilson Bull. 73:5–10.
1961. Helpers among Birds. Condor 63:198–226.
1961. To Make a Better World. The Voice of Ahinsa (Aliganj, India) 11:201–4.
1961. Youth's Aspirations. Aryan Path (Bombay, India) 32:352–56.
1961. "The Ant-thrush Chicks," in *Discovery*, edited by John K. Terres. J. B. Lippincott Company, Philadelphia.
1962. How Nestlings Defend Themselves. Animal Kingdom 65:6–9.
1962. Life Histories of Honeycreepers. Condor 64:92–116.
1962. The Constancy of Incubation. Wilson Bull. 74:115–52.
1962. Life History of the White-tailed Trogon *Trogon viridis*. Ibis 104:301–13.
1962. Vegetarianism and the Evil of Predation. Aryan Path (Bombay, India) 33:298–302.
1962. On the Habits of the Queo, *Rhodinocichla rosea*. Auk 79:633–39.
1962. Economic Individualism and Spiritual Individualism. Actas Segundo Congreso Extraordinario Interamericano de Filosofía (San José, Costa Rica) pp. 233–35.
1962. The Woodcreepers of Tropical America. Animal Kingdom 65:151–55.
1963. Life History of the Little Tinamou. Condor 65:224–31.
1963. Life History of the Rufous-tailed Jacamar *Galbula ruficauda* in Costa Rica. Ibis 105:354–68.
1963. Habits of the Chestnut-winged Chachalaca. Wilson Bull. 75:262–69.
1963. Los Ideales Básicos del Género Humano. Revista de Filosofía de la Universidad de Costa Rica, 4:27–34.
1964. Life Histories of Hermit Hummingbirds. Auk 81:5–25.
1964. Life History of the Scaly-breasted Hummingbird. Condor 66:186–98.
1964. Life History of the Blue-diademed Motmot *Momotus momota*. Ibis 106:321–32.
1964. Life Histories of Central American Pigeons. Wilson Bull. 76:211–47.
1964. Articles on Jacamar, Motmot, Puffbird, Shrike-Vireo, Sunbittern, Tanager, and Toucan in *A New Dictionary of Birds*, edited by Sir A. Landsborough Thomson. Thomas Nelson and Sons, London.
1965. The Message of Beauty. Aryan Path (Bombay, India) 36:109–11, 169–72.
1965. Life History Notes on Two Tropical American Kites. Condor 67:235–46.
1965. The Advancement of Biology in the Tropics. The Association for Tropical Biology, Inc., Bull. 4:31–34.

1965. The Silky-Flycatcher. Animal Kingdom 68:22–27.
1965. Life History of the Long-tailed Silky-Flycatcher, with Notes on Related Species. Auk 82:375–426.
1965. Birds in a Costa Rican Garden. Animal Kingdom 68:168–72.
1966. A Breeding Bird Census and Nesting Success in Central America. Ibis 108:1–16.
1966. Life Histories of Three Tropical American Cuckoos. Wilson Bull. 78:139–65.
1966. Western Kingbird and Inca Dove in Costa Rica. Auk 83:669.
1967. Cape May Warbler in Costa Rica. Wilson Bull. 79:118–19.
1967. The Thornbird and its Many-chambered Nest. Animal Kingdom 70:44–51.
1967. Family Life of the Golden-naped Woodpecker. Animal Kingdom 70:106–11.
1967. Adaptive Limitation of the Reproductive Rate of Birds. Ibis 109:579–99.
1967. Life History Notes on the Oriole-Blackbird (*Gymnomystax mexicanus*) in Venezuela. Hornero 10:379–88.
1968. The Nesting of Some Venezuelan Birds. Condor 70:66–82.
1968. Organs of the Universe. Aryan Path (Bombay, India) 39:2–6.
1968. Notes on eight species in *Life Histories of North American Cardinals, Grosbeaks, Buntings, Towhees, Finches, Sparrows, and Allies*, by Arthur Cleveland Bent and Collaborators, edited by Oliver L. Austin, Jr. Bull. U.S. Natl. Mus. 237.
1968. The Cotingas: A Study in Contrasts. Animal Kingdom 71:4–9.
1968. The Challenge of Tropical America. Bull. Texas Ornith. Soc. 2:30–33.
1969. A Study of the Rufous-fronted Thornbird and Associated Birds. Wilson Bull. 81:5–43, 123–39.
1969. Every Child's Birthright. Aryan Path (Bombay, India) March.
1969. Nunbirds. Animal Kingdom 72:8–11.
1969. Notes on the Possible Migration and the Nesting of the Black Vulture in Central America. Auk 86:726–31.
1969–70. Articles on Tinamidae, Cracidae, Meleagridinae, Momotidae, Ramphastidae, Dendrocolaptidae, Tyrannidae, Ptilogonatinae, Thraupinae, Catamblyrhynchinae, and Dacnidinae in *Grzimeks Tierleben*. Kindler Verlag, München.
1970. The Display of the Yellow-billed Cotinga *Carpodectes antoniae*. Ibis 112:115–16.
1970. Life History of the Common Potoo. The Living Bird, Ninth Annual, pp. 265–80.
1970. Jacamars: Insect-eaters of the American Tropics. Animal Kingdom 73:21–24.
1970. Asceticism: An Appraisal. Aryan Path (Bombay, India) 41:7–11.
1970. Migrations of the American Moth *Urania fulgens*. Entomologist (August) 192–97.
1971. Life History of the Keel-billed Toucan. Auk 88:381-96.
1971. The Birds of Nosara, Florida Naturalist 44:11-12.
1971. Life History of the Broad-billed Motmot, with Notes on the Rufous Motmot. Wilson Bull. 83:74-94.

The Author's Published Writings since 1970

Books

1971. *A Naturalist in Costa Rica*. University of Florida Press, Gainesville, 378 pp.
1972. *Studies of Tropical American Birds*. Publications of the Nuttall Ornithological Club, No. 10. 228 pp.
1973. *The Life of the Hummingbird*. With paintings by Arthur B. Singer. Crown Publishers, New York. 95 pp.
1976. *Parent Birds and Their Young*. University of Texas Press, Austin. 503 pp.
1977. *A Bird Watcher's Adventures in Tropical America*. With drawings by Dana Gardner. University of Texas Press, Austin. 327 pp.

1977. *Aves de Costa Rica*. With 100 photographs in color by John S. Dunning. Editorial Costa Rica, San José. 148 pp.
1979. *The Imperative Call: A Naturalist's Quest in Temperate and Tropical America*. University Presses of Florida, Gainesville. 331 pp.
1980. *A Naturalist on a Tropical Farm*. With drawings by Dana Gardner. University of California Press, Berkeley. 397 pp.
1981. *New Studies of Tropical American Birds*. With drawings by Dana Gardner. Publications of the Nuttall Ornithological Club, No. 19. 281 pp.
1983. *Birds of Tropical America*. With drawings by Dana Gardner. University of Texas Press, Austin. 305 pp.
1983. *Nature through Tropical Windows*. With drawings by Dana Gardner. University of California Press, Berkeley. 392 pp.
1985. *Life Ascending*. University of Texas Press, Austin. 268 pp.
1985. *Life of the Woodpecker*. With paintings by Dana Gardner. Ibis Publishing Company, Santa Monica, California, and Cornell University Press, Ithaca, New York. 136 pp.
1985. *La Finca de Un Naturalista*. (*A Naturalist on a Tropical Farm*, translated into Spanish, and with an introduction, by Raúl Elvir.) Asociación Libro Libre, San José, Costa Rica. 466 pp.
1987. *Helpers at Birds' Nests: A Worldwide Survey of Cooperative Breeding and Related Behavior*. With drawings by Dana Gardner. University of Iowa Press, Iowa City. 298 pp.
1987. *A Naturalist amid Tropical Splendor*. With drawings by Dana Gardner. University of Iowa Press, Iowa City. 232 pp.
1989. *Life of the Tanager*. Illustrated by Dana Gardner. Cornell University Press, Ithaca, New York. 114 pp.
1989. *Birds Asleep*. With drawings by John Schmitt. University of Texas Press, Austin. 224 pp.
1989. *A Guide to the Birds of Costa Rica* (with F. Gary Stiles). Illustrated by Dana Gardner. Cornell University Press, Ithaca, New York. 656 pp.
1991. *Life of the Pigeon*. Illustrated by Dana Gardner. Cornell University Press, Ithaca, New York. 130 pp.
1991. *El Ascenso de la Vida*. (Spanish translation by Raúl Elvin of *Life Ascending*.) Editorial Costa Rica, San José. 347 pp.
1992. *Origins of Nature's Beauty*. Illustrated by Dana Gardner. University of Texas Press, Austin.

Articles

1971. Life History of the Bright-rumped Attila *Attila spadiceus*. Ibis 113:316-22.
1973. Rivalry in the Nest. Animal Kingdom 76:8-14.
1974. South America: The Neotropical Realm in *The Mitchell Beazley World Atlas of Birds*, edited by Martyn Bramwell. Mitchell Beazley Publishers Ltd., London.
1977. The Incubation Patterns of Birds (from Ibis 99:69-93, 1957) in *Parental Behavior of Birds*, edited by Rae Silver. Benchmark Papers in Animal Behavior 11. Dowden, Hutchinson and Ross, Stroudsburg, Pennsylvania.
1977. Helpers at the Nest (from Auk 52:257-73, 1935) in *Parental Behavior of Birds* (see preceding entry).
1980. Arils as Food of Tropical American Birds. Condor 82:31-42.
1980. The Resplendent Quetzal. Americas 32:13-21. El Resplandeciente Quetzal. Américas 32:13-21. Reprinted in Bird Watcher's Digest, January-February 1981, pp. 56-65.
1981. Troupials and Thornbirds. American 33:52-56. Turpiales y Guatíes. Américas 33:52-56.
1982. La Guatusa, un Roedor Silvestre de America. Geomundo 6:529-35.
1982. Resplendent Myth. Audubon 84:74-84.
1982. Costa Rica's Golden-voiced Yigüirro. Americas 34:18-21. El Canto Melodioso del Yigüirro. Américas 34:18-21.

1983. Articles on *Columbina talpacoti, Geotrygon montana,* and *Herpetotheres cachinnans* in *Costa Rican Natural History,* edited by Daniel H. Janzen. University of Chicago Press, Chicago.
1983. Miniatures and Giants (from *Nature through Tropical Windows*). The Sciences, pp. 18-21.
1983. The Naturalist's Progress (from *Nature through Tropical Windows*). Defenders 58:37-39.
1985. Articles on Jacamar, Motmot, Puffbird, Shrike-Vireo, Silky-flycatcher, Sunbittern, Tanager, Toucan in *A Dictionary of Birds,* edited by Bruce Campbell and Elizabeth Lack. T. and A. D. Poyser, Calton, England.
1985. Articles on Toucans, Jacamars, Puffbirds, Tanagers, Swallow-Tanager, Cardinal Grosbeaks in *The Encyclopaedia of Birds,* edited by Christopher M. Perrins and Alex L. A. Middleton. George Allen and Unwin, London.
1985. Clutch Size, Nesting Success, and Predation on Nests of Neotropical Birds, Reviewed in *Neotropical Ornithology,* edited by P. A. Buckley, Mercedes S. Foster, Eugene S. Morton, Robert S. Ridgely, and Francine G. Buckley. American Ornithologists' Union Monograph No. 36. Washington, D.C.
1989. Courtship of the Rufous Piha *Lipaugus unirufus.* Ibis 131:303-4.
1989. Synchronized Flowering and Seed Dispersal in *Miconia.* Brenesia 29:83-94 (for March 1988).
1989. Flowering and Seed-production of *Fischeria funebris.* Brenesia 30:13-19 (for September 1988).
1991. Bird Song and Philosophy in *The Philosophy of Charles Hartshorne,* edited by Lewis Edwin Hahn. Open Court, La Salle, Illinois.

Appendix 3

The Author's Honors and Awards

1946. Fellow, American Ornithologists' Union
1947. Honorary Member, British Ornithologists' Union
1960. Honorary Member, Cooper Ornithological Society
1964. Corresponding Member, Asociación Ornitológica del Plata
1979. Honorary Fellow, American Ornithologists' Union
1979. Honorary President, International Council for Bird Preservation, Costa Rican Section
1989. Honorary Member, the Linnaean Society of New York

1950. William Brewster Medal of American Ornithologists' Union
1963. Diploma from Licéo Unesco of San Isidro de El General for contributions to ornithology
1971. Parchment from The Union of American Women, Costa Rican Chapter, for "thirty years of uninterrupted study of Costa Rican nature" and promulgating knowledge of its fauna
1977. Aquiléo J. Echeverría Award from the Costa Rican Ministry of Culture, Youth, and Sports for *Aves de Costa Rica*
1981. Parchment from the Costa Rican Ministry of Culture, Youth, and Sports on the occasion of the fiftieth anniversary of the establishment of the Municipality of San Isidro de El General
1983. Medal of the John Burroughs Memorial Association for *A Naturalist on a Tropical Farm*

1983. Arthur A. Allen Medal from the Cornell University Laboratory of Ornithology for "outstanding service to ornithology"
1983. Medal from II Iberoamerican Congress of Ornithology, Xalapa, Veracruz, Mexico
1983. Parchment from the Section of Forestry, Costa Rican Ministry of Agriculture and Cattle-breeding, for conservation of renewable natural resources
1986. Parchment from the Costa Rican Association of Travel Agents for studies of the avifauna of the Valley of El General
1987. Plaque from the agricultural cooperative Coopeagri El General for promoting conservation
1989. Plaque from Editorial Costa Rica for contributions to Costa Rican culture
1989. Hal Borland Award from editors of Audubon Magazine for "a lasting contribution to the understanding, appreciation, and protection of nature through writing"
1990. Plaque from the Community of San Isidro de El General for the author's "constant search for equilibrium between man and nature" and designating him a "Distinguished Citizen"

Index

Acorns, 31; storage by Acorn Woodpeckers, 32
Actinote anteas (butterfly): sleeping habits, 296–99; biennial abundance, 299
Agouti, *Dasyprocta punctata*, 138, 338; food, 150–51, 217; habits, 216–17
Agriculture: in El General, 37, 46, 279, 337; primitive practices, 280; tools, 280; preparation of land, 281; effects on soil fertility, 282–83; fertility restored by native vegetation, 283; burning for planting, 284–87; milpa system, 287; grasses deleterious to, 287; storing grains, 288; animals in, 289–91; scientific improvement of, 291–92; need of perennial food plants in humid tropics, 292–93; integration with the culture, 294–95
Aguacatillo, *Persea skutchii* (Lauraceae): floral behavior, 185–87. See also picture section, Part II

Agua dulce (beverage), 62
Airlines: in El General, 9, 46–47
Akee, *Blighia sapida* (Sapindaceae): treacherous arils, 333
Alchornea costaricensis (Euphorbiaceae): arillate seeds eaten by birds, 332
—*latifolia*: arillate seeds eaten by birds, 332
Allamanda cathartica, 152, 181
Almendro tree, *Dipteryx panamensis* (Leguminosae), 317
Almirante Bay region, Panama: author's sojourn in, 3
Amazonia, forests of, 226–27
Amazon River, 129
American Museum of Natural History, 4
Ani, Groove-billed, *Crotophaga sulcirostris*: communal nesting, 330–31
—Smooth-billed, *Crotophaga ani*, 331
Animals: protection of free, 289; domestic, 290–91

369

Annatto, *Bixa orellana* (Bixaceae), 150
Ant, army, *Eciton burchelli*: followed by birds, 235; attack wasps' nests, 272–75; eaten by domestic chickens, 275; plunder leaf-cutting ants' nest, 275–76; rarely attack vertebrates, 276–77
—Fire, *Solenopsis geminata*, 276
—gardener, *Azteca* sp.: aerial gardens, 258–59
—leaf-cutting, *Atta* spp.: fungus gardens, 257–58; wasted effort, 258
—parasol. See Ant, leaf-cutting
—spinning, *Camponotus senex*: nest and habits, 256–57. See also picture section, Part II
Antbird, Bare-crowned, *Gymnocichla nudiceps*, 313
Antbirds (Formicariidae), 237
Anting by birds, 257
Antpitta, Streaked-chested, *Grallaria perspicillata*: voice and habits, 228–29
Ants: in newly felled forest, 39; abundance and variety, 255–56; battle with bees, 260–61; eaten by birds, 319
Ant-Tanager, Red-crowned, *Habia rubica*, 237
Antthrush, Black-faced, *Formicarius analis*, 217
Antvireo, Streaked-crowned, *Dysithamnus striaticeps*, 319
Aphelandra tetragona (Acanthaceae), 118
Apinagia myriophylla (Podostemonaceae), 197
Araçari, Collared, *Pteroglossus torquatus*, 320; helpers at nest, 330
—Fiery-billed, *Pteroglossus frantzii*, 12, 297, 338; habits, 25, 148
Arils: as food for men and birds, 332–34
Aroids, 195, 318; eaten by spider monkey, 92
Atelopus varius (frog), 118
Atta ants. See Ant, leaf-cutting
Avocado, *Persea americana* (Lauraceae): floral behavior, 184–85

Bacon, Francis, 149, 291
Bacopa salzmanni (Scrophulariaceae): short-lived flowers, 176
Bahareque construction, 131, 143, 146
Balance of nature, 139–40
Balsa trees, *Ochroma* spp. (Bombacaceae), 221
Baltimore, Maryland; author's visit to, 100

Bamboo, climbing, *Chusquea* sp.: flowers and dies, 206–7
—dwarf (*Chusquea subtessellata*), 60
Bamboos, 59, 60, 64, 67
Banana plant: used to decorate Christmas garden, 50
Bananaquit, *Coereba flaveola*, 242
Barba, Volcán, 9, 87, 313
Barba amarilla (snake), *Bothrops atrox*, 220
Barbet, Prong-billed, *Semnornis frantzii*, 97
—Red-headed, *Eubucco bourcierii*: visits feeder, 163
Barro Colorado Island, Canal Zone, 339
Barú, Río, 106–9
Basilisk. See Lizard
Bat, Vampire, 43
Bats: as pollinators, 161
Bayberry, *Myrica* spp. (Myricaceae), 92
Bayon (author's horse), 16, 55–59, 68, 69, 94, 100, 105–7, 113–15, 135
Beans, 46; sowing and harvesting, 280, 281; storing, 288
Beebe, William, 275
Bees: in newly felled forest, 39; taking their honey, 39–40; pollinate coffee, 242; abundance, 259; battle with ants, 260–61; gather gum from Clusia flowers, 261; plunder hives of other species, 262
—euglossid: annoying habits, 259–60
Begonia cuspidata (Begoniaceae), 118
Begonias, 105, 118
Bellbird, Three-wattled, *Procnias tricarunculata*: voice, 67, 96; altitudinal movements, 94, 96; display, 96
Belt, Thomas, 87, 269
Biologia Centrali-Americana, 298
Birds: author's determination to study, 3; flying above forest, 11; sleeping habits, 22–25, 94, 330; helpers at nests, 24–25, 32, 324–32; song, 28, 104–5; breeding season, 68, 110, 332; rewards for finding nests, 72; number of species identified, 83, 319, 344; number of nests found, 83, 344; tameness in remote mountains, 97–98; singing in winter home, 103, 202; winter territories, 104; migrations, 126–29, 308; nuptial feeding, 159, 165, 320, 323, 329; as pollinators and seed disseminators, 159–60; at feeder, 162–67; mated throughout year, 165, 200; seasonal plumage changes, 166–67; census of nests, 167–68; success of

nests, 168–69, 237; responsive singing, 200; "mob" snakes, 201; the enigma of small broods in tropics, 230–31; leisurely schedule of reproduction in tropics, 231; follow army ants, 235; behavior at nests in forest, 237; longevity in forest, 237–38; in coffee plantation, 244; eat Cecropia spikes, 245; forest dwellers enter clearing to nest, 246; eat Pejibaye fruits, 247–48; anting, 257; build nests beside vespiaries for protection, 268–69; nest inside vespiary, 269–70; devour immature wasps, 270–71; dust-bathing, 288; and butterflies, 302–4; excited by large moths, 306–7; bring food for vanished nestlings, 327–28; eagerness for arillate seeds, 332–34; changes in avifauna at Los Cusingos, 338–39. See also Ani, Antbird, etc.
Blackbird (European), *Turdus merula*, 63, 333
Black Locust tree, *Robinia pseudo-acacia* (Leguminosae), 154
Blood: drops from roof, 41–43
Bocaracá (snake), *Bothrops schlegelii*, 220
Books, author's, 147
Botanical collecting, 4, 9, 29–30, 32–34, 38–39, 82–83, 94, 113, 176
Bracken fern, *Pteridium* spp., 35, 40–41, 67
Brassia gireoudiana (Orchidaceae), 169
Bromeliads, 67, 188, 195; pond life in, 234; in birds' nest, 328
Broomweeds, *Sida* spp. (Malvaceae): ephemeral flowers, 175
Brush-Finch, Gray-striped, *Atlapetes assimilis*: eats dead leaves, 217; nesting, 245
Buena Vista, Río, 7, 15, 16, 26, 31, 33, 56, 337
Buenos Aires de Osa, Costa Rica, 9; visited by author, 94
Burial ground: at Rivas, 44, 53; Indian, 223
Burío trees, *Heliocarpus appendiculatus* and *H. excelsior* (Tiliaceae), 221–22
Burning of forests and fields, 40–41, 60, 64, 66, 67, 280, 284–87, 291–92
Bushmaster (snake), *Lachesis muta*, 220
Butterflies: sleeping habits, 296–302; and birds, 302–4, 320
Butterfly, Monarch, *Danaus plexippus*, 302
—Morpho, *Morpho* spp., 118, 212
—sleepy blue-wing, 301–2
—Viceroy, *Basilarchia disippus*, 302

Cabuya, *Furcraea cabuya* (Amaryllidaceae): source of cordage, 21
Cacao plantation, 316; abundance of birds in, 319
Cacique, Chisel-billed, *Amblycercus holosericeus*, 301
—Scarlet-rumped, *Cacicus uropygialis*, 323; eats immature wasps, 271
—Yellow-rumped, *Cacicus cela*: nests plundered by snake, 269
Cacique tree, *Myrciara floribunda* (Myrtaceae), 144
Calabash tree, *Crescentia cujete* (Bignoniaceae), 150, 169, 170
Calcium oxalate: raphides of, 247
Calinguero grass, *Melinis minutiflora*, 15, 285, 287
Campana tree, *Laplacea semiserrata* (Theaceae), 144, 211; decrease of, 211, 338
Camponotus senex (ant): silken nest, 256–57
Canaán, Costa Rica, 18, 33–34
Cañas Gordas, Costa Rica: visit to, 313
Candela tree, *Virola koschnyi* (Myristicaceae), 144
Candelillo tree, *Cassia spectabilis* (Leguminosae), 309
Cane, Wild, *Gynerium sagittatum* (Gramineae): used for house construction, 20, 146
Capulín tree, *Brunellia costaricensis* (Brunelliaceae): as food for Two-toed Sloth, 89
Caracara, Red-throated, *Daptrius americanus*: attacks wasps' nests, 271; disappearance of, 338
Carao, *Cassia grandis* (Leguminosae), 152
Cardinal, Common, *Richmondena cardinalis*: eats flowers, 161
Caribbean lowlands: author's studies in, 313–14
Caribbean Sea, 87
Carludovica leucocarpa (Cyclanthaceae), 34
Cartago, Costa Rica, 68, 309
Cascabel Muda (snake), *Lachesis muta*, 220
Castlebuilder, Pale-breasted, *Synallaxis albescens*: extends range, 339
—Slaty, *Synallaxis brachyura*, 245
Caterpillars, stinging: eaten by birds, 327

Cavendishias, *Cavendishia* spp. (Ericaceae), 95
Cecropia trees, *Cecropia* spp. (Moraceae): foliage eaten by sloths and monkeys, 89, 91; fruit eaten by birds, 245; inhabited by ants, 319
Ceiba tree, *Ceiba pentandra* (Bombacaceae), 316
Centropogon sp. (Lobeliaceae), 251–52
Cephaelis elata (Rubiaceae), 212
—*pittieri*, 212
—*tomentosa*, 212
Cerillo tree, *Symphonia globulifera* (Guttiferae), 213
Cerro de la Muerte, El: journey over, 55–70; vegetation of, 60–63; birds of, 60, 63, 64–65; meaning of name, 61–62; night on, 62; view from, 63–64; appearance, 114, 221
Cerro de las Vueltas, El, 66–67
Cestrum sp. (Solanaceae): nocturnal blooming, 176
Chachalaca, Chestnut-winged, *Ortalis garrula*: enter garden for Guava fruits, 150
Chapman, Frank M., 162
Chavarría, Rafael, 315
Chickens, domestic: eat flowers, 161; and army ants, 275
Chigoes, 52
Chinilla. See Bocaracá
Chirripó, Río, 18, 31. See also picture section, Part I
Chirripó Grande, Cerro, 64, 147, 193, 221
Chisholm, A. H., 269
Chonta palm, *Socratea durissima*, 135, 215–16, 338. See also picture section, Part II
Christmas: gardens, 50–51; celebrations, 51–52
Chumico tree, *Pourouma aspera* (Moraceae): leaves used as sandpaper, 213
Church: at Rivas, 17; support of, 49
Chusquea sp. (Gramineae): gregarious flowering, 206–7
—*subtessellata*, 60
Cicadas, 118
Climate, 27–28, 40–41, 88, 102, 112–13; at Montaña Azul, 88, 92, 93–94, 95, 96, 97; at La Selva, 321. See also Seasons in Central America
Climbing Bittersweet, *Celastrus scandens* (Celastraceae), 333
Clusia flava (Guttiferae): on mountaintop, 34; fragrant flowers, 34, 51
Clusias, *Clusia* spp., 118; attract pollinating bees with gum, 261–62; arillate seeds sought by birds, 334. See also picture section, Part II
Coatimundi, *Nasua narica*, 162, 219, 289, 338
Coconut, *Cocos nucifera* (Palmae), 107; floral behavior, 175
Codiaeum, *Codiaeum variegatum* (Euphorbiaceae), 151
Coffee: a beautiful shrub, 240; specialized branches, 241; pruning, 241; flowering, 242–43; processing the beans, 243–44; birds in plantation, 244–46; increased production, 337
Colombia, author's visit to, 129
Colorado tree, *Nectandra concinna* (Lauraceae), 144
Columnea ornata (Gesneriaceae): discovery of, 118
Comenegro tree, *Hieronyma oblonga* (Euphorbiaceae), 144
Compsoneura spp. (Myristicaceae), 334
Cóncavas, Las: author's visit to, 100
Conservation of nature, 289–90, 339–40
Convalescence: compared to adolescence, 110
Cook, O. F., 287
Cooking: arrangements, 22; Central American, 52
Copalchí tree, *Croton glabellus* (Euphorbiaceae), 309
Copey, El, Costa Rica, 67–68
Cordillera Central of Costa Rica: topography, 86–87
Cormorant, Olivaceous, *Phalacrocorax olivaceus*, 198
Corn, Indian. See Maize
Cornus disciflora (Cornaceae), 89
Coronillo, *Bellucia costaricensis* (Melastomaceae), 217
Costa Rica: revolution in, 4; floral and faunal wealth, 7–8; the country and its people, 8; agriculture, 293; rainfall, 321
Cotinga, Turquoise, *Cotinga ridgwayi*, 12
—Yellow-billed, *Carpodectes antoniae*, 115
Cotingas, blue, *Cotinga* spp., 96
Courtesy: of Central Americans, 53–54
Cowbird, Giant, *Psomocolax oryzivorus*: in oropéndolas' colony, 106
—Red-eyed, *Tangavius aeneus*, 339
Cow dung: uses of, 146
Cuckoo, Squirrel, *Piaya cayana*, 199; eats stinging caterpillars, 327

—Striped, *Tapera naevia*: parasitic habits, 339
Cuphea, River, *Cuphea utriculosa*, 116
Cusingos, Los (author's farm), 133; first view, 136–37; purchase, 137–39; topography, 139; origin of name, 148
Cyclanthus bipartitus (Cyclanthaceae): leaves that split, 318

Dacnis, Scarlet-thighed, *Dacnis venusta*: discovery of nest, 229–30
Darwin, Charles, 173
Davilla kunthii (Dilleniaceae): ephemeral flowers, 173–74. See also picture section, Part II
Deer, Forest, *Mazama sartorii*, 151, 219, 338
Dendrobates pumilo (frog), 318
Dickcissel, *Spiza americana*: sings in winter home, 103
Dieffenbachia spp. (Araceae), 318
Dio Chrysostom, 306
Dodson, C. H., 262
Dog: flagellation of, 138; disastrous to wildlife, 217–18
Dominical, Punta, 100; trip to, 105–8; accident at, 107–8
Don Chico. See Mora, Francisco
"Dracaena," *Taetsia fruticosa* var. *ferrea* (Liliaceae), 151
Dragonflies, 118, 303, 320
Dulce (crude sugar), 49, 62
Durian, *Durio zibethinus* (Bombacaceae), 333

Eagle, Harpy, *Harpia harpyja*, 80
Eciton ants. See Ants, army
Ecuador: author's visits to, 112, 129
Education: in backwoods, 49–50
Efraim Flores, 102, 103, 105–10, 113, 114, 119
Egret, Cattle, *Bubulcus ibis*, 323
El General, Valley of: topography, 11; Indians in, 44–45; settlement of, 45–46; agriculture, 46, 279–80; character of inhabitants, 47–54, isolation, 55; author's returns to, 100–101, 113; seeking a farm in, 134–39; helpers at birds' nests in, 331–32; changes in (1935–1970), 335–39
Elleanthus capitatus (Orchidaceae), 195
Entada gigas (Leguminosae): aggressiveness, 213
Epidendrum imatophyllum (Orchidaceae): on nests of gardener ant, 169, 258

Epiphytes: abundance, 15, 95, 105, 195, 244; destroyed by flood, 204; and by monkeys, 218
Esmeraldas, Río, 129, 311
Espavé, *Anacardium excelsum* (Anacardiaceae), 106
Estera de vena, 21
Estrella, La, ridge of, 68
Eupatorium macrophyllum (Compositae), 300
Euterpe sp. (Palmae), 10, 33–34, 56–57, 216. See also Palmito; frontispiece
Evolution, 223–24

Fairs: to support church and school, 49
Falcon, Laughing, *Herpetotheres cachinnans*, 71–72, 338. See also Guaco
Farming, 280. See also Agriculture
Faulkner, Edward H., 291
Fer-de-lance (snake), *Bothrops atrox*, 220
Ferns, 29–30, 34–35, 63, 67, 195; tree, 208; twining, 213–14
Fig, *Ficus paraensis* (Moraceae): on nests of gardener ants, 258–59
Figwort family: evanescent flowers, 176
Fire, runaway, 284–85. See also Burning of forests and fields
Fish: bombing of, 203–4
Flame-of-the-forest tree, *Spathodea campanulata* (Bignoniaceae), 152; water-filled buds, 187
Flatbill, Eye-ringed, *Rhynchocyclus brevirostris*, 319
—Sulphury, *Tolmomyias sulphurescens*: builds beside wasps' nest, 268–69
Fleas, 68, 92
Flies, bloodthirsty, 57
Flower-of-an-hour, *Hibiscus trionum* (Malvaceae), 175
Flower-piercer, Slaty, *Diglossa plumbea*, 65
Flowers: abundance early in dry season, 27–28; in forest, 28, 33, 118; on high ridges, 60; at Montaña Azul, 96; changes in color, 151; in author's garden, 151–55; destroyed by birds, 158; as human food, 160–62; eaten by birds and horses, 161; pollinated by bats, 161; services to plants, 172–73; short lives, 173–77; nocturnal blooming, 176; gregarious blooming, 177; pigments, 177–79; causes of color changes, 178–79; structure of petals, 179–80; their optical properties, 180–83; arrangements for cross-pollination,

184–87; aquatic, on terrestrial plants, 187–90
Flycatcher, Fork-tailed, *Muscivora tyrannus*: roosting, 94
—Gray-capped, *Myiozetetes granadensis*: builds beside wasps' nest, 268–69
—Piratic, *Legatus leucophaius*: steals trogons' nest, 270
—Royal, *Onychorhynchus mexicanus*: nest, 116, 229; and butterflies, 303
—Slaty-capped, *Leptopogon superciliaris*: nesting, 124
—Sulphur-bellied, *Myiodynastes luteiventris*, 249
—Torrent, *Serpophaga cinerea*: habits, 200
Forest: extent of, in Costa Rica, 8, 87, 135–36, 316, 335–36; edge of, favorable for observation and collecting, 18; flowers in, 28, 33, 118; lost in, 35–36; felling, 37–39; burning, 40–41, 60; on high mountains, 64–65; physiognomy related to climate, 95; bought by author, 138–39; entering the, 208; at Los Cusingos, 208–20; distribution of rain forest on American continents, 225–26; its uniform aspect, 227; a realm of mysteries, 227–33; collecting trees in, 233–34; vast diversity of organisms in, 234; monotony of, 234; perils in, 235–36; its quiet and changelessness, 236; its ceaseless strife, 236–38; we find what we seek in it, 238; it reduces us to submission, 238–39; widespread destruction of, 337; puzzling changes in composition, 338
Forest-Falcon, Barred, *Micrastur ruficollis*, 338
Frogs, poisonous: *Atelopus varius*, 118; *Dendrobates pumilo*, 318
Frost: on high mountains, 62
Fruitcrow, Purple-throated, *Querula purpurata*, 319
Frullania sp. (liverwort), 170
Fuchsia arborescens (Onagraceae): eaten by Two-toed Sloth, 89
Furniture-making, 146–47

Gallinazo tree, *Jacaranda copaia* (Bignoniaceae), 5, 222
Gallinule, Purple, *Porphyrula martinica*: eats fruits of *Heliconia*, 189–90
Gamboa, Humberto, 37, 50–51, 53
Gavilán tree, *Pentaclethra macroloba* (Leguminosae), 316–17
General, El. See El General, Valley of

General, Río, 135, 144
General Viejo, Costa Rica, 135, 145
Gnatcatcher, Tropical, *Polioptila plumbea*: feeds nestling tanagers, 331
Goethalsia meiantha (Tiliaceae): winged fruits, 207
Goldman, Edward A., 250
Granadillas, 333
Grasses: injurious to agriculture, 287
Grassquit, Blue-black, *Volatinia jacarina*: eclipse plumage, 167
—Yellow-faced, *Tiaris olivacea*, 314
Greenlet, Tawny-crowned, *Hylophilus ochraceiceps*, 319
Grosbeak, Black-faced, *Caryothraustes poliogaster*: nesting, 328–29; helper at nest, 329
—Blue-black, *Cyanocompsa cyanoides*: habits, 237, 246–47
Ground-Dove, Blue, *Claravis pretiosa*: nesting, 245
—Ruddy, *Columbigallina talpacoti*: roosting, 94
Guaco, *Herpetotheres cachinnans*: appearance, 71–72; voice, 72, 75, 77, 81; takes snakes to nest, 73, 75, 77, 80; nest, 74; nestling, 76; guarded by female, 76–77, 78; failure to protect it from Tayra, 78; she eats her nestling, 79–80
Guan, Black, *Chamaepetes unicolor*, 314
—Crested, *Penelope purpurascens*: voice, 119; with young, 119; disappearance, 219, 338
Guanacaste, Province of: visit to, 94; trees in, 95
Guanacaste tree, *Enterolobium* sp. (Leguminosae), 106
Guarumo trees, *Cecropia* spp. (Moraceae): food of sloths, 89; of monkeys, 91
Guatemala: author's visits to, 3–4, 35, 47; treeline in, 64; Quetzal in, 83–85
Guatuso. See Agouti
Guava tree, *Psidium guajava* (Myrtaceae), 33, 144, 150, 221
Guayacán tree, *Tabebuia chrysantha* (Bignoniaceae), 144
Guillemot, Black, *Cepphus grylle*: attempt to reach nest, 109
Guinea Grass, *Panicum maximum*, 287
Guitarróns. See Wasp, Guitarrón

Haberlandt, G., 183
Hamelia patens (Rubiaceae): changes in floral color, 179

Hawk, Broad-winged, *Buteo platypterus*: migration, 129
—Swainson's, *Buteo swainsoni*: migration, 126–29, 315; fasting, 128
—White, *Leucopternis albicollis*: food, 71
Heliconia elongata (Musaceae): aquatic flowers, 188–89; damaged by Purple Gallinule, 189–90. See also picture section, Part II
Heliconias, *Heliconia* spp., 207; and hummingbirds, 189, 208
Heliconius petiveranus (butterfly): sleeping habits, 300–301
Hen: damages botanical driers, 29
Heredia, Costa Rica, 314
Heron, Green, *Butorides virescens*, 218
—Little Blue, *Florida caerulea*, 115
Herpetotheres cachinnans, 72. See also Guaco
Hibiscus mutabilis (Malvaceae): change in floral color, 151
Hidalgoa ternata (Compositae): chromoplasts, 178–79
Higuera, *Gunnera insignis* (Halorrhagaceae), 314
Hoja de guaco, *Mikania guaco* (Compositae), 77
Holdridge, Dr. and Mrs. Leslie R., 315–16
Honey, wild, 39–40
Honeycreeper, Blue, *Cyanerpes cyaneus*: at feeder, 166; eclipse plumage, 166–67; feeds young of other species, 167, 331; eagerness for arillate seeds, 333–34
—Green, *Chlorophanes spiza*: at feeder, 166; eagerness for arils, 333
—Red-legged. See Honeycreeper, Blue
—Shining, *Cyanerpes lucidus*, 313; eagerness for arils, 333
Horses: as lawn mowers, 154; eat flowers, 161. See also Bayon
House: building author's, 141–47
Household arrangements, 21–22, 29
Huacas (Indian graves), 45
Humboldt, Alexander von, 211
Hummingbird, Band-tailed Barbthroat, *Threnetes ruckeri*: song, 214–15; singing assembly, 215
—Blue-chested, *Amazilia amabilis*, 156
—Blue-crowned Woodnymph, *Thalurania colombica*, 156, 212
—Blue-throated Goldentail, *Hylocharis eliciae*, 156

—Brown Violet-ear, *Colibri delphinae*, 156
—Green Hermit, *Phaethornis guy*: nest, 30–31; courtship, 31
—Green Violet-ear, *Colibri thalassinus*, 55, 60, 65
—Little Hermit, *Phaethornis longuemareus*, 156, 242; nesting 252–53; courtship, 253–54
—Long-billed Starthroat, *Heliomaster longirostris*: at Poró trees, 157; nesting, 168
—Long-tailed Hermit, *Phaethornis superciliosus*, 156; pollinates Heliconia flowers, 189
—Purple-crowned Fairy, *Heliothrix barroti*: at Madera Negra trees, 155; a nectar-thief, 158
—Ruby-throated, *Archilochus colubris*, 157
—Rufous-tailed, *Amazilia tzacatl*, 156, 168, 242, 245
—Scaly-breasted, *Phaeochroa cuvierii*, 156, 157
—Snowcap, *Microchera albo-coronata*, 156
—Snowy-breasted, *Amazilia edward*, 156, 223, 245
—Violet-headed, *Klais guimeti*: nesting, 121–24; curiosity, 122–23; courtship assemblies, 123; at Stachytarpheta hedge, 156
—White-crested Coquette, *Paphosia adorabilis*, 156
—White-necked Jacobin, *Florisuga mellivora*, 156
—White-tipped Sicklebill, *Eutoxeres aquila*: visits Heliconia flowers, 208
"Hummingbirds' Brook," 120–26
Hydrangea, climbing, *Hydrangea peruviana* (Saxifragaceae), 95–96

Ibis, Green, *Mesembrinibis cayennensis*: voice and habits, 323–24
Impatiens sultani, 181
Indians: in Costa Rica, 44–45; burials, 45, 223; killed in machete fight, 135–36; former occupants of Los Cusingos, 142; cover bodies with Annatto paste in Ecuador, 150; rock pictographs, 244; agriculture, 287
Infant mortality, 53
Inga trees, *Inga* spp. (Leguminosae), 33; edible seed coats, 217, 218–19; shade for coffee, 241; visited by *Urania* moths, 309

Insects: insensitive to pain, 274. See also Ants; Bees; Butterflies; etc.
Inter-American Highway, 47, 70
Invierno (rainy season), 28
Ionopsis utricularioides (Orchidaceae), 170
Ira Chiricano tree, Vantanea barbourii (Humiriaceae), 135
Irazú, Volcán, 9, 68, 87; eruption, 113
Itabo, Yucca elephantipes (Liliaceae): edible flowers, 160. See also picture section, Part II

Jacamar, Great, Jacamerops aurea: catch butterflies, 319–20; carve nest in termitary, 319–20
—Rufous-tailed, Galbula ruficauda, 148; nesting, 212, 327; disappearance, 339
Jacamars: bills specialized for catching butterflies, 303; influence on evolution of butterflies, 303–4
Jacaranda. See Gallinazo
Jack-in-the-Pulpit, Arisaema triphyllum (Araceae), 247
Jaguar, Felis onca, 46–47, 235, 335
Jamaica: author's visit to, 3
Jamesonia glutinosa (fern), 63
Jay, Steller's, Cyanocitta stelleri, 88
—White-tipped Brown, Psilorhinus mexicanus· helpers at nests, 32, 330
Johns Hopkins University, 3
John Simon Guggenheim Memorial Foundation, 4
José ———, 20, 29–30, 38–39, 48, 52
Junco, Volcano, Junco vulcani, 64–65
Jussiaea suffruticosa (Onagraceae), 180

Kallima spp. (butterfly): protective coloration, 303
Kingbird, Eastern, Tyrannus tyrannus, 128
—Tropical, Tyrannus melancholicus: buffets hawk, 128
Kingfisher, Amazon, Chloroceryle amazona, 112; bathing, 197–98
—Green, Chloroceryle americana, 197
—Half-collared, Alcedo semitorquata: bathing, 198
—Ringed, Ceryle torquata, 197
Kinkajou, Potos flavus: habits, 116–17; sleeps in woodpecker's hole, 215–16; a mother with young, 249–51
Kite, Plumbeous, Ictinia plumbea, 105
—Swallow-tailed, Elanoides forficatus: building nest, 105; food, 105–6

Labidus praedator (army ant): fails to injure nestling birds, 276
Lagartillo trees, Xanthoxylum spp. (Rutaceae): arillate seeds sought by birds, 333
Lankester, Charles Herbert, 147, 152
Lantana camara (Verbenaceae), 179
La Selva: studies at, 313–16, 332
Laurel tree, Cordia alliodora (Boraginaceae), 319
Leaf-tosser, Scaly-throated, Sclerurus guatemalensis: habits and nesting, 212
Leaves: rich colors in deep shade, 183–84; decaying, eaten by Agoutis and birds, 217; shapes of, in tropical and temperate-zone forests compared, 233
Lianas, 38, 237; embedded in trunk, 145; aggressiveness, 213, 222. See also picture section, Part II
Liquor, moonshine, 337
Liverworts, 170
Lizard, Gray Basilisk, Basiliscus basiliscus: at bird's table, 162, 203; habits and food, 202–3. See also picture section, Part II
—Green Basilisk, Basiliscus plumifrons, 203
Lizards, 42–43
Lluvia de oro, Oncidium spp. (Orchidaceae), 32–33, 169
Lomaria wercklei (fern), 67
Lories, brush-tongued: as pollinators, 159
Lucia (lizard), Leiolopisma cherriei, 42–43
Lycopodium saururus, 63

Macaw, Scarlet, Ara macao, 107, 152–53, 298, 339
Madera Negra, Gliricidia sepium (Leguminosae): as living fence posts, 154–55; edible flowers, 160
Madre de Cacao. See Madera Negra
Maine, State of: author's studies on coast, 109
Maize, 46; storing, 279, 288; sowing, 280–81; a wasteful crop, 293
Mallow family: ephemeral flowers, 175
Mammals: elusiveness, 117, 232; changes in fauna at Los Cusingos, 338
Man: his cosmic significance, 341–42
Manakin, Black and White, Manacus manacus: survival rate, 238
—Blue-crowned, Pipra coronata, 12

—Orange-collared, *Manacus aurantiacus*, 12; nesting, 245
—Thrush-like, *Schiffornis turdinus*: voice, 33, 228
—White-collared, *Manacus candei*, 332
Mangosteen, *Garcinia mangostana* (Guttiferae), 333
Mano de Piedra (snake), *Bothrops nummifer*, 220
Marañon, Río, 318
Marathrum schiedeanum (Podostemonaceae), 196–97
—*utile*, 197
Marsh-Tit, *Parus palustris*: eats flowers, 161
Mastate. See Milk Tree
Maxillaria ctenostachys (Orchidaceae), 170. See also picture section, Part II
—*divaricata*; attracts pollinators with wax, 261-62
—*neglecta*, 170
—*oreocharis*, 170
—sp.: carrion-scented flowers, 170
—*vitariifolia*, 170
Maxon, William R., 9
Maya culture, 287
Mayo Colorado tree, *Vochysia ferruginea* (Vochysiaceae), 222–23
Mayo tree, *Vochysia aurea*, 222–23
Mayo trees, *Vochysia* spp., 159
Melastome, Flowering (*Miconia scorpioides*), 149
Mendoncia lindavii (Acanthaceae): water-filled buds, 187
Mica (snake), *Spilotes pullatus*, 77, 123–24, 269
Migration: of birds, 126–29, 308, 315; of moths, 307–12
Mikania guaco (Compositae), 77
Milk Tree, *Brosimum utile* (Moraceae), 136, 144, 210–11, 217; source of bark cloth, 211; increase of, 211, 338
Mimicry: in butterflies, 302, 303–4
Mockingbird, Common, *Mimus polyglottos*: eats flowers, 161
Mongoose, *Herpestes nyula*, 77
Monkey, Black Howler, *Alouatta palliata*, 90, 105
—Red Spider, *Ateles geoffroyi*, 90: incessant activity, 91; food, 91–92
—White-faced, *Cebus capucinus*, 90, 135, 338; food, 150, 218, 289; habits, 218–19; games, 219
Montaña Azul, Costa Rica: author's residence at, 86–99, 307; view from, 87; climate, *passim* 88–97; abundance of epiphytes, 95; changes at, 314. See also picture section, Part I
Mora, Francisco ("Don Chico"): sells farm to author, 137–39; mentioned, 141, 152, 153, 244, 281, 284
Moreau, R. E., 198
Morpho butterflies, *Morpho* spp., 118, 212
Moths: protective devices, 304–6; "mobbed" by birds, 306–7; migration, 307–12
Motmot, Blue-diademed, *Momotus momota*, 45; at feeder, 164; nesting, 212
Motmots: eat butterflies, 303; and arillate seeds, 334
Mountain of Death, The. See Cerro de la Muerte, El
Muñeco tree, *Cordia bicolor* (Boraginaceae), 229
Murray, Eric, 9
Museo Nacional de Costa Rica, 111–12, 129
Myiobius, Sulphur-rumped, *Myiobius sulphureipygius*: nesting, 121

Naturalists: character of, 1–2; pioneer, in tropics, 2; contemporary, 2–3; author's work as, 3–4
Neighbors: in El General, 44–54
Nicaragua, 87
Nicaraguan Gap: effect on distribution of organisms, 87–88
Nightingale-Thrush, Black-billed, *Catharus gracilirostris*, 60, 66
—Orange-billed, *Catharus aurantiirostris*, 301
Norby, Darwin, 147
Nunbird, Black-fronted, *Monasa nigrifrons*, 324
—White-fronted, *Monasa morphoeus*: choruses, 325; nesting, 325–28; helpers at nests, 326. See also picture section, Part II
Nutmeg, *Myristica fragrans* (Myristicaceae), 333

Oaks, *Quercus* spp. (Fagaceae), 31, 57, 60, 67, 68
Ocelot, *Felis pardalis*, 217
Oleandra costaricensis (fern), 34
Oliganthes discolor (Compositae), 28
Olivo tree, *Simaruba amara* (Simarubaceae): as food for Two-toed Sloth, 89
Oncidium spp. (Orchidaceae), 32–33, 169. See also picture section, Part II
—*titania*, 33

Opossum, Wooly, *Philander laniger*: at bird's table, 163
Orange: grows spontaneously, 153; eaten by birds, 165–66
Orchids, 32–33, 169–70, 195; floral behavior, 176–77
Oriole, Baltimore, *Icterus galbula*, 298; roosting, 94; in garden, 155; splits Poró flowers, 158; at feeder, 164
—Orchard, *Icterus spurius*: sings in winter home, 104; in garden, 155
Oropéndola, Chestnut-headed, *Zarhynchus wagleri*: nesting colony, 106. See also picture section, Part I
—Montezuma, *Gymnostinops montezuma*, 106
Orthrosanthus chimboracensis (Iridaceae), 66
Otter, Tropical, *Lutra annectens*, 198–200, 322
Ox: falls from bridge, 144–45
Oystercatcher, American, *Haematopus palliatus*, 107

Paca, *Cuniculus paca*, 138
Pacific Ocean, 10, 64, 105, 106–8
Packsaddle: first experience with, 20–21
Pacuar, Río, 114–15, 126
Palicourea guianensis (Rubiaceae), 152
Palm, Oil, *Elaeis guineensis*, 159
Palm-Chat, *Dulus dominicus*: eats flowers, 161
Palmito, *Euterpe* sp., 216; destruction of, 216, 337–38. See also *Euterpe*
Palms, 10, 33–34, 55–56, 135, 215, 216, 247, 252, 318; upper limit of, 67; floral behavior, 174–75; destruction of, 215, 216
Panama: author's visits to, 3, 310
Parakeet, Orange-chinned, *Brotogeris jugularis*, 339; destroy Poró flowers, 158
Páramo, 61, 64, 67
Parental self-sacrifice: restrained by natural selection, 80, 277–78
Parrot, Gray, *Psittacus erithacus*, 159
—Mealy, *Amazona farinosa*: voice, 91
—Red-lored, *Amazona autumnalis*, 153, 298; nuptial feeding, 323
—White-crowned, *Pionus senilis*: and ripening Poró seeds, 159; nuptial feeding, 159
Parrots: destructive of flowers and seeds, 159–60
Paulson, Dennis, 325
Pauraque, *Nyctidromus albicollis*, 117

Peccary, Collared, *Pecari angulatus*, 235
—White-lipped, *Tayassu pecari*, 235–36
Pedregoso, Río, 101
Pejibaye, *Guilielma utilis* (Palmae): ephemeral male flowers, 174–75; heat production by flowers, 174–75; seedless fruits, 175; edible fruits, 247–48; sought by squirrels and birds, 247–48. See also picture section, Part II
Pelican, Brown, *Pelecanus occidentalis*, 107
Peña Blanca, Peñas Blancas, Río, 135, 136–37, 147, 191–205; islands in, 204–5; floods, 204–5; view over valley, 221
Peperomia macrostachya (Piperaceae): on nests of gardener ant, 259
Peregrine (Falcon), *Falco peregrinus*, 80
Pernettia coriacea (Ericaceae), 63
Peru: author's visit to, 129, 143
Pescatorea cerina (Orchidaceae), 170
Pigeon, Band-tailed, *Columba fasciata*, 67
Pigeons, fruit, 333
Pigs, 49, 61, 69, 289
Piha, Rufous, *Lipaugus unirufus*: abundance in forest, 339
Pillows, 21
Pine trees: absent from Costa Rica, 13
Pipromorpha, Oleaginous, *Pipromorpha oleaginea*, 319, 333; nesting, 120–21; eagerness for arils, 333
Pittier, Henri, 207
Plantains, wild, *Heliconia* spp. (Musaceae), 188
Poás, Volcán, 9, 87; visited, 92–93. See also picture section, Part I
Podostemonaceae, 116, 196–97
Poikilacanthus macranthus (Acanthaceae), 208
Pokeberry, *Phytolacca* sp., 67
Policeman: at Rivas, 69
Polypodium fraxinifolium (fern), 35
Population problem, 53, 340–41, 342
Poró (orange-flowered), *Erythrina poeppigiana* (Leguminosae), 158, 181
—(red-flowered), *Erythrina berteroana*: flowers visited by birds, 157–58; puzzling seeds, 159–60; edible flowers, 160–61. See also picture section, Part II
Portal (Christmas garden), 50–51
Potoo, Common, *Nyctibius griseus*: voice, 90
Predation: a miscarriage of evolution, 231–32; and the reproductive rate, 232
Predators: habitual prudence of, 277

Privet, *Ligustrum vulgare* (Oleaceae), 156, 157
Psittacanthus sp. (Loranthaceae): parasitic on Mayo trees, 223
Psychotria sp. (Rubiaceae): colorful leaves of young shoots, 212
Puerto Viejo, Costa Rica, 314
Puerto Viejo, Río, 315, 321. *See also* picture section, Part II
Puma, *Felis concolor*, 217, 335
Pumpkin: edible flowers, 161
Puya dasylirioides (Bromeliaceae), 67

Quail-Dove, Ruddy, *Geotrygon montana*, 216
Quebracho tree. *See* Gavilán tree
Quebrada de las Vueltas, La: author's residence beside, 100–111
Quercus oleoides (Fagaceae), 31
Quetzal, *Pharomachrus mocinno*: national bird of Guatemala, 83; as symbol, legend, and source of plumes, 83–85; first view of, 84; in Costa Rica, 86, 88, 314; temporary disappearance, 94; voice, 96; nesting, 96–97, 98–99; song flight, 97; food, 98; plumage wear, 98–99
Quioro. *See* Toucan, Chestnut-mandibled
Quiriguá, ruins of, 287
Quizarrá, El, Costa Rica: arrival at, 136; purchase of farm at, 137–39; "a land of promise," 142; improvements at, 336

Rabbit, 151
Razisea spicata (Acanthaceae), 208
Recino. *See* Mayo Colorado tree
Redstart, Collared, *Myioborus torquatus*: tameness, 98
Religion: and agriculture, 294
Rice, 46, 101, 103; sowing, 280, 282; storing, 288
Río de la Paz: waterfall in, 314
Rivas, Costa Rica, 14–18, 56, 69, 72, 82–83, 94, 100. *See also* picture section, Part I
Riverweeds (Podostemonaceae), 116, 196–97
Riverwood tree. *See* Sotacaballo
Roads, 8, 336. *See also* Inter-American Highway
Robin, American, *Turdus migratorius*, 63
Robinson, T. Ralph, 184
Rotifers: in leaves of *Frullania*, 170
Rounds, Dean, 100

Saint-John's-wort, *Hypericum selenoides* (Guttiferae), 61, 63
—*Hypericum strictum*, 63
Salpichlaena volubilis (twining fern), 213–14
Saltator, Buff-throated, *Saltator maximus*: eats flowers, 161; at feeder, 164; nesting, 245
Salvin, Osbert, 85
San Antonio, Río: author's sojourn by, 114–29
Sandpiper, Spotted, *Actitis macularia*, 202
San Isidro del General, Costa Rica: journey to, 7, 9–12; described, 13–14; hospital at, 110; distance from author's farm, 137–38; changes at (1935–1970), 335–36
San José, Costa Rica, 7–8, 68, 112–13, 129, 309, 314
San Juan, Río, 87
San Pedro, Costa Rica, 135
Santa Cruz, Costa Rica, 31
Santa Elena, Costa Rica, 336
Santa-María, Juan: national hero, 17
Santa Rosa, Costa Rica, 113
Sarapiquí, Río, 87, 314, 315
Sassafras, *Sassafras officinale* (Lauraceae), 185
Satyria elongata (Ericaceae), 195
Sauvagesia erecta (Ochnaceae): ephemeral flowers, 176
Savage, E. M., 184
Schneirla, T. C., 277
Schroeder Frutos, Juan, 14–15, 42–43, 69, 86, 100, 113–14, 135–37
Season in Central America, 27–28, 69, 104, 286. *See also* Climate
Secretary-bird, *Sagittarius serpentarius*, 71
Securidaca sp. (Polygalaceae), 116
Seedeater, Variable, *Sporophila aurita*: nesting, 245
Seriema, *Cariama cristata*, 71
Shrike-Vireo, Green, *Smaragdolanius pulchellus*: a bird of mystery, 228, 313
Sida acuta (Malvaceae): short-lived flowers, 175
Silk-cotton tree. *See* Ceiba tree
Silky-Flycatcher, Long-tailed, *Ptilogonys caudatus*, 65
Singing-Wren, 22–24, 43
Skull-cap, Costa Rican, *Scutellaria costaricana* (Labiatae), 251

Skunk Cabbage, *Symplocarpus foetidus* (Araceae), 318
Skutch, Edwin, 147–48, 314, 322, 326, 329
—Pamela, 147, 314
Skutchia caudata (Moraceae), 82–83
Sloth, Three-toed, *Bradypus griseus*, 89
—Two-toed, *Choloepus hoffmanni*: at high altitudes, 89; food, 89; young, 89–90: voice, 90
Slud, Paul, 128, 319
Snake-eater. *See* Guaco
Snakes: eaten by birds, 71–81; one threatens hummingbird's nest, 123–24; in Peña Blanca valley, 142; "mobbed" by birds, 201; attacked by small birds, 201–2; one seizes adult bird, 201–2; venomous, 220, 235; pillage birds' nests, 237; held aloof from birds' nests by wasps, 269; increase of, 338
Snow, David W., 238
Sobralia pleiantha (Orchidaceae), 169, 172; ephemeral flowers, 177
—spp., 169; gregarious flowering, 177. *See also* picture section, Part II
Soils, tropical: fertility of, 279, 282–83, 337
Solitaire, Black-faced, *Myadestes melanops*: song, 57, 60, 105
Sotacaballo tree, *Pithecolobium longifolium* (Leguminosae), 15, 115–16, 194–95, 204–5, 300, 315. *See also* picture section, Part II
South America: author's visits to, 4, 129
Spadebill, Golden-crowned, *Platyrinchus coronatus*, 319
Sparrow, Black-striped, *Arremonops conirostris*: at feeder, 164, 166
—House, *Passer domesticus*: eats flowers, 161
—Orange-billed, *Arremon aurantiirostris*, 216
—Rufous-collared, *Zonotrichia capensis*, 65, 314
Spathiphyllum sp. (Araceae), 318
Sphagnum moss: on mountaintop, 34
Spigelia humboldtiana (Loganiaceae), 118
Spruce, Richard, 175
Squirrel, Grey, *Sciurus carolinensis*, 104, 247, 289, 317
—Pygmy, *Microsciurus alfari*: a mother with young, 104
—Red-tailed or Cinnamon-bellied, *Sciurus granatensis*, 104, 247, 289, 317
Stachytarpheta, *Stachytarpheta mutabilis* (Verbenaceae): attractive to hummingbirds, 155–57. *See also* picture section, Part I
Standley, Paul, 67, 82–83
Stanhopea spp. (Orchidaceae), 170
Stemodia verticillata (Scrophulariaceae): short-lived flowers, 176
Stout, A. B., 185
Strawberry Bush, *Evonymus americanus* (Celastraceae), 333
Sugarcane: leaves used for thatching, 19–20
Sunbittern, *Eurypyga helias*: habits, 119–20; nest, 120; disappearance, 339
Sungrebe, *Heliornis fulica*: habits, 322
Surá tree, *Terminalia lucida* (Combretaceae), 316. *See also* picture section, Part II
Swallow, Bank, *Riparia riparia*: migration, 126
—Barn, *Hirundo rustica*: migration, 103, 126
—Cliff, *Petrochelidon pyrrhonota*: migration, 103, 126
Swift, Black, *Cypseloides niger*, 125
—White-collared, *Streptoprocne zonaris*: behind waterfall, 125
Symbolanthus pulcherrimus (Gentianaceae), 50

Talamanca, Cordillera de, 10, 11, 12, 15, 17, 63–64, 114, 221, 336, 337
Tanager, Blue, *Thraupis episcopus*: nuptial feeding, 165; eat Pejibaye fruits, 247
—Dusky-faced, *Mitrospingus cassinii*: helpers at nest, 329–30
—Golden-masked, *Tangara larvata*: at feeder, 166; helpers at nests, 330, 331
—Gray-headed, *Eucometis penicillata*: habits, song, and nesting, 245–46
—Palm, *Thraupis palmarum*: nuptial feeding, 165; eat Pejibaye fruits, 247
—Plain-colored, *Tangara inornata*: helpers at nest, 330
—Scarlet-rumped Black, *Ramphocelus passerinii*: racial differences, 12; roosting, 157, 301; at feeder, 162, 164, 165, 166; young fed by Blue Honeycreeper, 167; seized by snake, 201–2; nesting, 245; eat Pejibaye fruits, 245; "mob" large moths, 306
—Silver-throated, *Tangara icterocephala*: nuptial feeding, 165
—Speckled, *Tangara chrysophrys*: nuptial feeding, 165
—Summer, *Piranga rubra*, 298; winter

territories, 104; at feeder, 164; devours immature wasps, 270–71
—Yellow-browed. *See* Tanager, Speckled
Tangerine, sour: an aggressive weed, 153–54
Tapir, *Tapirella bairdii*, 335, 338
Tayra, *Tayra barbara*: kills nestling Guaco, 78–79; food, 79; disappearing, 219, 338
Teeth, human: in backwoods, 52–53
Tennyson, Alfred Lord, 94
Tepiscuinte, Tepiscuintle. *See* Paca
Terciopelo (snake), *Bothrops atrox*, 220
Térraba, Río Grande de, 11
Thompson, Francis, 208
Thoreau, Henry David, 285
Thornbird, Rufous-fronted, *Phacellodomus rufifrons*, 313; attack snake, 201
Thrush, Black, *Turdus infuscatus*, 63
—Gray's, *Turdus grayi*, 245
—Olive-backed or Swainson's, *Hylocichla ustulata*: sings in El General, 103; follows army ants, 103; migration, 126; eats arillate seeds, 332
—Sooty, *Turdus nigrescens*: song, 63, 66
Thunbergia erecta, 176
Tigra (snake), *Spilotes pullatus*, 201
Tigre (Jaguar), 46–47, 235
Tijereta (folding cot), 21
Tiles, roof, 145–46
Timbers, tropical: qualities of, 144
Tinamou, Great, *Tinamus major*: voice, 119, 209; roosting, 209–10; nesting, 210; wariness, 219, 339
—Little, *Crypturellus soui*, 209–10
Tinbergen, Niko, 302
Tiquisqui, *Xanthosoma violaceum* (Araceae), 247
Tityra, Masked, *Tityra semifasciata*, 25
Tobacco, 46, 337
Tortillas, 56, 293–94
Toucan, Chestnut-mandibled, *Ramphastos swainsonii*: curiosity, 30; voice, 209; disappearance, 338
—Rainbow-billed, *Ramphastos sulphuratus*: eats arillate seeds, 332
Toucanet, Blue-throated, *Aulacorhynchus caeruleogularis*, 97
—Yellow-eared, *Selenidera spectabilis*: bathing, 320–21; voice, 321
Trigona fulviventris, 260n
Tristicha hypnoides (Podostemonaceae), 196–97
Trogon, Black-throated, *Trogon rufus*, 98

—Violaceous, *Trogon violaceus*: carves nest in vespiary, 269–70
—White-tailed, *Trogon viridis*, 98
Trogons: appearance and habits, 85; eat arillate seeds, 332, 334; persistence, 339
Trophis chorizantha (Moraceae), 83
Trumpeters, *Psophia* spp., 71
Turnos (rural fairs), 49
Turrialba, Volcán, 87
Tussacia friedrichsthaliana (Gesneriaceae): water-filled calyces, 188. *See also* picture section, Part II
Twittering-Wren, 22–24

United Nations, 336
Urania fulgens (moth), 296; migration, 307–12; visits flowers, 308–9; in Ecuador, 311
—*leilus*, 311
Urquhart, F. A., 302

Vandellia diffusa (Scrophulariaceae): short-lived flowers, 176
Van der Pijl, L., 160, 161, 262
Vanilla pfaviana (Orchidaceae), 33
Vara Blanca, Costa Rica, 86, 95
Venezuela: visited, 313
Veracity: in backwoods, 48
Verano (dry season), 28, 112
Vergil: quoted, 292
Vireo, Blue-headed or Solitary, *Vireo solitarius*: singing in winter home, 104
—Philadelphia, *Vireo philadelphicus*, 245; eats arillate seeds, 332
—Yellow-green, *Vireo flavoviridis*: its young fed by Blue Honeycreeper, 167
—Yellow-throated, *Vireo flavifrons*: eats Poró seeds, 160; and seeds of *Alchornea*, 332
Virola spp. (Myristicaceae): arillate seeds, 334
Volcán de Buenos Aires, Costa Rica: journey to, 135–36
Volcanoes, 9, 68, 86–87, 92–93
Vulture, Turkey, *Cathartes aura*: migration, 315

Walker, William, 17
Warbler, Black and White, *Mniotilta varia*: winter territories, 104
—Blackburnian, *Dendroica fusca*, 244
—Buff-rumped, *Basileuterus fulvicauda*, 116, 119, 306–7; habits, song, and nesting, 252

—Chestnut-sided, *Dendroica pensylvanica*, 244; eats arils, 332
—Myrtle, *Dendroica coronata*, 94
—Tennessee, *Vermivora peregrina*: at feeder, 164, 166; in coffee shade trees, 244–45
—Wilson's or Black-capped, *Wilsonia pusilla*, 60
—Yellow, *Dendroica aestiva*: winter territories, 104
Warning coloration: in frog, 118
Warszewiczia coccinea (Rubiaceae), 318
Washington, State of, 286
Wasp, Banded, *Polybia fasciata*, 257, 263, 271
—Guitarrón, *Synoeca septentrionalis*: build nest, 101–2; torpid on cool morning, 102–3; nest, 255; nest attacked by Red-throated Caracara, 271; and by army ants, 272–74; stupid persistence in building, 274
—Polistes, *Polistes erythrocephalus*: home life, 266–68
—Sticky-nest, *Parachartergus championi*: curious nest, 265–66; and army ants, 274–75. See also picture section, Part II
—Windowmaker, *Metapolybia aztecoides*: nest construction, 264–65. See also picture section, Part II
Wasps: nest architecture, 263–66; kill impaled bird, 269; nests attacked by birds, 270–71; and by ants, 272–75
—feltmaker, *Apoica thoracica* and *A. pallens*: nest and nocturnal habits, 263–64; nests plundered by army ants, 275
Water systems: installation of, 336
Waterthrush, Louisiana, *Seiurus motacilla*, 202
—Northern, *Seiurus noveboracensis*, 202
Wercklea insignis (Malvaceae), 314
Whimbrel, *Numenius phaeopus*, 107
Whippoorwill, *Caprimulgus vociferus*, 59
Witch Hazel, *Hamamelis virginiana* (Hamamelidaceae): odor of, 252
Woodcreeper, Buff-throated, *Xiphorhynchus guttatus*, 313
—Spotted-crowned, *Lepidocolaptes affinis*, 97
—Streaked-headed, *Lepidocolaptes souleyetii*: sleeping habits, 25

—Wedge-billed, *Glyphorhynchus spirurus*, 316
Woodpecker, Acorn, *Melanerpes formicivorus*: storage of acorns, 32; social nesting, 32, 331
—Cinnamon, *Celeus loricatus*: extracts ants from Laurel tree, 319
—Golden-naped, *Tripsurus chrysauchen*, 12, 334; helpers at nest, 24, 331; habits, 24–25; at feeder, 164; eats Pejibaye fruits, 247; brings food for vanished nestlings, 328
—Hairy, *Dendrocopos villosus*, 60, 97
—Lineated, *Dryocopus lineatus*, 319, 339
—Pale-billed, *Phloeoceastes guatemalensis*, 216, 338–39
—Red-bellied, *Centurus carolinus*, 25
—Red-crowned, *Centurus rubricapillus*: habits, 25; at feeder, 164; eats Pejibaye fruits, 247
—Rufous, *Micropternus brachyurus*: breeds in ants' nest, 269
—Smoky-brown, *Veniliornis fumigatus*, 313
Woodpigeon, *Columba palumbus*: eats flowers, 161
Wood-Quail, Marbled, *Odontophorus gujanensis*, 73, 339
Wood-Rail, Gray-necked, *Aramides cajanea*: habits, voice, and nesting, 248–49, 323
Wood-Wren, Lowland, *Henicorhina leucosticta*: voice, 119
Wren, Banded-backed, *Campylorhynchus zonatus*: helpers at nests, 330
—Nightingale, *Microcerculus philomela*, 313
—Riverside, *Thryothorus semibadius*, 12, 119; habits, 200–201; attacks snake, 201
—Southern House, *Troglodytes musculus*: habits, 22–24; helpers at nests, 24, 331; in roof, 42–43

Yavarí, Río, 324
Yew, *Taxus baccata* (Taxaceae), 333
Yos, *Sapium* sp. (Euphorbiaceae), 95
Yucca elephantipes (Liliaceae). See Itabo

Zunil, Volcán: lost on, 35–36

www.ingramcontent.com/pod-product-compliance
Lightning Source LLC
Chambersburg PA
CBHW022057150426
43195CB00008B/171